www.wadsworth.com

wadsworth.com is the World Wide Web site for Wadsworth and is your direct source to dozens of online resources.

At *wadsworth.com* you can find out about supplements, demonstration software, and student resources. You can also send email to many of our authors and preview new publications and exciting new technologies.

wadsworth.com
Changing the way the world learns®

From the Wadsworth Series in Speech Communication

Communication Between Cultures

Fourth Edition

Larry A. Samovar
San Diego State University

Richard E. Porter
*California State University,
Long Beach, Emeritus*

Wadsworth
Thomson Learning™

*Australia • Canada • Mexico • Singapore • Spain
United Kingdom • United States*

Executive Editor: Deirdre Cavanaugh
Publisher: Clark Baxter
Marketing Manager: Stacey Purviance
Print Buyer: Mary Noel
Permissions Editor: Susan Walters
Production Service: Vicki Moran, Publishing
    Support Services

Text and Cover Designer: Ellen Pettengell
Cover Image: Corbis
Copy Editor: Martha Ghent
Compositor: TBH Typecast, Inc.
Text and Cover Printer: Custom/VHP

Printed in the United States of America
1 2 3 4 5 6 7 04 03 02 01 00

For permission to use material from this text, contact
us by
    Web: http://www.thomsonrights.com
    Fax: 1-800-730-2215
    Phone: 1-800-730-2214

For more information, contact
Wadsworth/Thomson Learning
10 Davis Drive
Belmont, CA 94002-3098
USA
http://www.wadsworth.com

International Headquarters
Thomson Learning
International Division
290 Harbor Drive, 2nd Floor
Stamford, CT 06902-7477
USA

UK/Europe/Middle East/South Africa
Thomson Learning
Berkshire House
168-173 High Holborn
London WC1V 7AA
United Kingdom

Asia
Thomson Learning
60 Albert Street, #15-01
Albert Complex
Singapore 189969

Canada
Nelson Thomson Learning
1120 Birchmount Road
Toronto, Ontario M1K 5G4
Canada

Library of Congress Cataloging-in-Publication Data
Samovar, Larry A.
        Communication between cultures / Larry A. Samovar, Richard E. Porter.
    —4th ed.
            p.   cm.
        Includes bibliographical references and index.
        ISBN 0-534-53460-0
        1. Intercultural communication.   2. Communication and culture.
    I. Porter, Richard E.   II. Title.
    P94.6 .S26 2000
    303.48'2—dc21   00-035176

Contents

Preface

Culture, the acquainting ourselves with the best that has been known and said in the world, and thus with the history of the human spirit.

MATTHEW ARNOLD

Every tale can be told in a different way.

GREEK PROVERB

We approached the occasion of a fourth edition with three very different responses: gratification, excitement, and caution. Our pride and egos were delighted that our previous efforts were successful enough to warrant this new edition. We were also excited over the prospects of tinkering with what we had done in the earlier editions. We knew we had to be prudent when advancing additional perspectives and material so that we did not abandon the orientation that contributed to the popularity of the last three editions. We believe that in this fourth edition we have been able to balance the past, present, and future of intercultural communication. We have retained the core of the field, added current thinking and research, and staked out some new territory.

This book is still about the unique relationship between communication and culture. More specifically, it is about what happens when people from different cultures come together to share ideas, feelings, and information. Because communication and culture work in tandem we have tried to incorporate the basic principles from both topics throughout this book.

This text is intended for those whose professional or private life is likely to include encounters with people from cultures or co-cultures different from their own. We, therefore, deal with both communication among international cultures and communication among co-cultures in the United States.

RATIONALE

Worldwide interest in intercultural communication grows out of two assumptions. First, you live in an age when changes in technology, travel, economic and political systems, immigration patterns, and population density have created a world in which you increasingly interact with people from different cultures. And whether you like it or not, those interactions will continue to grow in both frequency and intensity. Huston Smith said much the same thing when he wrote: "When historians look back on our century they may remember it most, not for space travel or the release of nuclear energy, but as the time when the peoples of the world first came to take one another seriously."[1]

Second, people now know that culture affects communication in subtle and profound ways. Your cultural backgrounds and experiences help determine how the world looks to you and how you interact in that world.

APPROACH

Fundamental to our approach to intercultural communication is the belief that *all forms of human communication involve action*. Put in slightly different terms, communication is an activity that affects you as well as other people. Whether you are generating or receiving words or movements, you are creating and producing action. Any study of communication, therefore, must include information about the choices that you make in selecting your messages, as well as a discussion of the consequences of those choices. Hence, this book takes the view that engaging in intercultural communication is pragmatic, philosophical, and ethical. We have attempted throughout to translate ideas and concepts into practices that can improve your communication and help you attain your communication goals. We also continue to remind you in each chapter about the consequences of your choices.

PHILOSOPHY

A dual philosophy has guided us in the preparation of this book. First, it is to the advantage of all 6 billion of us who share the planet to improve our interpersonal and intercultural communication abilities. The world has grown so small that we all depend on each other now. What happens in one place in the world affects other places. Second, most of the obstacles to understanding can be overcome with motivation, knowledge, and appreciation of cultural diversity. We hope to supply you with all three.

Culture and communication, we have come to believe, involve personal matters, and we have, therefore, developed our own philosophy about intercultural interaction that can be summarized by the notion that the First Commandment of any civilized society must be: Let people be different. At times, as you read this book, you will observe that we have openly stated our own positions, and we make no apologies for them. We have also made a conscious effort to keep our own ethnocentrism in check, but for those instances in which it has accidentally emerged, we do apologize.

ORGANIZATION

We have organized the book in manageable increments that build on each other. What you learn in one chapter, you will carry into the next. The book is divided into four interrelated parts. Part 1 introduces you to the study of communication and culture. After pointing out the importance of intercultural communication in Chapter 1, we use Chapter 2 to examine communication, culture, and intercultural communication.

[1]Huston Smith, *The World's Religions* (New York: HarperCollins, 1991), 7.

Part 2 focuses on the ability of culture to shape and modify your view of reality. Chapter 3 examines how your culture influences perception and communication. In that chapter we identify some specific cultural patterns that are reflected during human interaction. In Chapter 4, we examine the sources of those perceptions, behaviors, and patterns by looking at cultural differences in world view, family experiences, and history.

Part 3 puts the theory of intercultural communication into practice. Chapters 5 and 6 explore differences between verbal and nonverbal messages. Chapters 7, 8, and 9 explain the ways in which cultures respond differently to business, educational, and health care settings.

In Part 4, we extend what you have learned throughout the preceding chapters by converting knowledge into action. In Chapter 10, we offer guidelines for improvement as well as a philosophy for a future that we believe will be filled with intercultural experiences.

NEW FEATURES

The fourth edition of *Communication Between Cultures* brings a number of significant changes and new features. Our addition of new content has been guided by the excellent feedback provided by our readers and reviewers. We have, of course, infused a great deal of current material that reflects our own interpretation and vision of the field of intercultural communication. Although some of the new features will be obvious to users of the third edition, many other changes are less visible. Let us mention a few of the alterations from both categories.

- Because of our strong belief that an understanding of culture must be at the heart of any study of human interaction, we have added three new sections to our discussion of the deep structure of culture. First, we have now included a detailed analysis on *cultural identity* and the roots of that identity in Chapter 4. Second, because of the increased contact between Americans and the people from Mexico, we have added a section on *Mexican History*. Third, while we alluded to the role of Confucianism in intercultural communication throughout the last edition, in this new volume we greatly augmented our discussion and have placed the world view of *Confucianism* alongside the other religious traditions.
- Due to the increased racial tensions in the United States and abroad, we have added new material in the areas of racism, stereotyping, prejudice, discrimination, and ethnocentrism.
- In addition to adding new material to the fourth edition we have expanded numerous portions of the book. For example, new material has been added to our critique of culture shock, ethics, social perception, intercultural competence, cultural adaptation, and the social contexts in which intercultural communication occurs.
- As more immigrants move from one culture to another, the issues of cultural adaptation take on added significance. Hence, we have added a new section on that particular topic. This edition also offers an increased focus on the role of co-cultures in North America.
- As with prior editions, we have integrated fresh examples throughout the book. We have also added hundreds of new references to this current volume.

ACKNOWLEDGMENTS

No book is the sole domain of the authors. Many people contributed to this new edition, and we would like to thank them. We begin by thanking our publisher, Wadsworth Publishing Company. In this day of fads and short-lived friendships, we greatly appreciate an association that spans nearly thirty years and includes fourteen books. The staff and editors at Wadsworth have offered us support, sound advice, and the freedom to advance new ideas. We especially acknowledge the editorial direction provided by Deirdre Cavanaugh.

We thank Connie Ruzich of Robert Morris College in Pittsburgh, Pennsylvania, for writing the InfoTrac College Edition questions that appear at the end of each chapter.

We are grateful to our manuscript reviewers for their many helpful suggestions:

Peter Oehlkers, Emerson College

Lisa M. Orick, Albuquerque Technical-Vocational Institute

Susan Mallon Ross, SUNY-Potsdam

Liliana Castaneda Rossman, Texas A&M University

Gustavo Yep, San Francisco State University

Finally, we express our appreciation to the thousands of students who have read past editions. They have allowed us to "talk to them" about intercultural communication and, by finding something useful in our exchange, have justified yet another edition of *Communication Between Cultures*.

Larry A. Samovar

Richard E. Porter

part 1

Communication and Culture

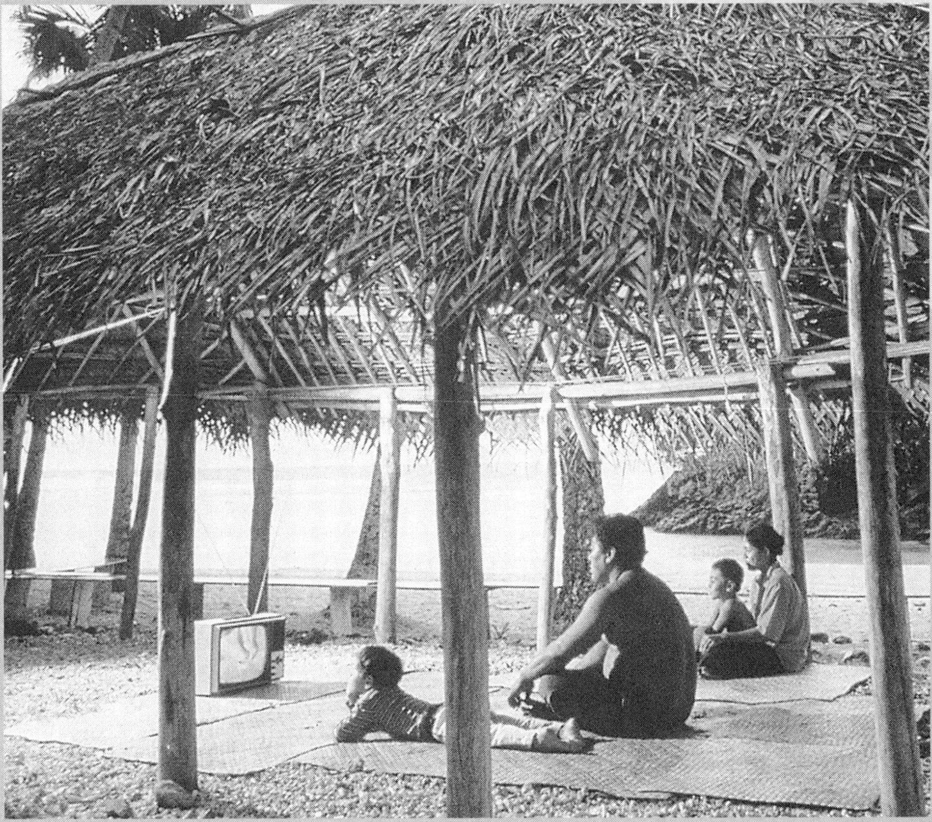

chapter 1

The Challenge of Intercultural Communication: Interaction in a Diverse World

Human beings draw close to one another by their common nature, but habits and customs keep them apart.

CONFUCIAN SAYING

There is no longer division between what is foreign and what is domestic—the world economy, the world environment, the world AIDS crisis, the world arms race—they affect us all.

WILLIAM JEFFERSON CLINTON, INAUGURAL ADDRESS, 1993

THE CHALLENGE OF INTERCULTURAL COMMUNICATION

You are about to embark on an intellectual adventure that will prove challenging as you acquire the knowledge and develop the skills necessary to be successful in almost any endeavor you undertake—skills and knowledge that will serve you well for the rest of your life. That challenge is to become a successful and effective intercultural communicator. The world into which your parents were born, and the world in which you now live, is undergoing continuous change—change that puts you into contact with people from diverse cultures and co-cultures. And, if you are going to function successfully in this world, you must be able to communicate with people whose entire backgrounds, whose very way of viewing the world and doing things may be completely different from yours. This is the challenge of the twenty-first century, and we hope to help you effectively meet that challenge.

INTERCULTURAL COMMUNICATION

Intercultural communication is the circumstance in which people from diverse cultural backgrounds are engaged in communication. You might wonder what is significant or unique about this. The answer is that the diversity of backgrounds, experiences, and assumptions resident in communicators due to their culture has the potential to make communication very difficult—and in some instances essentially impossible.

The crucial element in this form of communication is culture and the impact it has on your communicative behavior. Culture helps determine your beliefs, values, and world views; your use of language; your nonverbal behavior; and how you relate to others. It shapes your relationships with your family and friends, teaches you how to raise your children, and provides you with prescriptions for forms of communication appropriate to a variety of social situations. As you can see, culture is elaborate, multidimensional, and all pervasive; it constitutes a complete pattern of living. Aspects of culture are acted out each time members of different cultures come together to share ideas and information. In Chapter 2, we will consider communication and culture in depth and show how they intertwine in the form of intercultural communication.

Your intercultural communication will have two major points of contact: international and domestic. International contacts are those between people from different countries and cultures. Cultural differences between Chinese and Israelis, for instance, are easy to discern. It is also at the international level that perhaps the greatest cultural diversity will be found. Imagine, if you will, the vast differences in backgrounds and experiences between an Aleut villager of northeastern Canada and a Tutsi villager living in Uganda. Try to imagine how those differences lead to different perceptions of the world and different ideas about how people should lead and live their lives, and how they should communicate.

Also important is for you to understand that within each culture there are numerous co-cultures and specialized cultures. These provide the opportunity for domestic points of intercultural contact. In this situation we are referring to communication between people of diverse cultural backgrounds that live within a societal group. This includes communication involving such diverse co-cultures as African Americans, Asian Americans, Native Americans, and Latinos as well as women, gays and lesbians, and the disabled. We will investigate domestic contacts in greater depth later in this chapter.

THE IMPORTANCE OF INTERCULTURAL COMMUNICATION

Intercultural communication, as you might suspect, is not a new human endeavor. Since the dim beginnings of civilization when the first humans formed tribal groups, intercultural contact occurred whenever people from one tribe encountered others and found them to be different. Later, as civilization developed, sojourners, religious missionaries, and conquering warriors also encountered alien people different from themselves. Alien differences have long been recognized, but in the absence of accompanying cultural knowledge, this recognition most often elicited the human propensity to respond malevolently to those differences. This reaction to aliens—to those who are physically or socially different—was well expressed over two thousand years ago by the Greek playwright Aeschylus who wrote, "Everyone is quick to blame the alien." This penchant to blame the alien is still a powerful element in today's social and political rhetoric. For instance, it is not uncommon in today's society for you to hear that *immigrants cause all of the social and economic problems in the United States*.

From a historical perspective, successful intercultural communication has been the exception rather than the rule. The history of humankind details an ongoing antipathy and hostility toward those who are different. The twentieth century, for instance, witnessed two world wars that saw the introduction and use of chemical, biological, and nuclear weapons with the potential to destroy humankind. The world also witnessed the Holocaust, various smaller scale conflicts such as Korea, Vietnam, Kuwait, Rwanda, Bosnia, and Kosovo, as well as numberless ongoing religious, ethnic, and tribal clashes that seem to be without resolution. "Ethnic cleansing" in Kosovo, ethnic fighting between Hutus and Tutsis in Uganda and Rwanda, or a recent skirmish in the Indian village of Sindani between upper-class and lower-class Hindus that left twelve dead[1] are examples of ongoing conflicts that seem almost to be beyond resolution.

Perhaps as a reaction to these events, the latter third of the twentieth century also spawned the systematic study of intercultural communication. Although a recognition and understanding of the dynamics of culture in human interaction has begun, widespread successful intercultural communication is yet an unfulfilled challenge. The dawning of the twenty-first century greets you with the opportunity to meet that challenge and learn to overcome the difficulties that can arise when people from diverse cultural backgrounds meet and communicate.

Intercultural encounters today differ from earlier meetings. They are more abundant and, because of the physical and social interconnectedness of people, nations, and the world, more significant. The rain forest on Kaui in the Hawaiian Islands, for instance, exists in nutrient poor soil but is nourished by phosphorus blown to the island from the Takla Makan desert located some 3700 miles away in western China.[2] In a dissimilar vein, during 1998, El Niño–driven winds created a band of fires that stretched from Mexico to El Salvador, Honduras, Guatemala, and Nicaragua causing smoke that drifted north into Texas, Oklahoma, Florida, and even Wisconsin.[3]

The social realm, however, is where your interconnectedness most affects intercultural communication. These relationships can be seen in such diverse arenas as international business, international education, tourism, and cultural blending. In the arena of business, for instance, 60 percent of all shoes and more than half the toys sold in the United States bear a "Made in China" label.[4] With respect to international education, the number of U.S. students studying abroad has grown in both numbers and locations. During the 1994–1995 academic year, some 645,000 U.S. students were studying abroad in Great Britain, France, Spain, Italy, Mexico, Germany, Australia, Israel, Costa Rica, Japan, Austria, Russia, and China.[5] International tourism leads both to intercultural contact and to increased economic gain. According to the World Tourism Organization, in 1996 the top ten tourist countries were the United States, Spain, France, Italy, the United Kingdom, Austria, Germany, Hong Kong, China, and Switzerland with tourist industry earnings ranging from 6.64 billion in the United States to 9.09 billion in Switzerland.[6] Perhaps one of the most telling examples of social interdependence comes through cultural blending, which is the emergence of a sense of community among people from diverse cultures. This is occurring in the Asia-Pacific region with the emergence of a Pacific community. This community will be a completely new creation—neither Asian nor American—fusing together the best practices and values from many rich civilizations both Asian and Western.[7]

You can now board a plane and fly anywhere in the world in a matter of hours, and the reality of a global economy makes today's contacts far more commonplace than in any other period of the world's history. For example, between 1993 and 1997, the private investment flow from the United States to developing countries and multinationals exceeded $253 billion.[8] The web linking us together becomes vivid when we see a newspaper headline that tells us "American Ground Troops Bound to Kosovo." Additionally, the emergence of the information age has allowed us the opportunity to expand our knowledge so that the recognition of cultural differences need not result in hostile encounters. Think of the message sent to the world when U.S. and Russian astronauts—whose countries a decade ago were archenemies—began construction of the new international space station. That message signified a New World order.

The world, people, and societies are *always* in a state of change. This ongoing process continually produces new social dynamics with which we must learn to deal. Intercultural communication is about that change—changes in the world's fabric of social relationships that challenge us to keep pace with the changing world order. These changes at both the international and domestic levels have brought us into direct and indirect contact with people who, because of their cultural diversity, often behave in ways that we do not understand. With or without our consent, the last four decades have thrust us into social and professional situations with people who often appear alien, exotic, and perhaps even wondrous. These people may live thousands of miles away or right next door.

This book is about those changes and the challenges they present. In this chapter, we explore these changes. Many of you will be able to verify the examples we offer to document these alterations in intercultural contact, for some of you have had firsthand experiences with people whose cultures are different from your own.

Our rationale for looking at these changes is threefold. First, as the familiar gives way to a new and different world, the entire human race is affected. Second, many of the events that have brought diverse groups together have been too subtle to detect and have taken place over a long period. Hence, we believe that many of them may have been overlooked. Finally, by learning about these changes, you will learn to understand the role and impact of culture on communication and rise to meet the intercultural communication challenges posed in the twenty-first century. We begin by looking at intercultural contacts, both abroad and at home, and their implications to the study of intercultural communication. Next, we alert you to some of the problems inherent in the study of intercultural communication. Finally, we offer a brief preview of the remaining chapters so that you know what lies ahead.

POINTS OF CONTACT

In both your work and leisure activities, there are two principal points of contact where you may find yourself engaged in intercultural communication. The first is the *international arena* where you may find yourself interacting with people from different countries in a variety of work, travel, and social contexts. The other is the *domestic arena* where you may encounter people from a variety of co-cultures at work, where you live, where you go for entertainment, or where you vacation.

International Contacts

Because of international contacts, we are beginning to realize that a symbiotic relationship ties all people together. No nation, group, or culture can remain aloof or autonomous. If you touch one part of the world, you touch all parts. Three international developments have made intercultural contact more axiomatic and pervasive: (1) new technology and information systems, (2) changes in the world's population, and (3) a shift in the world's economic arena.

Tourism often introduces people to cultures that are very different from their own.

New Technology and Information Systems

Technology has accelerated intercultural contact by spurring development in two areas of human endeavor: transportation systems and communication systems. Travel, once taking days, is now measured in hours. Supersonic transports can place a traveler anywhere in the world within hours. Business executives and government officials can now attend a breakfast meeting in San Francisco and a dinner conference in Paris—during the same day. One result of these expanded travel opportunities is that people are encountering cultures that sometimes seem bizarre and even mysterious. Sources of differences now go far beyond eating utensils, traditional attire, and modes of travel. People are exposed to cultural idiosyncrasies in the perception of time and space, the treatment of women and the elderly, the ways and means of conducting business, and even the discovery and meaning of truth.

Business travelers are not the only people enjoying the increased mobility brought about by technical advances in transportation systems. Tourism is one of the fastest-growing industries in the world. But tourism, like other aspects of the dynamic world social order, is undergoing change. In 1997, the top five tourist destinations were France, the United States, Spain, Italy, and the United Kingdom. By 2020, predictions suggest the top five destinations will be China, the United States, France, Spain, and Hong Kong.[9]

Other developments in transportation technology are on the horizon—developments that will further increase cultural contact. Aerospace companies such as Boeing have experimental vehicles designed to power themselves vertically into Earth's orbit and then return to land in the same position. This means that travel time measured in hours today may some day be measured in minutes: Instead of taking twelve or more hours to fly from Los Angeles to Beijing, you may be able to do so in ninety minutes. With an increased ease of mobility, you will surely encounter new cultures at a greater rate than before.

New and advanced communication systems continue to encourage and facilitate cultural interaction. Communication satellites, sophisticated television transmission equipment, and fiber optic or wireless connection systems permit people throughout the world to share information and ideas instantaneously. Cellular telephone service is expanding rapidly with as many as 50,000 new subscribers each day. The world now has 180 million personal computers and 1.2 billion television sets.[10]

The continued development and improvement of communication satellites has driven the expansion of the World Wide Web and the Internet computer network. Between 1988 and 1997, the number of Internet hosts grew from a few thousand to over 15 million.[11] Currently, Internet traffic doubles every 100 days. A recent article in *Newsweek* made the same point: "The information revolution began in the United States, and the Internet is gradually spreading it around the world."[12] Although half of the computers on the Internet are in the United States, the rest are spread out among connected networks in more than 100 countries.[13]

In addition to fixed household and business Internet and computer usage, the development of portable laptop computers has added a degree of mobility to Internet access. This, however, is subject to rapid improvement as new technology is developed. For instance, IBM and Daimler-Chrysler have developed an office on wheels for mobile workers. In Europe, owners of new Mercedes V-class vans have an option to upgrade to a console that fits like a countertop in the backseat. It comes equipped with voice-recognition technology and an IBM Think Pad that allows passengers in the front seat or back to dictate messages aloud. It also has an inkjet printer and a Nokia cell phone.[14]

Computer education for children is on the rise worldwide. "Children are being educated in ways never conceived. They are linked across the globe through computer literacy. Some will grow up never knowing a time when they did not use the computer."[15] As a result of these computer links, many children may relate more to their global peers than to their local counterparts.

New Population

The second impetus to international communication has been a rapid increase in and redistribution of the world's population. The world's population increases at a rate of approximately 80 million every year. Eighty million babies born annually is enough to repopulate the state of California two times over each year.[16] The U.S. Census Bureau reported that in July 1999 the world population passed the 6 billion mark.[17]

Not only is the world's population growing rapidly, it is also on the move. As many as 100 million people are living outside the country of their birth, and millions more latter-generation immigrants maintain their ethnic identities. As Myron Weiner points out:

> More than ever before, migration is a global phenomenon. In search of employment, higher wages, educational opportunities for themselves and their children, and escape from persecution and violence, millions of people cross international borders each year. Countries that had few immigrants in the past now have growing immigrant populations. Nearly every major city in the world has a sizable immigrant community. Frankfurt has its Turks,

Many millions of people, from hundreds of cultures, have contact through the Internet.

Vancouver its Chinese, Marseilles and Paris their Algerians, London its West Indians, Kuwait, Dubai and Abu Dhabi their Indians, New York its Russian Jews, Dacca its Biharis, Bangkok its Burmese, and Tokyo its Iranians.[18]

Noncitizens now typically constitute more than 5 percent of the population in industrialized societies.

In addition to voluntary immigration is the immigration forced upon refugees. The United Nations High Commissioner for Refugees currently tends to more than 27 million people displaced by war and human rights violations. In the Balkans, more than 1.5 million Kosovos fled their homes during the Serbian "ethnic cleansing" campaign. As the global population continues to increase and relocate, three areas of concern will lead to potential competition, conflict, and needed intercultural communication: *finite natural resources*, the *environment*, and *international conflict*.

Finite Natural Resources. Over the next half century, it is predicted that water, our most precious natural resource, will replace oil as the prime trigger for international conflict. "At least 170 million people living in cities worldwide lack access to clean water for drinking, cooking, and washing; in rural areas, the number exceeds 855 million."[19] Nations are also beginning to confront each other over the dwindling supply of fish in the world's oceans. As *U.S. News & World Report* suggests:

Fish are the reason that Russians are shooting at Japanese, Tunisians are shooting at Italians and a lot of people are shooting at Spaniards. Heated conflicts are occurring on the high seas between aggressive fishing fleets and well-armed navy and coast guard vessels that are jealously protecting a lucrative and declining resource. Fisheries are a classic example of the economic dilemma of a commonly held resource. Nations have no incentive to conserve on their own, because their competitors will swoop in and plunder the excess.[20]

The decrease in food sources, in part brought about by the world's burgeoning population, is another example of how limited resources produce intercultural friction. Appropriately, the historian Linden notes, "As the global population climbs by nearly 100 million a year, starker limits appear on the horizon, and the potential for strife and disorder rises."[21] Although successful export-based economies can generate the money to buy food, someone has to produce it. Currently, China is too populous to count on exports to release its economy from inherent agricultural and resource limitations. Though the largest grain producer in the world, China is the second largest importer of grain.[22]

Negotiating these "limits" and avoiding "strife and disorder" are among the goals of intercultural communication. When we consider that 1 billion people worldwide lack sufficient food to meet energy and protein requirements for a productive and healthy life, it is easy to see how food insecurities could pit nation against nation.[23] Finite natural resources provide yet another reason for people to come together for international understanding.

Environment. Environmental problems do not observe geographic and cultural boundaries and thus affect all cultures. A 150-nation summit meeting held in Tokyo in 1997 identified global warming, depletion of the protective ozone shield, deforestation, soil erosion, toxic materials, water scarcity, and acid rain as some of the top worldwide environmental issues.[24] From China to Central America, weather-related flooding events resulted from deforestation that left many hillsides bare, causing rainfall to run quickly into rivers rather than being absorbed, thus leading to devastating landslides and floods. Also, population pressures have led many people to settle on flood plains and hillsides placing them in harm's way.[25] Although nations are beginning to realize that we must work together to solve environmental problems, progress is slow. In June 1997, a United Nations–sponsored meeting on the environment resulted in few solutions. Although nonstop speeches went on in the hall of the General Assembly, committees of nations bickered for days but were unable to agree on concrete proposals in the critical areas of global warming, deforestation, and annual emissions of carbon dioxide from fossil fuels.[26] The importance of a healthy environment to the well-being of all people provides yet another important reason to develop facility as an intercultural communicator.

International Conflict. Conflict among nations and peoples provides yet another reason to encourage effective intercultural communication. Ineffective communication can lead to increased tensions and violence with the ultimate outcome of failed communication being the use of military force. Karl von Clausewitz, a nineteenth-century Prussian military theorist, aptly described war as a political instrument used to continue policy when all other means have failed. It should be obvious to you that effective intercultural communication is the superior means of reducing international conflict.

As the population of the world continues to increase, it becomes more difficult for nations to remain detached and isolated from global tensions and conflicts. The end of the cold war redefined the world in a new light—cultural divisions among groups of

For the first time in history, people are beginning to realize that population growth is a serious problem.

people bound by certain shared values that are in conflict with the values of other groups. In short, it could very well become a world of the Christian West against the rest: such cultures as Islam, Confucian East Asia, the orthodox pan-Slavs.[27] *Global Trends 2010*, a study by the CIA's National Intelligence Council, finds that growing populations, widening gaps between the rich and the poor, and continuing revolutions in communication technology will incite new ethnic and civil conflicts. If intercultural communication cannot resolve these conflicts, U.S. military intervention may be required with increasing frequency.[28]

Recent events have given credence to the axiom that hostility anywhere has the potential to become hostility everywhere. Distance no longer matters. The United States, although thousands of miles away, is also a "neighbor" to the world. Peacekeeping missions in Bosnia and Haiti, and intervention against "ethnic cleansing" in Kosovo reflect but a few of the cases of U.S. involvement in international conflicts. Continued tensions between Israel and Palestine, conflict between China and Taiwan, famines in Africa and North Korea, as well as continued conflict in Russia, increased terrorism, and civil, religious, and tribal wars in third-world countries all present possibilities for global conflict and worldwide military involvement. Again, the need for effective intercultural communication is apparent.

Abroad, car bombs are planted in populated shopping areas and outside government offices. These are the urban equivalents of the guns and machetes of tribal warfare in the deserts and jungles. The recent bombings of the American embassies in Nairobi and Dar es Salaam underscore a trend in terrorism toward large-scale indiscriminate violence. The concept of "international terrorism" as a mutual problem for all nations is being used to build international consensus and a framework for cooperation.[29]

Nuclear capability also presents unlimited potential for global conflict. During the cold war, the nuclear weapons standoff between the United States and the Soviet Union was scary but stable. Nuclear weapons were limited to the United States, the Soviet Union, China, France, and Britain. Now, the nuclear club includes Israel, India, and Pakistan with Iran, Iraq, and North Korea vigorously seeking nuclear capability.[30] The detonation of a nuclear bomb by India has introduced a more chaotic world order. This situation represents yet another example of how events in one part of the world touch all parts of the world and underscores the need to communicate.

Tension, conflict, and hostility are not new to humankind. As Schlesinger points out, "The hostility of one tribe for another is among the most instinctive human reactions."[31] When people of different nationalities and ethnic origins, who frequently speak different languages and hold different convictions, attempt to work and live together, conflicts can easily arise. "Unless a common purpose binds them together," Schlesinger said, "tribal hostilities will drive them apart. Ethnic and racial conflict, it seems evident, will now replace the conflict of ideologies as the explosive issue of our times."[32]

The increasing levels of terrorism and the expansion of nuclear weapons capabilities sorely indicate the need for effective intercultural communication. People must discover that the resolution of conflict by communication is superior to the use of force. Unfortunately, such issues as ethnic pride, religious fervor, famine, and economic concerns often act as barricades to effective communication. And, when communication fails, other political means invariably follow. In numerous attempts to dissuade terrorism or the pursuit of nuclear weapons, the United States has imposed economic sanctions. In the past eighty years, economic sanctions have been imposed about 120 times. But sanctions seldom work and, as French president Jacques Chirac has argued, only increase the suffering of the poor.[33]

The New Economic Arena

A Russian proverb states, "Boris has one custom and Sergei another." This saying can easily be extended to the cultural context of the business setting, where different cultures come together to engage in commerce and, of course, communicate. For many years, the United States prospered by relying primarily on its huge internal market. In the early 1960s, the market expanded from the United States to the world. Consumers in developing countries in Asia, Latin America, and Central Europe will soon outnumber those in the West. By the year 2000, the number of consumers in developing-world countries earning the equivalent of $10,000 per year—the income threshold that marketers target—had surpassed those in the United States, Japan, and Europe combined.[34]

Changes in the international business community, coupled with new alignments among import and export countries, have compelled the United States to adapt to a changing world economic order. The United States is heavily involved in multinational corporations and now participates in various international business arrangements such as joint ventures, licensing agreements, turnkey projects, subcontracts, and management contracts. Recently, notable mergers and acquisitions took place between U.S. and foreign businesses. Among these were the merger of Daimler-Benz and Chrysler, the acquisition of Smith Kline Beckman by the British Beecham Group, the German

Bertelsmann A.G. acquisition of U.S. publisher Random House, and the Japanese Sony acquisition of Columbia Pictures. All of these changes thrust U.S. businesspersons into contact with businesspersons from other cultures.

Globalization of the U.S. economy is tied to fortunes of other economies. The interrelations between economies were vividly illustrated on August 27, 1998, when the Russian fiscal crisis shook stock and commodity markets from Tokyo to Toronto. The capitalization value of these markets plunged as fears that Russia's deepening crisis threatened the entire world economy.[35] Although this may have been what analysts call a knee-jerk reaction, it vividly illustrates the interconnectedness of the world economy.[36] As Miller says, "There's growing recognition of the inter-connectiveness of all this, of corporate decisions made here with results happening a long ways away."[37] These and countless other economic ties mean that it would not be unusual for you to work for an organization that does business in many countries or for you to conduct business in remote parts of the world. In Chapter 7, we say more about your role in the business setting.

Domestic Contacts

The second major point of contact for intercultural interaction is the domestic arena. Before we begin looking at the intercultural contacts you may make with members of co-cultures in the United States, we want to pause and look briefly at the dominant American culture.

Dominant Culture

It is important for you to understand that within each society there is a dominant culture and numerous co-cultures and specialized cultures. These groupings provide the opportunity for domestic points of intercultural contact. Before we discuss the impact of co-cultures in the United States, we need to clarify what our reference is when we use the term *culture*. When we refer to culture, we are applying the term to the *dominant culture* found in most societies. Although many discussions of culture use the terms *umbrella culture*, *mainstream culture*, or *European Americans*, when speaking of the United States, we prefer the term *dominant*, which clearly indicates that the culture we are talking about is the one in power.

The people in power are those who historically have controlled, and who still control, the major institutions within the culture: church, government, education, military, mass media, monetary systems, and the like. As McLemore notes:

> The dominant group in American society was created as people of English ethnicity settled along the Atlantic seacoast and gradually extended their political, economic, and religious control over the territory. This group's structure, values, customs, and beliefs may be traced to (a) the English system of law, (b) the organization of commerce during the sixteenth century, and (c) English Protestant religious ideas and practices.[38]

In the United States, white males must meet the requirements of dominance. They are in positions of power in every single major institution in this country. They are at the center of culture because their power enables them to determine and manipulate the content and flow of the messages produced by those institutions. By controlling most of the cultural messages, they are also controlling the images presented to the majority of the population. Whether it be the church, mass media, or the government, the dominant culture sets goals, perpetuates customs, establishes values, and makes the major decisions affecting the bulk of the population. Their power allows them to influence what people think, what they aspire to be, and what they talk about. As Folb noted, "Power is often defined as the ability to get others to do what you want."[39] It should be noted that all cultures are marked by a dominant group that greatly influences perceptions, communication patterns, beliefs, and values. What these groups use for their power may differ, but they all lead the way. Folb made the same point when she wrote:

> High status and attendant power may be accorded those who are seen or believed to be great warriors or hunters; those invested with magical, divine, or special powers; those who are deemed wise; or those who are in possession of important, valued and/or vital societal resources and goods.[40]

Regardless of the source of power, certain people within every culture have a disproportionate amount of influence, and that influence gets translated into how people behave.

Interaction with Co-Cultures

As changes have taken place throughout the world during the last few decades, so too has the cultural landscape of the United States been altered. Within our own boundaries, people are redefining and rethinking the meaning of being a member of the U.S. population. What once was considered a homogeneous group has changed. Recognition that the U.S. population comes in different colors and from diverse cultural backgrounds has had a profound effect on national identity. From all over the world, people from a large variety of cultures are now calling the United States their home. Simultaneously, co-cultures that, for a host of reasons, have remained silent for years, now ask—and at times demand—to be heard. The members of these co-cultures, like the members of the dominant culture, share perceptions, values, modes of communication, and lifestyles that make them unique. To better understand the impact of these groups, we look first at the immigrants and then examine some co-cultures in the United States. Finally, we consider two primary arenas for domestic intercultural contact between these groups and the dominant culture.

Immigration. The United States has made it relatively easy for people from other countries to move here. The United States permits more legal immigration than the rest of the world combined. Many observers believe that there will continue to be an increase in immigration to America because the rest of the world does not welcome foreigners to the degree found in the United States. In any one year, there are about 800,000 new immigrants—of which perhaps 300,000 are illegal. This number doesn't much alter social conditions. But the cumulative impact is significant. And, when you count their American-born children, the immigration effect is amplified.[41] This fact was emphasized in a special issue of *Time* magazine entitled "The New Face of America" that labeled the United States as "the first universal nation, the first truly multi-cultural society marked by unparalleled diversity."[42]

The U.S. population contains a higher proportion of foreign-born individuals than at any time in the past sixty years. In 1997, 9.7 percent of the nation's population were foreign born.[43] Unlike previous immigrants who came mainly from Europe, today's immigrants come primarily from Latin America, Asia, and the Indian subcontinent. In the ten-year period between 1985 and 1995, 335,000 Indians immigrated to the United States raising the Indian American population to more than a million.[44] At present, nearly one-half of all foreign-born U.S. residents are natives of Mexico, Central America, or the Caribbean. Only one in five currently come from Europe.[45]

Hence, many of the world's current 15 to 18 million refugees will immigrate to the United States. If current demographic trends persist, by the middle of the twenty-first century, whites will no longer make up a majority of the U.S. population. Latinos will have overtaken African Americans as the largest minority group. Asians and Pacific Islanders will more than double their number to 19.6 million by 2020.[46]

This change in the ethnic face of the United States has altered intercultural contacts among members of the U.S. population. The 1980 census showed 24 million people five years or older speak a language other than English in their homes. In 1998, the number is estimated at close to 38 million. More than half of the residents not using English at home speak Spanish. Four additional languages—Chinese, French, German, and Italian—are each spoken by roughly 5 percent of the total group.[47] Thus, immigration has not only brought us into contact with more and varied cultures, but has increased the number of interactions with people who do not use English as a first language.

Co-cultures and Recognition. Co-cultures are those groups within a society that share many common cultural attributes—world views, beliefs, values, commonality of language, nonverbal behaviors, and identity—yet do not share power with the dominant culture. In the United States there are numerous co-cultures that have become increasingly prominent because of their numbers and partly because many of their members do not subscribe or conform to many of the dominant cultural beliefs, values, and attitudes. Although there are many other co-cultures in the United States, the five we consider—Latinos, African Americans, Asian Americans, Muslim Americans, and mixed races—have become conspicuous because of their demands for recognition and equality. The values and beliefs from these co-cultures often complicate relational dynamics within the United States. We examine those dynamics as we consider each co-culture.

Latinos comprise the fastest growing population in the United States. Nearly 28 million people—1 in 10—consider themselves of Latino origin. Roughly 60 percent have their roots in Mexico. Fifty-eight counties in the United States have a Latino majority.[48] Although Latinos in the United States come from a wide variety of national origins, two prominent issues common to this co-culture create turbulence in the quality of interactions in American society: (1) illegal immigration and (2) English as a national language.

First, at least 300,000 Latinos enter the United States illegally each year—half by crossing into cities like San Diego, half by entering legally and overstaying their visas. Although most Latino immigrants come here legally, those who arrive illegally receive far more attention. Nonetheless, the large number of illegal immigrants constitutes an intercultural crisis, since they are the target of anti-Latino feeling and rhetoric.

Second, many Latinos have retained their native language rather than adopting English. The city of Los Angeles has more Spanish speakers than Madrid; only Mexico City has more. If current trends persist, in two generations half of the U.S. population will speak Spanish.[49] Many North Americans believe that lack of a shared national language is detrimental to a unified society. As we see in later chapters, businesses, schools, and health care organizations are struggling to find an equitable solution to the issue of language diversity. Communication will be a crucial part of orchestrating a solution.

African Americans now number over 30 million and account for 12 percent of the total U.S. population. Prior to the Civil Rights Act of 1964, African Americans and members of the dominant culture had only limited contact. Since that time, both groups have interacted with much greater regularity. As is often the case, however, when two diverse cultures come into contact, not all the encounters are successful. Two important perceptual issues are at the heart of many of these problems. The first issue is racism. Many African Americans believe that racism causes the economic disparity between themselves and members of the dominant culture. In addition, whites and African Americans continue to argue over the role racism plays in both the legal and educational institutions of the United States. When the results of legal trials bring riots and deep-seated ill feelings, we know that racism influences perception and communication. Hence, it is a topic that demands our attention. We return to this topic throughout the book and suggest ways to deal with this intercultural problem.

Asian Americans—particularly of Chinese and Japanese ancestry—have been present in the United States since the late 1800s. It is recent arrivals who pose the most perplexing communication problems. Take the case of one immigrant. She was born in a refugee camp in Thailand but immigrated to California at the age of four. She isn't quite Asian, and she isn't quite American. She speaks to her mother in their native Mien, her friends in English, and her children in "Mienglish," a blend of the two languages. She is considered to be a member of the 1.5 generation, or one-fivers. This term grew out of the Korean American community to describe Americans born in Korea but raised in the United States. Today, it's finding new meaning among Southeast Asian teens born in war-torn Asia but bred on jeans and Generation X.[50] Another example involves a Hmong widow who lives in Sacramento, California. Her five youngest children, ages two to twelve, live with her. Her three oldest children are scattered living with friends who do not have telephones. Like many Hmong tribe members, she came here with no job skills, no command of English, and no idea of how to pay bills, fill out medical forms, or deal with landlords and public officials.[51]

Not only are these people finding it difficult to cope living in the United States so far away from both their homelands and their cultures but they also pose difficult and unique communication problems for those who must relate to them.

Muslim Americans number an estimated 6 million and are increasing steadily. Considered by race or ethnic grouping, Arabs constitute 12 percent, African Americans 42 percent, South Asians 24 percent, and others 21 percent.

The children of Muslim immigrants who came to the United States in the 1960s are coming of age. Both pious and modern, they are the future of the Islamic faith in the United States. These children, however, are emerging as a co-culture: young Islamic Americans that are a blend of traditional Muslim and American institutions. These children might know it is time to pray, not by a muezzin's call from a mosque minaret, but because his or her PowerMac has chimed. Copies of *Wired* magazine and Jack Kerouac novels may share space with an Arabian prayer rug equipped with a sewn-in plastic compass so it may be oriented toward Mecca during prayer. Yet, at the programmed call, a young Islamic begins his or her prayers—the same as those recited across the globe from the Gaza Strip to Amarakand.[52]

Mixed races are a phenomenon of an increasingly diverse and multicultural society that leads to increases in personal intercultural relationships. As a result of these new-found friendships, marriages between members of different races and cultures are on the increase. A study released in July 1996 revealed that 12 percent of all new marriages involving an African American were interracial. That is almost double the number in 1980 and almost five times as many as in 1970.[53] In 1960, mixed-race marriages totaled about 150,000; in 1995, the number was 1.4 million or 1 in 40 married couples. Of those, about 328,000 were marriages between blacks and whites while nearly 1 million other were between whites and races other than black.[54]

The number of children produced by these marriages continues to grow. In 1990, "there were nearly 2 million children under 18 whom the census classified as 'of a different race than one or both of their parents.'"[55] As you might suspect, the complex relational dynamics of interracial marriages and child rearing place an additional burden on communication.

Each time two people of different races get together, there is a ripple effect. Their family members, friends, and neighbors have the opportunity to know someone who is different from themselves. On the other hand, many people dislike the notion of interracial marriages and often act in hostile ways when they observe people from different ethnic backgrounds together in a social setting. Such relationships can also bring stares, insults, isolation, and even cross burnings. The children of these racial unions often face antagonistic reactions from members of other cultures as well as their own. Still, many mixed-race couples and their children hold that the rewards are worth the challenges.[56]

One issue of growing concern to many mixed-race Americans is the matter of identity. The current system of racial classification forces them to deny part of their heritage by choosing a single race or by checking off "other." A government task force representing some thirty government agencies has been looking into adding a "multiracial" category to the year 2000 census form. This movement got a large boost from professional golfer Tiger Woods when on the *Oprah Winfrey* show he called himself a "Cablinasian," a term he coined to reflect his Caucasian, black, American Indian, and Asian heritage.[57]

There are many additional co-cultures in the United States such as women, gays and lesbians, the deaf, the incarcerated, gangs, the homeless, prostitutes, the disabled, and the elderly. Many members of these groups do not subscribe to all of the mainstream beliefs, values, and attitudes shared by the dominant culture.

STUDYING INTERCULTURAL COMMUNICATION

If we have been successful in our endeavors thus far, you have been convinced that learning to become successful in intercultural interactions is a necessary and worthwhile pursuit. We must now alert you to some of the problems as you face the challenge of intercultural communication.

Understanding the characteristics of diverse cultures and co-cultures as well as your own culture is the first step toward meeting the challenge of successful intercultural communication. The need to understand such significant differences as social relations, concepts of the universe, and views of suffering is a major theme of this book. We ask you to remain open-minded throughout your intercultural inquiry and consider the following Arab proverb: "The eyes are of little use if the mind is blind."

Although many intercultural interactions are synchronous and harmonious, friction, conflict, and numerous misunderstandings complicate others. Differences in language, food, dress, attitudes toward time, work habits, social behavior, and the like can cause many of our intercultural contacts to be frustrating or even unsuccessful. These issues, however, account for only some of the problems associated with intercultural communication; most misunderstandings go beyond these superficial differences. The deep structure of a culture primarily determines how a person responds to events and other people. What members of a particular culture value and how they perceive the universe are usually far more important than whether they eat with chopsticks, their hands, or metal utensils. The deep structures of culture will cause you the greatest problems in being an effective intercultural communicator. Most of these problems, however, stem from two factors: (1) the failure to recognize the uniqueness of the individual and (2) the inability to be objective. We will discuss each of these briefly in order to give you an insight into the work that lies ahead.

Individual Uniqueness

All human beings—and thus all cultures—share common universal experiences just by being alive. Everyone shares the commonality of being human. Each of you is a member of the human species sharing universal needs, a member of a specific culture sharing common cultural patterns, and at the same time a distinct person with an individual psychology following a unique script. Regardless of your culture, you all share such common emotions as fear, love, anger, hostility, shame, envy, guilt, grief, and joy. Each culture has its forms of ethnocentrism, face-saving, ego defense, pride, and forms of play. And in every culture people stress manners and civility to one another, practice sexual taboos, adhere to mating practices, and follow specific gender roles. But, *you are much more than your culture*.

Although this book focuses on the cultural influences that moderate human interaction, you must keep in mind that at your basic core you are not captives of your culture. You are, instead, thinking individuals with the rationality and potential to engage in free choice. Consequently, the values and behaviors of a particular culture may not be the values and behaviors of all the individuals within that culture. Each human being is unique and shaped by countless factors, culture being but one. At any given moment, our behavior is the product of millions of years of evolution; our genetic makeup; the social groups we have been in; our gender, age, individual history, political affiliation, perceptions of others, and current circumstances; and many other factors. As the Roman playwright Terence noted over two thousand years ago, "As many men, so many minds; every one his own way."

Although culture offers you a common frame of reference, your uniqueness allows you to learn continuously and to develop the philosophic perspectives necessary for intercultural communication. From these perspectives, you can learn to modify appropriately your perceptions, thinking, and communicative behavior when engaged in the process of interacting with culturally diverse peoples. You can, to paraphrase Weinberg, learn to value discrete groups of people regardless of race, ethnicity, religion, country of origin, gender, or sexual preference.[58]

Objectivity

The inability to be truly objective in intercultural encounters is a problem impossible to completely overcome. In this instance *you* are the problem—or as the comic-strip character Pogo once announced, "We have met the enemy, and he is us." The issue is simply this: *You study other cultures from the perspective of your own culture*, so your observations and your conclusions are tainted by your personal and cultural orientations. It is difficult, if not impossible, to see and to give meaning to words and behaviors with which you are not familiar. How, for example, do you make sense of someone's silence if you come from a culture that does not value silence? You might make the mistake of thinking "How could someone be so insensitive as to be silent at a time like this?" Your ethnocentrism not only impedes intercultural communication, but also is often difficult to identify because it is unconscious. We encourage you to be aware of your ethnocentrism so that it does not limit your perceptions.

Objectivity requires the elimination of both overt and subtle hostility or ambivalence by members of one culture against members of another culture or co-culture. This negative behavior not only is contrary to the ideals of most cultures, but it cripples both the perpetrators of the behavior and the target. To discriminate against someone simply because he or she has skin of a different color, lives in a different country, prays to a different god, has a dissimilar world view, or speaks a different language diminishes everyone. James Joseph, a U.S. ambassador to South Africa, was referring to the role South Africa is playing in nation building, but he could have been talking about your views toward diversity in the United States when he said:

> There are new democracies everywhere, but if a functioning, non-racial democracy can finally prevail in South Africa, it will give new hope to many around the world who are eager to demonstrate that diversity need not divide; that the fear of difference is a fear of the future; that inclusiveness rightly understood and rightly practiced is a benefit and not a burden.[59]

As we enter the twenty-first century, numerous forces are converging to drive people as never before across national boundaries, thus making intercultural contact a major concern in the century that lies ahead. We have stressed the necessity that all cultures must work together to preserve humankind. We are beginning to see the validity of John F. Kennedy's observation that ancient prejudices and other barriers to intercultural understanding can fall quickly to the wayside when survival itself is at stake.

PREVIEW OF THE BOOK

We have divided this book into four interrelated parts. Part I, which has two chapters, introduces the study of intercultural communication. Chapter 1 has three objectives: (1) to present you with the challenge of intercultural communication, (2) to convince you of the importance of intercultural communication, and (3) to convince you that *you* have a part to play in improving intercultural communication and contributing to a better global community. Chapter 2 examines communication, culture, and intercultural communication in some detail. We define communication and discuss its major components. In the course of that discussion, we note that although culture tends to separate people, the ways in which we communicate tend to unite us. In Chapter 2, we also define culture, discuss its salient characteristics, and relate it directly to communication.

Part II examines cultural patterns of behavior and then looks at the deep structures as the basic roots of cultural behavior. Chapter 3 examines the cultural patterns of behavior that people depend on to define their identity and their reality. These patterns are important to the study of intercultural communication in that they are manifested both in and out of the culture. Chapter 4 explores the deep structures at the root of cultural behavior: perception and behaviors revealed in a culture's world view, interaction patterns within the family, and cultural history.

Part III moves us from the theoretical to the practical by analyzing the mechanisms of intercultural interaction. Chapter 5 looks at people involved in intercultural communication and their attempts to communicate through verbal messages. Examining the kinds of messages that are exchanged will help us appreciate the responses those messages produce. Chapter 6 canvasses the effect of cultural diversity on nonverbal communication and the ways in which nonverbal messages support verbal communication in a variety of cultures. Chapters 7, 8, and 9 acknowledge the importance of two communication principles: first, that communication is rule governed, and second, that those rules are often tied to a particular cultural context. Hence, our investigation looks at cultural variations in business, education, and health care settings. Chapter 7 looks at intercultural communication in the business setting, Chapter 8 focuses on education in a multicultural setting, and Chapter 9 explores communication in the multicultural health care setting.

Part IV is concerned with the improvement of intercultural communication skills. In a sense, our entire study focuses on the issue of improvement, but Chapter 10 contains specific advice and recommendations—remedies for the problems that often plague the individual who comes into contact with members of different cultures or co-cultures. In addition, the final chapter suggests new philosophical and ethical ways to think about the topic of intercultural communication.

SUMMARY

- Intercultural communication presents you with a challenge you must meet if you are to become an effective communicator in today's world.
- Today, intercultural communication encounters are different from encounters of the past.
- New technology, growth in the world's population, and shifts in the global economic arena have contributed to increased international contacts.
- Domestic contacts are increasing because new immigrants and co-cultures are growing in numbers.
- Settings that are most affected by these cultural changes are the educational system, the workplace, and interpersonal relationships.
- The hazards of studying intercultural communication are overgeneralizing and forgetting how complex the nature of human behavior is.
- We are more than our culture. We are independent, thinking individuals with the ability to analyze and modify our behavior so that we can adapt to intercultural encounters.
- Part I serves as an introduction to the study of intercultural communication.
- Part II introduces specific examples of culture and describes the deep structure of culture that is primarily responsible for an individual's world view, values, and perceptions.
- Part III moves from the theoretical to the practical by examining language, nonverbal communication, and the business, educational, and health care settings.
- Part IV is concerned with the improvement of intercultural communication skills and the development of a new orientation.

INFOTRAC® COLLEGE EDITION EXERCISES

1. Accompanying your text is a valuable research and learning tool, the *InfoTrac College Edition*. This is a good time to explore the site and investigate the ways in which *InfoTrac College Edition* can make your learning more effective and relevant. Access the *InfoTrac College Edition* Web page at http://www.infotrac-college.com/wadsworth, and type in the password from the free subscription card that you received with your text. After registering, you will automatically enter the EasyTrac search option and be asked to enter the search term. Type "Communication and Culture" (the "subject guide" is

automatically selected as the default option) and click on the "Search" icon. Read the titles of the articles listed to gain a sense of the variety of issues and themes that are related to communication and culture. Select an article that interests you and write a one-paragraph summary of the article to share with the class.

The specific articles suggested in the InfoTrac College Edition *questions at the end of each chapter in this text are available via* InfoTrac College Edition *for a three-year period. If any of the articles suggested in the* InfoTrac College Edition *questions in this text are not available, please check at Wadsworth's Communication Cafe:* http://communication.wadsworth.com/samovar_cbc/index.html

2. This chapter discusses the ways in which we are becoming a "global village," a world of increasing interactions with diverse cultures. Using the Power-Trac option, locate the article "The Battle in Seattle: Antiglobalization Forces Are Threatening to Turn the WTO's Meeting on Free Trade into a Free-for-All" (Hint: Use "Seattle" and "World Trade Organiztion" as key word search terms). Read the article, noting both the benefits and the threats to increased global cooperation. As you see it, what are the key advantages and the key risks to participating in "the global village"?

ACTIVITIES

1. Seek out someone from another culture who is willing to answer questions about his or her culture for the duration of this course. If your class has a good cultural mix, pair up with a classmate; you may also have a friend or relative from another culture. If not, try an international students' organization or an English-as-a-second-language program on your campus or in your community. To make an even exchange, you may want to find someone who wants to practice English conversation or who needs tutoring.

2. Attend an intercultural event (e.g., foreign students' reception on your campus, international night, or

international students' dinner) involving persons from several countries. Try to meet some persons from foreign countries and find out the purpose of their visit, their intercultural adjustment experiences, and their future plans. Keep track of your communication experiences with each person.

3. Visit your career counseling or placement center and ask about job opportunities in foreign countries. If possible, interview some people who have worked abroad recently. Select a job opportunity that interests you and investigate the types of intercultural contacts or communication situations involved.

DISCUSSION IDEAS

1. Describe your current intercultural contacts (international and/or domestic). To what degree do you interact with people from other cultures? In what settings? How successful are your attempts at intercultural communication? If you have problems, to what do you attribute them? How might you improve these interactions?

2. In small groups, identify your culture or co-culture. The typical group should have members of at least two co-cultures. After identifying yourselves, attempt to answer the following questions: How many in the group identify with the dominant culture of North America? What has been the quality of the communication that you typically have had with each other? In what settings—for example, the workplace, the

family—do problematic issues arise? Take this opportunity to find out as much as you can about each other's cultural identity.

3. Give an example of a co-cultural behavior that you do not understand. See if anyone in the class can explain it to you. Give an example of a behavior from your culture that someone from another culture might have difficulty understanding.

4. How might new technology, population changes, the new economic arena, immigration, and so on affect you personally? Consider, among other things, your plans for furthering your education and pursuing a career.

5. Discuss the major analytical issues particular to each co-culture mentioned in the text.

chapter 2

Communication and Culture: The Voice and the Echo

How shall I talk of the sea to the frog, if he has never left his pond? How shall I talk of the frost to the bird

of the summerland if he has never left the land of his birth? And how shall I talk of life with the sage

if he is a prisoner of his doctrine?

CHUNG TZU

About 150,000 years ago our first "relatives" initiated an activity that would have a profound and everlasting effect on all of our lives. While it took another 140,000 years to refine the process, these early ancestors evolved the vocal tracts necessary for human communication. This extraordinary accomplishment was one of the major precursors for the development of culture around 6,000 years ago. From that day until now, communication and culture have been inseparable. Although communication and culture are two different words, and in some ways different concepts, they are directly linked. They are so inextricably bound that some anthropologists (as well as the authors of this book) believe the terms are virtually synonymous. As Smith noted, "Whenever people interact they communicate. To live in societies and to maintain their culture they have to communicate."[1] Culture is learned, acted out, transmitted, and preserved through communication. Although communication and culture work in tandem, we separate them here for purposes of our discussion. We begin by examining communication because to understand intercultural interaction, you must first recognize the role of communication in that process. Later in the chapter, we discuss culture.

THE IMPORTANCE OF COMMUNICATION

Communication—your ability to share your ideas and feelings—is the basis of all human contact. Whether you live in a city in Canada, a village in India, a commune in Israel, or the jungles of Brazil, you all participate in the same activity when you communicate. The results and the methods might be different, but the process is the same. The over 6 billion people that live on this planet communicate so that they can share their realities with other human beings. As we noted in Chapter 1, many of those human beings are now from cultures very different from your own. We open our study of intercultural communication with an analysis of human communication so that you will be better able to improve your own communication behavior and more fully appreciate that of others.

DEFINING COMMUNICATION

There was good reason for the English statesman Benjamin Disraeli to say "I hate definitions." While definitions are necessary, they can also be troublesome. For example, it is nearly impossible to find a single definition of human communication. Over twenty-six years ago, Dance and Larson canvassed the literature on communication and found 126 definitions of communication;[2] since then, countless others have been added to their list. Isolating the commonalties of those definitions, and being concerned with the intercultural dimensions of communication, we hold to the definition advanced by Ruben and Stewart: *"Human communication is the process through which individuals—in relationships, groups, organizations, and societies—respond to and create messages to adapt to the environment and one another."*[3]

SOME PRINCIPLES OF COMMUNICATION

To better understand Ruben and Stewart's definition, and the process of communication itself, we pause at this point to examine some basic principles of communication that are in operation each time you attempt to share your internal states with someone else.

There are a few points to keep in mind before we attempt to catalog some of the basic principles of communication. First, *communication has more characteristics than we can discuss in the next few pages.* Just as a description of the forest that mentions only the trees and flowers, but omits the lakes and streams, does not do justice to the entire setting, our inventory is not exhaustive. We, too, are forced to leave out some of the landscape.

Second, *our discussion of communication, like many other aspects of this book, often reflects a Western orientation.* Although we have tried to keep this cultural disposition in check, it often creeps into some of our descriptions of communication and culture. For example, many of the characteristics we discuss in the next section place a high premium on verbal messages as the carrier of ideas and feelings. Although verbalization might be important in America, in many parts of the world silence is often a more important way of communicating. There is even a Japanese proverb that states "A boy living near a Buddhist temple can learn an untaught lesson."

Communication Is a Dynamic Process

Communication Is Ongoing

Notice that very early in the Rubin and Stewart definition they refer to communication as a *process.* We would simply now add that it is a *dynamic process.* The phrase *communication is a dynamic process* carries more than one meaning. First, it means that communication is an *ongoing activity.* It is not fixed. Communication is like a motion picture, not a single snapshot. A word or action does not stay frozen when we communicate; it is immediately replaced with yet another word or action. As participants in communication, we too experience its dynamic nature. We constantly are affected by other people's messages and, as a consequence, are always changing. From the moment of conception through the instant of death (and some cultures believe even after death), we experience an almost endless variety of physical and psychological changes, some too subtle to notice, others too profound to ignore. As we shall see later in the chapter, culture too is dynamic. It is no wonder that twenty-five hundred years ago the Greek philosopher Heraclitus wrote, "There is nothing permanent except change."

Communication Is Transitory

Communication is dynamic because once a word or an action is employed, it cannot be retracted. T. S. Eliot might well have been referring to this *transitory* aspect of communication when he wrote, "In the life of one person, never the same time returns." Once an event takes place, we cannot have it again—perhaps we can experience a similar event, but not an identical one. The judge who advises the jury to "disregard the testimony just given" knows full well that this is impossible. The words were spoken, and they cannot be unspoken. An Asian proverb makes much the same point: "Once the arrow has been shot it cannot be recalled."

Communication is a dynamic process.

The Elements of Communication Interact with Each Other

The word *dynamic* also testifies to the idea that all the elements of communication constantly *interact* with each other. You send words, create actions, watch the response of those around you, and listen to your partners all at the same time.

Inattention Brings Change

Communication is also dynamic because *inattention* pervades your communication behavior. Briefly survey your own actions and you will realize that your mind often does not like what it is doing and hence dashes from idea to idea, seeking something it does like. People often shift topics in the middle of a sentence, and research shows that when they listen, their attention span is brief. This trait of communication is so common that in the writings of the Buddha it is said, "The mind is fickle and flighty, it flies after fancies wherever it likes: it is difficult indeed to restrain."[4]

Communication Is Symbolic

Inherent in our definition of communication is the fact that humans are symbol-making creatures. It is this symbol-making ability that allows for everyday interaction. It also enables culture to be passed on from generation to generation. You employ symbols to share your internal states. Other animals may participate in the communication process, but none of them has the unique communication capabilities of people: through millions of years of physical evolution, and thousands of years of cultural evolution, you are able to generate, receive, store, and manipulate symbols. This sophisticated system allows you to use a symbol—be it a sound, a mark on paper, a statue, Braille, a movement, or a painting—to represent something else. Reflect for a moment on the wonderful gift you have that allows you to hear the words "The kittens look like little cotton balls" and, like magic, have an image in your head. Or what about the joy you experience when you see the smile of your dearest friend? These two sets of symbols—words and actions—help you let other human beings know how you experience the world and what you think about that world.

In terms of intercultural communication it is important to keep in mind the fact that the symbols you use are discretionary and subjective. As Gudykunst and Kim remind us, "The important thing to remember is that symbols are symbols only because a group of people agree to consider them as such. There is not a natural connection between symbols and their referents: the relationships are arbitrary and vary from culture to culture."[5] What is being said here is that although all cultures use symbols, they usually assign their own meanings to them. Not only do Mexicans say *perro* for dog, but the image they form when they hear the sound is quite different from the one Americans may form. In addition to having different meanings for symbols, cultures also use these symbols for different purposes. In America and much of Europe, the prevalent view is that communication is used to get things done. Or as Trenholm and Jensen noted, "Communication is a powerful way of regulating and controlling our world."[6] In contrast, people in Japan, Taiwan, and China believe that information is internalized by most members of the culture, so not much needs to be coded. Because symbols are at the core of communication, we return to them throughout the book. For now, we remind you that symbols, by virtue of their standing for something else, give you an opportunity to share your personal realities.

Communication Is Systemic

We are using the word *systemic* to define the idea that communication does not occur in a vacuum, but rather is part of a larger system. We will briefly look at just a few of the elements of this system so that you will appreciate the interconnections within it.

Setting

You do not send and receive messages in isolation, but in a specific *setting*. According to Littlejohn, "Communication always occurs in context, and the nature of communication depends in large measure on this context."[7] Put more simply, setting and environment help determine the words and actions you generate and the meanings you give the symbols produced by other people. Context provides what Shimanoff calls a "prescription that indicates what behavior is obligated, preferred, or prohibited."[8] Dress, language, topic selection, and the like are all adapted to context. For example, under most circumstances, males would not, even in hot weather, attend a university lecture without wearing a shirt. The rules for each context, be it boardroom, classroom, or courtroom, are culturally based and therefore relative. As you will see later in this book, many of these contextual rules are directly related to your culture.

All cultures have stated and unstated rules regarding who takes part in the decision-making process during meetings. In the United States, the rule tells us it is the "boss." The simple American proverb "The buck stops here" gives us a clue as to the operational rule regarding decision making in the United States. In Japan, nearly everyone is consulted as part of the decision-making process. The Japanese proverb "Consult everyone, even your knees" demonstrates their approach to decision making.

When we speak of communication being systemic, we are referring to much more than the place of the interaction. Other elements associated with the systemic nature of communication are place, occasion, time, and number of participants. Even though these are found in all communication encounters, culture influences how we respond to them.

Location

People do not act the same way in every environment. The *location* of your interaction—whether an auditorium, restaurant, or office—provides guidelines for your behavior. Either consciously or unconsciously, you know the prevailing rules, many of which are rooted in your culture. Nearly all cultures, for example, have religious buildings, but the rules of behavior in those buildings are culturally based. In Mexico, men and women go to church together and remain quiet. In Iran, men and women do not worship together, and chanting instead of silence is the rule.

Occasion

The *occasion* of a communication encounter also controls the behavior of the participants. You know from your own experience that an auditorium can be the occasion for a graduation ceremony, pep rally, convocation, play, dance, or memorial service. Each of these occasions calls for a distinctly different type of behavior, and each culture has its own specifications for these behaviors. For example, in one culture the occasion of a wedding calls for solitude and silence (as would be the case of a royal wedding in Japan), yet in the Jewish culture the same occasion calls for loud music, dancing, and a great deal of merriment.

Time

The influence of *time* on communication is so subtle that its impact is often overlooked. To understand this concept, answer these questions: How do you feel when someone keeps you waiting for a long time? Do you respond to a phone call at 2:00 A.M. the same way you do to one at 2 P.M.? Do you find yourself rushing the conversation when you know you have very little time to spend with someone? The answers to these questions show that the clock often controls our actions. Every communication event takes place on a time–space continuum, and the amount of time allotted, whether it be for social conversation or a formal speech, affects that event. Cultures as well as people use time to communicate. In the United States, schedules and time constraints are ever present. As Hall and Hall note, "For Americans, the use of appointment-schedule time reveals how people feel about each other, how significant their business is, and where they rank in the status system."[9] Because time influences communication and the use of it is culture-bound, we treat the topic in greater detail in Chapter 6.

Number of People

The *number of people* with whom you communicate also affects the flow of communication. You know from personal experience that you feel and act differently if you are speaking with one person, in a group, or before a great many people. Cultures also respond to changes in number. For example, people in Japan find group interaction much to their liking, yet feel extremely uncomfortable when they have to give a formal public speech.

Cultural Setting

A still more general part of the communication event is the *cultural setting*. Wood notes, "The largest system affecting communication is our culture, which is the context within which all our interactions take place."[10] The rules, values, norms, traditions, taboos, and customs of a culture all affect the other areas of the communication system.

Communication Involves Making Inferences

Because there is no direct mind-to-mind contact between people, you cannot access the thoughts and feelings of other human beings, *you can only infer what they are experiencing*. You make these inferences from a single word, from silence, from long speeches, from simple head nods, and from glances in your direction or away from you.

This characteristic of communication has always frustrated human beings, for in a very real sense everyone is isolated from one another by the enclosure of their skin. What you know and feel remains inside of you, unless you communicate. It is as if you lived in a house with doors and windows that never opened. Perhaps the day will come when one of the futuristic devices from *Star Trek* becomes a reality and another human being can have direct access to what you are experiencing, but for now you must live in a kind of solitary confinement. An African proverb makes this point figuratively: "The earth is a beehive; we all enter by the same door but live in different cells."

Although the inability to have direct mind-to-mind contact is universal, the methods used to adjust to this limitation are culturally based. Some cultures believe that because they share a common pool of history and many similar experiences, they do indeed know what their partners are feeling and thinking. Yet in many Western cultures, the lack of direct access to another's mind places great demands on such communication behaviors as asking questions, engaging in self-disclosure, and oververbalizing.

You can well imagine some of the problems that might arise when people from these two orientations come together. We will discuss some of these problems later in the book.

Communication Is Self-Reflective

The American philosopher Emerson once wrote, "Wherever we go, whatever we do, self is the sole subject we study and learn." Emerson, whether he employed communication terminology or not, was referring to the idea that human beings have an ability to think about themselves, to watch how they define the world, and to reflect on their past, present, and future. This focus on self can, and usually does, take place while you are communicating. Ruben expresses it this way: "Because of self-reflectiveness, we are able to think about our encounters and our existence, about communication and human behavior."[11] This unique endowment lets you be participant and observer simultaneously: you can watch, evaluate, and alter your "performance" as a communicator at the very instant you are engaged in the act. Humans are the only species that can simultaneously be at both ends of the camera.

There is, as you have learned by now, an intercultural dimension to your capacity to be self-reflective, though this capacity may not always be manifest. Some cultures are much more concerned with the self than are others, and therefore devote a great deal of energy to watching and even worrying about the self. The "I" is at the heart of Western religion and psychology. For example, from Locke who said rationality meant you could know the answer to *all* questions, to modern self-help "experts" who speak of "personal power," Americans grow up believing the individual is at the center of the universe. Cultures that are more group oriented focus on other people, so although they can engage in self-reflective activity during communication, their main concern is with the other not with the self.

Communication Has a Consequence

As has been the case with all of the characteristics we have examined to this point, the next characteristic is woven throughout every chapter. This characteristic implies that when you receive a message, something happens to you. Also, all of your messages—to one degree or another—do something to someone else. This is not a philosophical or metaphysical theory, but a biological fact. It is impossible not to respond to the sounds and actions of others.

The responses you have to messages vary in degree and kind. It might help you to visualize your potential responses as forming a continuum (see Figure 2-1). At one end of the continuum lie responses to messages that are overt and easy to understand. Someone sends you a message by asking directions to the library. Your response is to say,

Figure 2-1 *Communication Responses*

```
1 ———————— 25 ———————— 50 ———————— 75 ———————— 100
Overt              Covert           Unconscious          Biological
```

"It's on your right." You might even point to the library. The message from the other person has thus produced an observable response.

A little farther across the continuum are those messages that produce only a mental response. If someone says to you, "The United States doesn't spend enough money on higher education," and you only think about this statement, you are still responding. Your response does not have to be an observable action.

As you proceed across the continuum, you come to responses that are harder to detect. These are responses to messages you receive by imitating, observing, and interacting with others. Generally, you are not even aware that you are receiving these messages. Your parents act out their gender roles, and you receive messages about your gender role. People greet you by shaking hands instead of hugging, and without being aware of it, you are receiving messages about forms of address.

At the far end of the continuum, you find the responses to messages that are received unconsciously. That is, your body responds even if your cognitive processes are kept to a minimum. Messages that come into you can alter your chemical secretions, increase or decrease your heart rate, change the temperature of your skin, modify pupil size, and trigger a host of other internal responses. Although these chemical and biological responses are the most difficult to classify, they give credence to our assertion that communication has a consequence. If your internal reactions produce chaos to your system, as is the case with severe stress, you can become ill. So regardless of the content of the message, it should be clear that the act of communication produces change in people.

All of you receive and respond to messages, yet the nature of your responses is rooted in your culture. The grief associated with the death of a loved one is as natural as breathing; each culture, however, determines ways of coping with and sharing that grief. These responses to the outside world range from outwardly wailing to maintaining a stoic exterior.

The response you make to someone's message does not have to be immediate. You can respond minutes, days, or even years later. For example, your second-grade teacher may have asked you to stop throwing rocks at a group of birds. Perhaps the teacher added that the birds were part of a family and were gathering food for their babies. She might also have indicated that birds feel pain just like people. Perhaps twenty years later, as you think about eating an animal, you remember those words from your teacher and decide to become a vegetarian.

It is important to remember the power of your messages and to consider the ethical consequences of your communication actions. For whether or not you want to grant those consequences, you are changing people each time you exchange messages with them. In the final chapter of the book, we offer some guidelines that you can employ as you evaluate your ethical responsibilities.

Communication Is Complex

One point should be obvious by now: *Communication is complex*. Think for a moment of all the bodily and mental activity that accompanies even the simple act of saying "hello" to a friend. From the stimulation of your nerve endings, to the secretion of chemicals in your brain, to the moving of your lips to produce sound, thousands of components are in operation (and most of them at the same time). Notice how the notion of complexity is clearly captured in the following observation advanced by Smith: "Human communication is a subtle and ingenious set of processes. It is always thick with a thousand ingredients—signals, codes, meanings—no matter how simple the message or transaction."[12] Communication becomes even more complex when cultural dimensions are added. Although all cultures use symbols to share their realities, the specific realities and the symbols employed are often quite different. In one culture you smile in a casual manner as a form of greeting, whereas in another you bow formally in silence, and in yet another you acknowledge your friend with a full embrace.

Another often overlooked reason why communication is complex is that *people are alike and they are different*. As you would suspect, this notion is difficult to explain. You need only reread the last sentence to begin appreciating our difficulty: we have to explain a statement that, at first glance, contains two contradictory ideas. We solve this problem by treating this apparent contradiction as a statement of two ideas that are both true.

People Are Alike

Let us start by talking about the premise that in many ways we are *like* every other human being. If you reflect for a moment, this entire section has focused on how people are alike: Each of you communicates by employing the same basic communication components—you construct symbols to represent your internal states, and other people receive and respond to those symbols. Your commonalties as a species, however, go far beyond the ways in which you share ideas and information. Because people are more alike than they are different, any inventory of these common qualities will be incomplete. Nevertheless, let us highlight a few commonalties so that you can better appreciate our starting premise.

People are identical in numerous physiological and chemical ways. We all have a heart, lungs, brain, and the like. You are also literally made of the same "stuff": Water, salt, and so on. Your genes and culture cause you to seek pleasure and avoid pain. That is, every human being—and all of the other animals with which we share this planet—devotes a great deal of energy to trying to avoid physical discomfort. Should you experience pain, you will suffer in much the same way as everyone else. Although the medical treatment might be different, a wound to the arm in Peru is much like a wound to the arm in Beverly Hills.

People also seek emotional pleasure and dislike injury to their feelings. Although the word ego may be very Western, the concepts behind it (self-respect, admiration, vanity, and the like) are common to all cultures. Ego may be called face-saving in China, *macho* in Mexico, and pride in Jordan, but the feelings evoked are very much the same.

You are also alike because *all of you*, regardless of your culture, must, at some point in life, face and attempt to resolve four fundamental truths. First, everyone realizes at some point that *life is finite:* You will not go on, at least in your present form, forever. As Shakespeare wrote in the *Tempest:* "We are such stuff / As dreams are made on, and our little life / Is rounded with a sleep." Second, everyone discovers early in life that they are *isolated from all other human beings*. As we noted earlier, the envelope of your skin separates you so that no one knows your exact internal states. Third, all of you, regardless of your culture, are thrown into a world that forces you to *make choices*. In the face of peer pressure and cultural and legal constraints, you have to make choices every instant of your life. Finally, the world has no built-in scheme that gives it meaning. It is, at the moment of birth, a meaningless world. Everyone *must give it meaning*.

We should add that cultures as well as individuals contribute to the pool of similarities. For example, every culture has a language, rules and norms about age and gender, a system of government, religions, economic systems, recreational and play activity, art, music, and the like.

There are, of course, numerous other commonalties, even those that relate to perception. People find the act of childbirth a dazzling and near mystical event. Nearly everyone belongs to a family, enjoys play and laughter, desires a mate, and wants someone to love and care for them. These and other universal experiences support the notion that people are very much alike. Having said that, we now move to a discussion of how they are different.

People Are Different

The English statesman Lord Chesterfield once wrote, "There never were, since the creation of the world, two cases exactly parallel." He might have also said that there have never been two people *exactly alike*. This belief is predicated on the simple fact that your experience of the world is both internal and unique. When you hear a word, or someone touches you, your body reacts from the inside out. The significance of this is apparent if you think about just two of the many actions in which people engage when they receive messages. First, the external world impinges on your nerve endings, causing something to happen within you. Second, you think about what is happening by employing symbols from your past (although you might have similar backgrounds, you have experienced each event in a unique way). We admit that this explanation is rather elementary, but it is nevertheless accurate. We have already noted that symbols, for example, do not mean the same thing to everyone—their interpretations are subjective. If you write the simple phrase "I like going to the race track," it can elicit a wide variety of responses depending on the listeners' background. One person might believe horse racing is "an evil form of gambling" and believe that you are foolish, yet another, reading the *same* words, could respond by saying, "I also like the races." *Subjectivity is always the rule*. A common beginning, anatomy, gender, age, culture, and the like may bind you, but your isolated minds and unique experiences keep you apart. The English essayist George Gissing captured the impossibility of knowing exactly what another person is experiencing: "It is the mind which creates the world about us, and even though we stand side by side in the same meadow, my eyes will never see what is beheld by yours, my heart will never stir to the emotions by which yours is touched."

Cultural, as well as individual, differences keep people apart. Although the philosophical issues of death, isolation, free choice, and meaning confront everyone, our resolutions for each issue have their roots deep in culture. For example, Hinduism tells its members that they will be reincarnated when they die. In Islam, death moves people into heaven or hell, depending on how they lived. Everyone thus deals with death in a personal way, but the options employed are cultural. Sitaram and Cogdell summarize this point:

> Members of different cultures look differently at the world around them. Some believe that the physical world is real. Others believe that it is just an illusion. Some believe everything around them is permanent while others say it is transient. Reality is not the same for all people.[13]

This notion of different realities, combined with the idea of cultural similarities, is at the heart of this book. That is why we repeatedly return to the theme that a *successful intercultural communicator appreciates similarities and accepts differences*.

UNDERSTANDING CULTURE

We now move from communication to culture. The transition should be a smooth one, for as Hall reminds us, "Culture is communication and communication is culture."[14] Or as the title of this chapter tells us, it is hard to distinguish which is the voice and which is the echo.

Some people in Korea and China put dogs in their ovens, but people in the United States put them on their couches and beds. Why? People in Tabriz or Tehran sit on the floor and pray five times each day, but people in Las Vegas stand up all night in front of slot machines. Why? Some people speak Tagalog; others speak English. Why? Some people paint and decorate their entire bodies, but others spend millions of dollars painting and decorating only their faces. Why? Some people talk to God, but others have God talk to them. And still others say there is no God. Why? The general answer to these questions is the same. People learn to think, feel, believe, and act as they do because of the messages that have been communicated to them, and those messages all bear the stamp of culture. This omnipresent quality of culture leads Hall to conclude that "there is not one aspect of human life that is not touched and altered by culture."[15] In many ways, Hall is correct: Culture is everything and everywhere. And more important, culture governs and defines the conditions and circumstances under which various messages may or may not be sent, noticed, or interpreted. As we noted elsewhere, you are born into a world without meaning. You do not arrive in this world knowing how to dress, what toys to play with, what to eat, which gods to worship, what to strive for, or how to spend your money and your time. *Culture is both teacher and textbook.* From how much eye contact you employ in conversations to explanations of why you get sick, culture plays a dominant role in your life. When cultures differ, communication practices also differ, as Smith pointed out:

> In modern society different people communicate in different ways, as do people in different societies around the world; and the way people communicate is the way they live. It is their culture. Who talks with whom? How? And about what? These are questions of communication and culture. A Japanese geisha and a New England librarian send and receive different messages on different channels and in different networks. When the elements of communication differ or change, the elements of culture differ or change. Communication and culture are inseparable.[16]

Because culture conditions you toward one particular mode of communication over another, it is imperative that you understand how culture operates as a first step toward improving intercultural communication. Although we will try to convince you that culture is a powerful force in how you see the world and interact in that world, you need to remember that in Chapter 1 we noted that a combination of elements contribute to the manner in which you communicate. We also told you that a specific individual may not always follow the dictates of his or her culture. Hanson offered a similar point of view when he wrote:

> Behavior is governed by many factors—socioeconomic status, sex, age, length of residence in a locale, education—each of which will have an impact on cultural practices as well. Finally, individuals may differ by the degree to which they choose to adhere to a set of cultural patterns. Some individuals identify strongly with a particular group; others combine practices from several groups.[17]

People are not born knowing what clothes to wear, what games to play, what foods to eat, or which gods to worship.

© Robert Fonseca

In this chapter, we (1) explain why cultures develop, (2) define culture, (3) discuss the major components of culture, and (4) examine the basic forms of intercultural communication.

The Basic Functions of Culture

The anthropologist Haviland suggests that "people maintain cultures to deal with problems or matters that concern them."[18] Nanda and Warms say "Culture is the major way in which human beings adapt to their environments and give meaning to their lives."[19] It is believed that culture evolved for the same reasons: *It serves the basic need of laying out a predictable world in which each of you is firmly grounded and thus enables you to make sense of your surroundings.* As the English writer Fuller wrote two hundred years ago, "Culture makes all things easy." Culture makes "things easy" for two important reasons.

First, culture helps facilitate the transition from the womb to this new life by providing meaning to events, objects, and people—thus making the world a less mysterious and frightening place. Second, culture makes life less confusing because, as we shall see later, most of culture is automatic and subconscious. Shapiro explains this idea:

> Thus, the influence of culture becomes habitual and subconscious and makes life easier, just as breathing, walking and other functions of the body are relegated to subconscious controls, freeing the conscious parts of the brain of this burden and releasing it for other activities.[20]

Culture, using the family as its first of many conduits, teaches the child how to behave in a manner that is acceptable to adults and that garners them rewards. There is no need for members of a culture to expend energy deciding what each event means or how to respond to it; usually, all those who share a common culture can be expected to behave correctly, automatically, and predictably. Hence, culture shields people from the unknown by offering them a blueprint for all of life's activities. Try to imagine a single day in your life without having the guidelines of your culture. From how to earn a living, to a systematic economic system, to how to greet strangers, to how to find a mate, culture provides you with structure. This structure supplies you with the skills and rules necessary to adapt to our world. We might even go so far as to agree with Harris that "our primary mode of biological adaptation is culture, not anatomy."[21]

In addition to making the world a less perplexing place, cultures have now evolved to the point where they are people's primary means of satisfying three types of needs: Basic needs (food, shelter, physical protection), derived needs (organization of work, distribution of food, defense, social control), and integrative needs (psychological security, social harmony, purpose in life).[22]

Definitions of Culture

As we have seen, culture is ubiquitous, multidimensional, complex, and all-pervasive. That combination of attributes makes culture hard to define. As was the case with communication, many definitions have been suggested for culture. As early as 1952, Kroeber and Kluckhohn listed 164 definitions of culture that they found in the anthropology literature.[23] And, of course, many new definitions have appeared since. Definitions of culture range from those that are all-encompassing ("it is everything") to those that are narrow ("it is opera, art, and ballet"). For our purposes, we are concerned with a definition that contains the recurring theme of how culture and communication are linked together. A definition that meets our needs is one advanced by Marsella:

> Culture is shared learned behavior which is transmitted from one generation to another for purposes of promoting individual and social survival, adaptation, and growth and development. Culture has both external (e.g., artifacts, roles institutions) and internal representations (e.g., values, attitudes, beliefs, cognitive/affective/sensory styles, consciousness patterns, and epistemologies.)[24]

We like Marsella's definition because it can include everything from rites of passage to concepts of the soul. Think for just a moment of all the cultural beliefs you hold that influence how you perceive the world and interact in it. How you respond to the American flag, as opposed to the Cuban flag, is part of your cultural membership. Your views on work, immigration, freedom, age, being graded by your teachers, cleanliness and hygiene, ethics, dress, property rights, etiquette, healing and health, death and mourning, play, law, magic and superstition, modesty, sex, status differentiation, courtship, formality and informality, bodily adornment, and the like are part of your cultural membership.

Characteristics of Culture

Regardless of how many definitions we could have examined, there would have been a great deal of agreement concerning the major characteristics of culture. Examining these characteristics will help you become a better communicator for two reasons. First, as we move through these characteristics, the strong connection between culture and communication will become apparent. You will discover that culture deals with matters of substance that influence communication. As Huntington notes, "The heart of culture involves language, religion, values, traditions, and customs."[25] Second, although we all hold memberships in various cultures, this might be the first time you have been exposed to the theory of culture. Remember, most of culture is in the taken-for-granted realm and below the conscious level. Learning about culture can therefore be a stimulating awakening as you give meaning to your actions and the actions of others. Shapiro offered much the same "pep-talk" when he wrote: "The discovery of culture, the awareness that it shapes and molds our behavior, our values and even our ideas, the recognition that it contains some element of the arbitrary, can be a startling or an illuminating experience."[26]

Culture Is Learned

Earlier in this chapter we noted that everyone is born into a world without meaning. From the moment of birth to the end of your life, you seek to define the world that impinges on your senses. This idea is often difficult to comprehend, for most of you cannot remember a world without definitions and meanings. Yet perhaps you can imagine what a confusing place this world must be to a newborn infant. After living in a peaceful environment, the child, with but a brief transition, confronts sights, sounds, tastes, and other sensations that, at this stage of life, have no meanings. It must be, as the psychologist William James noted, a bubbling, babbling mass of confusion that greets the newborn. But from that first moment on, the search for meaning becomes a lifelong endeavor. As you move from word to word, event to event, and person to person, you seek meaning in everything. The meanings you give to these experiences are learned and culturally based. In some ways, this entire book is about how different cultures "teach" their members to define the circumstances and people that confront them.

This notion of learning is the single most important characteristic of culture. Without the advantages of learning from those who lived before, you would not have culture. In fact, "the group's knowledge stored up (in memories, books and objects) for future use" is at the core of the concept of culture.[27] All of you are born with basic needs—needs that create and shape behavior—but how you go about meeting those needs and developing behaviors to cope with them is learned. As Bates and Plog note:

> Whether we feed ourselves by growing yams or hunting wild game or by herding camels and raising wheat, whether we explain a thunderstorm by attributing it to meteorological conditions or to a fight among the gods—such things are determined by what we learn as part of our enculturation.[28]

The term *enculturation* denotes the total activity of learning one's culture. More specifically, enculturation is, as Hoebel and Frost say, "*conscious or unconscious conditioning*

© Gloria Thomas

In European art the emphasis has been on the individual.

occurring within that process whereby the individual, as child and adult, achieves competence in a particular culture."[29] In social psychology and sociology, the term *socialization* is often used synonymously with enculturation. Regardless of which word is applied, the idea is the same. From infancy, members of a culture learn their patterns of behavior and ways of thinking until most of them become internalized and habitual. Enculturation usually takes place through *interaction* (your parents kiss you and you learn about kissing—whom, when, and where to kiss), *observation* (you watch your father do most of the driving of the family car and you learn about gender roles—what a man does, what a woman does), and *imitation* (you laugh at the same jokes your parents laugh at and you learn about humor).

The words *conscious* and *unconscious* used above in Hoebel and Frost's definition help us make our next assertion about learning. When you look at the word *learned* as it applies to culture, you find it has numerous meanings. Just as the word *pain* is used to denote the discomfort caused by a small splinter in the finger or the anguish felt by a burn victim, so too the word *learned* is asked to represent a host of variations. That is, *you learn your culture in many ways and from a variety of sources.* The little boy in the United States whose grandfather tells him to shake hands when he is introduced to a friend of the family is learning culture. The Arab baby who is read the Koran when he or she is one day old is learning culture. The Indian child who lives in a home where the women eat after the men is learning culture. The Jewish child who helps conduct the Passover ceremony is learning culture. The French child who is given hard cider at dinner is learning culture. The Egyptian child who is told by his uncle that his behavior brings shame to his family is learning culture. The Japanese girl who attends tea ceremony classes is learning about culture.

Conscious learning is easier to understand and to explain than is unconscious learning. In its simplest form, it is learning at the cognitive level. It is reading about or being told or shown what culture wants us to know. You see a film in your fourth-grade class about the courage people demonstrated in their attempt to save the Alamo, and you learn about patriotism and fortitude. A mother tells her young son to take a bath before he goes to bed, and he learns health habits and the importance of cleanliness. A father tells his daughter to thank someone who pays her a compliment, and she learns about manners. You read in the Bible about the compassion Jesus showed toward prostitutes, and you are introduced to values. The football coach admonishes his team to "take your punishment like men," and they learn gender roles. In these examples, people are told to think consciously about the messages they are receiving. Although this type of enculturation is part of the learning process, it is at the second level of learning—the unconscious—where you learn the bulk of what is called culture.

Because culture influences you from the instant you are born, you are rarely aware of many of the messages that it sends. As Keesing says, "It is a tenet of cultural anthropology that culture tends to be unconscious."[30] This *unconscious* or hidden dimension of culture leads many researchers to claim that culture is invisible. Ruben, for example, writes that "the presence of culture is so subtle and pervasive that it simply goes unnoticed. It's there now, it's been there as long as anyone can remember, and few of us have reason to think much about it."[31] Most of you would have a difficult time pointing to a specific event or experience that taught you about such things as direct eye contact, your use of silence and space, the importance of attractiveness, your view of aging, your ability to speak one language instead of another, and your preference for activity over meditation or for one mode of dealing with conflict over another. In short, while you would readily recognize that you had to learn how to solve a mathematics problem, you are apt to overlook the fact that you also had to learn how to worry and what to worry about, who to love and who not to love, who to touch and who not to touch.

A number of points should be clear by now. First, learning cultural perceptions, rules, and behaviors usually goes on without your being aware of it. Second, the essential messages of a culture get reinforced and repeated. And third, you learn your culture from a large variety of sources. In the next chapter, we examine how family, church, and state "teach" culture, and in Chapter 8 we discuss how schools are also a conduit for culture. But for now, let us touch on some of the more invisible "instructors" and their "instructions."

You Learn Your Culture Through Proverbs. In nearly every culture, proverbs, communicated in colorful and vivid language, offer an important set of instructions for members to follow. Because they are so brief (a line or two) their power as a "teacher" is often overlooked. Yet the great Chinese philosophers such as Confucius, Mencius, Chung Tzu, and Lao-tzu used proverbs and maxims to express their thoughts to their disciples—thoughts that still endure in the Chinese culture. These "words of wisdom" survive, so that each generation learns about what a culture deems significant. As Sellers tells us, "Proverbs reunite the listener with his or her ancestors."[32] Seidensticker notes that "They say things that people think important in ways that people remember.

They express common concerns."[33] Hence, "proverbs are a compact treatise on the values of culture."[34]

Proverbs are learned easily and repeated with great regularity. For this reason they soon become part of an individual's belief system. Because all people, regardless of their culture, share common experiences, many of the same proverbs appear throughout the world. However, there are also many proverbs that cultures use to teach important lessons that are unique to that particular culture. We can even learn about a culture by looking at these proverbs. The importance of proverbs as a reflection of a culture is underscored by the fact that "interpreters at the United Nations prepare themselves for their extremely sensitive job by learning proverbs of the foreign language" they will be translating.[35] As Mieder notes, "Studying proverbs can offer insights into a culture's world view regarding such matters as education, law, business, and marrage."[36]

Below are a few proverbs and sayings from the United States, each of which stresses an important American value—that is, a value held by the dominant culture.

Strike while the iron is hot. He who hesitates is lost. In the United States, we value people who take quick action. Even our problem-solving techniques are characterized by impulsive rather than reflective methods.

Actions speak louder than words. As noted in the next chapter, Americans are a "doing" culture, hence activity and "getting things done" are important to the dominant culture.

God helps those who help themselves. Pull yourself up by your boot straps. These sayings call attention to the strong belief in America that people should show initiative.

A man's home is his castle. This expression not only tells us about the value of privacy, but it also demonstrates the male orientation in the United States by implying the home belongs to the man.

The squeaky wheel gets the grease. In the United States, people are encouraged to be direct, "speak up" and make sure their views are heard.

Below are some proverbs from places other than the United States. You will see some of these proverbs again elsewhere in this book as we use them to explain the communication behavior of the cultures from which they come.

A proverb is like a swift horse. The Yorubas of Africa believe that people are not qualified to take part in communal discussions unless they are able to quote the proverbs relevant to each situation. The "swift horse" proverb simply underscores the importance of proverbs to this culture.

One does not make the wind but is blown by it. This saying, found in many Asian cultures, suggests that people are guided by fate rather than by their own devices.

The ill-mannered child finds a father wherever he goes. This African proverb demonstrates the value of the extended family, for it is saying that everyone takes a hand in raising the child.

Order is half of life. This expresses the value Germans place on organization, conformity, and structure.

Even if the bridge be made of stone, make sure it is safe. This Korean saying expresses the wisdom of going slowly and being cautious and reflective.

Nothing done with intelligence is done without speech. This Greek saying emphasizes the importance of talk as a means of communication.

Wisdom is better than jewels. This Jewish saying expresses the importance of learning and education.

A zebra does not despise its stripes. From the Maasai of Africa, this saying expresses the value of accepting things as they are, of accepting oneself as one is, and of not envying others.

A man's tongue is his sword. With this saying, Arabs are taught to value words and use them in a powerful and forceful manner.

Those who know do not speak and those who speak do not know. This famous doctrine, in the Analects of Confucius, stressing silence over talk, is very different from the advice give in the above Arab proverb.

Conversation is the food for the soul. In this Mexican proverb we see yet another view toward talking. The Mexican culture has a long tradition of valuing interaction among friends and family.

He who stirs another's porridge often burns his own. The Swedish, a very private people, teach the value of privacy with this proverb.

However crowded the way be, the hen will reach her eggs. The African proverb stresses the love of a mother for her children.

When spider webs unite they can tie up a lion. This Ethiopian proverb teaches the importance of collectivism and group solidarity.

We are all like well buckets, one goes up and the other comes down. This proverb expresses Mexicans' belief that life is a series of opposites—life and death, illness and health, pain and pleasure.

You Learn Your Culture from Folktales, Legends, and Myths. The stories each culture tells its people, whether in the form of folktales, legends, or myths, are all intended to transmit the culture from person to person and from generation to generation. Anthropologists Nanda and Warms highlight the importance of this form of cultural learning in the following paragraph:

> Folktales and storytelling usually have an important moral, revealing which cultural values are approved and which are condemned. The audience for folktales is always let, through the ways the tale is told, to know which characters and attributes are a cause for ridicule or scorn and which characters and attributes are to be admired.[37]

Whether it be Pinocchio's nose growing larger because of his lies, Columbus being glorified because he was daring, Captain Ahab's heroics as he seeks to overcome the power of nature, Abraham Lincoln learning to read by drawing letters on a shovel by the fireside, or the Power Rangers defending democracy and fighting for what is "right," folklore constantly reinforces our fundamental values. A case in point is the popular folk tale "Cinderella." Although nearly every culture has its own version of this story, the emphasis varies. In the American version, Cinderella's attractiveness is crucial; she is also rather passive and weak. In the Algonquin Indian tale, the virtues of truthfulness and honesty are the basis of Cinderella's character. The Japanese story accentuates intellectual ability and gentleness. In one Japanese version, there are only two sisters and they wish to go to a Kabuki play. In place of the famous slipper test is the challenge of having to compose a song extemporaneously. One sister manages only a simple, unimaginative song, which she sings in "a loud harsh voice." But Cinderella composes a song that has both meter and metaphor, and she sings it in "sweet gentle tones." Traits that are important to the specific culture are reflected in each version of the tale.

Every culture has hundreds of tales, each stressing a fundamental value. Americans revere the tough, independent, fast-shooting cowboy of the Old West; the English admiration of good manners, courtly behavior, and dignity is reflected in *The Canterbury Tales;* the Japanese learn about the importance of duty, obligation, and loyalty in the ancient story of *The Tale of the Forty-Seven Ronin;* and the Sioux Indians use the legend of *Pushing Up the Sky* to teach what people can accomplish if they work together. In Zaire children are told the *Myth of Invincibility.* In this story young boys learn that if they wrap green vines around their head the enemies weapons cannot hurt them.[38]

Legends, folktales, and myths do more than accent cultural values: "they confront cosmic questions about the world as a whole."[39] In addition, they can tell us about specific details of life that might be important to a group of people. Writing about Native American myths and legends, Erdoes and Ortiz make the following point concerning what stories can tell us about what was, and is, important to the Native American culture:

> They are also magic lenses through which we can glimpse social orders and daily life: How families were organized, how political structures operated, how men caught fish, how religious ceremonies felt to the people who took part, how power was divided between men and women, how food was prepared, how honor in war was celebrated.[40]

As we have seen, myths are useful tools for teaching culture because they cover a wide range of cultural concerns. Perhaps their most significant contribution is that they deal with the ideas that matter most to a culture—ideas about life, death, relationships, nature, and the like. Campbell tells us, "Myths are stories of our search through the ages for truth, for meaning, for significance. We all need to tell our story and to understand our story."[41] Because myths offer clues into culture, Campbell urges us not only to understand our story, but to "read other people's myths."[42] We strongly concur with Campbell—when you study the myths of a culture, you are studying the heart of that culture.

You Learn Your Culture Through Art. A trip to any museum in the world quickly reveals how the art of culture is yet another method of passing on culture. According to the art historian Gombrich, the Chinese have long "thought of art as a means of reminding people of the great examples of virtue in the golden ages of the past."[43] Nanda points out that the link between art and culture can be found in every culture:

> Art is a symbolic way of communicating. One of the most important functions of art is to communicate, display, and reinforce important cultural themes and values. The arts thus have an integrative function in society.[44]

One of the functions that Nanda is referring to is how the individual, through art, learns about himself or herself. In Asian cultures, most art depicts objects, animals, and landscapes, seldom focusing on people. American and European art, however, often emphasizes people. This difference reflects a difference in views: Asians believe that nature is more powerful and important than a single individual, whereas Americans and Europeans consider people as the center of the universe. In addition, in Western art, the artist tries to create a personal message. This is not the case with most Eastern artists. As Campbell notes, "Such ego-oriented thinking is alien completely to the Eastern life, thought, and religiosity."[45] The rule of the Eastern artist is not to "innovate or invent."[46]

As we already indicated, art is a relevant symbol, a forceful teacher, and an avenue for cultural values. Two more examples will further illustrate this point. We need only look at the art on totem poles to see what matters to Native Americans. The carvings on these poles tell us the story of a people who are concerned about their lineage and their identity. Hence, we see carvings that show relationships "between humans and animals, plants, and inanimate objects."[47] For many African cultures, art is used to call attention to the importance of such things as animals and "ancestor worship and reverence of royalty."[48]

You Learn Your Culture Through Mass Media. In the United States and in other Western cultures, the mass media do much more than supply entertainment. As Thompson tells us:

> Few people would deny that the nature of cultural experience in modern societies has been profoundly affected by the development of mass communication. Books, magazines and newspapers, radio, television and cinema, records, tapes and videos: These and other forms of mass communication occupy a central role in our lives.[49]

As the above quotation points out, the term *mass media* applies to a variety of sources, each helping to shape our perceptions of the world. While granting the importance of printed media, it is television, at least in the United States, that is most influential. Television contributes to what Williams calls "mass social learning," which has us "taking on the values of the images" we are exposed to on television.[50] Because exposure is five to six hours a day for the average American, it is easy to see how these images affect our attitudes toward sex, leisure time, and people of different ethnic, gender, and/or age groups. Mass media can even shape our views toward violence. In the United States, films, police stories, and many documentaries glorify violence. The language that we use in sports mirrors and sanctions violence. Sitting in front of a television set, one hears words and statements such as "kill," "head-hunter," "It's a war," and "They destroyed the offense."

Delgado offers us an excellent summary of the power of mass media by noting that they "help constitute our daily lives by shaping our experiences and providing the content for much of what we talk about (and how we talk) at the interpersonal level."[51]

As we have said elsewhere, the messages that are strategic for any culture are repeated, are reinforced, and come from various sources. Think for a moment of the thousands of ways you have been told the importance of being popular and well liked, or the many messages you have received concerning competition and winning. Our games, sports, toys, movies, and so on all fortify the need to win. A famous tennis player tells us that he "feels like dying when he comes in second." And the president of a major car company concludes his television pitch by announcing, "We want to be number one—what else is there?" Although the carriers of culture are nearly the same for all people, the messages they transmit, as we point out throughout this book, are specific to each culture.

We conclude our description of the first characteristic of culture by reminding you of three key points. First, most of the behaviors we label as cultural are not only automatic and invisible, but also engaged in without your being aware of them. For example, in American culture, women smile more often than men,[52] a behavior learned unconsciously and performed almost habitually. And to this day, Jews, while reading from the Torah, sway backward and forward like camel riders, having inherited this behavior unconsciously from centuries ago. Because Jews then were prohibited from riding camels, this imitation of riding was developed as a form of compensation.[53] Although the motive for the behavior is gone, the action has been passed on to each new generation by means of the silent, invisible power of culture. Such cultural behaviors, and there are thousands of them, tend to be unconscious in both acquisition and expression.

Second, it is important that we remind you that we have only mentioned some of the many ways we learn our culture. Space constraints have forced us to leave out many subtle yet powerful "teachers." For example, in every culture sports is much more than simple play. As Nanda and Warms tell us, "Football in America and bull fighting in Spain are both popular because they illustrate important themes of the respective cultures. They are exciting in part because they tell stories loaded with cultural meaning."[54] We will return to some very important cultural influences when we look at family, state, and religion in Chapter 4.

Finally, the methods and material of learning culture we discussed are important because they are available to most members of the culture—and have been for generations. One of the truisms of cultural studies is that common experiences usually produce common behaviors. The sharing of experience and behavior binds members and makes a culture unique. The Polish poet Stanislaw said it far more eloquently: "All of our separate fictions add up to a joint reality." Discovering those realities is what this book is all about.

Culture Is Transmitted from Generation to Generation

The American philosopher Thoreau once wrote, "All the past is here." For a culture to exist and endure, it must ensure that its crucial messages and elements are passed on. As Brislin said, "If there are values considered central to a society that have existed for many years, these must be transmitted from one generation to another."[55] As you saw in

Culture is transmitted from generation to generation.

our first characteristic, the means of transmitting the culture can take a variety of forms (proverbs, stories, art, etc.) and can have numerous "carriers" (family, peers, media, church, etc.), but the key elements of culture must be shared with each new generation. This idea supports our assertion that culture and communication are linked: Communication makes culture a continuous process, for once cultural habits, principles, values, attitudes, and the like are "formulated," they are communicated to each member of the culture. So strong is the need for a culture to bind each generation to past and future generations that, Keesing tells us, "Any break in the learning chain would lead to a culture's disappearance."[56]

Culture Is Based on Symbols

When you talk about symbols you are also talking about culture. Notice the link between symbols and culture in the definition of the word *symbol* advanced by Macionis: "A symbol is anything that carries a particular meaning recognized by people who share culture."[57] So important are symbols to a culture that the anthropologist Clyde Kluckhohn once wrote, "Human culture without language is unthinkable."[58] The emergence of language was the giant step that made possible the remarkable and intricate system we call culture. Your cerebral cortex and all the neurological structures associated with it have developed in a way that enables you to use symbols at a level of sophistication not shared by any other creature. Not only can you transmit knowledge from person to person, you also can pass ideas from generation to generation—a characteristic of culture we just examined. At our disposal are the speculations, observations, facts, experiments, and wisdom accumulated over thousands of years—what the linguist Weinberg called "the grand insights of geniuses which, transmitted through symbols, enable us to span the learning of centuries."[59] Through language—be it verbal, nonverbal, or iconic—it is, as Goodenough says, "possible to learn from cumulative, shared experience."[60] An excellent summary of the importance of language to culture is offered by Bates and Plog:

The important elements of a culture get transmitted through a variety of symbols.

© Gloria Thomas

Language thus enables people to communicate what they would do if such-and-such happened, to organize their experiences into abstract categories ("a happy occasion," for instance, or an "evil omen"), and to express thoughts never spoken before. Morality, religion, philosophy, literature, science, economics, technology, and numerous other areas of human knowledge and belief—along with the ability to learn about and manipulate them—all depend on this type of higher-level communication.[61]

As we have already indicated, the symbols any culture employs take a variety of forms. Cultures can use the spoken word as a symbol and tell people about the importance of freedom. They can use the written word as a symbol and let others read about the War of Independence. They can use nonverbal actions, such as shaking hands or bowing, as symbols to greet one another. They can use flags as symbols to claim territory or demonstrate loyalty. They have the means to use automobiles or jewelry as symbols of success and status. They can use a cross, crescent, or six-pointed star to show the love of God.

The portability of symbols allows us to package and store them as well as transmit them. The mind, books, pictures, films, videos, computer disks, and the like enable a culture to preserve what it deems to be important and worthy of transmission. This makes each individual, regardless of his or her generation, heir to a massive repository of information that has been gathered and maintained in anticipation of his or her entry into the culture. *Culture is therefore accumulative, historical, and perceivable*. As the French novelist Marcel Proust wrote, "The past remains the present."

Culture Is Subject to Change

The Greek philosopher Heraclitus might well have been talking about culture, when, over two thousand years ago, he observed: "You cannot step twice into the same river, for other waters are continually flowing in." What he was telling us then is true even today—cultures do not exist in a vacuum; they, because of "other waters continually flowing in," are subject to change. As Ethington notes, they are in a never-ending "process of reinvention."[62] Part of that reinvention stems from cultures coming in contact with one another. From the wandering nomad of thousands of years ago to millions of people all watching the same news event on CNN, cultures are constantly being confronted with ideas and information from outside sources. As we demonstrate in Chapter 1, today, because of the spread of Western capitalism and the availability of electronic information systems, cultures are being bombarded with new ideas that are often being presented by a host of "strangers." These "foreigners" may live next door or across the globe, but contact and change, whether in small increments or dramatic bursts, are now inevitable.

Change through contact is another example of how communication and culture are alike. Communication is not static, but rather is dynamic and constantly changing. Cultures are also subject to fluctuations, seldom remaining constant. Although cultures change through several mechanisms, the three most common are (1) innovation, (2) diffusion, and (3) acculturation.

Innovation is usually defined as the discovery of new practices, tools, or concepts that many members of the culture eventually accept and that may produce slight changes in social habits and behaviors.[63] In the United States, television, the computer, and the women's rights movement are good examples of products and concepts that reshaped culture. As you can see by the three examples we cited, change occurs much faster, and there is more of it, in modern and technological cultures.[64]

Because much of culture is habitual, and because many people fear change, you can find examples in every culture of how innovation sometimes does not gain complete acceptance. For example, there are still countless individuals in America who dislike computers and others who rail against women having rights equal to those of men.

Diffusion, another mechanism of change, is the borrowing by one culture from another. Historically, diffusion has been part of cultural contact for as long as cultures have existed. Whether it be the sugar from a plant of Middle Eastern origin taken to the New World or the McDonald's hamburger now being sold throughout the world, diffusion is everywhere.

Because cultures want to endure, they usually adopt only those elements that are compatible with their values and beliefs or that can be modified without causing major disruption. The assimilation of what is borrowed accelerates when cultures come into direct regular contact with each other. For example, as Japan and the United States have more commerce, we see Americans assimilating Japanese business practices and the Japanese using American marketing tactics.

Acculturation, as a type of cultural change, "occurs when a society undergoes drastic culture change under the influence of a more dominant culture and society with which it has come in contact."[65] Usually acculturation is in response to extended and intensive firsthand contact between two or more previously autonomous cultures or cocultures. This type of change is common to international immigrants, who for a variety of reasons find themselves in another culture. These people, as part of the acculturation process, need to cope with a considerable amount of cultural change. In most instances, they "begin to detect new patterns of thinking and behavior and to structure a personality relevant to adaptation to the host society."[66] Inherent in acculturation is the idea that most people, as they are adapting, are also holding on to many of the values, customs, and communication patterns found in their primary culture.

How successful people are in coping with a new culture is contingent on a host of factors. We focus on two here. First, how well one adapts is related to one's primary culture. That is, an English-speaking immigrant from Wales would have an easier time adapting to American culture than would someone from rural China. Second, acculturation is influenced by the specific behavior that is being modified. As Bates and Plog point out, "A society that gradually adopts the practices of another culture does not adopt every behavior or belief of that culture."[67] You can well imagine how much easier acculturation is when it involves utensils for eating instead of religious beliefs.

We return to the topic of acculturation in Chapter 10 when we offer some concrete advice as to how the transition from one culture to another can be made less stressful.

We conclude by pointing out a major consideration when analyzing cultural changes: *Although many aspects of culture are subject to change, the deep structure of a culture resists major alterations.* That is, changes in dress, food, transportation, housing, and the like are compatible with the existing value system. However, values associated with such things as ethics and morals, work and leisure, definitions of freedom, the importance of the past, religious practices, the pace of life, and attitudes toward gender and age are so deeply embedded in a culture that they persist generation after generation—a point Barnlund makes when he writes, "The spread of Buddhism, Islam, Christianity, and Confucianism did not homogenize the societies they enveloped. It was usually the other way around: Societies insisted on adapting the religions to their own cultural traditions."[68] In the United States, studies conducted on American values show that most contemporary core values are similar to the values of the last two hundred years. In short, when assessing the degree of change within a culture, you must always consider what is changing. Do not be fooled because downtown Tokyo looks much like Paris or New York. Most of what you call culture is below the surface, or like the moon: You observe the front, which appears flat and one-dimensional, but there are other dimensions that we cannot see.

Culture Is an Integrated System

Throughout this chapter, we have broken down and isolated various pieces of culture and talked about them as if they were discrete parts. The nature of language makes it impossible to do otherwise; yet in reality, culture functions as an integrated whole—it is, like communication, systemic. That is, culture "is composed of parts that are related to each other."[69] Think of all the important ingredients of culture in operation when families take children to church where they learn some of the key cultural values that they act out at school and even outside in the playground. As Hall said, "You touch a culture in one place and everything else is affected."[70] Values toward materialism will influence family size, the work ethic, spiritual pursuits, and the like. A complex example of the interconnectedness of cultural elements is the civil rights movement in the United States. This movement has brought about changes in housing patterns, discrimination practices, educational opportunities, the legal system, career opportunities, and even communication. Hence, this one aspect of culture has altered American attitudes, values, and behaviors.

Culture Is Adaptive

As has been shown from our discussion of cultural change, cultures are quite adaptive. History abounds with examples of how cultures have changed because of laws, shifts in values, natural disasters, wars, or other calamities. Changing sex roles in the United States is a case in point. For most of the history of this country, women were expected to remain in the home and raise the children. When they did work, they usually were either secretaries, nurses, or teachers. However, forces in the culture, as well as economic considerations, dramatically altered the role of women in this country. Both men and women have made major adaptations to this cultural change. There are, of course, countless other examples. Events in the last few hundred years have scattered Jews throughout the world, yet their culture has adapted and survived. And think for a moment about the major changes made by the Japanese to their society: Their government and economy were nearly destroyed during World War II, yet because they could adapt, their culture has endured and they are now a major political and economic force in the world.

We conclude this section on the characteristics of culture by reminding you that the pull of culture is so strong because teaching begins at birth and continues throughout life. Using the standard language of her time (sexist by today's standards), anthropologist Ruth Benedict offered an excellent explanation of why culture is such a puissant influence on all our lives:

> The life history of the individual is first and foremost an accommodation to the patterns and standards traditionally handed down in his community. From the moment of his birth the customs into which he is born shape his experience and behavior. By the time he can talk, he is the little creature of his culture, and by the time he is grown and able to take part in its activities, its habits are his habits, its beliefs his beliefs, its impossibilities his impossibilities.

Every child that is born into his group will share them with him, and no child born into the opposite side of the globe can ever achieve the thousandth part.[71]

The important point to take away from the preceding paragraph, and this entire discussion of culture, is beautifully expressed in the following simple sentence: "God gave to every people a cup, a cup of clay, and from this cup they drank life. . . . They all dipped in the water, but their cups were different."[72] Or as we said earlier in the chapter, we are all alike and we are all different, and culture represents part of those differences.

INTERCULTURAL COMMUNICATION

We have spent the bulk of this chapter demonstrating the link between communication and culture. Underlying our entire analysis has been the premise that the individual and his or her culture are interlocking systems. Barnlund summarized this important idea: "The individual and society are antecedent and consequent of each other: Every person is at once a creator of society and its most obvious product."[73] Hence, having developed fusion between culture and communication, we now are ready to discuss how that coalition produces the study of intercultural communication. We begin with a definition of intercultural communication and conclude the chapter by mentioning some of the forms that this type of communication can take.

A Definition of Intercultural Communication

In its most general sense, intercultural communication occurs when a member of one culture produces a message for consumption by a member of another culture. More precisely, *intercultural communication is communication between people whose cultural perceptions and symbol systems are distinct enough to alter the communication event.* Frequently, the term *cross-cultural communication* is used when referring to communication between people from different cultures. Because this term implies a comparison between cultures (for example, different styles of leadership), we find it too restrictive. There are, however, other terms that we can use to focus on various dimensions and forms of intercultural communication.

Forms of Intercultural Communication

The words and labels *race, ethnic groups,* and *co-cultures* are often used in discussions of intercultural communication. Although we believe that all three of these are actually forms of intercultural communication, we nevertheless will briefly define each of them.

Interracial Communication
Interracial communication occurs when the source and the receiver exchanging messages are from different races. Most scholars now reserve the word *race* for physical features rather than cultural traits. As Macionis notes, "People classify each other racially based on physical characteristics such as skin color, hair texture, facial features, and body shape."[74] There is even some argument supporting the notion that because physical traits are beginning to blend, especially in the United States, race will not be distinct

enough to warrant separate categories. But for now it needs to be remembered that physical differences frequently do influence communication—and in a very profound way. From avoiding people of color to using race to act out strong prejudices and discrimination, race does influence human interaction. Throughout this book in general ways, and very specifically in Chapter 10, we will try to focus on both the causes and cures of racism.

Interethnic Communication

Ethnic groups usually form their own communities in a country or culture. These groups share a common origin or heritage that is apt to influence common ancestors, family names, language, religion, values, and the like. What is unique about ethnicity is that ethnic groups share the "same social environment" with members of the dominant culture and with other ethnic groups.[75] Cubans living in Miami, Mexicans in San Diego, Haitians in New York City, and Chinese in San Francisco might all be citizens of the United States, yet their ethnic culture is transferred intergenerationally. This transfer enables the members of these, and other ethnic groups, to preserve their identity to some degree while living within the dominant culture.[76]

Much like race, one's ethnic background is often an issue in intercultural communication. Think for a moment about the intercultural implications of the term *ethnic cleansing*. In Bosnia, Kosovo, Southern Africa, and elsewhere, we can see vivid examples of what happens when people use ethnicity as a method of deciding social stratifications. We will, throughout this book, talk about how these negative views of someone's ethnicity are both unethical and harmful to intercultural understanding.

Co-cultural Communication

Although we have been using the word *co-culture* since Chapter 1, it might be helpful if we explain the term in a little more detail, and also offer the rationale behind our preference for the word *co-culture* over the word *subculture*.

The key to co-cultures is twofold. First, it should be obvious that people often hold dual or multiple memberships, and that these affiliations have behaviors and perceptions that are learned. For a number of years, the social scientific literature employed the word *subculture* when referring to individuals and groups of people who, while living in the dominant culture, had membership in another culture. In recent years, however, the term has been replaced and the concept itself reformulated. The term *co-culture* is now used because the prefix *sub* implies that members of the nondominant group are deficient and inadequate. *Subculture* also carries connotations implying "better and worse and superior and inferior."[77] We believe this switch in terms from *subculture* to *co-culture* is a sound one. Therefore, we use the word **co-culture** *when talking about groups or social communities exhibiting communication characteristics, perceptions, values, beliefs, and practices that are significantly different enough to distinguish them from the other groups, communities, and the dominant culture.* Before we move on, we need to stress one more time that members of co-cultures, because they live within the dominant culture, also share some patterns and perceptions with the larger population.

Co-cultures As Cultures. We need only return to our general analysis of culture to see why co-cultures have distinct patterns of communication. Most, in fact, meet many of the characteristics that we applied to cultures earlier in the chapter. As Lane notes, "Deaf culture provides its members with traditions, values, and rules for behavior that are handed down from generation to generation."[78] Even gays, as Goodwin points out, have their own language, traditions, and behavioral codes.[79] What is important about all co-cultures is that being gay, disabled, Mexican American, African American, or female exposes a person to a specialized set of messages that helps determine how he or she perceives some aspects of the external world. It also significantly influences how members of that co-culture communicate those perceptions. As we already noted, these co-cultural affiliations can be based on race, ethnic background, gender, age, sexual preference, and so forth.[80] For example, referring to the African American co-culture, Smith notes, "Black Americans have evolved certain language and other behavior characteristics that constitute a co-culture manifestation."[81] According to Hecht, Ribeau, and Sedano we could offer the same conclusions with regard to the Mexican American co-culture.[82]

All of the co-cultures we mentioned, as is the case with the dominant culture, have numerous "carriers" (such as media, churches, schools, parents, religion) that transmit the experiences that are learned by each new set of members—be they children or adults. In the next paragraph we try to explain this important point by looking at but one American co-culture—women. We have selected the issue of gender for our extended example because, as Wood tells us, "we know more about it than other co-cultures."[83] It is important, however, to keep in mind that we could do much of the same analysis for any co-culture composed of individuals who had shared common messages and experiences over a long period.

Gender As a Co-culture. If, as Bate stated, culture is "a relatively organized set of beliefs and expectations about how people should talk, think, and organize their lives,"[84] we can understand how women and men grow up in two distinct communication cultures. Although at first glance it may appear that they share common environments and experiences, such as judicial systems, homes, schools, churches, and media, the messages they receive from these institutions are often quite different. Think for just a moment about what is being "taught" to women in the United States by the following messages. A woman usually gives up her name once she gets married. Schools, according to the research reported by Wood, "tend to encourage dependence, quietness, and deference and frown on assertiveness in female students" and "reward independence, self-assertion, and activity in boys."[85] Girls are expected to do indoor chores and boys outdoor chores. Girls have to stay near the house while boys can go exploring. Boys and girls grow up playing very different games.[86] Girls' games are calm and restrictive; boys engage in games that are active, aggressive, combative, and competitive.[87] And think of the messages embedded in the selection of toys: Dolls for girls, and cars and guns for boys. Books, magazines, movies, and television offer stories and images that encourage gender-specific views of what is important and even *who* is important. For example, a 1996 *Time* magazine listed "the ten most powerful" people in the United States—all ten were white males.[88] These messages, and thousands of others, produce two groups of people who perceive themselves differently (women have lower self-esteem than do men), see the world differently (women view the world with more anxiety and hostility), act differently (92% of all people in prison are men), relate to people differently (women are more empathetic than men), talk differently (women use more tag lines and interrupt less), and make different use of nonverbal cues (women smile more, engage in more eye contact, and use smaller gestures). Our list of distinctions could fill this book, but that is not our point. What needs to be remembered is the idea that unique experiences generate unique modes of behavior that influence communication.

Finally, although we have discussed racial, ethnic, and co-cultural communication, we believe they *all share the same processes and elements*. That is, specialized alliances and associations create shared perceptions, comparable norms and values, and distinctive verbal and nonverbal codes. Therefore, the words *intercultural communication* seem best suited to refer to the interaction process—which is at the center of this book.

SUMMARY

- Human communication is the process through which individuals—in relationships, groups, organizations, and societies—respond to and create messages and adapt to the environment and one another.
- Communication is dynamic; it is ongoing and ever changing.
- Communication is symbolic.
- Communication is systemic and is therefore influenced by setting, location, occasion, time, number of participants, and cultural setting.
- We can only infer what another is experiencing, and we do this by using the symbols that we and other people have produced.
- Communication is reflective: We can watch ourselves and evaluate how we are communicating while we are doing it.
- Our communication behavior has consequences.
- Communication is complex.
- The world is a confusing place until we can make some sense of it, so the basic function of culture is to explain the world to each new member of the culture. By telling us what to expect, culture reduces confusion and helps us predict the future.
- Culture is shared learned behavior that is transmitted from one generation to another for purposes of promoting individual and social survival, adaptation, and growth and development.
- The characteristics of culture that most directly affect communication are that culture is (1) learned, (2) transmitted from generation to generation, (3) based on symbols, (4) dynamic, (5) integrated, and (6) adaptive.
- Intercultural communication is communication between people whose cultural perceptions and symbol systems are distinct enough to alter the communication event.
- Interracial communication occurs when source and receiver are from different races.
- Interethnic communication refers to situations in which the parties are of the same race but of different ethnic origins.
- Co-cultural communication is communication between members who hold two or more cultural experiences that might influence the communication process.

INFOTRAC® COLLEGE EDITION EXERCISES

1. This chapter discusses the ways in which myths, proverbs, folktales, and legends transmit cultural values and give meaning to choices and events. Using the PowerTrac option, locate the article "The Contents of Our Character" by Lindsey Brink et al. (Hint: Use "Personality and Culture" as your subject search term,

or search by author or title.) After reading the article, choose both a book and a movie that you feel would most clearly portray the American character and culture to those who are not Americans. Come to class prepared to explain your selections.

2. Using the PowerTrac option, locate the article "Keepers of Community in a Changing World" by Amanda Smith Barusch and Peter Steen. (Hint: Use "Culture Diffusion" as your subject search term.) This article discusses the ways in which grandparents and elders transmit culture. What are the challenges that grandparents face in the Chamorro culture of Guam and the Navajo culture of the American Southwest? What challenges have your grandparents or elders faced in their attemps to share stories and life lessons with you? Provide examples of stories and wisdom that grandparents/elders have shared with you and consider what meanings were intended to be shared with these stories.

ACTIVITIES

1. Ask your partner from another culture to relate a folktale (or a song, a work of art, or something similar) from his or her culture. What cultural values does it convey? Compare it to one from your culture. Do they stand in opposition to each other, or are there similarities?

2. In small groups, list the American cultural values mentioned in this chapter. Try to think of others. Then find examples from American advertising campaigns that illustrate these values. For example, the advertising slogan from an athletic-shoe manufacturer, "Just do it," reflects the American value of accomplishment.

3. Find out as much as you can about the history of your partner's culture. Try to isolate examples of how his or her cultural values have been determined by historical events.

4. In small groups, play a word-association game. Your instructor will compose a list of potentially culture-bound words such as *motherhood, freedom*, and *sex*, then say the words one at a time. Write down the first thing that comes into your mind as you hear each word. Compare your reactions. Are there any major differences within the group? Discuss them. Then compare your answers with the entire class and discuss.

5. Attend a meeting (church, lecture, etc.) of a culture or co-culture different from your own. Try to notice the various ways that you can see specific cultural characteristics of that culture being acted out.

DISCUSSION IDEAS

1. What is meant by the phrase "much of culture is invisible"?

2. Explain how the statement "People are alike, and people are different" relates to intercultural communication.

3. Inferring is another characteristic of communication. Give examples of situations in which you inferred what someone else was experiencing. Were your inferences correct? How do you know?

4. Explain American views toward these elements of culture: Work, dress, hygiene, courtship, sex, and status.

5. Describe a typical day from morning to night in terms of the cultural values that govern your actions. For example:

Action	Value
Brush teeth, take shower	Personal odors are offensive in American culture
Put on jeans and T-shirt	Comfort and informality are acceptable in educational settings.

6. Give additional examples, from recent history, of cultures that have changed as a result of invention, diffusion, and calamity.

7. How would you explain the link between culture and communication?

part 2

The Influence of Culture

© Gloria Thomas

chapter 3

Cultural Diversity in Perception: Alternative Views of Reality

There never were, in the world, two opinions alike, no more than two hairs, or two grains; the most universal quality is diversity.

MONTAIGNE

No object is mysterious. The mystery is in your eye.

ELIZABETH BOWEN

The moon is a rocky physical sphere that orbits the Earth; yet when looking at this object, many Americans often see a man in the moon, many Native Americans perceive a rabbit, Chinese claim a lady is fleeing her husband, and Samoans report a woman weaving. In the United States children have a tooth fall out and place it under their pillow. The Japanese child tosses it on the roof of the house. For Americans, a "V" sign made with two fingers usually represents victory. Australians equate this gesture with a rude American gesture usually made with the middle finger. Most Asians respond negatively to white flowers because white is associated with death. For Peruvians, Iranians, and Mexicans, yellow flowers often invoke the same reaction.[1] In these four examples, the external objects (moon, tooth, hands, flowers) were the same, yet the responses were different. The reason is perception, and that is what this chapter is about. More specifically, this chapter deals with how distinct cultures have "taught" their members to look differently at the world around them. We will begin with a definition of perception; link perception to culture; briefly discuss beliefs, attitudes, and values; and than spend the bulk of the chapter looking at various cultural patterns that influence intercultural communication.

DEFINING PERCEPTION

Perception is the means by which you make sense of your physical and social world. As the German novelist Hermann Hesse states, "There is no reality except the one contained within us"—and it has been placed in us, in part, by our culture. The world inside of us "includes symbols, things, people, ideas, events, ideologies, and even faith."[2] Your perceptions give meaning to all those external forces. As Gamble and Gamble state, *"Perception is the process of selecting, organizing, and interpreting sensory data in a way that enables us to make sense of our world."*[3] In other words, perception is an external process whereby people convert the physical energy of the world outside of them into meaningful internal experiences. Because that outside world embraces everything, we can never completely know it. As Singer notes, "We experience everything in the world not as it is—but only as the world comes to us through our sensory receptors." [4] Although the physical dimension is an important phase of perception, you must realize *it is the psychological aspects of perception that help you understand intercultural communication.*

PERCEPTION AND CULTURE

As we indicated, your individual make-up (personality, education, emotions, beliefs, values, traits, attitudes, motives, etc.) has much more impact on how you perceive your environment and how you behave in regard to it than does your physical handling of incoming stimuli. Once you bring the outside world inside you begin to put your own personal touch and interpretation on what you have taken in. This, of course, sees you tinkering, tampering, and even fictionalizing your views of the world.

We have already mentioned that your perceptions of the world are representations you make from both the nerve impulses that reach your brain and your unique set of experiences supplied to you as a member of a particular culture. Whether you feel delighted or ill at the thought of eating the flesh of a cow, fish, dog, or snake depends on what your culture has taught you about food. Whether you are repulsed at the sight of a bull being jabbed with sharp swords and long steel spears, or believe it is a poetic sport, often depends on culture. By exposing a large group of people to similar experiences (such as foods or sports), culture generates similar meanings and similar behaviors. This does not mean, of course, that everyone in a particular culture is exactly the same. As we note in Chapter 1, *there is significant diversity within cultures just as there is diversity among cultures.* However, because this is a book about culture, we offer a few examples of how culture affects perception and communication.

In a classic study by Bagby, Mexican children from a rural area and children from the dominant culture in the United States viewed, for a split-second, stereograms in which one eye was exposed to a baseball game while the other was exposed to a bullfight. In the main, the children reported seeing the scene according to their culture; Mexican children tended to report seeing the bullfight and American children tended to report the baseball game.[5] What should be obvious is that the children made selections based on their cultural background; they tended to see and to report what was most familiar. This study would, of course, yield different results with Mexican children from a large city, for they are familiar with baseball.

In yet another experiment Caucasian mothers tended to interpret as positive those aspects of their children's speech and behavior that reflected assertiveness, excitement, and interest. Navajo mothers who observed *the same* behavior in their children reported them as being mischievous and lacking discipline. To the Navajo mothers, assertive speech and behavior reflected discourtesy, restlessness, self-centeredness, and lack of discipline; to the Caucasian mothers, the same behaviors reflected self-discipline and were, therefore, beneficial for the child.[6]

Personal credibility is yet another perceptual trait that is touched by culture. People who are credible inspire trust, know what they are talking about, and have good intentions. Americans usually hold that expressing one's opinion as openly and forcefully as possible is an admirable trait. Hence, someone is perceived as being highly credible if he or she is articulate and outspoken. For the Japanese, a person who is quiet and spends more time listening than speaking is more credible because they regard constant talking as a sign of shallowness. Among Americans, credible people seem direct, rational, decisive, unyielding, and confident. Among the Japanese, credible persons are perceived as being indirect, sympathetic, prudent, flexible, and humble.[7] In Japan, social status is a major indicator of credibility, but in the United States it has only modest import.

Even the perception of something as simple as the blinking of one's eyes is affected by culture, as Adler and Rodman note: "The same principle causes people from different cultures to interpret the same event in different ways. Blinking while another person talks may be hardly noticeable to North Americans, but the same behavior is considered impolite in Taiwan."[8]

How we perceive the elderly is also tempered by culture. In the United States, we find a culture that "teaches" the value of youth and rejects growing old. In fact, "young people view elderly people as less desirable interaction partners than other young people or middle-aged people."[9] This disapproving view of the elderly is not found in all cultures. For example, in the Arab, Asian, Latin American, and Native American cultures, old people are perceived in a very positive light. And notice what Harris and Moran tell us about the elderly in Africa:

> It is believed that the older one gets, the wiser one becomes—life has seasoned the individual with varied experiences. Hence, in Africa age is an asset. The older the person, the more respect the person receives from the community, and especially from the young.[10]

It is clear from these few examples that culture strongly influences our subjective reality and that there are direct links among culture, perception, and behavior. As Triandis noted, "cultural factors provide some of the meaning involved in perception and are, therefore, intimately implicated with the process."[11] We would summarize how culture is "implicated with the process" in two ways. First, as we have pointed out, perception *is selective*. This simply means that because there are too many stimuli impinging on your senses at the same time you "allow only selected information through [y]our perceptual screen to our conscious mind."[12] What is allowed in, as discussed earlier, is in part, determined by culture. Second, your perceptual patterns *are learned*. As pointed out in Chapter 1, everyone is born into a world without meaning, and it is culture that gives meaning to most of our experiences. As Adler points out, "perception is culturally determined. We learn to see the world in a certain way based on our cultural background."[13]

As is the case with all of culture, *perceptions are stored within each human being in the form of (1) beliefs, (2) attitudes, (3) values, and (4) cultural patterns*. Understanding how these four elements impact intercultural communication will occupy the reminder of this chapter. Our rationale for including this information is simple—knowledge of these

What makes belief systems important is that they are learned, endure, and are subject to cultural interpretations.

four elements will help you interpret your own communication behavior as well as the actions of people from different cultures.

BELIEFS

The Spanish poet Antonio Machado once noted that "Under all that we think, lives all we believe, like the ultimate veil of our spirits." Although not directly saying so, he was, of course, talking about our belief systems. Belief systems are significant to the study of intercultural communication because they are at the core of your thoughts and actions. According to Rogers and Steinfatt, "Beliefs serve as the storage system for the content of our past experiences, including thoughts, memories, and interpretations of events. Beliefs are shaped by the individual's culture."[14] What is important about beliefs is that they are usually reflected in your actions. If, for instance, you believe that snakes are slimy, you avoid them. On the other hand, if you believe that only through the handling of snakes can you find God (as do some religious sects), you handle them and believe your faith will protect you from venomous bites.

Belief systems are significant to students of intercultural communication because they are learned and hence subject to cultural interpretation and cultural diversity. We might embrace the *New York Times* or the *CBS Evening News* as sources of what is true and what we should believe because we respect them. If you highly value the Islamic tradition, you will believe that the Koran is an infallible source of knowledge and thus accept the miracles and promises that it offers. Whether you trust as sources of truth and knowledge the *Times*, the Bible, the Koran, the entrails of a goat, tea leaves, Madonna, the Dalai Lama, the visions induced by peyote, or the changes specified in the Taoist *I Ching* depends on your cultural background and experiences. If someone believes that sitting quietly for long periods of time can guide him or her along the proper path, you cannot throw up your hands and declare the belief wrong. You must be able to recognize the fact that cultures have different realities and belief systems. People from parts of Africa, North Korea, Cuba, or certain Native American tribes may very likely believe that business and the means of production should belong to the state or to the people collectively. On the other hand, someone born in the United States or Canada most likely grew up believing that the means of production should belong to individuals in sole proprietorships, or to several individuals in partnerships, or to numerous people in corporations. People who grow up in cultures where Christianity is the predominant religion usually believe that salvation is attainable only through Christ. People who are Jewish, Islamic, Buddhist, Shinto, or Hindu do not subscribe to that belief. They hold their own beliefs about salvation or what happens to the human spirit when the body dies. What is enthralling about beliefs is that they are so much a part of culture that in most instances we do not demand proof or question them. We simply accept them because we "know they are true." The French novelist Saint-Exupery wrote, "To know is not to prove, nor to explain."

Beliefs are such an influential factor in intercultural communication because they affect your conscious and unconscious minds, as well as the manner in which you communicate. Your beliefs originate as you grow up in your culture. At early ages, you are not prepared to question our social institutions (family, church, school, state), so you accept freely what they teach you about truth and how to live in your society. Because there seems to be, at least in most cultures, consensus about how to dress, how to speak to your elders, how to eat, how to attain peace.and tranquillity, how you should earn your living, and what the proper social structure is, you grow up firmly believing these things. When you do question the core beliefs of your culture, you usually receive such strong negative reactions that you immediately put aside your questions and either accept what you have been told or become a social outcast. In other words, as you grow up in a culture, that culture conditions you to believe what it deems to be worthy and true.

ATTITUDES

Attitudes represent yet another perceptual dimension that influences how you experience and interact with that world. Specifically, "an attitude is a combination of beliefs about a subject, feelings toward it, and any predisposition to act toward it."[15] The intensity of your attitudes is based on the degree of conviction that your beliefs and evaluations are true and correct. This certainty of conviction creates a psychological state of readiness to react to the objects and events you confront in your environment. Thus, if you believe, for instance, that physically abusing another person is wrong or fear being hurt when it happens, and further believe boxing has a high probability of producing physical abuse, you may have an internalized negative predisposition toward boxing (an attitude) which manifests itself in the fact that you would not attend or participate in a boxing match.

As was the case with beliefs, attitudes are learned within a cultural context. Whatever cultural environment surrounds you helps to shape and form your attitudes, your readiness to respond, and ultimately your behavior. You will recall that earlier we mentioned the Bagby study concerning bullfighting. We return to that study to explain how attitudes get acted out. A vast number of North Americans believe that cruelty to animals is wrong and the systematic wearing down and killing of a bull is an example of that cruelty. Consequently, many North Americans view bullfighting within a negative attitude—an attitude that keeps most North Americans from attending bullfights. For most Latin Americans, however, bullfighting is not cruelty to animals, but rather a display of extraordinary courage, skill, and physical agility. You will notice once again that we have used "most" not "all" when we speak of any cultural group. The reason for our equivocation is obvious, and one we have stressed throughout the book—all members of a culture are not alike.

There are three important points that we can take away from our discussion of attitudes: (1) attitudes have to be learned, (2) culture is often the source of the "learning," and (3) attitudes eventually get put into action.

VALUES

One of the most important functions of belief and attitude systems is that they are the basis of our values. *Values are*, according to Rokeach, *"a learned organization of rules for making choices and for resolving conflicts."*[16] As Nanda and Warms point out, "Values are shared ideas about what is true, right, and beautiful that underlie cultural patterns and guide society in response to the physical and social environment."[17] Albert highlights that importance of values when he notes, "a value system represents what is expected or hoped for, required or forbidden. It is not a report of actual conduct but is the system of criteria by which conduct is judged and sanctions applied."[18]

An individual's cognitive structure consists of many values, which are arranged into a hierarchical order that is highly organized and that, Rokeach says, "exist[s] along a continuum of relative importance."[19] That is to say, some values are of greater importance than others. Values can be classified as *primary*, *secondary*, and *tertiary*. Primary values are the most important: they specify what is worth the sacrifice of human life. In the United States, democracy and the protection of oneself and close family are primary values. Secondary values are also quite important. In the United States, the relief of the pain and suffering of others is a secondary value. The securing of material possessions is also a secondary value for most Americans. We care about such values, but we do not hold the same intense feeling toward them as we do with primary values. Tertiary values are at the bottom of our hierarchy. Examples of tertiary values in the United States are hospitality to guests and cleanliness. Although we strive to carry out these values, they are not as profound or consequential as values in the other two categories.

While each of us has a unique set of individual values, there also are values that tend to permeate a culture. These are called *cultural values*. Cultural values are derived from the larger philosophical issues that are part of a culture's milieu. As we saw in preceding chapters, they are transmitted by a variety of sources (family, media, school, church, state, etc.) and therefore tend to be broad-based, enduring, and relatively stable. Cultural values generally are *normative* and *evaluative* in that they inform a member of a culture what is good and bad, and right and wrong. Cultural values define what is worthwhile to die for, what is worth protecting, what frightens people, and what are proper subjects to study and which derive ridicule.

As already indicated, values are learned within a cultural context. For example, the outlook of a culture toward the expression of emotion is one of the many values that differ among cultures. In the United States people are encouraged to express their feelings outwardly, and also taught not to be timid about letting people know they are upset. Think for a moment about what is being said by the proverb we cited in the last chapter: "The squeaky wheel gets the grease." This positive value toward the expression of emotion is very different from the one found in China. As Gao and Ting-Toomey note, "Chinese are socialized not to openly express their own personal emotions, especially strong negative ones."[20] There is even a Chinese proverb that states "A harsh word dropped from the tongue cannot be brought back by a coach and six horses."

As was the case with cultural beliefs, cultural values guide both perception and communication. That is, *your values get translated into action.* An understanding of cultural values helps you appreciate the behavior of other people. Knowing, for instance, that the Japanese value detail and politeness might cause you to examine carefully a proffered Japanese business card, as the Japanese do, rather than immediately relegate it to a coat pocket or purse. An awareness of cultural values also helps you understand your own behavior. Impatience, for example, can be associated with your value of time, aggressiveness with your value of competition, and self-disclosure with your twin values of friendship and sociability.

CULTURAL PATTERNS

People and cultures are extremely complex and consist of numerous interrelated cultural orientations besides beliefs, attitudes, and values. A useful umbrella term that allows us to talk about these and other orientations collectively instead of separately is *cultural patterns. Cultural patterns refers to both the conditions that contribute to the way in which a people perceive and think about the world, and the manner in which they live in that world.* These cultural patterns are useful in the study of intercultural communication because they are systematic and repetitive instead of random and irregular.[21] They are also widely shared by most members of the culture and influence how people within the culture behave. You can see cultural patterns being acted out in something as simple as how cultures perceive the elderly. It is not fortuitous or by chance that most people in Mexico give respect and merit to elderly people, while in the United States the dominant culture values youth and all of the trappings associated with being young.

Before we open our discussion of cultural patterns, we need to offer a few cautionary remarks that will enable you to better use the cultural patterns that we present in the remainder of this chapter.

We Are More Than Our Culture

We begin with the most obvious, yet most often overlooked, imperfection in using cultural patterns in communication: *The value of the culture may not be the value of all individuals within the culture.* How you see the world and how you communicate in that world are influenced by factors as divergent as age, gender, status, occupation, and political, group, and co-culture affiliations. One study pointed out that although Americans share a great many values, beliefs, and communication patterns, variations in region can affect perception and communication.[22] However, although we grant the complex nature of human behavior, we suggest that culture has the strongest influence on your communication behavior because all of your other experiences take place within a cultural context. As we shall point out in the next chapter, family structure is a major component of each culture. It is that same cultural family that is a dominant force that helps shape your beliefs, attitudes, and values.

Cultural Patterns Are Points on a Continuum

As we move through our discussion of cultural patterns it would be useful if you *try to visualize each culture's response to a specific pattern as a point on a continuum rather than one of only two possible responses*. As Rokeach said, people "everywhere possess the same values to different degrees."[23] Every culture teaches their young people to be civil and well mannered, yet the importance of that common value, and how it gets acted out, is a matter of degree. This idea will become clear later in this chapter when you observe the manner in which the Dutch researcher Geert Hofstede ranks, on a scale of one to forty, different cultures across the *same dimension*.

Cultural Patterns Are Interrelated

The patterns are interrelated with a host of other values and do not operate in isolation. For example, a pattern that stresses a spiritual life over materialism also directs values toward age, status, social relationships, greeting behavior, the use of time, and the like.

Heterogeneity Influences Cultural Patterns

Any attempt to delineate a national culture or typical cultural patterns for any culture is extremely hazardous because of the heterogeneity of many societies. For example, it is estimated that together the United States and Russia contain over 125 ethnic groups. The *Encyclopedia of American Religions* identifies nearly 1,200 different religions in the United States. Although the United States might be an extreme example of ethnic variety, we assure you it is found in all countries (for example, Romania has Hungarians, Germans, Serbs, Croats, and Turks; Peru has Indians, whites, blacks, Japanese, and Chinese). Hence, *common cultural patterns that could be said to hold for the whole country must be limited to the dominant culture in each country*.

There Are Numerous Cultural Patterns in Each Culture

There are literally hundreds of cultural patterns found in every culture. What we have done in this chapter, because this is a book about communication, is present those patterns that are most manifest during interaction. For example, in the United States the powerful pattern of individuality influences the way in which we perceive such things as status, leadership, nonverbal communication, speaking, competition, and assertiveness.

Cultural Patterns Change

As we note in Chapter 2, *cultures change and therefore so do the values of the culture*. The "women's movement," for example, has greatly altered social organizations and some value systems in the United States. With more women now getting college degrees than men we can see how the workplace and classrooms have changed in the United States during the last 20 years.[24] And as Western capitalism and culture move through much of Asia, we see many young people in some traditional countries now wearing Levi's and dancing at disco clubs. However, even granting the dynamic nature of culture and value systems, we again remind you that the deep structure of a culture resists change.

Cultural Patterns Are Often Contradictory

In many instances, we find contradictory values in a particular culture. In the United States, we speak of "all people being created equal," yet we observe pervasive racial prejudice and violence directed against gays. Individualism is at the heart of American culture, yet the United States is the most humanitarian country in the world. Americans claim to be a moral and honorable group of people, yet the United States is one of the world's most violent societies. These sorts of contradictions are found in all cultures. In China, where Confucianism and Buddhism stress interpersonal harmony, you will witness human rights violations. The Koran teaches brotherhood among all people, yet in many Arab cultures there is a vast gulf between the very rich and the very poor.

Even with the reservations we have just offered, it is our contention that study of cultural patterns is a worthwhile pursuit. Although some deviations exist, there are patterns at the core of all cultures. Knowing these patterns will help you know the culture. Therefore, we will now turn our attention to a variety of taxonomies that have attempted to classify and catalog various cultural patterns that can be found in nearly every culture. Specifically, we will now examine dominant American cultural patterns, Hofstede's value dimensions, Bond's Confucian dynamism, Kluckhohn and Strodtbeck's value orientations, Hall's high- and low-context orientation, and two additional patterns (informality/formality and assertiveness/interpersonal harmony) that are not directly treated by Hofstede, Kluckhohn, or Hall.

DOMINANT AMERICAN CULTURAL PATTERNS

Although this textbook is used in many foreign countries, we nevertheless believe that a section on American cultural patterns would be helpful for all of our readers. For people who are not members of the dominant culture we would trust that our discussion of cultural patterns would offer insights into that culture. For those who are members of the dominant culture, we offer our analysis of cultural patterns for three reasons. First, as we have said throughout this book, people carry their culture wherever they go, and that culture influences how they respond to the people they meet. To understand the communication event in which you find yourself, you must appreciate *your* role in that event. Therefore, any analysis of cultural patterns must include the patterns that *both* participants bring to the encounter. Second, examining one's own cultural patterns can reveal information about culture that is often overlooked. As the anthropologist Hall notes, "Culture hides more than it reveals, and strangely enough what it hides, it hides most effectively from its own participants." Finally, one's cultural patterns can also serve as reference points and bases of comparison with other cultures. At the conclusion of this section, we compare American patterns with those found in other cultures. We limit our discussion to the dominant American culture as we define it in Chapter 1. You will recall we said that the dominant culture is that part of the population, regardless of the culture being studied, that controls and dominates the major institutions, and determines the flow and content of information. In the United States that group has been, and continues to be, white, male, and of European heritage.[25]

Individualism

The single most important pattern in the United States is *individualism*. Broadly speaking, individualism refers to the doctrine, spelled out in detail by the seventeenth-century English philosopher John Locke, that each individual is unique, special, completely different from all other individuals, and "the basic unit of nature."[26] The basic premise of Locke's view is a simple one: the interests of the individual are or ought to be paramount, and that all values, rights, and duties originate in individuals. This emphasis on the individual, while found elsewhere in the world, has emerged as the cornerstone of American culture. As Huntington points out, this "sense of individualism and a tradition of individual rights and liberties is unique among civilized societies."[27]

As is the case with most cultural patterns, the origin of this value has had a long history and a variety of champions. Benjamin Franklin told us that "God helps those who help themselves" and Herbert Hoover reminded us that "the American system was based on rugged individualism." Individualism manifests itself in personal initiative

© Larry Samovar

The importance of individualism can be seen in how Americans use space.

("Pull yourself up by your own boot straps"), independence ("Do your own thing"), individual expression ("The squeaky wheel gets the grease"), privacy ("A man's home is his castle"), and individual responsibility ("You made your bed, now lie in it"). Whether it be in sexual, social, or ethical matters, the self for Americans holds the pivotal position. So strong is this notion that some Americans believe that there is something wrong with someone who fails to demonstrate individualism. Think of the power of the concept in the words of former Supreme Court justice Felix Frankfurter: "Anybody who is any good is different than anybody else." Whether it be literature, art, or American history, the message is the same: Individual achievement, sovereignty, and freedom are the virtues most glorified and canonized. American role models, be they the cowboys of the Old West or action heroes in today's movies, videos, or computer games, are all portrayed as independent agents who accomplish their goals with little or no assistance. The result of these and countless other messages is that most Americans believe that each person has his or her own separate identity, which should be recognized and reinforced. From their strong belief in democracy to the ease with which they go to war to preserve freedom, individualism dominates American culture. As we see later in the chapter, individualism is not the driving force in all cultures. A 1996 poll among Russians, for example, indicated that 77 percent of the polled preferred "social order" over individual democracy.[28]

Equality

Closely related to individualism is the American value of *equality*, which is emphasized in everything from government (everyone has the right to vote) to social relationships ("Just call me by my first name"). Americans believe that all people have a right to succeed in life and that the state, through laws and educational opportunities, should ensure that right.

The value of equality is prevalent in both primary and secondary social relationships: For instance, most of the primary social relationships within a family tend to advance equality rather than hierarchy. Formality is not important, and children are often treated as adults. In secondary relationships, you find that most friendships and co-workers are also treated as equals. As we note later in this chapter, the value of equality in American social relationships creates communication problems in intercultural settings. Americans like to treat others as equals and choose to be treated in the same manner when they interact in school, business, or social environments. People from cultures that have rigid, hierarchical social structures often find it disconcerting to work with Americans, who they believe negate the value of hierarchical structures within a society.

We would be remiss if, when describing the dominant culture in the United States, we did not once again remind you of some of the contradictions that often exist when we speak of individualism and equality. As Macionis points out, "Despite prevailing ideas about individualism and freedom, many people in the United States still evaluate others according to their sex, race, ethnicity, and social class."[29] He adds, "Although we describe ourselves as a nation of equals, there is little doubt that some of us rank as 'more equal than others.'"[30]

Materialism

For most Americans, *materialism* has always been an integral part of life. As Stewart and Bennett note, "Americans consider it almost a right to be materially well off and physically comfortable."[31] Americans even judge other people by their material possessions. Materialism shows itself in a host of ways. A popular bumper sticker proclaims, "The person who dies with the most toys wins." Americans expect to have swift and convenient transportation—preferably controlled by themselves—a large variety of foods at our disposal, clothes for every occasion, and comfortable homes equipped with many labor-saving devices. As the philosopher Lionel Trilling observed, "In the American metaphysic, reality is always material reality."

Science and Technology

For most Americans, *science* and *technology* take on the qualities often associated with a god. The following inscription, found on the National Museum of American History in Washington, D.C., echoes the same idea: "Modern civilization depends on science." Americans believe that nothing is impossible when scientists, researchers, engineers, and inventors put their minds to a task or problem. From fixing interpersonal relationships to walking to the moon, science has the answer.

The American respect for science is based on the assumptions that reality can be rationally ordered by humans and that such an ordering, using the scientific method, allows people to predict and control much of life. Very broadly, this emphasis on science reflects the values of the rationalistic-individualistic tradition that is so deeply embedded in Western civilization. From John Locke to Francis Bacon, Rene Descartes, Bertrand Russell, and Albert Einstein, Western cultures have long believed that all problems can be solved by science. This emphasis on rationality and science, according to Macionis, helps "explain our cultural tendency (especially among men) to devalue emotion and intuition as sources of knowledge."[32]

While Westerners tend to prize rationality, objectivity, empirical evidence, and the scientific method, you will see in the next chapter when we discuss world views, that these views often clash with cultures that value and believe in fatalism, subjectivity, mysticism, and intuition.

Progress and Change

Perhaps more so than any other people, Americans have always placed great importance on *progress* and *change*. From changing their personalities with the assistance of self-help gurus, to changing where they live at a faster rate than any other people in the world, they do not value the status quo. Nor have they ever. "Early Americans cleared forests, drained swamps, and altered the course of rivers in order to 'build' the country. Contemporary Americans have gone to the moon in part to prove they could do so."[33] The French writer Alexis de Tocqueville, after visiting the United States over a hundred years ago, reached much the same conclusion when he wrote that the people in the United States "all consider society as a body in a state of improvement, and humanity as a changing scene." From the culture's earliest establishment as a distinct national entity, there has been a diffuse constellation of beliefs and attitudes that may be called the cult of progress. These beliefs and attitudes produce a certain mind-set and a wide range of behavior patterns. Various aspects of this orientation are optimism, receptivity to change, emphasis on the future rather than the past or present, faith in an ability to control all phases of life, and confidence in the perceptual ability of the common person. Belief in progress fosters not only the acceptance of change, but also the conviction, true or false, that changes tend in a definite direction and that the direction is good. Each new generation in the United States wants its opportunity to be part of that change.

So strong is the belief in progress and change that Americans seldom fear taking chances or staking out new and exciting territories. The writer Henry Miller clearly captured this American spirit when he wrote, "Whatever there be in progress in life comes not through adaptation but through daring, through obeying blind urge."

As we discuss later in the chapter, many older and more traditional cultures, which have witnessed civilizations rise and fall and believe in fatalism, do not sanctify change, progress, and daring and often have difficulty understanding the way Americans behave. As Althen notes:

> This fundamental American belief in progress and a better future contrasts sharply with the fatalistic (Americans are likely to use that term with a negative or critical connotation) attitude that characterizes people from many other cultures, notably Latin, Asian, and Arab, where there is a pronounced reverence for the past. In those cultures the future is considered to be in the hands of "fate," "God," or at least the few powerful people or families that dominate the society. The idea that they could somehow shape their own futures seems naive or even arrogant.[34]

Work and Leisure

Whether motivated by ego gratification, material possession, or the Puritan ethic, Americans value *work*. When people meet each other for the first time, a common question is "What do you do?" Embedded in this simple question is the belief that working (doing something) is important. For most Americans, work is a desired and desirable expenditure of energy, a means of controlling and expressing strong affective states, and an avenue to recognition, money, or power. It represents a cluster of moral and affective conditions of great attractiveness to Americans, whereas voluntary idleness often constitutes a severely threatening and damaging social condition. That is, although Americans are humanitarian and charitable to those whom they perceive as deserving assistance, they look with displeasure and intolerance on anyone who can work but does not.

A major reward of hard work, and an important American value, is *leisure*. Most Americans seem to have embraced the words of the American poet and philosopher George Santayana: "To the art of working well a civilized race would add the art of playing well." For Americans, play is something they have earned. It is relief from the regularity of work; it is in play that we find real joy. This emphasis on recreation and relaxation takes a variety of forms. Each weekend people rush to get away in their recreational vehicles, play golf or tennis, go skiing, ride their mountain bikes, or "relax" at a gambling casino.

Competition

Competition is part of an American's life from early childhood on. Whether it be through the games they play or their striving to be more attractive than the person they are sitting next to in class, a competitive nature is encouraged in the United States. People are ranked, graded, classified, and evaluated so that everyone will know if they are "the best." In sports and at work, we are told the importance of "being number one." Young people are even advised that if they lose and it does not bother them, there is something wrong with them. As is the case with all the patterns found in a culture, the origin of a specific pattern has a long history. Notice the call for competition in the following proverb—written at the beginning of the first century by the Roman philosopher Ovid: "A horse never runs so fast as when he has other horses to catch up and outpace." The message was clear then and it is clear now—you need to "outpace" all the other horses.

Competition is yet another pattern that often causes problems for Americans when they interact with people who do not espouse this value. Harris and Moran offer an explicit example of this problem as it applies to the French:

> When confronted with individuals with a competitive drive, the French may interpret them as being antagonistic, ruthless, and power-hungry. They may feel threatened, and overreact or withdraw from the discussion.[35]

DIVERSE CULTURAL PATTERNS

In Chapter 2, we looked at various universal cultural characteristics and elements, and in the preceding pages of this chapter, we examined some cultural patterns as they applied to the dominant American culture. We are now ready to make some comparisons. Many anthropologists, social psychologists, and communication scholars have devised taxonomies that can be used to analyze key behavioral patterns found in particular cultures. We have decided on those classifications that are most helpful in understanding how cultures perceive the world and communicate within that world. The first classification, developed by Hofstede, identifies four value dimensions that are influenced and modified by culture. The second is based on the research of the cross-cultural psychologist Michael Bond. The third grows out of the anthropological work of the Kluckhohns and Strodtbeck. Our fourth taxonomy was advanced by Hall and looks at how high-context and low-context cultures respond to various message systems. Our final classification discusses some cultural patterns that we deem to be important, but that are not directly included in the other taxonomies.

Hofstede's Value Dimensions

Hofstede has identified four value dimensions that have a significant impact on behavior in all cultures.[36] *These dimensions are individualism-collectivism, uncertainty avoidance, power distance, and masculinity and femininity.* Hofstede's work was one of the earliest attempts to use extensive statistical data to examine cultural values. During the 1980s, he surveyed over a hundred thousand workers in multinational organizations in forty countries. After careful analysis, each country was assigned a rank of one through forty in each category, depending on how it compared to the other countries (see Table 3-1). The results yielded a clear picture of what was valued in each culture.

Individualism-Collectivism

Researchers for many years have maintained that "self-orientation versus collective orientation is one of the basic pattern variables that determine human action."[37] Even today, as Ting-Toomey notes, "Individualistic and collective value tendencies are manifested in everyday family, school, and workplace interactions."[38]

Table 3-1 *Ranking of Forty Countries on Individualism and Collectivism*

Country	Ranking*	Country	Ranking*
Argentina	23	Japan	22
Australia	2	Mexico	29
Austria	18	Netherlands	5
Belgium	8	New Zealand	6
Brazil	25	Norway	13
Canada	4	Pakistan	38
Chile	33	Peru	37
Colombia	39	Philippines	28
Denmark	9	Portugal	30
Finland	17	Singapore	34
France	11	South Africa	16
Germany	15	Spain	20
Great Britain	3	Sweden	10
Greece	27	Switzerland	14
Hong Kong	32	Taiwan	36
India	21	Thailand	35
Iran	24	Turkey	26
Ireland	12	U.S.A.	1
Israel	19	Venezuela	40
Italy	7	Yugoslavia	31

*A high score means the country can be classified as collective; a lower score is associated with cultures that promote individualism.

Source: Adapted from Geert Hofstede, *Culture's Consequences: International Differences in Work-Related Values* (Beverly Hills: Sage, 1980).

Although Hofstede is often given credit for investigating the concepts of individualism and collectivism, he is not the only scholar who has researched these crucial intercultural dimensions. Triandis, for example, has derived an entire cross-cultural research agenda that focuses on these concepts.[39] Therefore, we use Hofstede's work as our basic organizational scheme; we also examine the findings of Triandis and others. Although we speak of individualism and collectivism as if they are separate entities, it is important to keep in mind that all people and cultures have both individual and collective dispositions.

Individualism. Having already discussed *individualism* earlier in the chapter, we need only touch on some of its constituents: (1) the individual is the single most important unit in any social setting, (2) independence rather than dependence is stressed, (3) individual achievement is rewarded, and (4) the uniqueness of each individual is of paramount value.[40] According to Hofstede's findings, the United States, Australia, Great Britain, Canada, the Netherlands, and New Zealand tend toward individualism. Goleman highlights some of the characteristics of these and other cultures that value individualism:

> People's personal goals take priority over their allegiance to groups like the family or the employer. The loyalty of individualists to a given group is very weak; they feel they belong to many groups and are apt to change their membership as it suits them, switching churches, for example, or leaving one employer for another.[41]

Collective cultures see the group as the most important social entity.

In cultures that tend toward individualism, competition rather than cooperation is encouraged; personal goals take precedence over group goals; people tend not to be emotionally dependent on organizations and institutions; and every individual has the right to his or her private property, thoughts, and opinions. These cultures stress individual initiative and achievement, and they value individual decision making. When thrust into a situation that demands a decision, people from cultures that stress this trait are often at odds with people from collective cultures. This point is made by Foster:

> At the negotiating table, differences in this dimension can clearly cause serious conflict. Individual responsibility for making decisions is easy in individualistic cultures; in group-oriented cultures this can be different. Americans too often expect their Japanese counterparts to make decisions right at the negotiating table, and the Japanese are constantly surprised to find individual members of the American team promoting their own positions, decisions, and ideas, sometimes openly contradicting one another.[42]

Collectivism. *Collectivism* is characterized by a rigid social framework that distinguishes between in-groups and out-groups. People count on their in-group (relatives, clans, organizations) to look after them, and in exchange for that they believe they owe absolute loyalty to the group. Triandis offers an excellent summary of this situation:

> Collectivism means greater emphasis on (a) the views, needs, and goals of the in-group rather than oneself; (b) social norms and duty defined by the in-group rather than behavior to get pleasure; (c) beliefs shared with the in-group rather than beliefs that distinguish self from in-group; and (d) great readiness to cooperate with in-group members.[43]

In collective societies such as those in Pakistan, Colombia, Venezuela, Taiwan, and Peru, people are born into extended families or clans that support and protect them in exchange for their loyalty. A "we" consciousness prevails: Identity is based on the social system; the individual is emotionally dependent on organizations and institutions; the culture emphasizes belonging to organizations; organizations invade private life and the clans to which individuals belong; and individuals trust group decisions even at the expense of individual rights. Regarding China as a collective culture, Meyer notes, "With individual rights severely subordinated, group action has been a distinctive characteristic of Chinese society."[44] This view toward working as a group is also expressed in the Chinese proverb, "No matter how stout, one beam cannot support a house." We see this same attitude toward collectivism in African societies, where according to Richmond and Gestrin "individual needs and achievement, in contrast to the West, take second place to the needs of the many."[45]

Collective behavior, like so many aspects of culture, has deep historical roots. Look at the message of collectivism in these words from Confucius: "If one wants to establish himself, he should help others to establish themselves at first."

As is the case with all cultural patterns, collectivism influences a number of communication variables. Kim, Sharkey, and Singles, after studying the Korean culture, believe that traits such as indirect communication, saving face, concern for others, and group cooperation are linked to the collective orientation found in the Korean culture.[46]

Collectivism is also contextual. That is to say, we can observe the collective pattern in various settings and contexts. For example, in collective classrooms, such as those found in Mexico, harmony and cooperation in learning are stressed instead of competition.[47] Think of what is being said in the Mexican saying, "The more we are the faster we finish." The medical environment also reflects the pattern of individualism and collectivism. Schneider and Silverman offer the following view of the health care context in Egypt:

> Even in illness, Egyptians prefer company. A man who has a headache, or a fever, will be surrounded by a stream of friends and relatives who bring him soda, food, aspirin, and advice. Hospitals are crowded with residents and friends visiting patients.[48]

Numerous co-cultures in the United States can be classified as collective. Mexican Americans, for example, have most of the characteristics of collectivism mentioned by Triandis; and the research of Hecht, Collier, and Ribeau concludes that African Americans also have the characteristics of collective societies.[49]

Triandis estimated in 1990 that "about 70% of the population of the world lives in collective cultures."[50] This fact alone should be sufficient motivation for members of other cultures to understand the perceptions and communication behaviors of these collective cultures. It is easy to imagine how differently cultures might approach the intercultural setting—whether that setting be a classroom or a factory. Knowing these and other differences in communication styles could facilitate successful intercultural communication.

Uncertainty Avoidance

At the core of uncertainty avoidance is the inescapable truism that the future is unknown. Though we may all try, none of us can accurately predict the next moment, day, year, or decade. As the American playwright Tennessee Williams once noted, "The future is called 'perhaps,' which is the only possible thing to call the future." As the term is used by Hofstede, *uncertainty avoidance* "defines the extent to which people within a culture are made nervous by situations which they perceive as unstructured, unclear, or unpredictable, situations which they therefore try to avoid by maintaining strict codes of behavior and a belief in absolute truths."[51]

High-Uncertainty Avoidance. *High-uncertainty-avoidance cultures* try to avoid uncertainty and ambiguity by providing stability for their members, establishing more formal rules, not tolerating deviant ideas and behaviors, seeking consensus, and believing in absolute truths and the attainment of expertise. They are also characterized by a higher level of anxiety and stress: People think of the uncertainty inherent in life as a continuous hazard that must be avoided. There is a strong need for written rules, planning, regulations, rituals, and ceremonies, which add structure to life. Nations with a strong uncertainty-avoidance tendency are Portugal, Greece, Peru, Belgium, and Japan (see Table 3-2).

Low-Uncertainty Avoidance. At the other end of the scale we find countries like Sweden, Denmark, Ireland, Norway, the United States, Finland, and the Netherlands, which have a *low-uncertainty-avoidance* need. They more easily accept the uncertainty inherent in life and are not as threatened by deviant people and ideas, so they tolerate the unusual. They prize initiative, dislike the structure associated with hierarchy, are more willing to take risks, are more flexible, think that there should be as few rules as possible, and depend not so much on experts as on themselves, generalists, and common sense. As a whole, members of low-uncertainty-avoidance cultures are less tense and more relaxed—traits reflected in the Irish proverb "Life should be a dance, not a race."

As was the case with our first value dimension, differences in uncertainty avoidance affect intercultural communication. In a classroom composed of children from weak,

Table 3-2 *Ranking of Forty Countries on Uncertainty Avoidance*

Country	Ranking*	Country	Ranking*
Argentina	10	Japan	4
Australia	27	Mexico	12
Austria	19	Netherlands	26
Belgium	3	New Zealand	30
Brazil	16	Norway	28
Canada	31	Pakistan	18
Chile	6	Peru	7
Colombia	14	Philippines	33
Denmark	39	Portugal	2
Finland	24	Singapore	40
France	7	South Africa	29
Germany	21	Spain	9
Great Britain	35	Sweden	38
Greece	1	Switzerland	25
Hong Kong	37	Taiwan	20
India	34	Thailand	22
Iran	23	Turkey	11
Ireland	36	U.S.A.	32
Israel	13	Venezuela	15
Italy	17	Yugoslavia	5

*A high score means the country can be classified as one that does not like uncertainty; a low score is associated with cultures that do not feel uncomfortable with uncertainty.

Source: Adapted from Geert Hofstede, *Culture's Consequences: International Differences in Work-Related Values* (Beverly Hills: Sage, 1980).

uncertainty-avoidance cultures we might expect to see students feeling comfortable in unstructured learning situations and students also being rewarded for innovative approaches to problem solving.[52]

Approaches to uncertainty avoidance would also affect negotiation sessions involving members from both groups. High-uncertainty-avoidance members would most likely want to move at a rather slow pace and ask for a greater amount of detail and planning. Some older members might also feel uncomfortable with young members of the group. There would also be differences in the level of formality with which each culture would feel comfortable. Low-uncertainty-avoidance members would not become frustrated if the meeting was not highly structured. The negotiation process would see differences in the level of risk taking on each side. Americans, for example, would be willing to take a risk. Writing about American business practices, Harris and Moran point out, "In light of their history, their perceptions of their rugged individualism, and the rewards of capitalism, Americans have embraced risk and are not risk avoidant."[53]

Power Distance

Another cultural value dimension is *power distance*, which classifies cultures on a continuum of large- to small-power distance. Hofstede is talking about the distance between power and the members of a particular culture. The premise of the dimension deals with the extent to which a society prefers that power in relationships, institutions,

Table 3-3 *Ranking of Forty Countries on Power Distance*

Country	Ranking*	Country	Ranking*
Argentina	25	Japan	22
Australia	29	Mexico	2
Austria	40	Netherlands	28
Belgium	12	New Zealand	37
Brazil	7	Norway	34
Canada	27	Pakistan	21
Chile	15	Peru	13
Colombia	10	Philippines	1
Denmark	38	Portugal	16
Finland	33	Singapore	6
France	9	South Africa	24
Germany	30	Spain	20
Great Britain	31	Sweden	35
Greece	17	Switzerland	32
Hong Kong	8	Taiwan	19
India	4	Thailand	14
Iran	18	Turkey	11
Ireland	36	U.S.A.	26
Israel	39	Venezuela	3
Italy	23	Yugoslavia	5

*A low score means the country can be classified as one that prefers a large-power distance; a high score is associated with cultures that prefer a small-power distance.

Source: Adapted from Geert Hofstede, *Culture's Consequences: International Differences in Work-Related Values* (Beverly Hills: Sage, 1980).

and organizations is distributed unequally. Although all cultures have tendencies for both high- and low-power relationships, one orientation seems to dominate. Foster offers a clear and condensed explanation of this dimension:

> What Hofstede discovered was that in some cultures, those who hold power and those who are affected by power are significantly far apart (high-power distance) in many ways, while in other cultures, the power holders and those affected by the power holders are significantly closer (low-power distance).[54]

Large-Power Distance. This dimension is reflected in the values of the less powerful members of society as well as in those of the more powerful members. People in *large-power-distance* countries such as India, Brazil, Singapore, Greece, Venezuela, Mexico, and the Philippines (see Table 3-3) believe that power and authority are facts of life. Both consciously and unconsciously, these cultures teach their members that people are not equal in this world and that everybody has a rightful place, which is clearly marked by countless vertical arrangements. Social hierarchy is prevalent and institutionalizes inequality.

In the organizations within large-power-distance cultures you find a greater centralization of power, great importance placed on status and rank, a larger proportion of supervisory personnel, a rigid value system that determines the worth of each job, and the bypassing of subordinates in the decision-making process.[55]

Small-Power Distance. *Small-power-distance* countries such as Austria, Finland, Denmark, Norway, New Zealand, and Israel hold that inequality in society should be minimized. People in these cultures believe they are close to power and should have access to that power. To them, a hierarchy is an inequality of roles established for convenience. Subordinates consider superiors to be the same kind of people as they are, and superiors perceive their subordinates the same way. People in power, be they supervisors or government officials, often interact with their constituents and try to look less powerful than they really are. The powerful and the powerless try to live in concert.

We can observe signs of this dimension in nearly every communication setting. Within the educational context Calloway-Thomas, Cooper, and Blake offer the following summary:

> In large power distance societies, the educational process is teacher centered. The teacher initiates all communication, outlines the path of learning students should follow, and is never publicly criticized or contradicted. In large power distance societies, the emphasis is on the personal "wisdom" of the teacher, while in small power distance societies the emphasis is on impersonal "truth" that can be obtained by any competent person.[56]

Masculinity-Femininity

Masculinity. Hofstede uses the words *masculinity* and *femininity* to refer not to men and women, but rather to the degree to which *masculine* or *feminine* traits are valued and revealed. *Masculinity* is the extent to which the dominant values in a society are male oriented. These cultures are associated with such behaviors as ambition, differentiated sex roles, achievement, the acquisition of money, and signs of manliness. Ireland, the Philippines, Greece, South Africa, Austria, Japan, Italy, and Mexico are among countries that tend toward a masculine world view (see Table 3-4). In a masculine society,

Table 3-4 *Ranking of Forty Countries on Masculinity and Femininity*

Country	Ranking*	Country	Ranking*
Argentina	18	Japan	1
Australia	14	Mexico	6
Austria	2	Netherlands	38
Belgium	20	New Zealand	15
Brazil	23	Norway	39
Canada	21	Pakistan	22
Chile	34	Peru	31
Colombia	11	Philippines	10
Denmark	37	Portugal	33
Finland	35	Singapore	24
France	29	South Africa	12
Germany	9	Spain	30
Great Britain	8	Sweden	40
Greece	16	Switzerland	5
Hong Kong	17	Taiwan	27
India	19	Thailand	32
Iran	28	Turkey	26
Ireland	7	U.S.A.	13
Israel	25	Venezuela	3
Italy	4	Yugoslavia	36

*A high score means the country can be classified as one that favors feminine traits; a low score is associated with cultures that prefer masculine traits.

Source: Adapted from Geert Hofstede, *Culture's Consequences: International Differences in Work-Related Values* (Beverly Hills: Sage, 1980).

men are taught to be domineering, ambitious, and assertive. In Japan, for instance, despite the high level of economic development, the division of labor still finds most men in the role of provider and most women as, says Meguro, "homemaker and breeder."[57]

Femininity. Cultures that value *femininity* as a trait stress caring and nurturing behaviors. A feminine world view maintains that men need not be assertive and that they can assume nurturing roles; it also promotes sexual equality and holds that people and the environment are important. Gender roles in feminine societies are more fluid than in masculine societies. Interdependence and androgynous behavior are the ideal, and people sympathize with the unfortunate. Nations such as Sweden, Norway, Finland, Denmark, and the Netherlands tend toward a feminine world view.

Placing a greater value on masculine over feminine traits can even be been seen in the type of person a culture selects to "lead" them. For example, in Sweden, which had the highest ranking in Hofstede's femininity category, women occupy 41 percent of legislative positions; in Japan, ranked the highest in masculine traits, only 5 percent of legislative offices are held by women.[58]

As you might suspect, the acting out of gender roles influences communication. In masculine cultures, men do most of the talking and take an active role in decision making. We say more about the role of gender in intercultural communication when we examine the topic in the business (Chapter 7), educational (Chapter 8), and health care (Chapter 9) settings.

Over the years there has been some criticism leveled against Hofstede's work. First, since Hofstede's original study, numerous other studies have focused on individualism and collectivism; but the other three dimensions he studied lack what Draguns called "systematic investigation."[59] Second, because the people Hofstede surveyed were middle managers in large multinational organizations, most of his findings are work related. Third, many important countries and cultures were not included in Hofstede's study. For example, there were no Arab countries, and Africa was represented by only South Africa. Finally, Hofstede conducted his extensive study a great many years ago. Hence, many critics question the pertinence of his findings as they apply to today's cultures. We do not agree with this last charge. Although cultures change, we suggest, as we do in Chapter 2, that their deep structures are resistant to change. The values Hofstede studied were of those deep structures.

Confucian Dynamism

The cross-cultural psychologist Michael Bond, and his research group at the Chinese Cultural Connection, extended the work of Hofstede by adding another dimension known as *Confucian dynamism*.[60] The main goal of their research was to discover specific work-related values. Data for their study was drawn from the cultures of Hong Kong, Taiwan, Japan, South Korea, and Singapore. The research team isolated six key values found within the five cultures of their study. The primary values included "a dynamic long-term orientation, perseverance, ordering relationships by status, being thrift centered, having a sense of shame, and emphasizing collective face-saving."[61] It is easy to see how these patterns would influence interaction in a variety of settings. In organizations, for example, employees reflecting these values would have a strong work ethic and show great respect to their employers. We would also expect individuals who are members of these cultures to value social order and long-range goals.

Because Confucianism is at the core of Bond's analysis, and also the basic world view of much of Southeast Asia, we will return to a detailed discussion of Confucianism in the next chapter.

Kluckhohns and Strodtbeck's Value Orientations

The Kluckhohns and Strodtbeck supply us with yet another taxonomy for analyzing cultural patterns. These patterns are called "value orientations" in that they "tell" the members of the culture what is important and also offer guidance for living their life. [62] Since their work was completed, other researchers have added to the findings of the Kluckhohns and Strodtbeck.[63] The Kluckhohns and Strodtbeck were anthropologists, who after examining numerous cultures, reached the conclusion that all people turn to their culture to answer the same basic questions. Let us list the five questions before we look at some specific cultural answers to these common concerns (see Table 3-5).

1. What is the character of human nature?
2. What is the relation of humankind to nature?
3. What is the orientation toward time?
4. What is the value placed on activity?
5. What is the relationship of people to each other?[64]

These five orientations might best be visualized as points on a continuum.[65] As you move through these five orientations, you will undoubtedly notice some of the same

Table 3-5 *Five Value Orientations for Analyzing Cultural Patterns**

Orientation	Values and Behaviors		
Human Nature	Basically Evil	Mixture of Good and Evil	Basically Good
Human Kind and Nature	People Subject to Nature	People in Harmony with Nature	People the Master of Nature
Sense of Time	Past Oriented	Present Oriented	Future Oriented
Activity	Being	Being in Becoming	Doing
Social Relationships	Authoritarian	Group Oriented	Individualistic

*Based on Kluckhohn, Kluckhohn, and Strodtbeck. See notes for Chapter 3 at end of book.

characteristics discussed by Hofstede. This is very understandable because both approaches are talking about meaningful values found in all cultures. Hence, both sets of researchers were bound to track many of the same patterns.

Human Nature Orientation

Nearly all judgments about human behavior, be they moral or legal, begin with this core question: What is the character of human nature? Was Anne Frank right when she wrote in *The Diary of a Young Girl*, "In spite of everything, I still believe that people are really good at heart"? Or was the philosopher Immanuel Kant correct when he observed, "Out of the crooked timber of humanity no straight thing can ever be made"? Our answer to the question of human nature is that it is a powerful force in how we live our life. As Stevenson and Haberman tell us, "Different conceptions of human nature lead to different views about what we ought to do and how we can do it."[66] Although all of us have personal answers to this question of human nature, there are also cultural explanations for why people act as they do. Understanding these cultural responses is directly linked to the study of intercultural communication.

Discussions of human nature usually deal with questions of goodness and rationality, so we will look briefly at each of these issues. People have raised questions about good and evil for almost as long as humans have had a sense of self. Because answers differ, it is best to place cultures on a continuum that has three logical divisions: evil at one end of the scale, good and evil in the middle, and good at the other end of the continuum.

Evil. Cultures that begin with the premise that people are intrinsically *evil* and therefore cannot be trusted seek to control the actions of their members with institutions ranging from the religious to the political. As we shall see in the next chapter, Islam came to the Middle East at a time when the Bedouin culture was plagued with immorality and hedonism. Allah was needed, the people thought, to save these "sinners." In the United States, our orientation, inherited from our Puritan ancestors, is based on the concept of original sin. However, we are "perfectible." By following certain rules we can change, improve, and "be saved." According to this view, with constant hard work, control, and self-discipline, we can achieve goodness. This is one reason education and training are a part of the American mosaic. We can also see this "self-help" approach to life in other aspects of Christianity. For Christians, God is the "Father" and humans are his children. As is the case with all children, we get guidance but must also make choices. According to Christianity, "We are rational beings, we have self-consciousness, and we have free choice."[67] Through those choices, we can move from being corrupt to being good.

Good and Evil. Toward the middle of the continuum is the orientation that people can be *evil and good*—that they are inherently malleable. How they end up depends on the events in their lives and how they handle those events. Much of Europe, with its strong tradition of learning and education, holds this view.

Goodness. Perhaps the most extreme view of innate *goodness* of human nature can be found in the philosophies of Confucianism and Buddhism. Most interpretations of the writings of Confucius maintain that he was "very optimistic" about human nature.[68] Hundreds of years later we see this same view toward the innate goodness of people in the words of the Chinese philosopher Lu Wang: "Human nature is originally good." As we discuss in Chapter 4, Buddhism also maintains that we are born pure and are closest to what is called "loving kindness" when we enter this world. Hence, people are good, and our culture is what makes us evil.

Cutting across the arguments concerning the good and evil of human nature has been the question of the essential rationality of human nature. Throughout history, there has been tension between those who believe in fate or mystic powers and those who believe that the intellect can solve any problem and discover any truth. Imagine for a moment your perceptions of reality if you are French and take the rational approach characteristic of Descartes' philosophy, or if you are Native American and believe that forces outside you control much of your thinking and behavior. And for the Hindu, mysticism, intuition, and spiritual awareness are needed to understand the nature of reality. A belief in fate, as opposed to one that stresses free will, is bound to yield different conclusions. We say more about the sway of science versus the power of intuition when we discuss various world views in the next chapter.

Person-Nature Orientation

Human Beings Subject to Nature. The differences in conceptions of the relationship between humanity and nature produce distinct frames of reference for human desires, attitudes, and behaviors. At one end of the scale devised by the Kluckhohns and Strodtbeck is the view that maintains *human beings are subject to nature*. Cultures that hold this orientation believe that the most powerful forces of life are outside their control. Whether the force be a god, fate, or magic, a person cannot overcome it and must therefore learn to accept it. This orientation is found in India and parts of South America. For the Hindu, because everything is part of a unified force, "the world of distinct and separate objects and processes is a manifestation of a more fundamental reality that is undivided and unconditional."[69] This "oneness" with the world helps create a perceptual vision of a harmonious world.

"Cooperation" with Nature. The middle or so-called *cooperation view* is widespread and is associated with East Asians. In Japan and Thailand there is a perception that nature is part of life, and not a hostile force waiting to be subdued. This orientation affirms that people should, in every way possible, live in harmony with nature. The desire to be part of nature and not control it is also strong among Native Americans. This orientation is eloquently summarized by Chief Seattle: "Humankind has not woven the web of life. We are but one thread within it. Whatever we do to the web we do to ourselves. All things are bound together—all things connect."

Controlling Nature. At the other end of the scale is the view that compels us to *conquer and direct the forces of nature* to our advantage. This value orientation is characteristic of the Western approach, which, as we noted earlier in the chapter, has a long tradition of valuing technology, change, and science. Americans have long believed that nature was something that could and had to be mastered. The early immigrants to North America found a harsh and vast wilderness that they needed to "tame." Even today we use terms such as "conquering" space. For people with this orientation there is a clear separation from nature. There are even some religious underpinnings to the American view of nature. There is a belief that it is God's intention for us to make the earth our private domain. As an article in *Newsweek* magazine noted, "Environmentalists have long blamed Biblical tradition—specifically God's injunction to man in Genesis to 'subdue the earth'—for providing cultural sanction for the Industrial Revolution and its plundering of nature."[70]

We can often find examples of cultures clashing because of divergent views on how to relate to nature. A case in point is the ongoing controversy between the dominant American culture and some Native American tribes who object to widespread strip mining of coal because it disfigures the earth and displaces spirits worshipped by the tribes. Our cultural orientation of controlling nature can be seen in a host of other instances. Adler highlights some of these:

> Some other examples of the North American dominance orientation include astronauts' conquest (dominance) of space; economists' structuring the market; sales representatives' attempts to influence buyers' decisions; and, perhaps most controversial today, bioengineering and genetic programming.[71]

Time Orientation

As a species, our fixation with time and the power we give it are rather obvious. Over two thousand years ago, the Greek philosopher Sophocles observed, "Time is a kindly God." As is the case with most of the issues discussed in this book, cultures vary widely in how much they want to "give in" to that "God." *Where they differ is in the value placed on the past, present, and future and how each influences interaction.* So important is a culture's use of time that we develop the subject in great detail in Chapter 6, but for now let us simply highlight some of the major cultural differences.

Past Orientation. *Past-oriented* cultures believe strongly in the significance of prior events. History, established religions, and tradition are extremely important to these cultures, so there is a strong belief that the past should be the guide for making decisions and determining truth. You can see this orientation in China, which because of its long and resplendent history continues to respect the past. Even today, Chinese historical dramas lead box-office sales. And, as Adler notes, "Chinese children have no space-age superman to emulate. Even at play they pretend to be the Monkey King, the supernatural hero of a medieval epic."[72] There is even a famous Chinese proverb that states, "The past is as clear as a mirror, the future as dark as lacquer." In Japan, where

© Gloria Thomas

Past-oriented cultures place a high value on traditions.

Shintoism is strong and ancestor worship important, the past remains paramount. Great Britain, because of its extensive devotion to tradition, including the continuation of a monarchy, resists change as it attempts to cling to the past.

France is yet another culture that can be understood by exploring its view of the past. The French, on many levels, venerate the past. As Curtius notes, "The French live deeply in remembrance and the past."[73] Curtius maintains that you can see admiration for the past in the fact that the French have a feeling that they belong to an ancient civilization, and that "true patriotism is the love of the past."[74]

Within the United States, Native Americans—in part because of their strong oral tradition—also value the past. Many of the Native American stories in fact use the past to set examples and to "provide moral guidelines by which one should live."[75]

Present Orientation. *Present-oriented* cultures hold that the moment has the most significance. For them, the future is vague, ambiguous, and unknown and what is real exists in the here and now. For these cultures, enjoyment comes in the present. People of the Philippines, Mexico, and Latin America usually have these beliefs. Mexican Americans also "prefer to experience life and people around them fully in the present."[76]

Future Orientation. *Future-oriented* cultures, such as the one found in the United States, emphasize the future and expect it to be grander and nicer than the present. What is coming next holds the greatest attraction for most Americans because whatever we are doing is not quite as good as what we could be doing. The "next" thing can happen in one minute, one week, one month, one year, or in heaven, but the future is

Diverse Cultural Patterns **77**

where happiness is to be found. This does not mean that Americans have no regard for the past or no thought of the present, but it is certainly true that most of you, in thought or action, do not want to be "left behind." You all want to wear the most current fashions and to drive a brand new car.

Like many other orientations, our view of time is related to a host of other values. For example, Americans' view of the future makes them optimistic. This is reflected in the common proverb "If at first you don't succeed, try, try, and try again." This optimistic view of the future also sees Americans believing they can control the future. The power to control the future was clearly spelled out by former president Lyndon Johnson when he told all Americans that "Yesterday is not ours to recover, but tomorrow is ours to win or to lose." Later in the book we will examine how these three orientations toward time can influence everything from business negotiations to activity within a classroom.

Activity Orientation

Activity orientation is the way a culture views activity. Three common modes of activity expression, as detailed by the Kluckhohns and Strodtbeck, are being, being-in-becoming, and doing.

Being Orientation. *Being orientation* refers to spontaneous activity. Most Latin cultures have the view that the current activity is the one that matters the most. In Mexico, for example, people take great delight in the simple act of conversation with family and friends. Mexicans will talk for hours with their companions, for they believe that the act of "being" is one of the main goals and joys of life.

Being-in-Becoming. *Being-in-becoming* orientations often correlate with cultures that value a spiritual life more than a material one. For example, in both Hinduism and Buddhism, people spend a portion of their lives in meditation and contemplation in an attempt to purify and fully advance themselves. For them, this inner or spiritual development represents one of the main purposes of life.

Doing Orientation. *Doing orientation* describes activity in which accomplishments are measurable by standards external to the acting agent. This orientation, which thrives on action, most characterizes the dominant American culture. Think of the notion of "doing" and "action" in the well-known proverb "No sooner said than done—so acts your man of worth." The high value placed on activity and doing is reflected in countless ways in American culture. For example, Americans plan and schedule nearly every activity in the day. This reverence for activity is expressed in the proverb "Idle hands are the devil's workshop."

African Americans are also a "doing" culture. Emotional vitality, activity, openness of feelings, and being expressive, which are part of the African American experience, all involve forms of "doing."[77]

Activity Orientation. The *activity orientation* of a culture impinges on many other beliefs and values. Your definition of activity affects your perception of work, efficiency, change, time, and progress. Even the pace at which you live your life—from how fast you walk to the speed at which you reach conclusions—is related to where you land on the being–doing scale. Americans have long admired and rewarded people who can make rapid decisions and "speak up" quickly, and they even become impatient with people who are too reflective. Writing about American education Newman notes, "The child who speaks when the teacher requests a response is rewarded. The one who ponders is often considered withdrawn, problematic. The educational system appears to favor students who have the immediate answer, not those who take time to consider other questions."[78] This attitude toward activity contrasts with that fostered by the Taoist tradition: The individual is *not* the active agent; he or she is to remain calm, and truth eventually will make itself apparent. Imagine members of these two cultures sitting down together at a business meeting—or occupying the same classroom.

Relational (Social) Orientation

This value orientation is concerned with the ways in which people perceive their relationships with others. We discussed the basic ideas behind relational orientations when we examined Hofstede's dimensions of individualism and power distance, so our explanations here are rather brief.

Authoritarian Orientation. As Table 3-5 shows, the value orientations on the continuum range from authoritarianism to individualism. Although most Americans find it difficult to believe, many cultures have had only *authoritarian* leaders, and therefore, believe this type of social relationship to be the norm. By American standards, Egypt might well be the only democracy in the entire Arab world. The people who live in the other Arab countries believe that some people are born to lead and others to follow, so authoritarian relationships—from those with the ruling family to those with the leaders of the church—are accepted. The Arab proverb "The eye cannot rise above the eyebrow" demonstrates this accepting attitude.

Collective Orientation. As we noted elsewhere, *collective* cultures (such as the Chinese, Indian, African, Native American, Mexican, Korean, and Latin American cultures) see the group as the most important of all social entities. Group affiliations take precedence over individual goals. In India, for example, the family influences a person's education, marriage, and occupation choice. So strong is the collective nature of some African tribes that "attempts to get Maasai students to raise their hands and participate in formal classrooms are often futile."[79] The reason is that they do not want to call attention to themselves in a group setting.

Individualism Orientation. Having already spent a number of pages on the topic of individuals we now simply remind you that cultures that value the *individual* believe all people should have equal rights and complete control over their destiny. Anything else, as most Americans hold, violates the will of God and the spirit of the Constitution.

Hall's High-Context and Low-Context Orientation

The anthropologist Hall offers us another effective means of examining cultural similarities and differences in both perception and communication. He categorizes cultures as being either high or low context, depending on the degree to which meaning comes from the settings or from the words being exchanged.[80] The assumption underlying Hall's classifications is that "one of the functions of culture is to provide a highly selective screen between man and the outside world. In its many forms, culture therefore designates what we pay attention to and what we ignore."[81] The study of high-context and low-context cultures therefore offers us some insight into not only what people pay attention to but what they ignore.

The word *context* needs to be understood if one is to appreciate the link between context and communication. Context can be defined as "the information that surrounds an event; it is inextricably bound up with the meaning of the event."[82] Although all cultures contain some characteristics of both high and low variables, most can be placed along a scale showing their ranking on this particular dimension (see Table 3-6). To call your attention to the fact that there are degrees of high and low context we have placed various cultures on a continuum rather than only using two rigid categories. The Halls define high and low context in the following manner:

> A high context (HC) communication or message is one in which most of the information is already in the person, while very little is in the coded, explicitly transmitted part of the message. A low context (LC) communication is just the opposite; i.e., the mass of the information is vested in the explicit code.[83]

Table 3-6 *Cultures Arranged Along the High-Context and Low-Context Dimension*

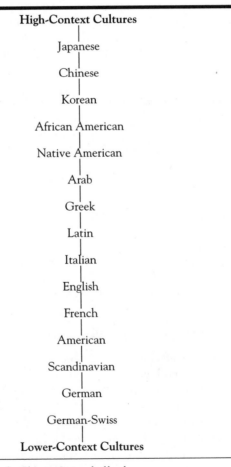

High-Context Cultures

Japanese

Chinese

Korean

African American

Native American

Arab

Greek

Latin

Italian

English

French

American

Scandinavian

German

German-Swiss

Lower-Context Cultures

Based on Edward T. Hall. See notes for Chapter 3 at end of book.

High Context

In *high-context* cultures (Native Americans, Latin Americans, Japanese, Chinese, and Korean), people are very homogeneous with regard to experiences, information networks, and the like. High-context cultures, because of tradition and history, change very little over time. These are cultures in which consistent messages have produced consistent responses to the environment. "As a result," the Halls say, "for most normal transactions in daily life they do not require, nor do they expect, much in-depth, background information."[84] Meaning, therefore, is not necessarily contained in words. In high-context cultures, information is provided through gestures, the use of space, and even silence. High-context cultures tend to be more aware of their surroundings and their environment and can communicate those feelings without words. As Andersen points out, "High-context cultures are more reliant on and tuned in to nonverbal communication."[85] As an indicator of this tendency to use nonverbal communication you can see how the Korean language contains the word *nunchi*, which means being able to communicate with the eyes. In high-context cultures, so much information is available in the environment that it is unnecessary to verbalize everything. For instance, statements of affection, such as "I love you," are rare because the message is conveyed by the context.

Meaning, in high-context cultures, is also conveyed "through status (age, sex, education, family background, title, and affiliations) and through an individual's informal friends and associates."[86]

Low Context

In *low-context* cultures (German, Swiss, and American), the population is less homogeneous and therefore tends to compartmentalize interpersonal contacts. This lack of a large pool of common experiences means that "each time they interact with others they need detailed background information."[87] In low-context cultures, the verbal message contains most of the information and very little is embedded in the context or the participants. This characteristic manifests itself in a host of ways. For example, the Asian mode of communication is often vague, indirect, and implicit, whereas Western communication tends to be direct and explicit—that is, everything needs to be stated, and if possible, stated well. Althen offers an excellent summary of Americans' fascination with language in the following paragraph:

> Americans depend more on spoken words than on nonverbal behavior to convey messages. They think it is important to be able to "speak up" and "say what is on their mind." They admire a person who has a moderately large vocabulary and who can express herself clearly and cleverly.[88]

Differences in perceived credibility are yet another aspect of communication associated with these two orientations. In high-context cultures people who rely primarily on verbal messages for information are perceived as less credible. They believe that silence often sends a better message than words, and anyone who needs words does not have the information. As the Indonesian proverb states, "Empty cans clatter the loudest."

Differences in this communication dimension can even alter how conflict is perceived and responded to. As Ting-Toomey has observed, the communication differences between high-context and low-context cultures are also apparent in the manner in which each approaches conflict. For example, because high-context cultures tend to be less open, they hold that conflict is damaging to most communication encounters. For them, Ting-Toomey says, "Conflict should be dealt with discreetly and subtly."[89]

Harris and Moran summarize this dimension as follows:

Unless global leaders are aware of the subtle differences, communication misunderstandings between low- and high-context communicators can result. Japanese communicate by not stating things directly, while Americans usually do the opposite—"spell it out." The former is looking for meaning and understanding in what is not said—in the nonverbal communication or body language, in the silences and pauses, in relationships and empathy. The latter places emphasis on sending and receiving accurate messages directly, usually by being articulate with words.[90]

Et Cetera

We have labeled this final examination of cultural patterns "et cetera" as a way of alerting you to the fact that any catalog of cultural patterns is indeed endless. In fact, the word *et cetera* actually means "other things." So we now turn to some of those "other things." That is to say, although Hofstede, Bond, the Kluckhohns and Strodtbeck, and the Halls have identified what might be some of the most important ways of studying cultures, there are still other dimensions that need to be considered. We have selected two of these—*informality and formality* and *assertiveness and interpersonal harmony*—that have been alluded to in the preceding taxonomies.

One more observation is in order before we begin. It should be clear at this stage that cultural patterns do not exist in isolation, but influence all aspects of life. Try to visualize major cultural patterns as a large stone cast into a pond. The stone (the pattern) will create countless ripples (other patterns) that will affect the entire pond (culture). Although we have examined but one pattern at a time, we have tried to point out how these patterns relate to other patterns and to communication. For example, when we discussed individualism and collectivism, we noted that individualism often has a ripple effect: it creates competition, impatience with group activity, a negative view of conformity, and so forth. To be consistent with the discussion of the other patterns, we have decided to again treat these last two values as points on a continuum.

Informality and Formality

From the way people dress, to their posture, to the language they use, the manifestations of informality and formality take many forms. These two dimensions, like our other patterns, are influenced by culture. Cultures tend to range from very informal to quite formal.

Informality. The United States is an *informal* culture, as Javidi and Javidi note:

In North America people tend to treat others with informality and directness. They avoid the use of formal codes of conduct, titles, honorific, and ritualistic manners in their interactions with others.[91]

American informality shows itself in a host of ways. Not only do Americans use first names when meeting strangers for the first time, but their standard of dress reflects their nonchalant outlook on life. Even the simple greeting "Hi" is a badge of informality. Althen offers the following summary of how informality is often reflected in American culture:

Idiomatic speech (commonly called "slang") is heavily used on most occasions, with formal speech reserved for public events and fairly formal situations. People from almost any station in life can be seen in public wearing jeans, sandals, or other informal attire. People slouch down in chairs or lean on walls or furniture when they talk, rather than maintaining an erect bearing.[92]

Although "Americans pride themselves on their informality, people from Asia and most other places in the world do not see this as a virtue."[93] Steward and Bennett offer some examples to buttress this important point:

> The degree of informality found in American communication patterns is uncommon in other cultures. In most Latin American and European societies, for instance, there are levels of formality attached to status difference. In Asian cultures, formal communication may be demanded by greater age as well as by higher status. In Japan, formality is also extended to strangers with whom a relationship is demanded. This formality is no joking matter, since failure to follow appropriate form may suggest to others a severe flaw in character.[94]

Formality. There are, of course, many specific examples of cultures that highly value formality. In Egypt, Turkey, and Iran, the student–teacher relationship is very formal. This may be seen in the Egyptian proverb "Whoever teaches me a letter, I should become a slave to him forever." In these countries, when the teacher enters the room, students are expected to stand. When students meet their teachers on the street, they are expected to bow to them. Contrast this with the relaxed, informal student–teacher relationships found in the United States.

The degree of formality in Germany is, from an American perspective, extreme. Germans address others and conduct themselves in a very formal manner. It is important for Germans to dress well even if just visiting friends or going to school, but especially when attending church. Formality is also evident in how cultures use forms of address. Not knowing these differences can cause problems. The Halls note, "American informality and the habit of calling others by their first names make Germans acutely uncomfortable, particularly when young people or people lower in the hierarchy address their elders or their superiors by their first names."[95] The use of personal titles is yet another way the Germans mark formality.[96] They use titles extensively to identify people and their positions in the social structure. If, for instance, a person is both a professor and a physician, he is referred to as Herr Professor Doktor Kaempfer. And because Germany has a male-oriented culture, women are not addressed by their surname, such as Frau (Mrs.) Kaempfer, but always by their husband's title. The wife of Herr Professor Doktor Kaempfer, for example, would be addressed as Frau Professor Doktor Kaempfer. Germany is not the only place where forms of address are directly linked to perception and values. Schneider and Silverman remind us that Mexicans are yet another culture that values formality:

> Mexicans also make heavy use of honorific titles to show respect. New acquaintances met at a party are addressed as *senor, senora,* and *senorita.* In business, people address managers with titles like director, doctor, *ingeniero* (engineer), or *licienciado* (someone who has a higher education degree).[97]

The significance of informality and formality in communication goes well beyond a culture's use of language. The number of friends you have and what you tell those friends are also affected. In a study on intercultural friendships Gareis noted "whereas Americans are easily accessible," Germans tend to be formal and private even when dealing with their friends.[98] There is even a German proverb that states, "A friend to everyone is a friend to no one." In yet another extensive study conducted on self-disclosure, Barnlund concluded that Americans tend to disclose much more about themselves than do members of cultures such as the Japanese, who value formality.[99] Linking this difference to the deep structure of the Japanese culture, Barnlund concluded:

> Permanently secure within the primary group, supported without qualification at every transition in life, a Japanese has little need to extend himself socially, to seek and cultivate endless series of friends to replenish those who make up his social circle.[100]

Assertiveness and Interpersonal Harmony

Our final pattern deals with the manner in which people "present" themselves to others. While there are many dimensions to our communication style, *assertive* and *interpersonal harmony* are two that influence intercultural interaction in a host of ways. Therefore, let us conclude this section by looking at these two cultural characteristics.

Assertiveness. *American culture* is known for its assertive and aggressive communication style. It is not uncommon for Americans to actually enroll in assertiveness training classes that encourage them to be frank, open, and direct when they are dealing with other people. This type of behavior is now so commonplace that *U.S. News & World Report* recently presented an essay titled "The American Uncivil Wars." The thrust of the article was to call attention to the variety of ways aggressive behavior is reflected in American culture:

> It is a time when schools use metal detectors to keep out guns and knives, when universities insist on speech and behavior codes to stem the tide of hatred and disrespect, when legal cases become shouting matches, when the Internet is lettered with raunch and menace, when political campaigns resemble food fights, when trash talk and head butts are the idiom of sports, and when popular culture tops itself from week to week with displays of violence, sex, foul language and puerile confession.[101]

The many signs of assertive and aggressive behavior in our culture, like all aspects of culture, did not develop by chance. A culture that has a long history of valuing nonconformity, individualism, competition, and freedom of expression is bound to encourage assertive behavior. We are a culture that turned a self-help book with the title *Confession of an S.O.B* into a best-seller. The reasons we value assertive communication, according to Nadler, Nadler, and Broome, are obvious: "North American individuals are expected to stand up for their rights, and this often involves open confrontation."[102] Barnlund adds: "The eloquent articulation of conviction is among the most valued virtues of [American] citizens, and the arts of argument and debate are encouraged in the home, school, and marketplace."[103] Wenzhong and Grove reinforce this idea:

> In a culture where individualism is as highly valued as it is in the United States, people are expected to take the initiative in advancing their personal interests and well-being and to be direct and assertive in interacting with others. High social and geographic mobility and the comparatively superficial nature of many personal attachments create a climate where interpersonal competition and a modest level of abrasiveness are tolerated and even expected.[104]

Harmony. As you can imagine, communication problems arise when cultures that value assertiveness come in contact with cultures that value accord and harmony. One of the authors recalls that at an international conference, members of the Israeli delegation, who were arguing their position in a dynamic manner, complained that the representatives from Thailand showed no interest in or enthusiasm for the meeting; they were "just sitting there." The Thai delegates, on the other hand, thought the professors from Israel were angry because they were "using loud voices." Both responses were, of course, a product of cultural experiences. As Cooper and Cooper point out, "The Thai learns how to avoid aggression rather than how to defend himself against it."[105] And members of the Jewish culture stress what they believe to be healthy disagreement. There is even a Yiddish saying that pokes fun at this confrontational style: "Where there are two Jews there are three arguments."

The Thais are not the only people who seek to avoid confrontation and strive for a communication style that values calmness, equanimity, and interpersonal harmony. Let us look at a few of these cultures so that you might be better able to understand their behavior and your reaction to that behavior.

For members of the Filipino culture, Gochenour says, "The ultimate ideal is one of harmony—between individuals, among the members of a family, among the groups and divisions of society, and of all life in relationship with God."[106] Filipinos have two words that express their conception of harmony: *amor propio* and *pakikisama*. *Amor propio* translates into English as "harmony" and refers to a very fragile sense of personal worth and self-respect. In interactions with others, it denotes being treated as a person rather than an object. This value makes the Filipino especially vulnerable to negative remarks that may affect his or her standing in society. Consequently, Filipinos seldom criticize or verbally confront others; and if they do, it is in the most polite manner.[107] They see bluntness and frankness as uncivilized traits. Instead, they value *pakikisama*, or smooth interpersonal relations.[108]

The Japanese also place a high value on interpersonal harmony. In fact, "Self is subordinated in the interests of harmony."[109] Like so many dimensions of culture, interpersonal harmony can be found in the deep structure of Japanese society. As Hendry notes, "The value attached to harmony in Japan dates back to at least the Seventeen-Article Constitution of Prince Shotoku (594–622), which esteemed concord above all things as the subject of the first article and the underlying theme of all the others."[110] It is a cultural pattern that touches all aspects of Japanese life, including child-rearing practices: "The concern of adults to create a secure and an attentive environment for a small child is part of this wider emphasis in Japanese society on harmony in social relationships."[111]

The cultural thinking that stresses harmony can clearly be seen in the method the Japanese employ when doing business. Perhaps exaggerating slightly, Harris and Moran suggest that harmony is "more important in business dealings for the Japanese, than achieving higher sales and profits."[112] To maintain harmony and avoid interpersonal clashes, Japanese business has evolved an elaborate process called *nemawashii*: "binding the roots of a plant before pulling it out."[113] In this process, any subject that might cause disorder at a meeting is discussed in advance. Anticipating and obviating interpersonal antagonism allow the Japanese to avoid impudent and discourteous behavior.

It is not our intent to imply that the Japanese people do not get insulted or angry just like everyone else, but as Schneider and Silverman point out, "in their society values and norms forcefully promote self-control and the avoidance of direct personal confrontation."[114]

Like Thais, Filipinos, and Japanese, the Chinese "tend to regard conflict and confrontation as unpleasant and undesirable."[115] Chen and Xiao underscore this same point when they state: "It is without a doubt that harmony is one of the primordial values of Confucianism and of the Chinese culture."[116] This principle also has a long and meaningful history in China. Its roots are in Chinese religion: "According to Confucianism, the ultimate goal of human behavior is to achieve 'harmony' which leads Chinese people to pursue a conflict-free and group-oriented system of human relationships."[117] Two Chinese proverbs speak to the issue of outward signs of anger: "The first man to raise his voice loses the argument" and "One hurtful word wounds like a sharp sword." We should add in closing that the Malaysians are another Asian culture that has an aversion to interpersonal anger.[118]

For reasons that are very different than those found in Asian cultures, Mexicans also seek smooth interpersonal relationships and try to avoid face-to-face confrontations. They often will say something that is not true or even slightly alter the facts if it makes the other person feel better. From the Mexicans' perspective, this shading of the truth is not a lie but simply part of a long cultural heritage going back to the early marketplaces where people would bargain and negotiate with friends by verbal bartering. These verbal exchanges were a kind of game whereby each person demonstrated his or her language skills. Condon suggests that even today we could learn a great deal about this attribute by visiting a marketplace.[119] This avoidance of discord is seen in a number of different settings. Ruch notes that in the business context, for example, "When a visitor asks for information that a Mexican doesn't have, the Mexican does his best to say something that will please the visitor."[120]

Co-cultures in the United States hold contrary views of assertive and aggressive communication. For example, North American Native Indians, say Moghaddam, Taylor, and Wright, "have developed a distaste for Western assertiveness and tend to avoid those who interact in assertive ways."[121] Cheyenne children are even removed from the tribe for short periods if they act aggressively toward other members of the tribe.[122]

You can also observe in the United States varying aggressive and assertive patterns as they apply to gender. "From childhood on, males learn to be aggressive."[123] This aggression takes the form of assertive and domineering communication patterns, and these patterns get acted out in a variety of situations. As Ivy and Backlund note, "Some men are verbally aggressive on their jobs."[124] They add that "aggressive behavior might take the form of emphatic sales pitches, interruptions of subordinates, or fevered attempts to persuade colleagues."[125] Reflect for a moment on how some of the cultures we discussed in this last section would perceive and respond to those communication techniques. We urge you to learn about the different cultural patterns we have highlighted throughout this chapter so that you will be able to understand, predict, and even adapt to the behavior of people from other cultures.

SUMMARY

- Perception is best defined as *"the process of selecting, organizing, and interpreting sensory data in a way that enables us to make sense of our world."*
- Although the physical process of perception is almost the same in everyone, culture influences how we interpret and evaluate incoming stimuli.

- An attitude is a combination of beliefs about a subject, feelings toward it, and any predisposition to act toward it.
- Beliefs are our convictions in the truth of something—with or without proof.
- Values are enduring attitudes about the preferability of one belief over another.
- Dominant American cultural patterns include individualism, equality, materialism, science and technology, progress and change, work and leisure, and competition.
- Cultures differ in their beliefs, attitudes and value toward (1) individualism and collectivism, (2) uncertainty avoidance, (3) power distance, (4) masculinity and femininity, (5) work, (6) human nature, (7) the perception of nature, (8) time, (9) activity, (10) relationships, (11) context, (12) informality and formality, and (13) assertiveness and interpersonal harmony.

INFOTRAC® COLLEGE EDITION EXERCISES

1. One of the cultural patterns discussed in this chapter is the individualism/collectivism continuum. Using the EasyTrac option, search the subject term "Individualism." Browse the articles listed as well as the subdivisions of this subject to gain a sense of the vigor of this research and its practical applications. Then, using the PowerTrac option, locate the article "Television, Individualism, and Social Capital" by Allan McBride (Hint: use author or title search terms to locate this article). According to McBride, what kinds of messages about authority, conflict, individualism, and collectivism are being transmitted by American television? From your own experience, provide specific examples of shows and episodes that further support the author's conclusion or that refute his ideas about the cultural messages sent by television.

2. Using the PowerTrac option locate *one* of the following articles:

   (a.) "The Influence of Culture on American and British Advertising: An Exploratory Comparison of Beer Advertising" by Zahna Caillat and Barbara Mueller.

   (b.) "Engaging in Kenson: An Extended Case Study of One Form of 'Common' Sense" by Bradford Hall and Mutsumi Noguchi (this article compares Japanese and Western concepts of modesty).

   Read the article you have selected and summarize the similarities and differences described between American values and the values of the other culture discussed. Imagine traveling to either Great Britain or to Japan: How might the information you've learned be useful in interacting with others?

3. Using the PowerTrac option, locate the article "Hofstede's Country Classification 25 Years Later" by Denise Rotondo Fernandez et al. How does this article extend the text's discussion of cultural differences?

ACTIVITIES

1. Ask your informant for English translations of sayings and proverbs from his or her culture that reflect important values in that culture. Alternatively, you may want to show the sayings and proverbs in this chapter to your informant and see if he or she has corresponding sayings.

2. In small groups, create an ideal culture and give it a name. Indicate which of the values discussed in this chapter would be primary in the value hierarchy of your culture. Try to accommodate the interests of all group members. Time permitting, describe the outward manifestations of your cultural values (for example, dress, work, play, food preferences, roles).

3. In a small group, conduct a mock business meeting at which half the members are from a high-context culture and the other half from a low-context culture.

4. Ask your friends and/or family members to list ten of the most important characteristics of American culture. Compile these lists to identify the most commonly mentioned American cultural patterns. Compare your list with all the patterns discussed in this chapter and try to identify similarities and differences.

DISCUSSION IDEAS

1. Discuss American cultural perceptions of color. What do Americans associate with the following colors? Ask three people from other cultures what they associate with the colors.

   black yellow

   white blue

   red

2. Find examples of sports and military terms that are used in American business settings. Interview a corporate employee and/or read a weekly business magazine or the business section of your local newspaper. Explain what the terms mean and why you think they are used in this context.

3. How does learning about one's own culture help in understanding other cultures?

4. Why do cultural patterns change over time? What American patterns tend to be relatively stable? Do cultural patterns change faster in America than in some other cultures? Why?

chapter 4

The Deep Structure: Roots of Reality

There is only one religion, though there are a hundred versions of it.

GEORGE BERNARD SHAW

The family is the nucleus of civilization.

WILL AND ARIEL DURANT

History is philosophy teaching by example.

HENRY ST. JOHN BOLINGBROKE

This book has been about the manner in which culture helps create and shape your realities. How particular cultures view reality determines how the members of that culture see the world, their place in it, and how they interact in that world. In the last chapter, we emphasized cultural variations in both the patterns and functions of those realities. With that information as a point of reference, we are now ready to discuss the important question of *why* cultures differ in their perceptions of and responses to reality. Why do members of some cultures seek solitude, whereas those of other cultures feel despondent if they are not continuously in the company of other people? Why do some cultures frantically cling to youth, whereas others welcome old age and even death? Why do some cultures worship the Earth, whereas others molest it? Why do some cultures seek material possessions while others believe they are a hindrance to a peaceful life? These and countless other philosophical, ideological, and metaphysical questions need to be answered if you are to understand how people from different cultures communicate. It is not enough to know that some people bow whereas others shake hands or that some value silence whereas others value talk. Although these behaviors are significant, you also need to know what motivates them. We believe the source of how a culture views the world can be found in its *deep structure*. It is this deep structure that unifies and makes each culture unique. It is also the focus of this chapter.

THE DEEP STRUCTURE OF CULTURE

Although many intercultural communication problems occur on the interpersonal level, most serious confrontations and misunderstandings can be traced to cultural differences that go to the basic core of what it means to be a member of one culture or another. In the United States when members of the racist sect the Aryan Nations engage in violence against Jews on the fourth of July,[1] when "a lunchroom fight pitting Arab and non-Arab students turns into an all-out brawl,"[2] when thousands of Native American Indians protest the use of Indian names for mascots or nicknames,[3] and when African Americans and members of the dominant culture employ racist language after the O. J. Simpson trial, it is the deep structure of culture that is being manifested. Elsewhere we find the same strife because of cultural collisions. Whether it be in Macedonia, Kosovo, or Bosnia-Herzegovina ethnic cleansing represents attacks on a culture's major institutions. When tribal warfare continues to rage in parts of Africa, or Christians face oppression around the world,[4] the deep structure of culture, not interpersonal communication, is also at the heart of these problems. What we are suggesting is that when there are ethnic and cultural confrontations in Boston, Belfast, Beirut, Burundi, and Bombay, the deep structure of culture is being acted out. Although some of our examples are drawn from the past, Huntington speaks to the future of intercultural contact and the potential problems that can arise when cultural beliefs clash: "The great divisions among humankind and the dominating sources of conflict will be cultural."[5] Huntington's reasoning reminds us of the basic theme of this book, as well as the rationale for this chapter:

> The people of different civilizations have different views on the relations between God and man, the individual and the group, the citizen and the state, parents and children, husband and wife, as well as differing views of the relative importance of rights and responsibilities, liberty and authority, equality and hierarchy.[6]

It is important to notice that all the issues Huntington cites penetrate deep into the culture—or what we refer to as the deep structure of a culture. Such issues (God, loyalties, family, state, liberty, etc.) have been part of every culture for thousands of years and help define each culture. Hence, our point is a simple one: *To better understand any culture, you need to appreciate that culture's deep structure.* The deep structure has its roots deep in the basic institutions of the culture. As Delgado points out, "Culture produces and is reproduced by institutions of society, and we can turn to such sites to help recreate and represent the elements of culture."[7] The aim of this chapter is to look at those "sites" so that we might better understand how and why cultures have different visions of the world.

The how and why behind a culture's collective action can be traced to its (1) world view (religion), (2) family structure, and (3) state (community, government). Since the conception of the world's first culture, these three social forces, working in combination, create, transmit, maintain, and reinforce the basic elements of collective behavior.

We suggest four interrelated reasons as to why our world view, family, and cultural history hold such a prominent sway over our actions. Let us look at these four so that you might be able to appreciate the importance of a culture's deep structure to any study of intercultural communication.

Deep Structure Institutions Carry a Culture's Most Important Beliefs

The three institutions of church, family, and state *carry the messages that matter most to people*. Your religion, parents, and government are given the task of "teaching" you what is important and what you should strive for. Whether it be a desire to gather material possessions, or a life that seeks spiritual fulfillment, the three institutions of church, family, and state help you make those major decisions. These institutions tell you how we fit into the grand scheme of things, whether you should believe in fate or the power of free choice, why there is suffering, what to expect from life, and even how to prepare for death. In short, these and other consequential issues fall under the domain of church, family, and state.

Deep Structure Institutions and Their Messages Endure

These institutions are important because *they endure*. From the early Cro-Magnon cave drawings in Southern France over forty thousand years ago until the present, we can trace the strong pull of religion, family, and community. Generation after generation of children are told about Moses, the Buddha, Christ, Muhammad, and the like. Whether it be the Eightfold Path, the Ten Commandments, or the Five Pillars of Islam, the messages of these writings survive. And just as every American knows about the values contained in the story of the Revolutionary War, every Mexican is aware of the consequences of the Treaty of Guadalupe Hidalgo.

The enduring quality of the major institutions of culture, and the messages they carry, is one of the ways in which cultures are preserved. Each generation is given the wisdom, traditions, and customs that make a culture unique. However, as students of intercultural communication you need to be aware of the fact that often deep-seated hatreds that turn one culture against another also endure. We see a vivid example of the longevity of bitterness and revenge in the following *U.S. News & World Report* caption: "For 600 years, violent nationalism has bloodied the Balkans."[8] In short, whether it be the clashes in Nazareth on Easter of 1999 that go back two thousand years, or seeing Pakistan name its first nuclear bomb after a sixth-century martyr who fought against India, scorn and distrust also endure.

Deep Structure Institutions and Their Messages Are Deeply Felt

The content generated by these institutions, and the institutions themselves, arouse deep and emotional feelings. Think for a moment about the violent reactions that can be produced by taking God's name in vain, calling someone's mother a dirty name, or burning the American flag. Countries and religious causes have been able to send young men to war, and politicians have attempted to win elections, by arousing people to the importance of God, country, and family. If we would make a hierarchy of the cultural values we discussed in the last chapter we would find that on the top of every culture's list would be love of family, God (whatever form it might take), and country.

Deep Structure Institutions Supply Much of Our Identity

We are born without a specific identity. However, as we interact with other people we begin to develop a variety of identities. Even now your identity, who you are, is composed of many facets. You are a man or a woman, a student at a specific college or university, you live in a specific region, and perhaps you are a member of a club. These, and countless other "memberships," help define you. However, the identities that mean the most to people are the ones gained through their deep structure institution. That is to say, family, church, and state *give each individual his or her unique identity*. When you think about yourself, you most likely conclude that you are a member of a family (my name is Jane Smith), that you have a religious orientation (I am a Mormon), and that you live in the United States. Regardless of the culture, each individual identifies himself or herself as a member of these cultural organizations. Those identities are important to the study of intercultural communication. As Lynch and Hanson point out, "A person's cultural identity exerts a profound influence on his or her lifeways."[9] The remainder of this chapter will look at those "lifeways" and their influence on perception and communication.

WORLD VIEW

We begin with world view for an obvious reason. As the two words tell you, your world view influences all aspects of life for it is "your view of the world." Each group of people has, from the very beginnings of civilization, felt the need to evolve a world view. The links among perception, culture, and world view are made clear in Hoebel and Frost's definition of world view as "the human being's inside view of the way things are colored, shaped, and arranged according to personal cultural preconceptions."[10] World view thus influences all aspects of our perception and consequently affects our belief and value systems as well as how we think. Dana offers an excellent summary of the importance of world view:

World view provides some of the unexamined underpinnings for perception and the nature of reality as experienced by individuals who share a common culture. The world view of a culture functions to make sense of life experiences that might otherwise be construed as chaotic, random, and meaningless. World view is imposed by collective wisdom as a basis for sanctioned actions that enable survival and adaptation.[11]

It might be useful to think of a culture's world view as its basic core. Speaking of this core, Hoebel writes, "In selecting its customs for day-to-day living, even the little things, the society chooses those ways that accord with its thinking and predilections—ways that fit its basic postulates as to the nature of things and what is desirable and what is not."[12] The pervasive impact of our world view has led Olayiwola to conclude that a culture's world view even influences the social, economic, and political life of a nation.[13]

Because world views deal with the topics that penetrate *all* phases of human existence, they start with questions about what we commonly call the meaning of life. Therefore, world view is a *culture's orientation toward God, humanity, nature, questions of existence, the universe and cosmos, life, suffering, sickness, death, and other philosophical issues that influence how its members perceive their world.* The importance of examining these crucial issues has been identified by Pennington: "If one understands a culture's world view and cosmology, reasonable accuracy can be attained in predicting behaviors and motivations in other dimensions."[14] For instance, the Islamic world view provides insight into the Islamic culture's perception of women. As Bianquis points out, "Generally speaking woman as an individual was subordinated to man both by the *Quran* and the *Hadith*. God created woman from a fragment of man's body that she might serve him."[15]

Knowledge of world view can even help you understand a culture's perception of nature. As we noted in the last chapter, many environmentalists disavow the biblical tradition which tells people that God wants them to be masters over the Earth: "And God said, Let us make man in our image, after our likeness: and let them have domain over the fish of the sea, and over the fowl of the air, and over the cattle, and over all the earth, and over every creeping thing that creepeth upon the earth." Other religious views produce different attitudes. The Shinto religion encourages an aesthetic appreciation of nature in which the focus is on reality and not heaven—a reality that makes nature supreme. Shintoism prescribes an aesthetic love of the land, in whole and in part. Every hill and lake, every mountain and river is dear. Cherry trees, shrines, and scenic resorts are indispensable to a full life. People perceive them as lasting things among which their ancestors lived and died. Here their ancestral spirits look on and their families still abide. People thus preserve nature so that nature can preserve the family.

Another link between world view and behavior can be seen in how a culture perceives the business arena. In two classic textbooks, Weber's *The Protestant Ethic and the Spirit of Capitalism* and Tawney's *Religion and the Rise of Capitalism*, the bond between religion, commerce, and production is examined. Their conclusion—there was a direct link. Bartels reaffirms that link to contemporary times when he tells us that "The foundation of a nation's culture and the most important determinant of social and business conduct are the religious and philosophical beliefs of a people. From them spring role perceptions, behavior patterns, codes of ethics and the institutionalized manner in which economic activities are performed."[16]

Even the manner in which a culture actually conducts its business can be reflected in its world view. For example, if a culture values "out-of-awareness" processes and intuitive problem solving, it might reach conclusions in a manner much different from that of a culture valuing the scientific method. Howell made this same point with a specific example:

> A Japanese manager who is confronted with a perplexing problem studies it thoroughly; once he feels he understands what the problem is, he does not attempt to collect data and develop hypotheses. He waits. He knows that his "center of wisdom" is in his lower abdomen, behind and somewhat below the navel. In due time a message will come from the center, giving him the answer he desires.[17]

What is interesting about Howell's example is that in the Buddhist tradition, where meditation is stressed, a common meditation technique is watching one's breath as it originates in the abdomen. Here again you can see the tie between world view and behavior.

We have attempted to make it very clear that world view, perception, and communication are bound together. Gold clearly illustrates this crucial link between one's spiritual view and how that world view determines the manner in which people live:

> Ask any Tibetan or Navajo about one's place in the scheme of things and the answer will inevitably be that we must act, speak, and think respectfully and reasonably toward others. Navajos say that we are all people: earth-surface walkers, swimmers, crawlers, flyers, and sky and water people. Tibetans know that we are humans, animals, worldly gods and demi-gods, ghosts and hell beings, and a host of aboriginal earth powers. Regardless of category or description, we're all inextricably connected through a system of actions and their effects, which can go according to cosmic order or fall out of synchrony with it.[18]

RELIGION AS A WORLD VIEW

We have already said that your world view originates in your culture, is transmitted via a multitude of channels, and can take a variety of forms. But what predominant element is found in every culture, and has for thousands of years, given people their world view? *Religion!* As Nanda and Warms note, "Religion is a human universal."[19] The human need to confront important issues is so universal that Haviland pointed out that "we know of no group of people anywhere on the face of the earth who, at any time over the past 10,000 years, have been without religion."[20]

For some unexplainable reason, the responsibility of generating and preserving the elements of world view has rested with either religious institutions (for example, the Catholic Church) or spiritual leaders (for example, the Buddha). Whether it be the teachings of the Bible, Vedas, Koran, Torah, or I Ching—or the signs of the stars—people have always felt a need to seek outside themselves the values by which they live their lives and guidance on how to view and explain the world. In a host of ways, religion has provided the peoples of the world with advice, values, and guidance since antiquity. It appears that for thousands of years billions of people have agreed with the Latin proverb that tells us that "A man devoid of religion is like a horse without a bridle."

Most experts agree that religions have endured because they endeavor to explain those notions about life that otherwise could not be understood or resolved. Religion, as Nanda observes, "deals with the nature of life and death, the creation of the universe, the origin of society and groups within the society, the relationship of individuals and groups to one another, and the relation of humankind to nature."[21] You will notice that the items highlighted by Nanda offer credence to the basic theme of this chapter: The deep structure of culture deals with issues that matter most to people.

Whether it be conceptions of the first cause of all things, or natural occurrences such as comets, floods, lightning, thunder, drought, famine, disease, or an abundance of food, people rely on religious explanations. The steadfast importance of religion to the psychological welfare of every individual is eloquently expressed by Smith:

> When religion jumps to life it displays a startling quality. It takes over. All else, while not silenced, becomes subdued and thrown into a supporting role. . . . It calls the soul to the highest adventure it can undertake, a proposed journey across the jungles, peaks, and deserts of the human spirit.[22]

The study of religion not only helps you in your quest for a meaning and purpose to life, but it also gives you clues into the social aspects of a culture. Haviland notes:

> The social functions of religion are no less important than the psychological functions. A traditional religion reinforces group norms, provides moral sanctions for individual conduct, and furnishes the substratum of common purpose and values upon which the equilibrium of the community depends.[23]

Religion then, be it theology or the everyday practices of a culture, gives us insight into the members of that culture. As Lamb observes, "It is clear that religion and culture are inextricably entwined."[24] Guruge takes much the same stance when he observes that "religion and civilization seem to have gone hand in hand in the evolution of human society to an extent that one could conclude that they are co-equal and co-terminus."[25] Studying religious distinctions can be helpful in that they often represent "a set of differences that make a difference."[26] We strongly believe that Paden was correct when he wrote:

> The study of religion, . . . prepares us to encounter not only other centers and calendars, and numerous versions of the sacred and profane, but also to decipher and appreciate different modes of language and behavior. Toward that end, knowledge about others plays its indispensable role.[27]

With thousands of religions and world views to choose from, how can we decide which orientations to examine? In the United States alone there are 700 to 800 denominations, and half of them are imported variants of standard world religions.[28] So the question remains—what do we include and what do we exclude in our treatment of world views? We have decided on two criteria—*numbers* and *relevance*. We agree with Carmody and Carmody: "When we speak of the great religions we mean the traditions that have lasted for centuries, shaped hundreds of millions of people, and gained respect for their depth and breadth."[29] These are the same religions that Smith says "are the faiths that every citizen should be acquainted with, simply because hundreds of millions of people live by them."[30] There are six religious traditions we "citizens" should be aware of: Christianity, Judaism, Islam, Hinduism, Buddhism, and Confucianism. Before we treat each of these religions in detail, we need to mention the similarities among these spiritual paths, for as we have said repeatedly, it is often your similarities rather than your differences that lead to intercultural understanding.

Religious Similarities

It should not be surprising that there are numerous similarities among the world's great religions. As we note in Chapter 2, every human being, from the moment of birth to the time of his or her death, asks many of the same questions and faces many of the same problems. It falls on a culture's religion to supply the answers to these universal questions. Although there are many similarities among all religious traditions, we have selected six parallel points that illustrate how in many ways cultures are alike in their search for a meaning to life and explanation to the experience of death.

Sacred Scriptures

At the heart of all the world's main religious traditions lies a body of sacred wisdom. As Crim points out, "Sacred scriptures express and provide identity, authorization, and ideals for the people of the tradition."[31] Each of these scriptures, be they oral or written, enables a culture to pass on the wisdom of that culture from generation to generation. We say more about these writings later in the chapter; for now, let us simply touch on the important religious texts for some of the religions we have chosen to discuss.

The Bible, consisting of the thirty-nine books of the Old Testament, written in Hebrew, and the twenty-seven books of the New Testament, written in Greek, serves as the written centerpiece of Christianity. For Jews, the Hebrew Bible, or Old Testament, is an important document that has lasted thousands of years and offers guidance to the present and future. The Koran, which Muslims believe was dictated to the prophet Muhammad by Allah, is written in classical Arabic. For Muslims, according to Crystal, "the memorization of the text in childhood acts simultaneously as an introduction to literacy."[32] In Hinduism, the sacred writings are found in the Vedas. These divine wisdoms cover a wide range of texts and are written in Sanskrit. The Pali Canon, based on oral tradition, contains the teaching of the Buddha. "Pali became the canonical language for Buddhists from many countries, but comparable texts came to exist in other languages, such as Chinese and Japanese, as the religion evolved."[33] For the Confucian tradition people will turn to the the Analects. This collection has for centuries helped shape the thoughts and actions for billions of people.

Authority

In nearly all cases, religious orientations have an authority figure who provides guidance and instruction. Whether the figure be a supreme all-knowing God such as Allah, a philosopher such as the Buddha, Jesus, "the Son of God," or the wise counsel of Confucius, all traditions have someone greater than the individual who can be turned to for emotional and spiritual direction.

Traditional Rituals

"Ritual is one of the oldest, most complex, and persistent symbolic activities associated with religions."[34] Rituals are not instinctive and therefore need to be passed on from generation to generation. Ritual "expresses the psychic, social, and religious world to its participants" while it is also providing "identity," and structure.[35] Rituals take a variety of forms. They range from the lighting of candles or incense, to the wearing of certain attire, to deciding whether to stand, sit, or kneel when you pray. There can be rituals dealing with "space" (Muslims going to Mecca) and others that call attention to "time" (Christians celebrating Christmas and Easter).

Rituals can also be indirect. A good example of an indirect ritual is the Japanese tea ceremony. At first glance, it would appear that the tea ceremony is simply the prepara-

Ritual is one of the oldest and most persistent symbolic activities associated with religions.

tion and drinking of tea, but the importance of the ritual to Buddhism is far greater. As Paden notes:

> Every detailed act, every move and position, embodies humility, restraint, and awareness. This framing of ordinary action in order to reveal some deeper significance—in this example the values are related to the Zen Buddhist idea of imminence of the absolute in the ordinary—is a common element of ritual behavior.[36]

Speculation

Every religion knows that all human beings seek answers to the great mysteries of life. As we noted earlier, each tradition, knowing that people usually are vexed by the great conundrums of life, attempt to address questions about mortality and immortality, death, suffering, the origins of the universe, and countless other events. From Genesis stories to detailed descriptions of heaven and hell, all traditions supply answers to timeless and overwhelming questions.

Ethics

Regardless of the tradition, "religion always includes an ethic."[37] It is intriguing that ethical standards are nearly the same for all cultures. In the case of ethics, according to Smith, the realm "pretty much tells a cross-cultural story."[38] For example, all religions say we should avoid murder, thieving, lying, and adultery.[39] In addition, they all stress the virtues of "humility, charity, and veracity."[40]

Security

All religions, as we have noted elsewhere, provide their members with a sense of identity and security. Religion unites people by asking them to share symbols, values, and norms. There is a strong feeling of security to know that you are part of a religious family that is feasting on the same day, wearing the same attire when they pray, bowing in one direction or another, or taking Holy Communion.

Religion has provided the peoples of the world with advice, values, and guidance since antiquity.

Part of the similarity of security can be found in the fact that all traditions provide meaning and purpose. Macionis, in the paragraph below, summarizes this sense of refuge and security found in all religious traditions.

> Religious beliefs offer the comforting sense that the vulnerable human condition serves a great purpose. Strengthened by such beliefs, people are less likely to collapse in despair when confronted by life's calamities.[41]

Six Religious Traditions

As we begin our discussion of the great religions of the world, it is important to keep three points in mind. First, religion is but one kind of world view, and even the person who says "There is no God" has answers to the large questions about life, death, suffering, and social relationships. Second, as Hendry says, "Religion pervades many spheres which we might call secular and it cannot easily be separated from them."[42] It is often difficult to draw a line between religion and a subtle manifestation of religion. What one person might call religion or world view another might call philosophy. For our purposes, the labeling is not nearly as important as the notion that a culture's heritage includes ways of dealing with timeless and fundamental questions. Finally, it is not our intent to offer a course on world religion, but rather to isolate those aspects of world view that are most manifest in how a culture perceives issues such as life, death, social relationships, community, ethics, and other matters that affect communication. In short, as the title of this chapter indicates, we are trying to demonstrate how a culture's deep structure serves as the "roots of their reality."

Christianity

We begin with Christianity, a religion of over a billion people scattered throughout the world. Christianity is also the dominant world view found in America. It is estimated that 86 percent of the U.S. population is Christian.[43] Although some of the specific precepts, rituals, and names applied to the term *Christianity* may vary (Protestant, Baptist, Methodist, Lutheran, Roman Catholic, and so on), they have a number of important characteristics in common.

Basic Assumption. At the heart of Christian faith is the assertion "that the crucified Jesus was resurrected by God and present in the church as 'the body of Christ.'"[44] As Noss and Noss note, "In the belief that Jesus is the clearest portrayal of the character of God all the rest of Christian doctrine is implied."[45] The key to this conception is that by actually submitting to death, "Jesus had destroyed its power, thereby making eternal life available to everyone."[46] Christians believe in a God who is manifest in the Trinity of the Father, the Son, and the Holy Spirit. This view is clearly summarized by Reverend Thomas Baima:

> There is one God who is almighty, whom Jesus called Father. The one God is the Creator of heaven and earth. Jesus is the divine and human, only son of this Father, and we call God Lord, we call Jesus Lord, for the Father is in him and he is in the Father.[47]

Of the thousands of directives Jesus and his apostles carried to the world, let us select a few of those that have most shaped the Christian tradition. As we examine these characteristics of Christianity you should remember that our purpose is not to explain Christian theology, but rather to demonstrate the link between religion, perception, and behavior.

Organized Worship. Christians believe strongly in organized worship as a means of proclaiming God's message.[48] As Carmody and Carmody note, "Jesus's view of the self was relational. The self was not a monad existing in isolation."[49] Jesus believed, "The closer people drew to God, the closer they could draw to one another."[50] This notion of organized worship may contribute to the social dimension of Western cultures. Americans are social creatures and belong to numerous clubs, committees, and organizations. The French historian de Tocqueville pointed out over two hundred years ago that Americans had a large series of networks and associations that went well beyond their family unit. Perhaps the stimulus for such behavior can be found in Christianity. In the East, one's spiritual life is conducted in solitude; in the West, God's "message" is shared with others.

Ethics. Jesus preached a system of ethics that has endured for two thousand years. Words and phrases such as *commandments*, *right* and *wrong*, *good* and *evil*, *morals*, and *ethics* are central to Christianity. And of course, "The central ethic Jesus taught was love."[51] The word "love" appears with astonishing frequency in the New Testament. We would even suggest that the following ethic regarding love may be the most repeated in history: "Love your neighbor as yourself. What you would like people to do to you do to them."[52] We see these ideas of love and compassion reflected in everything from the large amounts of charitable contributions Americans make to their willingness to go to foreign countries to improve the lives of strangers.

Individualism. Most religious scholars agree with the notion that "Christianity discovered the individual."[53] That is to say, the Western concept of the importance of the individual, which we have discussed throughout this book, can be linked partially to Christianity. As Woodward notes, "The Gospels are replete with scenes in which Jesus works one on one healing this woman's sickness, forgiving that man's sins and calling each to personal conversion."[54] Summarizing this important point, Woodward adds, "Christianity discovers individuality in the sense that it stresses personal conversion."[55] In addition, the Christian theology begins with the assumption that the world is real and meaningful because God created it. Human beings are significant because God created them in his image. God has a special relationship with each person in that God sees and hears, rewards, and punishes. Each person is important to him. The Christian God is a personal God, who desires a relationship with his creation.[56] In a culture that values individualism, Christianity is perhaps the perfect religion.

"Doing." Much of the Western "doing" orientation can be found in the life of Jesus. Peter, one of Jesus' disciples, once said, "He went about doing good."[57] For example, the Romans would throw people into the streets at the first sign of sickness because they were afraid of dying. Christians would take an active role and try to nurse the sick.[58] This is not an isolated instance. Anyone who has studied Christianity and knows the lessons of Jesus is aware that he was an active man and urged his followers to be dynamic. As we indicated, the Bible is full of accounts of how he traveled from place to place healing the sick and counseling misfits and ordinary people. In short, activity and Christianity are bound together.

Future. As noted when we discussed notions of "time" in Chapter 3, Americans are future oriented. Now we are suggesting that one of the "roots" of that reality can be found in Christianity. Put in slightly different terms, in comparison to other religions, one of the "lessons" of Christianity is that future is important. As Muck points out, for Christians "no matter what happened in the past, it is the future that holds the greatest promise."[59] Mistakes, regret, and remorse are forgiven by God. In this sense, the individual can always "move on." Even the notion of a heaven places emphasis on the future.

Language. In the last chapter when we talked about high- and low-context cultures we pointed out that Americans are a low-context culture. One of the reasons for this classification rested in the idea that most Americans placed a high priority on verbal communication. While there are countless reasons for every cultural trait, we are now offering the contention that Christianity stresses language.

Much of Christian religion is filtered through language. For Christians, language is not empty talk, but is God's gift to everyone. Language drives communication with others so we can be part of a "religious community." In addition, Christians believe that "God relies on language to reveal himself to humans in the Bible and through godly people."[60] You also see the importance of language revealed in the fact that most of the teachings in the Bible, and the act of "preaching," usually take the form of stories.[61]

Gender. The enduring legacy for women is, of course, the Garden of Eden story. This view of women is perhaps best illustrated when Paul speaks in 1 Timothy:

> I permit no woman to teach or to have authority over men; she is to keep silent. For Adam was formed first, then Eve; and Adam was not deceived, but the woman was deceived and became the transgressor.[62]

While this story is often used to justify placing women in second-class positions, more recent interpretations of the Bible reveal a view of women that is more consistent with current perceptions. For instance, some biblical scholars are asserting that Jesus might well have been a feminist. They offer some of the following examples to justify their claim. First, prior to the coming of Jesus, Roman society regarded women inherently inferior to men. Husbands could divorce their wives but wives could not divorce their husbands. Jesus banned all divorce. Men could even marry girls ten or eleven years old. Jesus challenged all of these practices. Wrote one biblical scholar, "The new religion offered women not only greater status and influence within the church, but also more protection as wives and mothers."[63]

Second, "although he called only men to be apostles, Jesus readily accepted women into his circle of friends and disciples."[64] Defying custom Jesus even invited women to join him at meals. All of this leads Murphy to note, "Women were often prominent in the accounts of his ministry, and he acknowledged the oppression they face."[65]

Finally, Jesus helped define a new role for women by giving them greater responsibility. For example, they "shared with men the cultural responsibility for teaching children, as reflected in the Proverbs: 'My son, keep your father's commandment, and forsake not your mother's teaching.'"[66]

Courage. A strong message in Christianity is courage. As Carmody and Carmody note, "Jesus was courageous."[67] A careful reading of the life of Jesus reveals a man who would not be intimidated by his opponents. On occasion after occasion, we have accounts of Jesus' strong personality emerging. His strength and courage are traits that all Christians are reminded of repeatedly. As you know from your own experience, these are also two powerful values in the American culture. Here again, you can see the link between world view and communication styles.

Judaism

Background. Judaism is the oldest of the religions being practiced today and is monotheistic, worshipping one supreme being. Abraham is thought to have founded it in approximately 1300 B.C. when twelve Israelite tribes came to Canaan from Mesopotamia. Later, many of them settled in Egypt where they were held as slaves until they fled to freedom under the leadership of Moses in about 1200 B.C. During the last five thousand years Judaism has spread throughout the world. Although Jews represent less than one-half of 1 percent of the world's population (approximately 13 million Jews), and only 2 percent of the entire population of the United States,[68] their interest in politics, the arts, literature, medicine, finance, and the law has, for thousands of years, made them important and influential. As Smith notes, "It has been estimated that one-third of our Western civilization bears the marks of its Jewish ancestry."[69]

Basic Concepts. The Jewish faith is unique in that it is both a culture and a religion. It is common, for example, to find nonreligious Jews who identify fully with the culture but not with the theology. Fisher and Luyster elaborate on this point: "Judaism has no single founder, no central leader or group making theological decisions; Judaism is a people, a very old family. This family can be defined either as a religious group or a national group."[70]

"At the heart of the Jewish religion," says Banks, "lies the existence of a covenant between God and his people."[71] Although Jews believe that God's providence extends to all people, they also hold to the notion God entered into this special covenant with them so that they could carry God's message by example. From circumcision to the keeping of the Sabbath, signs of the covenant abound in Jewish culture and religion.[72] It is this covenant that is at the heart of why Jews consider themselves God's "chosen people." In Jewish theology this special "consideration never meant advantages for the Jews, only increased responsibilities and hardships."[73]

The Jewish world view is expressed through a number of concepts basic to the faith: (1) God is one, (2) no human ever will be divine, (3) humans are free, (4) humans are the pinnacle of creation, (5) Jews belong to a group or nation whose goal is to serve God, and (6) humans must be obedient to the God-given commandments in the Torah and assume personal responsibility. These six concepts compose a belief system stressing the secular notion that order must be maintained if Jews are to have a collective life. The Ten Commandments in the Torah therefore give structure to and make possible a social world.[74] Judaism penetrates every area of human existence, providing humankind with a means of communicating with both the secular and transcendental worlds.[75] It is not simply a religion that serves spiritual needs but a guide to worship, ceremonies, justice, friendship, kindness, intellectual pursuits, courtesy, and diet. Although Jewish culture is defined to a large extent by its belief system, Judaism is more than a set of laws.

Oppression and Persecution. Historically, oppression and persecution have been part of the Jewish view of the world. Through the belief that God is using them "to introduce insights into history that all people need," suffering, oppression, and persecution seem to be built into the Jewish faith.[76] Prager and Telushkin offer an excellent summary of the long-standing persecution of Jews:

> Only the Jews have had their homeland destroyed (twice), been dispersed wherever they have lived, survived the most systematic attempt in history (aside from that of the Gypsies) to destroy an entire people, and been expelled from nearly every nation among whom they have lived.[77]

Even Moses, as Boorstin says, "felt righteous anger at the oppression of his people."[78] What we have then is a people who, for thousands of years before the Holocaust, have experienced murder, exile, and discrimination. This treatment makes it very difficult even today for many Jews to trust gentiles (non-Jews).

Learning. Of additional interest is the importance the Jewish religion places on learning. So strong is this value that the Jewish essayist Elie Wiesel quotes a Jewish saying that "Adam chose knowledge instead of immortality." The attitude helps determine how Jews perceive the world and function in it. For thousands of years Jews have made the study of the Talmud (a holy book that is over five thousand pages long) an important element of Jewish life.[79] Some Hebrew translations of the word *Talmud* actually contain the words "learning, "study," and "teaching."[80] So strong is the value of learning for Jews that the Jewish prayer book speaks of "the love of learning" as one of three principles of faith.[81] References to the importance of education are sprinkled throughout Jewish holy books. "As long ago as the first century, Jews had a system of compulsory education."[82] Even today there is a Jewish proverb that states "Wisdom is better than jewels."

Justice. The Jewish faith also teaches a strong sense of justice. As Novak notes, "the promotion of justice is a paramount concern" for the Jew.[83] In fact, one of the four categories of Jewish law is actually "To ensure moral treatment of others."[84] So strong is this basic precept that Smith believes much of Western civilization owes a debt to the early Jewish prophets for establishing the notion of justice as a major principle for the maintenance of "social order."[85]

Family. While all societies value the family, for the Jew kinship ties have both religious and cultural overtones. Rosten offers a clear synopsis of this link in the following paragraph:

> For 4,000 years, the Jewish family has been the very core, mortar, and citadel of Judaism's faith and the central reason for the survival of the Jews as a distinct ethnic group. The Jewish home is a temple, according to Judaic law, custom, and tradition.[86]

Islam

We believe Smith is right when he says "Islam is a vital force in the contemporary world."[87] Islam is the newest and fastest-growing religion in the world with more than 1 billion followers—6 million of them in the United States.[88] Many demographers say Islam will soon be the second-most-commonly practiced religion in the United States.[89] Yet in spite of these statistics most Americans know little about the Islamic religion. As Noss and Noss point out:

> The heart of Islam is well hidden from most Westerners, and the outer images of Islamic countries present bewildering contrasts: stern ayatollahs ordering the lash for prostitutes, camel drivers putting down prayer mats in the desert, a sophisticated royal prince discussing international investments, and fiery national liberators proclaiming equality and denouncing Western values.[90]

History. Islam, like Christianity and Judaism, is monotheistic. It believes in one God, and that God is Allah. The two main forms of Islam—Sunni and Shi'a—both accept that Muhammad was the heir to the religious mantle passed down by the prophets of the Bible. For Muslims, Muhammad (570–632) was the messenger of God. Muslims believe that their God, Allah, spoke to human beings many times in the past: to Adam, Abraham, Moses, and Jesus. Like many of the prophets, Muhammad was concerned with establishing a new social order as well as delivering a religious message. Muhammad, believing that community and religion were one and the same, established the city state that became known as Madinah. This fusion of church and state was unique to Muhammad's time. His accomplishments marked him as "one of the most remarkable and charismatic men in history."[91]

Koran. When Allah spoke to Muhammad the prophet wrote down, in Arabic, the divine words in the Koran (often spelled Qur'an), the holy book of Islam. To a Muslim, this 114-chapter book (*suras*) represents the unique word of Allah and is without comparison and beyond question. It is a map, a manual on how to live. Unlike the Hebrew Bible and the Christian New Testament, the Koran has very little narrative; instead, it deals with themes "regarding legal and social matters and the general conduct of life."[92] The Koran makes it clear that those who are cruel and undisciplined will be punished. It also promises, to those who have faith, that there will be great rewards waiting for them in heaven. Like so much of Islam, the Koran does not distinguish between religious, social, and political life. Some observers have suggested that the Koran is the most memorized book in the world. Muslims say that in the Koran, Allah has spoken completely and that he will not speak again. Hence, the book, says Wilson, is "seen as a perfect revelation from God, a faithful reproduction of an original engraved on a tablet in heaven which has existed from all eternity."[93]

Submitting to God. One of the keys to understanding the nature of the Islamic world view is the word *Islam*, which is the infinitive of the Arab verb meaning "to submit." The word *Muslim* is the present participle of the same verb. A Muslim, then, is one who accepts and submits to the will of Allah. So powerful is this belief in Allah that to become a Muslim, one only has to declare "I testify that there is no god but God, and that Muhammad is the Prophet of God."[94] Like Christians, Muslims worship a personal god with a profound interest in moral behavior. This god also created the universe, called forth a community of beings, and charged them with the responsibility to establish righteousness in the world. But the god of Islam is distinctive because he dominates the globe and acts in history. Muslims believe that everything, good or evil, proceeds directly from the divine will as it is irrevocably recorded on the Preserved Tablets. This orientation produces fatalism: whatever happens has been willed by Allah. The saying *"in sha'a Allah"* (if God wills it) looms large in the thinking of the average Muslim. The word *inshalle* is also used with great frequency. This word translates as "God willing." This usage is important for it represents the Islamic theological concept that destiny unfolds according to God's will.

A Complete Way of Life. Muhammad, who was Allah's messenger, was both a political and religious prophet. In Islam, religion and social membership are inseparable. In this sense it touches all aspects of the Arab's life. Nydell develops this idea when he notes: "An Arab's religion affects his whole way of life on a daily basis. Religion is taught in school, the language is full of religious expressions, and people practice their religion openly, almost obtrusively, expressing it in numerous ways."[95] Novak said it quite clearly when he wrote, "Contained within its teaching of the path to God is guidance for the entire range of human life—social, political, and economic."[96] Viewed from this perspective Islam is a codification of all values and ways to behave in every circumstance, from child rearing to eating, to the treatment of homosexuals, to views toward modesty. As Smith noted, Islam is a religion that guides human thought and practice in unparalleled detail.[97] For example, the Koran instructs women to "cover their adornments" and to "draw their veils over their bosoms."[98] This attitude is expressed today with the following proverb: "A woman is like a jewel: You don't expose it to thieves."

Like so many world views that are a complete way of life, Islam is taught from infancy. In fact, the first sentence chanted in the ear of a Muslim infant is "La ilaha illa 'llah" (There is no god but God). Lutfiyya summarizes Islam as a philosophy that stresses "(1) a feeling of dependency on God; (2) the fear of God's punishment on earth as well as the hereafter; and (3) a deep-seated respect for tradition and for the past."[99] This religious orientation provides one with guidelines that must be followed if one is going to strive for a life, a death, and an afterlife that will bring fulfillment. Hence, says Esler, the Islamic tradition has resulted in "an immense body of requirements and prohibitions concerning religion, personal morality, social conduct, and political behavior. Business and marital relations, criminal law, ritual practices, and much more were covered in this vast system."[100] What Islam did from its beginnings until today is bind "all its millions to a religion, a civilization, and pattern of history."[101]

Art and Architecture. The tandem relationship that Islam has to all phases of life has helped create a remarkable and brilliant civilization that is "as distinctive in its way as those of China or the Greco-Roman Mediterranean."[102] Part of that civilization is seen in the art and architecture associated with Islam. Many Arab countries are, as Crim notes, "rich in painting, sculpture, and the decorative arts."[103] What is interesting about the artistic magnificence of Arab art is that it reflects Islamic religion. The Koran "teaches that an object and its image are united."[104] This would, in part, help explain why so little Arab art is representational. You will notice that in most Arab art forms the emphasis is on shapes, form, design, style, and image—not people, landscapes, and other representations of reality.

The Five Pillars of Islam. Jews and Christians strive to observe the Ten Commandments, Buddhists attempt to adhere to the Eightfold Path of Buddha, and Muslims follow the Five Pillars of Islam. Referring to the Pillars, which, Fisher and Luyster maintain, "outline specific patterns for worship as well as detailed prescriptions for social conduct, to bring remembrance of God into every aspect of daily life and practical ethics into the fabric of society."[105] Here are the Five Pillars of Islam:

1. *Repetition of the creed*, "There is no God but Allah, and Muhammad is the Prophet of Allah." The first part of this pronouncement expresses the primary principle of monotheism, and the second element reinforces the Muslim belief in Muhammad, thus validating the Koran. These words are heard everywhere in the Muslim world.
2. *Prayer*, which is a central ritual, performed five times a day: on rising, at noon, in the midafternoon, after sunset, and before retiring. The prayer ritual is very structured: one must face Mecca, recite a prescribed prayer, and be prostrate, with the head to the ground. These prayers can be offered in a mosque, at home or work, or even in a public place. When observing someone in prayer, you should "avoid staring at, walking in front of, or interrupting" the person.[106]
3. *Almsgiving*, which began as a voluntary activity and has become codified. Muslims are required to give about 2.5 percent of their incomes to support Muslims in need and the Islamic faith. There is, like so much of religious ritual, a deeper meaning behind the act of almsgiving. Schneider and Silverman offer part of the rationale for almsgiving when they write: "Consideration for the needy is part of Islam's traditional emphasis on equality. In the mosque, all are equal; there are no preferred pews for the rich or influential—all kneel together."[107]
4. *Fasting*, a tradition observed during the holy month of Ramadan, which is the ninth month of the Islamic lunar calendar. During this period, Muslims do not eat, drink, or smoke between sunrise and sunset. The act of fasting is believed to serve a number of purposes. First, it eliminates bodily impurities and initiates a new spiritual awakening. Second, as Nydell, notes, "The purpose of fasting is to experience hunger and deprivation and to perform an act of self-discipline, humility, and faith."[108]

5. *Pilgrimage*. Once in a lifetime every Muslim, if financially able, is to make a pilgrimage to Mecca as evidence of his or her devotion to Allah. The trip involves a series of highly symbolic rituals designed to bring each Muslim closer to Allah.

From the Western perspective, the Islamic tradition is difficult to understand: It touches all aspects of life, emphasizes fatalism, is religiocentric, and in many areas limits, at least by American standards, the individual's freedom of choice. In the West, we believe that our senses keep us in touch with reality; however, Muslims, say Fisher and Luyster, "believe that our senses do not reveal all of reality."[109]

Hinduism

With over 1 billion followers Hinduism is perhaps the most difficult of all religious orientations for the Westerner to understand. As Esler notes, "The Hindu religion is extremely ancient, very complicated, and more than a little exotic to Western eyes."[110] One of the central reasons Westerners have trouble with Hinduism is supplied by Boorstin:

> Western religions begin with a notion that One—One God, One Book, One Son, One Church, One Nation under God—is better than many. The Hindu, dazzled by the wondrous variety of the creation, could not see it that way. For so multiplex a world, the more gods the better! How could any one god account for so varied a creation?[111]

Background. As we have already noted, from the Western perspective, Hinduism is difficult to grasp and explain because it is so unlike Western religions. Hinduism has developed over about four thousand years. At the heart is the following assertion: "Hinduism regards the multiplicity of gods and goddesses in its pantheon as manifestations of the one divine spirit, *Brahman*."[112] Jain and Kussman offer an excellent summary of this important concept of *Brahman*:

> *Brahman* is the ultimate level of reality, a philosophical absolute, serenely blissful, beyond all ethical or metaphysical limitations. The basic Hindu view of God involves infinite being, infinite consciousness and infinite bliss.[113]

In many respects, Hinduism is a conglomeration of religious thought, values, and beliefs without the benefit of a single founder like Abraham, Jesus, or Muhammad. It also does not have an organizational hierarchy, such as that of the Catholic Church. Among the Hindus, one may find magic, nature worship, animal veneration, and an unlimited number of deities. This view of a vast number of deities makes Hindus among the most religious people in the world because they find the divine in everything. As Boorstin notes, "The Hindu is dazzled by a vision of the holy, not merely holy people but places like the Himalayan peaks where the gods live, or the Ganges which flows from Heaven to Earth, or countless inconspicuous sites where gods or goddesses or unsung heroes showed their divine mettle."[114] Rituals are important for showing that God is in everything, and ritual significance can be found in everyday activities such as the lighting of incense, bathing, eating, and marriage ceremonies.

The Upanishads. The literature associated with the development of Hinduism can be found in the Upanishads. The word *upanishad* actually means instruction. Written in Sanskrit between 800 and 400 B.C., they represent the most sacred of all spiritual teachings and "instructions" found in Hinduism. There are more than a hundred Upanishads; however, it is the Bhagavad Gita that is the most influential. One of the many things they teach strikes at the very core of Hinduism. It is that God is an exalted, inspiring, and sublime force *within us*. Because God is within us, say the Hindus, we can rise above our mortal limitations.

A Complete Way of Life. As is the case with so many religions, Hinduism invades every part of existence. Radhakrishnan, the former president of India, observed that "Hinduism is more a culture than a creed."[115] This creed "forms the basis of a social system, and thereby governs the types of modalities of interaction even in contemporary society."[116] In this sense, as Venkateswaran points out, "Hinduism is not merely a religion. It encompasses an entire civilization and a way of life, whose roots date back prior to 3000 B.C.E."[117]

Another Reality. Hinduism is based on the fundamental assumption that the material world, the one we can touch and see, is not the only reality. Instead, they hold that there are other realities that reveal the true nature of life, the mind, and the spirit. According to Hinduism, "What we see as reality is the merest illusion, a game, a dream, or a dance."[118] Hence, Hindus are not satisfied with what they see or hear: "Him the eye does not see, nor the tongue express, nor the mind grasp."

This notion of other realities stems from the Hindu belief of deliverance from the misleading appearances and experiences of the physical world. Hindus believe that finding satisfaction in the material and physical world might gratify us for many lifetimes, but eventually the satisfaction will "wear out." To experience *Nirvana*, or liberation, one needs to discover the spiritual existence found outside traditional concepts of reality. In short, Hindus are certain that there are mental and spiritual realms of unshakable reality that guarantee eternal satisfaction once one discovers them; therefore, Hindus spend much of their lives in search of these realms.

Important Teachings. Several Hindu concepts specifically relate to world view and individual values and behavior. Hindu philosophy, says Hammer, begins with the premise that "the ultimate cause of suffering is people's ignorance of their true nature, the Self, which is omniscient, omnipotent, omnipresent, perfect, and eternal."[119] To help one discover "the Self," Hinduism offers its followers some specific recommendations. Non-Hindus can gain insight into this world view by looking at these historical guidelines.

First, *intellect is subordinate to intuition*. Truth does not come to the individual; it already resides within each of us. The same point is made in the Bhagavad Gita: "Meditation excels knowledge." Second, *dogma is subordinate to experience*. One cannot be told about God; one must experience God. Third, *outward expression is secondary to inward realization*. Communication with God cannot take place through outward expression; it must occur through internal realization of the nature of God. Fourth, *the world is an illusion* because nothing is permanent. All of nature, including humankind, is in an unending cycle of birth, death, and rebirth or reincarnation. Fifth, *it is possible for the human to break the cycle of birth, death, and reincarnation and experience an internal state of bliss called Nirvana*. One achieves Nirvana by leading a good life and thus achieving higher spiritual status in the next life. The more advanced one's religious life, the closer one is to Nirvana. This advancement can be assisted by holding materialism in abeyance and practicing introspection and meditation. The path toward Nirvana is also influenced by one's karma, an ethical standard that asserts, "Every act we make, and even every thought and every desire we have, shapes our future experiences."[120] In this way, karma is the link between a person's acts in one life and his or her acts in the next. As Jain and Kussman point out: "The present condition of each individual life is a product of what one did in the previous life, and one's present acts, thoughts, and decisions determine one's future states."[121]

Multiple Paths. Perhaps one of Hinduism's greatest appeals through the centuries has been its ability to offer various paths and to adapt to diverse needs. As Smith notes, "Hinduism abounds in directives to persons who would put their shoulders to the collective wheel. It details duties appropriate to age, temperament, and social status."[122] Recognizing four different types of people, Hinduism offers four distinct spiritual paths: (1) *jnana yoga*, the path of knowledge; (2) *bhkti yoga*, the path of devotion; (3) *karma*, the path of work; and (4) *raja yoga*, the path of meditation.[123]

Buddhism

A fifth major religious tradition that influences how its followers perceive the world and interact in it is Buddhism. Many Westerners find it difficult to understand Buddhism, in part because it requires abandonment of views generated by the use of ordinary words and scriptures. As Brabant-Smith notes, "Ordinary language tends to deal with physical things and experiences, as understood by ordinary man; whereas Dharma language (Buddha's teaching) deals with the mental world, with the intangible non-physical world."[124] This notion finds expression in two famous Buddhist statements: "Beware of the false illusions created by words," and "Do not accept what you hear by report."[125] These sayings reflect Buddhists' belief that there is a supreme and wonderful truth that words cannot reach or teach—that is transmitted outside of ritual and language. A Buddhist teacher expressed it this way: "A special transmission outside the scriptures; No dependence upon words or letters; Direct pointing at the mind of man; Seeing into one's nature and the attainment of Buddhahood."[126]

History. Buddhism was founded by an Indian prince named Siddhartha Gautama in about 563 B.C. The story of how this man became known as The Enlightened One has two essential parts that are both crucial to the study of Buddhism. First, when Gautama was twenty-nine he awoke to the recognition that man's fate was to suffer—to grow old and sick, then die. As Van Doren notes, "Overwhelmed with the sadness, he began to seek some means of allaying the pain of life."[127] Through meditation he found the solution and became known as the Buddha (The Enlightened One). Second, "After this momentous event the Buddha spent the next forty-five years of his life wandering up and down the Ganges Valley preaching the message to ascetic and lay persons alike."[128]

The fact that he was born an ordinary man is extremely important to Buddhism. The Buddha stressed during his entire life that he was not a god but a man, an extraordinary man who found enlightenment and then devoted his life to helping others achieve Nirvana, the state of spiritual and physical awakening and purity necessary to escape the continuing cycle of suffering and rebirth.

Basic Assumption. The basic assumption behind this world view is that life, for a host of reasons, is *suffering*. Accepting this premise, the Buddha taught that each individual has the power to overcome suffering. Although all world views try to offer comfort to their constituents through supernatural solutions, Buddhism is quite different. Fisher and Luyster say, "In its traditional form, it holds that our salvation from suffering lies only in our own efforts. The Buddha taught us that only in understanding how we create suffering for ourselves can we become free."[129]

Modern Buddhism directs itself to purification of life and consciousness, not to worship of a godlike figure. Its followers are taught to realize truth through meditation and correct living. Buddhism is at once a faith, a philosophy, and a way of life attempting to help the individual come to the end of suffering by discovering the true nature of reality—its impermanence, its inherent unsatisfactoriness, and its "emptiness."

From the Buddhist perspective, peace, enlightenment, and Nirvana do not come from God. Unhappiness, pain, and suffering are the result of believing in an illusory self or ego. The craving of this ego locks people into seeing and desiring one thing after another for their entire lives. For the Buddhist, one must identify, and at times destroy, those aspects of one's ego that contribute to suffering and obstruct happiness. This individual responsibility is often difficult for Westerners to understand, for many Western religions stress community and direction from the clergy. Buddhism, to the contrary, challenges each individual to do his or her own religious seeking: Direct personal experience is the final test of truth. A famous Buddhist saying states, "Be lamps unto yourselves."

Four Noble Truths. Much of the Buddha's message can be found in the Four Noble Truths, which include the Noble Eightfold Path. The Four Noble Truths represent Buddha's answers to the most important questions about life. "Together," says Smith, "they stand as the axioms of his system, the postulates from which the rest of his teachings logically derive."[130]

The First Noble Truth is that life is *dukka*, usually translated as "suffering." As the Buddha said in his early writings: "Birth is suffering, aging is suffering, illness is suffering, worry, misery, pain, distress and despair are suffering; not attaining what one desires is suffering."[131] Contrary to Western interpretation, the Buddha's philosophy is not pessimistic: He was, in fact, concerned with the cessation of suffering, so he strove to help others by teaching them to identify the causes of their suffering.

The Second Noble Truth concerns the origin of suffering. The Buddha taught that much of the suffering is caused by desire and craving. The Third Noble Truth is clearly summarized by Smith:

> The Third Noble Truth follows logically from the Second. If the cause of life's dislocation is selfish craving, its cure lies in the overcoming of *tanha* [desire], such craving. If we could be released from the narrow limits of self-interest into the vast expanse of universal life, we would be relieved of our torment.[132]

The Fourth Noble Truth indicates that the way to remove suffering is by means of the Noble Eightfold Path, which forms the basic teaching of Buddha.

The Eightfold Path. The tenets of the Eightfold Path are listed below:

1. *Right view* is understanding and accepting the reality and origins of suffering, and the ways leading to the cessation of suffering. Often referred to as "right knowledge," this first principle obviously implies an awareness of the Four Noble Truths.
2. *Right thought* is being free from ill will, cruelty, and untruthfulness toward the self and others. Buddha believed that we needed to be truthful even about our imperfections.
3. *Right speech* is abstaining from lying, tale bearing, and harsh language. Buddha stressed that we should "use communication in the service of truth and harmony."[133]

4. *Right behavior*, some have said, is Buddha's version of the Ten Commandments, for his fourth principle called for abstaining from the taking of life, from stealing, from sexual misconduct, from lying, and from drinking intoxicants.
5. *Right livelihood* is not harming any living thing and being free from luxury at the expense of others.
6. *Right effort* is avoiding and overcoming evil, and promoting and maintaining good.
7. *Right mindfulness* is the contemplation of the transitory nature of the body, of one's own and others' feelings, of the mind, and of phenomena. This principle calls attention to the crucial Buddhist thought that liberation is said to be through a mind that is aware of the moment.
8. *Right meditation* is complete concentration on a single object and the achievement of purity of thought, free from all hindrances and distractions. When the mind is still, according to the Buddha, "the true nature of everything is reflected."[134]

Important Teachings. To summarize the Buddhist tradition, we remind you of the following key points. First, the Buddha believed that to find enlightenment within oneself, a Buddhist must lead a life that focuses on some of the following behaviors. Through mindfulness, a Buddhist seeks to anchor the mind securely in the present. In achieving right mindfulness through concentration and meditation, the mind is trained to remain in the present: open, quiet, and alert while contemplating the present event. Says Thich-Thien-An, "If we keep our minds under control, if we can realize the meaning of what we are doing, if we can be what we do, this is meditation."[135]

Second, Buddhism stresses the impermanent nature of all things, both good and bad, which are always changing. Simplicity and freedom from want are states without stress. Envy and desire keep us from being happy and peaceful. A Buddhist must learn to let go of the things of the universe in order to be content. The impermanent and delicate nature of life is eloquently stated by the second-century Buddhist philosopher Narajuna: "Life is so fragile, more so than a bubble blown to and fro by the wind. How truly astonishing are those who think that after breathing out, they will surely breathe in again, or that they will awaken after a night's sleep."

Third, karma is important because it sets the tone for ethical standards. Karma is concerned with action–reaction and with cause and effect: Good deeds bring good results; corrupt deeds bring corrupt results. As is the case with so much of Buddhism, each individual—not a supernatural power—decides his or her karma. The Buddha stated:

> All beings are the owners of their deeds (Karma), the heirs of their deeds; their deeds are the womb from which they sprang. . . . Whatever deeds they do—good or evil—of such they will be the heirs.[136]

Fourth, as we alluded to earlier, Buddhism is directed at the individual. A famous Buddhist saying makes this very important point: "Betake yourself to no external refuge. Work out your own salvation with diligence."

Finally, in Buddhism we see a world view more concerned with humanism and the art of living daily life than supernatural authority or even metaphysical speculation. As Smith noted:

> Buddha preached a religion that skirted speculation. He could have been one of the world's great meta-physicians, but "the thicket of theorizing" was not for him. Whether the world is

eternal or not eternal, whether it is finite or infinite, whether the Buddha exists after death or not—on such questions the Buddha maintains a noble silence.[137]

Confucianism

Background. Confucianism is "the system of social, political, ethical, and religious thought based on the teachings of Confucius and his successors."[138] Although Confucianism has had a profound impact on the cultures of Korea and Japan, its greatest impact for thousands of years has been on the people of China. As Barry, Chen, and Watson note, "If we were to describe in one word the Chinese way of life for the last two thousand years, the word would be 'Confucian.'"[139] The roots of Confucianism are "planted" so very deep in China, that even during the anti-religious period of Communism the leaders borrowed the Confucian notions of selfishness, allegiance, and deference to help accomplish their purpose of controlling the masses.[140] In some ways this control was made easy by the fact that "Confucianism has no priests, no temples, no religious rituals."[141] It is "a rational, ethical system with strict norms, stressing loyalty to the ruler, obedience toward one's father, and proper behavior."[142]

At the heart of Confucianism is the belief in social harmony. As Yum notes, "Confucianism is a philosophy of human nature that considers proper human relationships as the basis of society."[143] As we shall see later, these correct relationships involved such things as the protection of "face," dignity, self-respect, reputation, honor, and prestige.

The Man. As was the case with Buddhism, Confucianism centers around the teachings of a particular man—Confucius. And like Buddha, Confucius was not a ruler, nor did he consider himself a god. In fact, he was not really even interested in the philosophical and ethereal dimensions of religion. Confucius was born in 551 B.C. in the small feudal state of Lu, which is now Shantung Province in China. Confucius dabbled at various careers early in his life; however, at the age of 30 he turned to teaching and by all accounts was very successful. According to McGreal, "People were impressed by his integrity, honesty, and particularly his pleasant personality and his enthusiasm as a teacher. Three thousand people came to study under him and over seventy became well-established scholars"[144] As is the case with so many great thinkers, what Confucius taught grew out of his observations about "the human condition" in China during his lifetime. As Crim notes, "Confucius was witness to the political disintegration of the feudal order, an era characterized by the hegemony of various states and almost constant internecine warfare."[145]

The Analects. Confucius did not write down his philosophy. Therefore, the details of his teaching have come to us through his disciples. The most influential and far reaching of these collections is the Analects. This book was not written in a systematic and structured fashion. Instead what it contains are the aphorisms, sayings, proverbs, and the like that the disciples believed to be the most salient ideas of Confucian philosophy, ideas so important that they helped shape the thoughts and actions of countless people through the centuries.

Important Teachings. As we have already indicated, in somewhat general terms Confucianism teaches that the proper and suitable foundation for society is based on respect for human dignity. That respect stressed the proper hierarchy in social relationships between family members, community, and superiors. Confucius set forth five ideals that structured much of his thought about these relationships. (1) *Jen* (humanism) is related to the concept of reciprocity. It is, for Confucius, "the ideal relationship which should pertain between individuals."[146] (2) *Chun tzu* (perfect person) means the kind of person in whom cultivated feeling has maximum development.[147] (3) *Li* (rituals, rites, proprieties, conventions) is the outward expression of good manners—the way things should be done. (4) *Te* literally means power. Confucius was concerned with how power was used. He strongly believed that "leaders must be persons of character, sincerely devoted to the common good and possessed of the character that compels respect"[148] (5) *Wen* refers to the arts. Confucius had great reverence for the arts. We can observe that veneration in the following paragraph:

> By poetry the mind is aroused; from music the finish is received. The odes quicken the mind. They induce self-contemplation. They teach the art of sensibility. They help to retrain resentment. They bring home the duty of serving one's parents and one's prince.[149]

Confucianism and Interpersonal Relationships. As is the case with all the world views we have examined, Confucianism influences perception and communication in a variety of ways. First, Confucianism teaches, both directly and indirectly, the notion of *empathy*. Smith tells us that for Confucius that part of *Jen* is "the capacity to measure the feelings of others by one's own."[150] This view toward others would, of course, make listening an important element of communication. Second, when communicating, those that follow Confucian philosophy would be concerned with *status relationships*. We can see this in everything from differentiated linguistic codes (words showing respect and rank)[151] to "paternalistic leadership" in business and educational settings.[152] Third, we could also except great concern for *ritual and protocol* when following Confucian principles. As we noted early, social etiquette was an important part of Confucian teaching. Novak reminds us that "In Confucius's view, attentive performance of social ritual and everyday etiquette shapes human character in accordance with archetypal patterns."[153] Finally, Confucian philosophy would tend to encourage the use of *indirect instead of direct* language. As you learned elsewhere, Americans often ask very direct questions, are blunt, often use the word "no," and like it when people "get to the point" rather quickly. However, Confucian philosophy encourages indirect communication. For example, "In Chinese culture, requests often are implied rather than stated explicitly for the sake of relational harmony and face maintenance."[154] Yum makes much the same point while demonstrating the link between Confucianism and "talk" in the following paragraph:

> The Confucian legacy of consideration for others and concern for proper human relationships has led to the development of communication patterns that preserve one another's face. Indirect communication helps to prevent the embarrassment of rejection by the other person or disagreement among partners.[155]

Numerous other world views have, because of space constraints, been omitted from our analysis. If you want to understand some of the other religions of East Asia, we urge you to learn about Taoism and Shintoism. To learn about the cultures of Africa, Australia, the Pacific Islands, and the Indian cultures of North and South America, we ask you to study the primal religions. In every instance, you will learn how collections of people, for thousands of years, have attempted to deal with the crucial questions centering on the meaning of life.

A COMPARISON OF WORLD VIEWS

Throughout this section, we have repeatedly returned to two ideas. First, that world view and communication work in tandem. And second, that world view is much more than a person's religion. In the next few pages, we reinforce these ideas by summarizing and comparing some of the characteristics of the American world view with those of other cultures. Hoebel and Frost offer an excellent condensation of the main forces driving the American world view:

> Historically, the American world view is a derivation of the Hellenistic-Judeo-Christian traditions as they were blended and modified through the Renaissance, the Reformation, and the industrial revolution in Europe. In the American setting, these traditions have taken on their own intensifications and selective qualities.[156]

The results of these forces on American perceptions and behaviors are numerous. We now look at two of the ways in which the Western world view differs from those of other cultures.

A Mechanistic View

The mechanistic world view is common in America and goes by many different names. Some refer to it as *reason versus intuition*, *objectivity versus subjectivity*, or *science versus religion*. Regardless of the headings researchers apply, what is being alluded to is the American world view of ways of knowing, summarized by Hoebel and Frost:

> American thought patterns are rational rather than mystic; the operative conception of the universe is mechanistic. The bedrock proposition upon which the whole world view stands is the belief that the universe is a physical system operating in a determinate manner according to discoverable scientific laws. . . . Because they view the universe as a mechanism, Americans implicitly believe that individuals can manipulate it. Human beings need not accept it as it is; they may work on it, and as they gain in knowledge and improve their techniques, they even redesign it so that it will be more to their liking.[157]

The mechanistic world view shows itself in a number of ways. For example, this view makes a sharp distinction between religion and science as alternative ways of discovering truth. In fact, going all the way back to the English philosophers Hobbes and Bacon, Westerners have held that reasoning is humankind's "highest faculty and achievement."[158] There is also a strong reliance on "facts." For Americans, facts are more reliable and dependable than subjective evaluations based on "feelings" and "intuition." As Althen notes, "Americans assume there are 'facts' of life, of nature, and of the universe that can be discovered by trained people (usually called 'scientists') using special techniques, equipment, and ways of thinking."[159] We even teach people "to disregard the emotional aspects of an argument."[160] In short, "mechanism is orthodoxy and remains a pervasive view in Western culture."[161]

The Western mechanistic world view is not found in all cultures. For example, the Eastern view of reality and truth is very different from the one found in the West. Elgin notes that the nonmechanistic world view is "a perspective that historically has emerged in countries such as India, Tibet, Japan, China, and Southeast Asia, and is exemplified by spiritual traditions such as Buddhism, Hinduism, Taoism and Zen."[162] Whereas the Western view tends to place intellect and rationality above other traits, the Eastern view often maintains, say Fisher and Luyster, that "intuition transcends the data of the senses and the manipulation of the mind to perceive truths that seem to lie beyond reason."[163] For this world view, Fisher and Luyster continue, "Intuitive wisdom cannot be verified by the senses or the scientific instruments that we use to extend the range of perception. It emerges into awareness in an entirely different way than does logical thought."[164] Eastern approaches, Fisher and Luyster further observe, "have developed meditation techniques that encourage intuitive wisdom to rise from the depths—or the voice of the divine to descend into individual consciousness."[165] This form of intuitive thinking is clearly summarized by Asuncion-Lande:

> Intuitive discovery allows for that "flash of insight" which leads to total involvement. It has been claimed that this type of cognitive approach is congruent to the predominant value of "man as harmony with nature," as well as the fatalist attitude. Truth will come but you have to wait for it patiently.[166]

A very clear anti-mechanistic view of truth is found in the poem by the Buddhist teacher Hui Neng. As you read this poem reflect for a moment on how different it is from the Western motivational saying "You don't just wait for information to come to you."

> *There is nothing true anywhere,*
> *The True is nowhere to be found.*
> *If you say you see the True,*
> *This seeing is not the true one.*
> *When the True is left to itself,*
> *There is nothing false in it, for it is Mind itself.*
> *When Mind in itself is not liberated from the false,*
> *There is nothing true; nowhere is the True to be found.*[167]

A Dualistic View

East and West also have differing world views in what is called dualism. Dualism is a philosophical system that seeks to explain all phenomena in terms of two distinct and irreducible principles. For example, in Plato's philosophy there is an ultimate dualism of "being" and "becoming" and ideas and matter. According to Smart, Western religions such as Judaism, Christianity, and Islam are also dualistic "because they see two separate parts to reality—God and creation."[168] Elgin makes much the same points when he notes: "Where the Western view is dualistic (viewing mind and body as separate, as well as God and humankind as separate), the Eastern view is profoundly nondualistic."[169] The West often perceives the world as being composed of separate pieces to be manipulated and examined.

Dualism distinguishes people from nature. The Eastern orientation, and also the one found among Native Americans, is characterized by a monistic world view. This philosophy sees the world as a unit—a world continuously creating and intimately infusing every aspect of the cosmos from its smallest detail to its grandest feature. Human beings in this orientation are at once body, mind, and spirit. This is a world that is profoundly holistic.

From our brief account of religion, mechanism, and dualism, it should be clear that a culture's world view touches every aspect of life. As Paden notes, "They speak from those places and times in conversation with the conceptual needs of a community. They create discourse that not only expresses but in some way tries to re-create those communities."[170] If you understand those world views, we trust that you now also understand those communities.

FAMILY

The Chinese say that if you know the family, you do not need to know the individual. There is a Jewish adage that states "God could not be everywhere and therefore he made mothers." And in Africa children learn the proverb that "What belongs to me is destroyable by water or fire; what belongs to us is not destroyable by neither water nor fire." Although these three ideas might differ slightly, they all call attention to the importance of family to every human being's life. The family is among the oldest and most fundamental of all human institutions. It is also a universal experience—found in every culture.[171] As Galvin and Brommel say, "We are born into a family, mature in a family, form new families, and leave them at our death."[172] In addition to these general responsibilities, Schneider and Silverman offer us a list of some specific duties that face every family:

> Families regulate sexual activities, supervising their members to be sure they conform to sexual norms. Families are in charge of reproduction to keep the society going, and they socialize the children they produce. Also families provide physical care and protection for the members. They also provide emotional support and caring.[173]

Perhaps what is most significant about families is that it is the family that greets us once we leave the comfort of the womb. This idea is eloquently stated by Swerdlow, Bridenthal, Kelly, and Vine:

> Here is where one has the first experience of love, and of hate, of giving, and of denying; and of deep sadness. . . . Here the first hopes are raised and met—or disappointed. Here is where one learns whom to trust and whom to fear. Above all, family is where people get their start in life.[174]

The family is where children are first introduced to culture.

The Importance of Families

As you see, families are important for a number of reasons. First, the family is charged with transforming a biological organism into a human being who must spend the rest of his or her life around other human beings. The family, say Nye and Berardo, "is the primary or basic institution of any society. . . . Without the family human society as we know it could not exist."[175] Second, although a culture's core values and world view derive primarily from its predominant religious views and cultural history, the family is the primary caretaker of these views and values and transmits them to new members of the culture. Finally, families are important because they supply all of us with part of our identity. Burguiere makes this point in the following way: "Before we become ourselves, we are a son or daughter of X or of Y; we are born into a family, and are identified by a family name before becoming a separate social being."[176] The family gives children knowledge about their historical background, information regarding the permanent nature of their culture, and specific behaviors, customs, traditions, and language associated with their ethnic or cultural group.[177] In short, the family tells us, and others, who we are and what groups we are part of.

Types of Families

Traditionally, all people encounter two families during the course of their life: the family they are born into (the *family of orientation*) and the family that is formed when, and if, they take a spouse (the *family of procreation*). Kinship bonds link these two families into more complex family systems. In recent years, definitions of family have begun to include a number of different configurations. Berko, Rosenfeld, and Samovar mention three of these:

> Live-in couples, heterosexual or homosexual, with or without child, who are unmarried but have a binding relationship; single-parent family, in which the parent—married, never married, widowed, or divorced—lives with her or his biological or adopted child; and blended family, consisting of two adults and their children, all, some, or none of whom may be the offspring from their union.[178]

For our purposes, we are most concerned with your family of origin—the family in which you grew up. For, regardless of the culture, it is primarily this family that "provides you with the foundation of your self-concept and communication competencies."[179]

Culture and Family

The American author William Thayer once wrote, "As are families, so is society." His words clearly express the importance of family to both culture and individuals. Culture alters the most fundamental of all human processes—including family. As Anderson notes, "The different cultures of our world have bequeathed to us a variety of forms of the family and specific roles that the family plays in society."[180] This subtle and yet powerful link between family, culture, and behavior is clearly highlighted by the famous anthropologist Margaret Mead:

> At birth, babies can grow up to be members of any society. . . . It depends on how they are trained and taught, loved and punished, whether they turn into one kind of person or another. So, if we make a study of this and find out the steps by which these human

babies become one kind of grown-up person instead of another, we learn a great deal about them . . . the details of a bath, or the way the baby is fed, the way it's punished or rewarded give us a great many clues about the way character is formed in that society.[181]

What is being said by Mead is one of the basic themes of this book: A human being's development can take any number of paths, and culture is one of the major determinants of that path. A child in India who lives with many people in one house learns about extended family. A Mexican child who is raised in a home with many elderly people learns about the treatment of the elderly. These seemingly insignificant experiences, when combined with thousands of other messages from the family, shape and mold children into members of their culture.

McGoldrick makes much the same point when she writes:

Families do not develop their rules, beliefs, and rituals in a vacuum. What you think, how you act, even your language, are all transmitted through the family from the wider cultural context. This context includes the culture in which you live, and those from which your ancestors have come.[182]

Thus, as McGoldrick says, "Our definitions of human development are culturally based."[183] Different cultures create different families. Cultures vary in everything from, says McGoldrick, "their definition of family" to "their definition of the timing of life cycle phases and the tasks appropriate at each phase."[184] Let us look at some of these ways so that we can appreciate their impact on intercultural communication.

We begin this section on the role of family in much the same way we started our analysis of world view—with a disclaimer. Because of space considerations, we do not present an in-depth exploration of the family. We simply want to make you more conscious of the cause-and-effect relationship existing between growing up in one's family and the manner in which one perceives and interacts with other people. The basic assumption of this section is simple: The interaction patterns in the family offer clues as to communication patterns found outside the family, or as the Swedish proverb tells us, "Children act in the village as they have learned at home."

Gender Roles

Perhaps one of the most important of all family patterns, and one that is found in all cultures, is the teaching of appropriate gender roles. Early in life, children learn to differentiate between masculine activities and feminine activities. In fact, studies reveal that "at 24 months children were aware that labels, such as boy, girl, mommy and daddy, applied to certain classes of people."[185] These perceptions are learned and influence how members of a culture interact with both sexes. What is intriguing about gender roles is that like all important aspects of a culture, specific perceptions can be traced to the deep structure issues we talked about earlier in the chapter. For example, in cultures such as the Japanese, Vietnamese, Chinese, and Korean, the history of these roles can be traced to the influence of Confucianism. Kim says of Korea: "Confucianism made men alone the structurally relevant members of the society and relegated women to social dependence."[186] In early Confucian families, boys studied the classics and played, while "girls were confined to the inner quarters of the house where they received instruction in womanly behavior and tasks, such as domestic duties, embroidery, cooking."[187] Even today, in Asian families, according to Davis and Proctor, "Males are primarily responsible for task functions, while females attend to social and cultural tasks."[188] Children see the father get served first at meals, get the first bath, and receive nods and deep bows from the rest of the family. What is interesting about gender roles in most Asian cultures, Hendry says, is that although the family system perceives men as being superior to women, "the duty of care within the family falls almost automatically to women, whether it be in times of sickness, injury or senility."[189] This is exemplified in the Chinese saying, "Strict father, kind mother."

The Mexican culture also places the father in the dominant role and the mother in the domestic role. This, of course, is not difficult to understand if you recall what we said about the role of Confucian philosophy in the shaping of Asian gender roles. That is to say, the conception of female roles within Christianity derives, in part, the masculine representation of God as "the Father."[190] We see this view toward gender roles being acted out when Mexican children learn very early in life that "within the family unit the father is the undisputed authority figure. All major decisions are made by him, and he sets the disciplinary standards. His word is final and the rest of the family looks to him for guidance and strength."[191] So strong is the pull of masculinity in the Mexican culture that "when the father is not present, the oldest son assumes considerable authority."[192] Not being the "leader" in one's home even carries negative consequences. Think for a moment what is being implied by the Spanish proverb that states, "Woe to the house where the hen crows and the rooster is still."

The female role within the Mexican family is an important one that is clearly defined by tradition and religion. As Schneider and Silverman write, "Women, as mothers, belong to the City of God, set apart in the protected and protecting home. Motherhood is a sacred value in Mexico."[193] Female children observe this value and early in life begin "to play the role of mother and homemaker."[194] Both children observe yet other female roles within the home. They see a mother who is willing to sacrifice, is strong, and has great perseverance. As Dana notes, these "behaviors ensure survival and power through the children."[195]

In India, males are also considered the superior sex. Male children are thought to be entrusted to parents by the gods. As Nanda points out, "Men make most of the important decisions, inheritance is through the male line, and a woman lives in her husband's village after she marries."[196] Very early in life, children begin to see how this belief is acted out: Boys are given much more freedom of expression than are girls; Boys are encouraged to take part in the religious festivals and activities as a means of introducing them to the spiritual world; and girls are asked to help with the chores that keep the family functioning.

Perhaps the earliest and clearest delineation of gender roles can be found in the Arab culture, which also treats males as the preferred sex. This partiality, as was the case with Confucianism and Christianity, can be traced to deep structure issues. As Anderson notes, "The Koran addresses men only."[197] Family desire for a male is so strong that, on the wedding day, friends and relatives of the newlyweds wish them many sons.[198] An Arab proverb states, "Your wealth brings you respect, your sons bring you delight." The socialization of the sexes even extends to weaning; as Patai says, "Weaning comes much earlier in the life of a girl than of a boy."[199] Through these and other practices, roles begin to evolve, and women learn to be subservient to men. Patai points out: "The destiny of women in general, and in particular of those within the family circle, is to serve the men and obey them."[200]

It is important to note that gender roles, like all aspects of culture, are subject to change. While change is often slow, you can observe shifts in gender roles throughout the world. In Africa young women are starting to question the notion of female circumcision. And in parts of the Middle East women are asking for the right to vote. The notion of a global economy has also contributed to a reevaluation of females roles within the family. As Nanda and Warms note, "Women are being increasingly incorporated into the world economy, especially working in multi-national corporations in developing countries."[201] As we have indicated, these new economic roles, of course, influence what happens in the family. For example, studies have shown that as Mexican American women secure employment outside the home there is, within the family, "joint decision making and greater equality of male and female roles."[202]

Individualism and Collectivism

In the last chapter we discussed the importance of individualism and collectivism to the study of intercultural communication. Favoring one of those values over another is not a matter of chance, but rather is part of the enculturation process. Hence, within each family, children begin to learn if they are from a culture that values individualism or one that stresses collectivism. The manifestations of these lessons take a variety of forms. Let us look at some of those forms as a way of understanding how our communication partners, and ourselves, might view other people.

Individualism and the Family. Anyone who has observed families in the dominant culture of the United States quickly concludes, as did Althen, that "for most Americans, the family is a small group of people, not an extended network."[203] As Moghaddam, Taylor, and Wright note: "In modern North America, 'family' is often described in terms of the isolated nuclear family."[204] This kind of family unit encourages all of the attributes associated with individualism. For example, because the individualism is fostered there is less support to the child, and he or she must quickly learn to be self-reliant. As Nomura and his colleagues point out, "children in America appear to be encouraged to 'decide for themselves,' 'do their own things,' 'develop their own opinion,' or 'solve their own problems.'"[205] Althen buttresses this view that children in America are taught the manifestations of individuals when he writes that "the parents' objective in raising a child is to create a responsible, self-reliant individual who, by the age of 18 or so, is ready to move out of the parents' house and make his or her own way in life."[206] Still speaking about American families he adds, "Notions about independence, individuality, equality, and informality are all embodied in what takes place in families."[207] You will recall that four of the values mentioned by Althen were discussed in detail in the last chapter when you looked at American cultural patterns. All that is being said now is that those patterns have their roots within the structure of the family.

In an individualistic culture such as that of the United States, loyalty is generally confined to the immediate family. The value placed on family loyalty has been influenced by the dramatic rise in the incidence of single-parent households headed by women. Haviland cites this statistic: "Currently there are twice as many households in the United States headed by divorced, separated, and never-married individuals as there are occupied by traditional nuclear families."[208] This, of course, means the child seeks affiliations outside the family.

Collectivism and the Family. There is an Indian proverb that states "An individual could not more be separated from the family than a finger from the hand." We see the proverb being acted out when Wolpert tells us that in India, people "share property, all material possessions, food, work and love, perform religious rituals together, and often live under the same roof."[209] The culture of Mexico presents yet another excellent contrast to that of the United States. Whereas in the United States one might say, "I will achieve mainly because of my ability and initiative," the emphasis in Mexico on family attachment leads the Mexican to say, "I will achieve mainly because of my family, and for my family, rather than myself."[210]

Individualism and collectivism are learned through the family, which teaches children whom they must obey and who the dominant figures are in their life. During the 1996 presidential campaign, one political party maintained that "it takes a village to raise a child" whereas the opposition advanced the view that "a family raises the child." The issue is *what* the child is being taught and *who* is doing the teaching.

Directly linked with this concept of obedience is the notion of dominance—who controls the child and who or what the child may control. In the Arab world, children learn that God controls them and must be listened to. In the United States, children learn to answer mainly to themselves or their parents. Among the Maasai of Africa, many people share in raising the child. A Maasai proverb says, "The child has no owner"—all members of the tribe are responsible for the socialization process.

While learning self-reliance and responsibility, the child, through the extended family, is also being taught the parameters of loyalty. For example, when speaking of the extended family in Africa, Richmond and Gestrin note, "The African extended family is extended indeed. Among its members are parents and children, grandparents, uncles and aunts, in-laws, cousins of varying degrees, as well as persons not related by blood."[211] We also find these large networks of loyalty in other cultures. Mexicans are also "intensely loyal to their families and pride themselves on their willingness to put their families first."[212] So important is this value toward family loyalty that even Mexicans living in the United States, as Valenzula tells us, have a "strong sense of loyalty." [213]

The Japanese also "hold loyalty in the highest esteem."[214] "This means" children are brought up "to seek fulfillment with others rather than individually."[215] The Chinese family also takes this approach to loyalty. For historical and geographical reasons, most Chinese have always felt detached from their central government. Hence, family loyalty comes first for them, as this Chinese proverb makes clear: "Heaven is high and the Emperor is far away." Chu and Ju make much the same point: "An important Chinese cultural value is filial piety. Traditionally Chinese children felt a lifelong obligation to their parents, ideally exemplified by an unreserved devotion to please them in every possible way."[216] And in the Arab culture, "Family loyalty and obligations take precedence over loyalty to friends or the demands of the job."[217]

Age

The family is also the first institution to introduce the child to the notion of age-grading, an important perceptual attribute that greatly influences the way individuals perceive youth as well as old age. It does not take a great deal of documentation to establish the assertion that the dominant American culture prefers youth to old age. From plastic surgery so Americans can look younger, to an active media that extols the values of youth, Americans do not applaud the benefits of growing old. This condition does not exist in all cultures. In the Arab culture, Lutfiyya says, a very different socialization process exists:

> Children are often instructed to kiss the hands of older people when they are introduced to them, to be polite in the presence of elders, and to stand up and offer them their seats.

Young people are encouraged to listen to and to learn from their elders. Only from the older people who have lived in the past can one learn anything of value, they are told.[218]

This same respect for the elderly is taught in most Asian cultures. In China, Wenzhong and Grove note, "Perhaps the chief determinant of relative power . . . is seniority."[219] The hierarchy associated with age in this culture is rather clear. After the father, the eldest male has most of the authority. Because of the influence of Confucian principles in Japan, Hendry says, the younger members of the house are taught to be "indebted to the older members for their upbringing."[220] There is even a Chinese proverb that states, "When eating bamboo sprouts, remember who planted them." The Filipino culture is yet another in which the family teaches admiration and respect for the elderly. Says Gochenour, "There is an almost automatic deference of younger to older, both within the family and in day-to-day interaction in school, social life, and work."[221]

Within the United States we see, says Rubel, how "respect for one's elders is a major organizing principle of the Mexican-American family."[222] Among Native American families, this same attitude is taught early in life. Elders, because of the oral tradition found in this culture, are the "carriers" of much of the knowledge that is deemed important. Writing as an American Indian, Arnold notes, "elders are responsible for passing on the collective and personal knowledge that our people have accumulated through thousands of years."[223]

The French are yet another culture that teaches young people that "mature age is preferred to youth."[224] Even the French language has no special word for "youth." As Curtius notes, "The values which French civilization prefer are the values of age."[225]

Social Skills

We can see the influence of the family on the development of social skills in the following paragraph offered by Anderson:

> Through socialization the family teaches the child to integrate into the community, to develop his potentials, and to form stable and meaningful relationships. The individual is not born with the ability to participate in group activities but must learn to take account of others, to share and to cooperate.[226]

Anderson's observations should be obvious. While children are very young and primarily under the influence of their immediate family, they acquire an understanding of basic social skills, including politeness, how to communicate to make friends, "what subjects can be discussed, and ways of expressing anger or affection."[227] Learning about these social skills comes from childern observing and participating in family interactions. As Turner and West note, "We tend to understand and create our sense of family through our perceptions of our family interaction patterns. Thus, we characterize our family as quiet, extroverted, jovial, and so forth, based on how we think we talk to one another."[228]

Although all cultures ask the institution of family to instruct children in the correct use of basic communication skills, the skills that are stressed vary from culture to culture. Studies of Western family life have shown that parents encourage, approve, and reward aggressive behavior.[229] In the traditional Mexican family, which highly values respect, the child is taught to avoid aggressive behavior and to use, says Murillo, "diplomacy and tactfulness when communicating with another individual."[230] One study found that "the Mexican parents were the most punitive for aggression against other children, while the American parents stand out as particularly tolerant of aggression against other children."[231]

In Chinese families, as we have already indicated, children learn the social skills necessary for group harmony, family togetherness, interdependence in relationships, respect for their place in the line of generations, and saving face.[232] In the Sioux culture, says McGoldrick, "talking is actually proscribed in certain family relationships."[233] The rationale for this behavior, she continues, is that "the reduced emphasis on verbal expression seems to free up Native American families for other kinds of experience—of each other, of nature, and of the spiritual."[234]

A vivid example of how each family teaches various social skills can also be seen in the Thai family. Cooper and Cooper offer an excellent summary of the Thai family role in teaching patterns of interaction:

> The child quickly learns that by behaving in a way that openly demonstrates consideration for the feelings of others, obedience, humility, politeness and respect, he can make people like him and be nice to him. This behavior may be summed up in one Thai word, *krengjai*. *Krengjai* is usually translated as consideration.[235]

We hope the examples we have provided have demonstrated the prominence of the family in the enculturation process. What is intriguing about this process is that, like most of the deep structure of culture, it is resistant to change. Although, for reasons we have already discussed, this may not apply to the United States, it does apply to most other cultures. In China, for example, in spite of the legal and cultural persecution of the traditional Chinese family, neither Mao's Cultural Revolution nor the Gang of Four could destroy it. As Chu and Ju declared, "They failed to remove the soil in which the Chinese family had been planted."[236] We can find the "deep soil" of the family in the United States among immigrants from different cultures. It appears, say Galvin and Brommel, that the force of the Chinese family is so great that "cultural/ethnic heritages are maintained across generations."[237] In fact, there is abundant evidence that the Chinese family retains ethnic values and identification for many generations after immigration to the United States.[238] The Chinese have a proverb, written long before we had studies to measure human behavior, that expresses both the strength and influence of the family: "To forget one's ancestors is to be a brook without a source, a tree without a root."

HISTORY

The importance of history to the study of culture can be represented by the assertion of English writer Edmund Burke that "history is a pact between the dead, the living, and the yet unborn." Burke's observation takes on added meaning for students of intercultural communication when we realize that we can substitute the word *culture* for the word *history*, for in a very real sense both are the conduits that carry the important messages a culture deems important.

Before we begin our discussion of how history and culture are interwoven, we remind you that our intention is simply to expose you to some historical examples that will enable you to appreciate the following advice: *The study of history needs to be part of the*

© Gloria Thomas

What a culture seeks to remember and pass on to the next generation tells us about the character of the culture.

study of intercultural communication. Yu underscores the importance of that advice when he writes, "we need to recognize that the history of every society or people deserves to be studied not only as part of world history but also on account of its intrinsic values."[239]

The influence of history is hard to pin down and define. When we are talking about history, we are talking about much more than historical events and specific dates. Granted these are important, but when we refer to history as one of the deep structures of a culture, we are also talking about a culture's formal and informal government, its sense of community, its political system, its key historical "heroes," and even its geography. All of these, working in combination, provide the members of every culture with their identity, values, goals, and expectations. For example, the history of the United States teaches young people that almost anything is possible—one can even become president. History books are full of stories about Abraham Lincoln's log-cabin background and the simple clothing-store clerk Harry Truman. Such history is deeply rooted in the American psyche.

The penetrating effect of a culture's history on perception and behavior can be seen in countless examples. The deep-seated hatred and killing in Bosnia-Herzegovina did not start in the 1990s. In a newspaper article appropriately titled "How the Seeds of

Hate Were Sown," one historian traces the roots of the conflict back to the fourteenth century.[240] Much of the enmity between Jews and Arabs, as well as between African Americans and the dominant culture in the United States, can be traced to a long and agonizing history. An editorial in *Time* magazine, discussing the tribal conflicts in Africa, reminded all of us that war and killing is seldom surprising "when ethnic enemies use the outbreak of fighting to settle scores that can stretch back for centuries."[241] And even in something as simple as Japan's low murder rate we can see the influence of history. As an article in *U.S. News & World Report* pointed out, "Japan's relatively low murder rate reflects its history and customs, just as America's relatively high numbers do. Since the 17th century, private ownership of most guns has been banned in Japan."[242]

Our interest in the study of history is predicated on two assumptions. First, *historical events help explain the character of a culture*. As the historian Basile noted, "For all people, history is the source of the collective consciousness."[243] From the earliest Western movement across the plains of the United States to explorations of outer space, Americans have agreed on a history of conquest. Second, *what a culture seeks to remember and pass on to the next generation tells us about the character of that culture*. American history books and folktales are running over with examples of how an individual can make a major difference in the world. We have all learned how Martin Luther King Jr. almost single-handedly shaped the civil rights movement.

Let us pause at this point and examine a few countries so that we might be able to further convince you that part of any study of culture must include a review of the historical events that helped shape the character of the members of that culture.

United States History

We begin our examination of history with the United States, which is unique in that the dominant culture is relatively young and was formed primarily through two processes. First, those who originally arrived on the Atlantic coast brought many English values, the English system of law, and the basic organization of commerce that was prevalent during the sixteenth century. Second, these settlers were immediately confronted with a wave of new citizens who arrived through migration. And as we noted in Chapter 1, these "new citizens" continue to arrive each and every day. This ongoing influx of immigrants, both legal and illegal, has produced what is sometimes referred to as the "melting pot," "stew," or "mixed salad" metaphor of culture.

Cultural integration did not come about easily. The shared, desperate desire of the American people to be separated from what was known as the Crown and Divine Right, as well as from the Church of England, provided the impetus to seek unity. This impetus led, in part, to the binding of Germans, Irish, and English together in a social fabric ample enough to contain Catholics, Congregationalists, and Methodists and to unite North, South, East, and West within a national framework. Americans wanted to separate alienable rights—those that could be voluntarily surrendered to the government—from inalienable rights, those that could not be surrendered or "taken away" even to a government of the people.[244] The fundamental American proposition became "life, liberty, and the pursuit of happiness" for each individual, whose liberties had to be secured against the potentially abusive power of government.

The people who settled the colonies valued individuality, a lack of formality, and efficient use of time. Centuries later, these values still endure. We can attribute this to the character of the people who emigrated to this new world to stake out a fresh life. Settling a new, undeveloped land required a great deal of attention to the daily activities of surviving, a situation that did not lend itself to formality or dependency. There was no time to waste on what was perceived to be the nonsense of rigid European and British rules of formality. Only the independent survived.

These environmental factors also had psychological effects on the settlers: After developing habits of survival based on individualism, a lack of formality, and efficiency, they soon also developed thought patterns, beliefs, values, and attitudes attuned to that environment. In this way, individualism became even more important for the American culture. We consider anything morally wrong that might violate our right to think for ourselves, judge for ourselves, make our own decisions, or live our own lives as we see fit. We have developed a pride in individualism that has become fixed in folk history as well as factual history: For instance, Daniel Boone's father knew it was time to move whenever a new neighbor was so close he could see smoke from the neighbor's fireplace.

Another aspect of American history that has shaped the culture is violence. Our history is filled with stories of violence: the taking of Native American lands by force; fighting the War of Independence and the Civil War; engaging in two World Wars, the Korean War, the Vietnam War, Desert Storm and recently the conflict in Kosovo. Guns are so much a part of our culture and history that the Constitution guarantees our right to bear arms—a right no other nation grants. It is not our intention here to debate the merit of this heritage but only to point out its impact on the development of our culture.

Americans have historically believed in the principle of Manifest Destiny. Although originally applied to Mexicans and Native Americans, this philosophy stressed that we were the people "who would inevitably spread the benefits of democracy and freedom to the lesser peoples inhabiting the region."[245]

Our notions of freedom and independence and the challenge of developing a sparsely populated land have produced a culture with a strong love of change and progress. "America," as *U.S News & World Report* said, "incorporates the yearnings of both Daedalus and Icarus, constructing miraculous contraptions of every type with the caution of the industrialist, yet audaciously believing there is no place we cannot reach."[246] In the same commentary, the editors remarked: "Being what we are, it was inevitable that Americans would quickly progress from boats to trains to planes. The constitutionally restless republic that trampled the American road was bound to clutter the American sky, expansionism being in their blood."[247]

A review of American history also offers us clues into the link between history, perception, and the role of women in the United States. For example, during the colonial period the legal status of women was influenced by English common law doctrine, under which a woman's legal identity was submerged with her husband's. Even the Constitution of the United States excluded women from equal rights. Women were prohibited from voting, owning land, executing contracts, and conducting business.[248] Even Thomas Jefferson, the great advocate of democracy, was part of the history that subjugated women. The historian Ambrose offers us an excellent summary of Jefferson's view of women—a view that in some ways is still part of American history.

> In America, Jefferson rejoiced, women knew their place, which was in the home and, more specifically, in the nursery. Instead of gadding frivolously about town as French women did, chasing fashion or meddling in politics, American women were content with "the tender and tranquil amusements of domestic life" and never troubled their pretty heads with politics.[249]

African American History

The dominant American culture is not the only group that American history has shaped. African Americans were also touched by the history of the United States. Africans were not willing immigrants. They and their ancestors were captured and enslaved in their own home, brought to the United States, and sold to the colonists as laborers and servants. As Segal notes, "The rule of slavery was forced labor," and the labor was difficult.[250] Life on the plantation was hard. Most slaves worked fifteen to eighteen hours a day and had few rights or privileges. As Esler notes, "they were property, to be bought and sold like farm animals."[251] Slave owners attempted to cut family and tribal links as soon as the slaves arrived in the United States. Yet, many important elements of West African cultures survived and have helped shape the African American experience. Bagwell states it in the following manner: "Our history of enslavement has defined who we are and what we believe today."[252]

Africans became a group robbed of much of their cultural identity: Slaves were forced to adopt a new language and religion and were even assigned new names. Being denied access to the culture of their captors while being told they could not preserve their own culture, they attempted to forge a new one. It was a culture that, in order to survive, stressed companionship and group solidarity. This solidarity was accomplished in part by maintaining historical traditions that had their roots in Africa. As is the case with so many customs, this social bonding still exists. Then and now, the bond of the extended families was communicated through the use of names: It became the custom to identify everyone as a member of the same family. As the poet and novelist Maya Angelou notes, "In slave society Mariah became Aunt Mariah and Joe became Uncle Joe. Young girls were called Sister, Sis, or Tutta. Boys became Brother, Bubba, and Bro and Buddy."[253] Angelou adds, "We have used these terms to help us survive slavery, its aftermath, and today's crisis of revived racism."[254] The terms *brother* and *sister* are still heard throughout African American communities.

During the years of enslavement and afterward, African men were often removed from their families and required to work apart. Thus, African women became a commanding force in the family, and the influence of mothers predominated. This, of course, as Patterson notes, was "an assault on the key roles of fathers and mothers."[255] Even today we see the impact of this phase of history on many African American families.

What is both sad and interesting about African American history is the fact that persecution, prejudice, and treatment as second-class citizens did not end with the Civil War and the passing of the Thirteenth Amendment. The historian Patterson states this point rather clearly when he notes, "The thing that makes African Americans special is the period of Jim Crow which was very much a kind of slave system except without individual masters. In others words, blacks were essentially in bondage into the 1960s."[256]

In the 1960s demonstrations, sit-ins, rallies, marches, and even violence, got the attention of the government, and in 1964 the Civil Rights Act was passed. The act, among other things, gave the attorney general power to protect citizens against discrimination and segregation in voting, education, and the use of public facilities.

Because most history is written by the dominant culture, African Americans, until recently, have had their stories told, and their identities defined, by historians who were mainly white. In many cases, this did not ensure an accurate or complete portrayal of their culture. In the 1960s, as a means of overcoming the problems of accuracy and identity, African Americans adopted the slogan "Black is beautiful" and demanded that other versions of their history be made known. In many instances, this concept of black pride frightened some whites and historically has contributed to increased racism.

Jewish History

Having already discussed the Jewish religion, we offer here just one or two examples of how history and culture fuse together to help form the character of the Jewish people. All Jews know that their history is a study of almost thirty-five hundred years of persecution. As the historian Van Doren notes, "The history of Judaism and the Jews is a long and complicated story, full of blood and tears."[257] What every Jew knows from this history of "blood and tears" is that the suffering and pain has been, almost since the inception of the Jewish culture, ongoing. In A.D. 66 Jews were sold as slaves and during the Spanish Inquisition thousands of Jews were massacred. And, of course, you know about Hitler's "Final Solution" for the Jews. During this period of history "Six million European Jews of both sexes and all ages and conditions of life were worked, starved, stripped, gassed, robbed of rings and the gold in their teeth, and trundled off to the crematoria."[258] That number represented about one-third of the world's Jewish population.

Because of this long history of persecution and oppression, Jews have come to believe that they must live with their eyes fixed on the past. When they are called on to make fundamental choices, they turn for guidance to the past, where they find persecution, genocide, and flight. Throughout their history, Jews have had to move from place to place to avoid persecution. As recently as sixty years ago, non-Jews in the United States were responsible for an event that many still remember: In 1939, a ship carrying Jewish people away from Germany landed in Miami but was turned back—an action that became symbolic of non-Jews' treatment of Jews.

The history presented to young Jewish children is full of other examples of persecution. The story of Hanukkah stresses how a relatively small band of Jews overcame the Greek-Syrians in the second century B.C. The message is clear, and one that is told over and over: A group of people thwarted persecution and put their lives on the line for religious freedom.

As is the case with the history of all cultures, the evidence of history can be seen in the present. Jewish history has helped create a people who value family as a crucial means for survival. Their history of being forced to move from one location to another has encouraged Jews to pursue and value occupations that could easily be transferred to new settings. Occupations using the mind (teacher, lawyer, doctor, writer, and so on) thus are popular occupations even today—thousands of years later.

Van Doren offers an excellent summary of Jewish history and how it "has been passed down from father to son for nearly four thousand years."[259] He writes:

> With all that, the Jews are still, essentially, the same stubborn, dedicated people, now and forever maybe, affirming the same three things. First, they are a people of the law as given in the holy books of Moses. Second, they are the chosen people of God, having an eternal covenant with him. Third, they are a witness that God is and will be forevermore.[260]

Russian History

Much of Russian history is similar to that of the Jews. The Russians have been subjected to invasion, persecution, and suffering. During the last thousand years, their country has been invaded and occupied time and again by the Mongols, Germans, Turks, Poles,

Swedes, French, and English. Russian cities have been brutally occupied and tightly governed, and entire towns and villages have been slaughtered for failure to pay tribute. Consequently, Russians have developed a perception of the world that incorporates the plundering of Mother Russia. It is difficult for most Americans to understand this national paranoia toward outsiders. The historian Daniels summarizes these differences in perception and history:

> It is of greatest importance for Americans to appreciate how different was Russia's international environment from the circumstances of the young United States. Russia found itself in a world of hostile neighbors, the United States in secure continental isolation. Living under great threats and equally great temptations, Russia had developed a tradition of militarized absolutism that put the highest priority on committing its meager resources to meet those threats and exploit those temptations.[261]

As is the case with all countries and cultures, historical and political heritage have helped mold the Russian people. Esler depicts those heritages in the following manner: "Russia's political tradition has historically been autocratic, from the legacy of the Byzantine emperors and Tatar khans, through the heavy-handed authoritarianism of Peter the Great, to the totalitarian regime of Joseph Stalin."[262]

The cultural experiences described by Esler created within the Russian people traits that made it easy for them to follow orders and accept the dictums of their leaders. Even today we see these qualities in the Russian people.

The link between the Russian people and their land is also an essential component in appreciating this culture. As Kohan tells us, "Any understanding of the Russian character must inevitably begin with the land, which covers roughly one-sixth of the globe."[263] The vast sweep of Russia's steppes and forests and the sheer enormousness of their country created a people that "would rather settle down by a warm stove, break out a bottle of vodka and muse about life."[264]

Chinese History

The Chinese proverb "Consider the past and you will know the present" clearly states how important history is to the study of their culture. Each Chinese derives his or her strongest sense of identity from history. Whatever people's qualities or quirks, whatever their circumstances or political allegiance, and whether they live in China itself or are scattered to distant lands, pride in China's history links all members of the culture. The Chinese assign near-mystical qualities to their history, as Sangren concluded: "For China, history itself is the text through which heaven's order can be known."[265] It is no wonder that history is important both to the Chinese people and to anyone seeking to understand the Chinese. As the historian Felipe Fernandez-Armesto tells us, "China appears as the home of an uniquely successful imperial experiment, which has endured for over two thousand years with not very conspicuous discontinuities."[266]

A number of specific aspects of China's history contribute to the shaping of their world view: First and foremost is China's long history of physical and cultural isolation. For centuries, China was isolated by immense natural barriers. To its north are the desolate Siberian and Mongolian plateaus and the Gobi Desert. To the west, high mountain ranges separate the country from Russia, Afghanistan, and Pakistan. The towering Himalayas form the southwestern border, secluding China from India and Burma. And high mountains and deep valleys separate the country from its southern neighbors. This geographical separation contributed to the formation of a number of familiar Chinese characteristics. Latourette mentions some of them:

> To [isolation] may partly be ascribed their intense national pride. All other civilizations with which the Chinese had close contact were derived from themselves and, they thought, were inferior to theirs. They were the source of the culture of most of their neighbors, but although they repeatedly profited by contributions from abroad, with the exception of Buddhism they thought themselves as having received but little. Theirs was the Middle Kingdom and all other peoples were barbarous.[267]

China's self-perception has prevailed for five thousand years. Even today, China believes that it is the "center of civilization." Esler summarizes the links among geographical separation, feelings of cultural supremacy, and modern-day China:

> This combination of isolation and predominance has fostered distinctive patterns of behavior and attitude among the Chinese. The unique combination, for instance, contributed substantially to the cultural continuity that marks Chinese history. In fact, twentieth-century China is still governed to a striking degree by ideas that first emerged two or three thousand years ago.[268]

Another historical idea that has lasted for thousands of years, and still continues, is the notion of the Chinese clan and family being more important than the state. As Stafford notes, "The Chinese dedication to family was among the gravest problems facing any attempt to construct Chinese nationalism."[269] Again and again the Chinese have made great sacrifices for the clans and families, but "for the nation there has never been an instance of the supreme spirit of sacrifice."[270]

The values of merit and learning, two traits that mark modern China, have a long historical tradition. As early as 200 B.C. one's merit would be determined by his or her fund of knowledge.[271] And successful candidates for public office and important bureaucratic positions of power and prestige would demonstrate their skills by passing examinations based upon the mastery of the Confucian classes.[272]

Granting that any culture's history is composed of thousands of elements, we offer another historical example that helps explain the bond that exists between a culture's history and its perception of the world. For some five thousand years, Chinese civilization has been built on agriculture, as Wenzhong and Grove note: "Generations of peasants were tied to the land on which they lived and worked. Except in times of war and famine, there was little mobility, either socially or geographically."[273] This agrarian lifestyle helps explain a number of Chinese cultural traits and values. For example, say Wenzhong and Grove, "The collective (group-oriented) nature of Chinese values is largely the product of thousands of years of living and working together on the land."[274]

Japanese History

Because it is basically a series of islands, Japan is yet another country that has had its history and character molded by isolation. According to Reischauer, this separation "has produced in the Japanese a strong sense of self-identity and also an almost painful self-consciousness in the presence of others."[275] So strong is this island nation mentality that school children learn the following phrase "surrounded by seas and enemies, so we must depend on each other."[276] Being isolated from much of the world has generated other traits as well. For example, Reischauer notes that isolation "has caused the Japanese to be acutely aware of anything that comes from outside and to draw special attention to its foreign provenience."[277] "Another by-product of isolation may be Japan's unusual degree of cultural homogeneity."[278] In addition, feelings of detachment from the rest of the world have also fostered, according to Schneider and Silverman, "feelings of loyalty and obligation to the nation"[279]; feelings which "are not of recent origin."[280]

Another important link between Japan's long history and some of its current values can be seen in its 250-year feudal period. A number of key Japanese traits grew out of this period. First, benevolent lords took care of the people and their needs. This has had a major impact on the development of modern industrial Japan. It was easy for the Japanese to transfer *loyalty* from the feudal lords to large companies because the companies, in a sense, have replaced feudalism: Companies care for their employees, providing them with lifelong employment and a kind of cradle-to-grave social environment. Second, from feudalism the Japanese learned *discipline and sacrifice*. The people were required to walk a certain way, to move their hands a certain way, and even to sleep with their head pointing in a specific direction. Third, this historical period is seen as contemporary by the high degree of *conformity* found in dress, manner and outlook.[281] Finally, Hays lists three other Japanese values that emerged from this period: the *lack of individualism*; *a sense of one's place in society* "so ingrained that all psychic life revolved around it"; and a way of life that generated a long *"series of obligations."*[282]

As we have said throughout this chapter, a culture's history is just one of many sources that contribute to the character of the people of that culture. This concept is clearly demonstrated with regard to the Japanese view toward collectivism. We have already noted that the Japanese family and world view helped create this value, and now we suggest that there are historical antecedents for this value. As far back as the second century A.D., Japanese agriculture depended on many "small dike-surrounded, water-filled plots of land, fed by an intricate man-made system of small waterways."[283] For this system to work, the people of Japan had to learn how to share water. As Reischauer pointed out, "Probably such cooperative efforts over the centuries contributed to the notable Japanese penchant for group identification and group action."[284] This desire to cooperate and conform is vividly expressed in the following Japanese proverb: "When you go to the village, go as the villagers go."

Mexican History

We agree with Griswold del Castillo when he writes, "Within the last few years Americans have become more aware of the importance of studying Mexico and its relationship to the United States."[285] Part of that study should include Mexican history. As we have noted throughout this chapter, the deep structure of a culture (religion, family, history) offers valuable insights into the makeup of the members of that culture. This is particularly true for Mexicans. As McKiniss and Natella note, "Mexicans tend to be very conscious of their past, to the extent of speaking of historical events as current issues."[286] Schneider and Silverman echo the same theme when they write, "Mexicans themselves believe that their history holds the key to their character."[287] It seems that "as much as the future pulls us forward, the past propels Mexican thought and action."[288] Let us now turn to some of that past so that we might better understand the Mexican culture.

The history of Mexico, and how that history has influenced the Mexican people, can be divided into six major periods: (1) the pre-Columbian period, (2) the invasion by Spain, (3) the independence from Spain, (4) the Mexican-American War, (5) the revolution, and (6) modern Mexico.

What is called the pre-Columbian period of Mexican history lasted from around 300 B.C. to A.D. 1519. The great cultures of the Olmec, Maya, Toltec, and Aztec tribes flourished in different parts of Mexico during this period. While each tribe made its own unique contribution to contemporary Mexican culture, collectively they are an important part of Mexico's view of the world and themselves. These groups produced civilizations that were equal to anything in Europe.[289] Even today their legends, artistic heritages, architecture, and their foods "are an integral part of the national identity." [290]

It is important to remember that Mexicans are extremely proud of this period of their history. They know, for example, that the Mayas were advanced in astronomy and mathematics. They developed the concept of zero before it was discovered in Europe; and they created one of the world's first calenders.[291] Mexicans are also well aware of the accomplishments of the Aztecs. Aztec art and social and religious structure have survived for thousands of years. The Aztecs were a very proud people and considered themselves the chosen people of the sun and war god. Feelings of great pride are a trait that is common to Mexicans even today.

The pre-Columbian period of Mexican history ended with the Spanish Conquest. On April 22, 1519, with cries of "God, Glory and Gold," Cortes invaded Mexico. This was, as Foster notes, "a collision of two totally foreign civilizations, each previously unknown to the other.[292] Cortes, because of his use of horses, guns, and interpreters who could speak Spanish, had very little trouble defeating the indigenous people of Mexico. The Spanish occupation of Mexico, and subsequent subjugation of the Mexican Indians, would change the country and the people for hundreds of years to come. Let us look at four of the major changes brought about by the Spanish military victory. First, of course, was the introduction of Catholicism to Mexico. In the beginning it was left to the Spanish army to smash Indian idols and replace them with crosses. However, it was the Spanish friars, not the soldiers, who "fanned out across the country" converting the conquered Indians.[293] Actually the conversions were rather easy. The Indians adapted the new religion to meet their needs. In addition, both cultures "believed in an afterlife and a world created by god(s)."[294]

The second outgrowth of the Spanish domination was the development of a rigid social class that many historians believe had negative consequences on the Indian people. As Foster observed, "The Spanish caste system spread illiteracy, racism, and official corruption through the land, setting one group against the others."[295] Third, Spain's occupation of Mexico resulted in large tracts of land being turned over to Spanish nobles, priests and solders. Finally, the Spanish conquest of Mexico saw the demise of millions of Indians. By some estimates, a combination of being exposed to European diseases, famine, and murder, reduced some Indian populations by 70 to 90 percent.[296]

For almost three hundred years Mexico suffered under Spanish rule. Mexico was a feudal and deeply Catholic country where landed aristocrats dominated a population of peasants.[297] In the summer of 1810 Miguel Hildago y Costilla, a creole parish priest, formed a group of his followers and started working and fighting for the independence of Mexico. Although Hidalgo was executed in 1811, he is known as the "Father of

Mexican Independence," an independence that came on February 24, 1821, in the form of the Plan of Iguala.[298] Final "freedom" did not arrive until 1824 when Mexico became a federal republic under its own constitution.

The next twenty years was a time of great upheaval in Mexico as the people attempted to adapt to a new form of government. It is during this period that the territory of Texas declared its independence from Mexico. This, of course, brought about the Mexican-American War in 1846. On May 13, 1846, President Polk declared war on Mexico. In addition to Texas, Polk, with the backing of the American people, wanted to acquire what amounted to half of Mexico's territory. The two countries fought over the land for two years in a war "that Americans hardly remember and that Mexicans can hardly forget."[299] The war ended with the Treaty of Guadalupe Hidalgo. For Mexicans the war was a bitter defeat. But for the United States it is an example of Manifest Destiny—"spreading the benefits of democracy to the lesser peoples of the continent."[300]

What the war between these "neighbors" did had an impact that is felt even today. Historians Samora and Simon speak of that impact when they write "The Mexican-American War created unparalleled bitterness and hostility toward the United States, not only in Mexico but throughout Latin America."[301] They add, "Even today, Latin American relationships with the United States are often marred by suspicion and distrust"[302] that goes back over a hundred years.

The next important phase of Mexico's history deals with the Revolution of 1910. After a long and tiring dictatorship under President Porfirio Diaz the Mexican people revolted—and with just cause. At the time of the revolution "90 percent of Mexico's *mestizos* and Indians were still desperately poor on the ranches and haciendas of a handful of wealthy landowners."[303] While the revolution "was an effort to bring about social change and equality for all Mexicans," it was also an attempt to return to local customs and tradition and to break away from European "culture and standards."[304]

When the revolution ended and the Constitution was produced in 1917, a new era was begun in Mexico. The revolution "ended feudalism and peonage and created labor unions and redistributed land."[305]

The last phase of Mexican history that is important to students of intercultural communication is called "Modern Mexico." Huge oil and natural gas reserves, manufacturing, agriculture, tourism, and the hundreds of *maquiladora* factories along the Mexican–U.S. border, have now made Mexico a major economic force in the world. And, of course, with the passage of the North American Free Trade Agreement (NAFTA) Mexico, the United States, and Canada are free-trade partners.

Although economic agreements have improved relations between the governments of Mexico and the United States, there are still historical wounds that influence intercultural interactions. Two recent ones are worth noting. First, there are different perceptions concerning undocumented immigrants. Many Mexicans resent the physical barriers that many border states have erected to "keep out" illegal immigrants. Second, hostility toward Americans was also increased when "A majority of Californians voted in 1994 to deny education and health services to immigrants who enter the state without proper documentation."[306] Many Mexicans perceived this vote as a sign of racism.

As we conclude this chapter we again remind you that there are thousands of examples of the tandem relationship between history, world view, family, and culture. We have offered but a handful of those. In each instance, our aim was to demonstrate that the study of intercultural communication must include a study of what Wolfe calls "The sacred trinity"—God, family, and country.[307]

SUMMARY

- World view is a culture's orientation toward God, humanity, nature, the universe, life, death, sickness, and other philosophical issues concerning existence. Although world view is communicated in a variety of ways, religion is the predominant element of culture that gives us our world view.
- The family, because it is the child's first introduction to culture, influences both perception and communication. Family teaches gender roles, views toward individualism and collectivism, perceptions toward aging, and social skills.
- History, by passing on stories of the past, influences perception and teaches group identity, loyalty, and what to strive for.

 INFOTRAC® COLLEGE EDITION EXERCISES

1. Using the PowerTrac option, locate the article "The West Unique, Not Universal" by Samuel P. Huntington (Hint: For more on related subjects, use the subject search term "values"). According to Huntington, what constitutes the "deep structure" of Western culture, and what surface realities are often confused with Western culture? What changes must non-Western societies make in order to modernize? What can Western cultures anticipate as non-Western cultures become more modern?

2. Using the PowerTrac option, locate and read the article "Top Ten Religion Stories of the Millennium." How many of these stories are you already familiar with? Choose one story to investigate further, examining the ways in which religion has far-reaching influence on human history and culture. What story (or stories) might you add to the list? If you'd like to read more about contemporary religious effects, locate the article "On-Line Religion" by Paul A. Soukup (Hint: For more on related subjects, use the subject search terms "Religion" and "Culture").

3. Much has been written about differences in world religions, but as the text notes, one can also say with George Bernard Shaw "There is only one religion, though there are a hundred versions of it." Using PowerTrac, locate and read the article "Universal Human Values: Finding an Ethical Common Ground" by Rushworth M. Kidder. Do you agree with Kidder that universal human values can be identified? If so, do you agree that each of the values that Kidder lists are universal? Would you add any other values to Kidder's list?

ACTIVITIES

1. Find out as much as you can about the history of your informant's culture. Try to isolate examples of how your informant's cultural values have been determined by historical events.

2. Ask someone from a culture different from your own specific questions about child-rearing practices. You might inquire about methods of discipline, toys, games, stories, topics discussed at the dinner table, and so forth.

3. Attend a church that is very different from your own, and try to isolate the rituals and messages that might influence perceptions of members of that church.

DISCUSSION IDEAS

1. Explain how understanding the religious aspect of a particular culture's lifestyle might help you better communicate with a member of that culture.

2. Explain the link between a culture's historical roots and some current perceptions and behaviors of that culture.

3. How are religion, family, and history linked together?

part 3

From Theory to Practice

chapter 5

Language and Culture: Words and Meanings

The notion that thought can be perfectly or even adequately expressed in verbal symbols is idiotic.

ALFRED NORTH WHITEHEAD

The sum of human wisdom is not contained in any one language, and no single language is capable of expressing all forms and degrees of human comprehension.

EZRA POUND

THE IMPORTANCE OF LANGUAGE

The importance of language to the study of intercultural communication is clearly captured in filmmaker Federico Fellini's simple sentence "A different language is a different view of life." His notion takes on added significance when you realize that one of the major characteristics identifying you as human is your ability to use language. "People can talk. Other animals can't. These skills make *Homo sapiens* a uniquely successful, powerful, and dangerous animal."[1] Yet language is more than just a skill; it has evolved a rich and expressive versatility that was recognized by Paul Tillich when he observed that "language has created the word 'loneliness' to express the pain of being alone and the word 'solitude' to express the joy of being alone."

Our ability to use words is indeed a remarkable gift. Over two thousand years ago, the Athenian poet Aristophanes glorified the beauty of words: "By words the mind winged." Everything that you are is inside your body. Most of this internal state is an electrochemical melange residing in your brain. Your beliefs, values, attitudes, world views, emotions, and myriad other aspects of yourself and personality is locked up inside. You can convey some aspects of yourself nonverbally through facial expressions, gestures, or touching. This nonverbal communication is explored in detail in Chapter 6. Our task in this chapter is to develop an understanding and appreciation of verbal language as it functions in intercultural communication.

Language enables us to have contact with other human beings.

To state that language is important is merely to acknowledge the obvious, yet the significant influence language has on human behavior is frequently overlooked. The ability to speak and write is often taken for granted. Through our use of sounds and symbols, we are able to give life to our ideas—as Henry Ward Beecher once wrote, "Thought is the blossom; language the opening bud; action the fruit behind it." Or as Cartmill has observed:

> Language lets us get vast numbers of big, smart fellow primates all working together on a single task—building the Great Wall of China or fighting World War II or flying to the moon. It lets us construct and communicate the gorgeous fantasies of literature and the profound fables of myth. It lets us cheat death by pouring out our knowledge, dreams, and memories into younger people's minds. And it does powerful things for us inside our own minds because we do a lot of thinking by talking silently to ourselves. Without language, we would be only a sort of upright chimpanzee with funny feet and clever hands. With, it we are the self-possessed masters of the planet.[2]

Functions of Language

Language is extremely important to human interaction because of its *labeling, interaction*, and *transmission* functions. The labeling function serves to identify or name a person, object, or act, so that he, she, or it may be referred to in communication. The interaction function is concerned with the sharing and communication of ideas and emotions. And transmission is the process by which you pass information to others. Although these functions are generally considered the primary purposes of communication, there are other functions and purposes that, nevertheless, are equally important.

In many instances of social interaction, the communication of ideas is a marginal or irrelevant consideration. Here, communication serves additional purposes that facilitate and maintain social and individual needs. Crystal has identified six such functions: *emotive expression*, *thinking*, *phatic interaction*, *control of reality*, *the keeping of history*, and *identity expression*.

Emotive Expression

Language permits you to express your internal emotional states. This form of expression may range from a simple statement such as "I feel sad" to the loud cursing of something that is not functioning properly. Whether in the absence of others or in their presence, this use of language serves as a means of getting rid of nervous energy when you are under stress.[3]

Thinking

People tend to be both visual and verbal thinkers and engage in both forms depending upon their activity. Verbal thinking, however, plays an extremely important role in human communication where language functions as an instrument of thought when you speak your thoughts out loud as an aid to problem solving or thinking.[4]

Phatic Interaction

Another function is phatic interaction where messages with no factual content help maintain a comfortable relationship between people. Such commentary as "Bless you" to a sneeze, and "Good morning" or "Nice day" as a greeting are examples of phatic messages. The topics of phatic communication can be culturally diverse. Rundi women in Burundi, Central Africa, for instance, are likely to say "I must go home now or my husband will beat me" as a phatic form of leave-taking.[5] In other cultures, such as the Paliyans of southern India or the Aritama of Columbia, people prefer silence and little is said in a phatic sense.[6]

Control of Reality

Communication may also function to assist in the control of reality. The use of prayers or blessings, which invoke supernatural beliefs, involves the use of language to control the forces that are believed to control one's life. For instance, in the Roman Catholic Mass, the speaking of the words "This is my body" is believed to identify the moment when the communion bread becomes the body of Christ.[7]

Keeping of History

Language also functions to record facts, which is represented by all kinds of record-keeping ranging from historical records, geographical surveys, and business accounts to scientific reports, legislative acts, and public record data banks. This arena "is an essential domain of language because the material guarantees the knowledge-base of subsequent generations which is a prerequisite of social development and the perpetuation of culture."[8]

Identity Expression

The last major function of language is the expression of identity. Many social situations involve the use of language that unites the participants rather than presenting information. Cheering at a football game or shouting names or slogans at public meetings can reveal a great deal about people—in particular their regional origins, social background, level of education, occupation, age, sex, and personality.[9]

Beyond shouting slogans or cheers, language functions to express and maintain your social identity. What you are can be very important in the eyes of society. Your sociolinguistic identity derives from the way in which people are organized into hierarchically ordered social groups or classes. The way people talk reveals a great deal about their social position and their level of education.[10]

Over millions of years, *Homo sapiens* have evolved the anatomy necessary to produce and receive sounds; in a much shorter span of time, they have created cultural systems in which those sounds have taken on meaning by representing things, feelings, and ideas. This combination of evolution and culture has led to the development of a four-part process that enables you to share your internal states with other human beings. In short, you can *receive, store, manipulate,* and *generate* symbols to represent your personalized realities. But, to a large degree, your language behavior is mediated by your culture. How you use language, the forms of language that you use, and the purposes to which you choose to apply language are subject to cultural diversity.

Cultural diversity in language behavior is perhaps one of the most difficult and persistent problems encountered in intercultural communication. For this reason, we will examine three prominent issues in language (1) the link between language and culture, (2) language translation, and (3) language diversity among co-cultures in the United States.

LANGUAGE AND CULTURE

Language is the key to the heart of a culture. So related are language and culture that language holds the power to maintain national or cultural identity. Language is important in ethnic and nationalist sentiment because of its powerful and visible symbolism; it becomes a core symbol or rallying point.[11] The impact of language as a strong symbol of national identity may be seen in the history of the Basques, an ethnic group in the north of Spain. The Spanish government from 1937 to the mid-1950s made an active attempt to destroy the Basque culture and forbid the use of the Basque language. Basque could not be taught in the schools or used in the media, church ceremonies, or in public places. Books in the language were publicly burned, and Basque names could not be used in baptism ceremonies. All Basque names in official documents were translated into Spanish, and inscriptions on public buildings and tombstones were removed.[12]

Because of this relationship between language and cultural identity, steps are often taken to limit or prohibit the influence of foreign languages. Costa Rica, for instance, recently enacted a new law that restricts the use of foreign languages and imposes fines on those who break it. Under the law, companies that advertise in a foreign language also must include a Spanish translation in larger letters.[13] Likewise, Iran has banned companies from using Western names. Turkey's government is considering fining anyone who uses foreign names on the airwaves. And France has a list of thirty-five hundred foreign words that cannot be used in schools, bureaucracies, or companes.[14]

Verbal Processes

As we have already alluded, and you should by now suspect, it is impossible to separate language from culture. In its most basic sense, language "is a set of characters or elements and rules for their use in relation to one another."[15] These characters or elements

Language clearly distinguishes one culture from another.

are symbols that are culturally diverse. That is, they differ from one culture to another. You may readily discover this when you study another language. Not only are the symbols (words) and sounds for those symbols different, but so are the rules (phonology, grammar, syntax, and intonation) for using those symbols and sounds.

Word differences are obvious in various languages. In English, you live in a *house*. In Spanish, you live in a *casa*. In Thai, people live in *bans*. Phonology also varies culturally. While in English there are 21 consonant sounds and 5 vowels that combine to form 38 various sounds, the Filipino language has 16 consonants and 10 vowels forming 26 phonemes. Grammatical structures are unique to each language as well. In English, there are both singular and plural nouns and pronouns, but in Korean, "the distinction between singular and plural is made by the context of the sentence."[16] In English, verb tenses express contrast between past, present, and future acts, but in Vietnamese, the same verb reflects all three and the time of the action is inferred from the context.[17] Syntax, or the word order and structure of sentences, also varies depending on the language. In the normal word order for simple sentences in Filipino the predicate is followed by the subject.[18] For example, the English sentence "The teacher died" would be *"Namatay ang guro"* or *"Died the teacher"* in Filipino. These examples tell you that if you want to communicate in another language, you must know not only the symbols (words) of that language, but also the rules for using those symbols.

Language is much more than just a symbol and rule system that permits communication with another person; it is also the means by which people think and construct reality. As Nanda and Warms point out: "Language does more than just reflect culture: It is the way in which the individual is introduced to the order of the physical and social environment. Therefore, language would seem to have a major impact on the way in which the individual perceives and conceptualizes the world."[19]

Patterns of Thought

You may easily assume that everyone speaks and thinks in much the same way—just in different languages. But this is not the case; how people think and how they ultimately speak is determined to a large extent by their culture. This process is known as linguistic relativity. As Rogers and Steinfatt suggest:

> The assignment of meaning to a message concerns human perceptions about the relationship between symbols and their referents. Language is used to think as well as to speak. *Linguistic relativity* is the degree to which language influences human thought and meanings. It proposes that in human thought language intervenes between the symbols and the ideas to which the symbols refer.[20]

And, as verbal behavior differs from one culture to another, thought processes and perceptions of reality also differ. The essence of linguistic relativity is exemplified in the theoretical formulations of Benjamin Lee Whorf, which suggest that language and thought are so intertwined that one's language determines the categories of thought open to him or her. As Whorf has indicated, "We cut up and organize the spread and flow of events as we do largely because through our mother tongue, we are parties to an agreement to do so, not because nature itself is segmented in exactly that way for all to see."[21] What has become known as the Sapir-Whorf hypothesis argues that language is not simply a means of reporting experience but, more important, it is a way of defining experience. Sapir, a student of Whorf, wrote:

> Human beings do not live in the objective world alone, nor alone in the world of social activity as ordinarily understood, but are very much at the mercy of the particular language which has become the medium of expression for their society. . . . The real world is to a large extent unconsciously built up on the language habits of the group. No two languages are ever sufficiently similar to be considered as representing the same social reality. The worlds in which different societies live are distinct worlds, not merely the same world with different labels attached.[22]

Nanda provides an excellent example of the Sapir-Whorf concept in practice:

> If my language has only one term—*brother-in-law*—that is applied to my sister's husband, my husband's brothers, and my husband's sisters' husbands, I am led by my language to perceive all of these relatives in a similar way. Vocabulary, through what it groups together under one label and what it differentiates with different labels, is one way in which language shapes our perception of the world.[23]

In a similar sense, in the Hindi language, there are no single words that are equivalent to the English words for uncle and aunt. Instead, Hindi has different words for your father's older brother, father's younger brother, mother's older brother, mother's older brother-in-law, and so forth.[24]

Another instance of how language defines experience can be seen in the Navajo language, which emphasizes the nature and direction of movement. Rather than saying, "One dresses," the Navajo would say, "One moves into clothing." Instead of saying, "One is young," the Navajo would say, "One moves about newly." Language is one aspect of the Navajo culture that coincides with the notion of a universe in motion.[25]

Although complete acceptance of linguistic relativity is controversial, its application to culture and language is clear: "There is the closest of relationships between language and thought. . . . Language may not determine the way we think, but it does influence the way we perceive and remember, and it affects the ease with which we perform mental tasks."[26] Thus, you can clearly see that culture influences language by way of its symbols and rules as well as your perceptions of the universe. Equally important is the fact that meaning takes different forms as you move from one culture to another.

Culture and Meaning

As children, you most likely asked your parents, "What does that word mean?" This question reflects the way language is viewed. It suggests that people tend to look for meaning in words themselves, but you are incorrect if you believe that words possess meaning. It is far more accurate to say that people possess meaning and that words elicit these meanings. The same word can elicit different meanings. For instance, to one person, the word *grass* might mean something in front of the house that is green, has to be watered, and must be mowed once a week; to another person, *grass* may mean something that is rolled in paper and smoked. All people, drawing on their backgrounds, decide what a word means. People have similar meanings only to the extent that they have had or can anticipate similar experiences. If your past experience includes baseball, then a *rope* is a line drive. If your background lies in the world of jazz music, the word *ax* does not indicate something used to chop wood but any horn or woodwind instrument. And it is quite likely that you and a physician will respond very differently to the word *cancer*.

A word, then, can elicit many meanings. Linguists have estimated that the five hundred most-used words in the English language can produce over fourteen thousand meanings. There simply are many more ideas, feelings, and things to represent than there are words to represent them. As the English poet Tennyson said, "Words, like Nature, half reveal and half conceal the Soul within." We add that what is "half concealed" often may be more important than what is revealed.

If culture is included as a variable in the process of abstracting meaning, the problems become all the more acute, for culture teaches us both the symbol (*dog*) and what the symbol represents (a furry, domesticated animal). When you are communicating with someone from your own culture, the process of using words to represent your experiences is much easier because within a culture people share many similar experiences. But when communication is between people from diverse cultures, different experiences are involved and the process is more troublesome. Objects, events, experiences, and feelings have the labels or names they do because a community of people arbitrarily decided to so name them. If this notion is extended to the intercultural setting, you can see that diverse cultures can have both different symbols and different responses. As an example, consider the word *pain*. In the United States, we avoid pain at all cost, and most of us would never consider even having a tooth filled without some form of painkiller. In other cultures, however, incisions are made without any anesthesia. *Pain* is a simple word. If you imagine shifting your cultural references for every word and meaning you know, you can begin to visualize the influence of culture on how we send and receive messages. Think for just a moment about the variety of meanings various cultures have for words such as *freedom, sexuality, trespassing, wealth, nature, leadership, assertiveness, security, democracy, outer space,* or *AIDS*.

The Hawaiian and Sami languages offer additional examples of the impact culture has on meaning. The Hawaiian language contains only about twenty thousand words, and only fifteen thousand of those are in dictionaries. The Hawaiian language is very ambiguous to outsiders because some words have up to five different meanings and some of the words can be used in a variety of ways and contexts. "Only a knowledge of all the possible meanings of a word and the probable intent of the speaker enables one to arrive at the correct interpretation."[27] The Sami language of Kiruna Sweden has five hundred words to explain *snow* and several thousand more to define *reindeer*, but no word for *computer*.[28] For example, one word describes snow "where reindeer have been digging and eating in one place and then left, so it's no use to go there."[29] Reindeer are a staple of the Sami economy, and snow is a prevalent weather condition in Kiruna. Because these words hold such significance for the Sami culture, their language has hundreds of words to represent them. However, computers play no part in the herding of reindeer, so the Sami language has no word to represent such common English terms as *computer, printer, hard drive, megabytes, Windows 2000,* or *software applications*.

There are even differences between British and American usage in word meanings. Although some words are spelled and pronounced the same, they have different meanings. For instance, the words *boot, bonnet, lift,* and *biscuit* in British English translate into American English as *car trunk, car hood, elevator,* and *cookie*. In the area of business, there are also some interesting differences. For example, the British term *annual gunnel meeting* translates in American English as *annual meeting of shareholders*. The British word *billion* translates as *trillion*, and the British term *superannuation scheme* translates as *pension plan*.[30] From these examples, you can see that culture exerts an enormous influence on language because culture teaches not only the symbols and rules for using those symbols, but more importantly, the meaning associated with the symbols. Further, culture influences the way people *use* language. In the next section, we examine some of the cultural variations in the use of language.

Culture and the Use of Language

Human language seems to be the only communication system that uses meaningless elements to create meaningful structures.[31] Yet, as Arensberg and Niehoff observe, "nothing more clearly distinguishes one culture from another than its language."[32] A comedic example of this diversity may be seen from the various ways in which a sign announces a broken vending machine. In the United Kingdom, the sign might read "Please Understand This Machine Does Not Take 10p Coins." In the United States, the translation would probably be "NO 10p COINS." The Japanese version would express sorrow at the inability to accept 10p coins and offer apologies to the consumer. Although the rules of a foreign language often appear arbitrary and nonsensical to non-native speakers, to the native speakers, the rules make perfect sense and seem more logical than those of other languages. For you to understand the diversity of language across cultures, we will examine characteristics of language use that are culturally diverse. These include *directness, formality, social relationships, emotive expression,* and *language enjoyment*.

Directness
Language usage reflects many of the deep structure values of a culture by its degree of directness. North American language, especially in the United States, is rarely reserved. Instead, it is characterized by direct bluntness and honesty, low-context explicitness, and a great deal of informality. Americans try to avoid vagueness and ambiguity and get directly to the point. If they mean no, they will say so without hesitation. Such direct

use of language is often viewed in other cultures as a disregard for others and can lead to embarrassment and injured feelings.

Most cultures of the world employ less direct language than do Americans in an attempt to preserve the dignity, feelings, and "face" of others. They frequently deem American directness and bluntness as impolite and possibly uncivilized.

Mexicans are very concerned about respecting the individual and preserving dignity. Their values of indirectness and face-saving are evident in their use of language. Direct arguments are considered rude. The Mexican usually attempts to make every interaction harmonious and in so doing may appear to agree with the other person's opinion. In actuality, the Mexican will retain his or her own opinion unless he or she knows the person well or has enough time to explain his or her opinion without causing the other person to lose face. This indirect politeness is often viewed by North Americans as dishonesty and aloof detachment when in actuality it is a sign of individual respect and an opportunity for the other person to save face.

Indirectness and ambiguity are an art in African languages, and imprecision is their first cousin. As Richmond and Gestrin indicate:

> Africans speak naturally, with eloquence, and without hesitation or stumbling over words, but their language is often imprecise and their numbers inexact. Every personal interaction becomes a discussion which establishes a basis for the relationship between the two parties. Westerners should probe gently for specific details until they are reasonably satisfied that they understand what is meant even if not stated.[33]

East Asian people tend toward language and verbalization involving fewer words supported by the aesthetics of vagueness. Cultures with this orientation tend to be concerned more with the overall emotional quality of the interaction than with the meaning of particular words and sentences. Chinese, Japanese, Korean, and Thai cultures, for example, employ language cautiously because they favor moderate or suppressed expression of negative and confrontational messages. Because of the collectivistic nature of their cultures, East Asian speech frequently does not reflect the use of personal pronouns in an effort to emphasize the importance of the group rather than the individual.[34]

In most East Asian cultures, the primary function of speech is the maintenance of social harmony. A Japanese saying states, "The mouth is the cause of calamity." The use of indirect language, therefore, facilitates face-saving helping to maintain social harmony. Members of these high-context cultures expect their communication partners to be able to read between the lines or decode messages from a holistic, context-based perspective.[35] Thus, courtesy may take precedence over truth.

The use of direct and indirect language is a major linguistic difference between North Americans and many East Asian cultures, such as the Chinese. Most North Americans learn to say *yes* and *no* as a means of expressing their individual views. But, being a collective culture, the Chinese usually use *yes* or *no* to express respect for the feelings of others. "In other words," says Ma, "to say *yes* for *no* or *no* for *yes* is largely a reflection of the indirect approach to communication, through which undesirable interpersonal communication can be avoided."[36] This *contrary-to-face-value* aspect of Asian verbal language behavior is often confusing to North Americans.

The use of indirect language is evident in ways other than the use of *yes* and *no*. For example, an American host or hostess, when complimented on his or her cooking, is likely to respond, "Oh, I'm so glad you liked it. I cooked it especially for you." In contrast, the Chinese host or hostess will "instead apologize profusely for giving you nothing even slightly edible and for not showing you enough honor by providing proper dishes."[37]

A final example of how the Chinese employ indirect language is evident in their use of offensive language. For many Americans the creation of an "immediate effect" is a major rhetorical goal. When you insult someone, they know its full impact immediately. The Chinese prefer a "corrosive effect" that is deferred and long-lasting. For the Chinese, the most powerful insult is to leave the insulted person unable to fall asleep at a later time because the more he or she thinks about the words, the more insulting the words become.[38]

Among Koreans, language behavior is also affected by a consideration of others. Face-saving is crucial, because Koreans do not want to be responsible for causing someone to feel shame.[39] The Korean philosopher Han Yongun maintained that interpersonal harmony was the key to virtuous "social action."

From an American perspective, the interpersonal communication of Koreans in the presence of family, work associates, and friends may seem strange. Confucian ethics govern most interpersonal relationships, following a basic premise that proper human relationships are the foundation of society. Proper interpersonal communication includes the expression of warm feelings and the placement of interpersonal relationships before personal interests.[40]

Social Relationships

Language serves to maintain and enhance appropriate social status and relationships between and among members of a culture. Again, this is an instance where language functions to preserve the deep structure values of a culture.

The Spanish language, for instance, expresses formality through separate verb conjugations for formal and informal speech. In Spanish, there are formal and informal pronouns for the English word *you*. In formal speech, the pronoun *usted* is used, whereas in familiar speech, the pronoun *tu* is appropriate.

The use of language to communicate social status is perhaps the most significant difference between Japanese and Western communication styles. In Japan, the very structure of the language requires the speaker to focus primarily on human relationships, whereas Western languages focus on objects or referents and their logical relationships.

Japanese culture and society are bound by rigid rules that govern social relationships and social status in all aspects of life. The Japanese language, therefore, differs substantially in various social situations. Separate vocabularies are used for addressing superiors, peers, and inferiors. When a Japanese is speaking to someone of lower social position, he or she must speak in a particular way. If a person is speaking to someone of higher status, however, then he or she must use other appropriate language even though the message content is identical.[41]

In the Japanese language, a number of words take different forms for different situations, sometimes depending on relationships between the speaker and the listener or the person being discussed. For example, there are many words for *you*: *omae, kimi, ariata, kisama,* and *anata-sama*. In addition, words that men and women use differ in Japanese. Certain words are used only between a husband and wife to express their delicate conjugal relationship. A man uses the word *omae* in two cases: when calling rudely to another man and when addressing his wife. Thus, *omae,* when the "you" is female, can be used only by a husband addressing his wife. Therefore, only one man in the world can call a woman *omae*: her husband.

The Thai culture places a great deal of importance on the individual's place in the social order. To facilitate this concern, the Thai language contains many forms of address for the various levels of social hierarchy. Different classes use different pronouns, nouns, and verbs to represent rank and intimacy. There are at least forty-seven pronouns, including seventeen forms for *I* and nineteen for *you*. Because the language contains different forms for different classes, it is possible to distinguish four Thai languages: the royal, the ecclesiastic, the common or familiar, and a slang.

Language also defines gender roles and relationships within a culture and provides many instances of males and females learning different styles of speech. Pronunciation, grammar, vocabulary, and context of use can all be affected by the gender of the speaker. This is especially evident in the speech of the Japanese. Females use a style known as *joseigno* or *onnakotoba* that evolved among upper-class women as a sign of their position in society. Japanese women have conscious control over their speech styles. Female speech forms are used when women wish to emphasize their femininity; on other occasions, they adopt a sexually neutral style. A Japanese woman may, therefore, use the feminine style when talking to other women about children and adopt the neutral style when talking to business colleagues.[42]

Male dominance is a characteristic of the Mexican culture, and it is revealed in the Spanish language through the use of gendered nouns and pronouns. A group of men, for instance, would be referred to as *ellos*, and a group of women as *ellas*, the *o* ending being masculine and the *a* ending being feminine. But if a group contains several men and one woman, it is called *ellos*, using the masculine gender; if a group contains several women and one man, the group is still called *ellos*. A group of girls is called *niñas*, but a group of girls that includes a single boy is called *niños*.

Emotive Expression

Koreans are far more reserved than Americans; verbally, their feelings are neither freely nor openly expressed. Love is neither expressed as warmly nor as sweetly as in the United States. For example, a Korean wife will maintain her reserve and not rush to embrace her husband at the airport even though he may have been absent for years.[43]

In Great Britain, the language is interspersed with euphemisms that enable the speaker to avoid expressing strong feelings. For instance, when English persons wish to disagree with someone, they are liable to preface their comments with phrases such as "I may be wrong, but . . ." or "There is just one thing in all that you have been saying that worries me a little." Another example of this subtle form of speech is the frequent use of an expression of gratitude to preface a request, as in "I'd be awfully grateful if . . ." or "Thank you very much indeed." This restraint is also evident in the differences between American and British word choice. Compare the following signs seen in the United States and England:

United States: "No dogs allowed."
England: "We regret that in the interest of hygiene, dogs are not allowed on the premises."
United States: "Video controlled."
England: "Notice: In the interest of our regular customers, these premises are now equipped with central security closed-circuit television."
United States: "Please keep hands off door."
England: "Obstructing the door causes delay and can be dangerous."

Enjoyment of Language

In many European and Latin American countries, people derive a great deal of pleasure from the art of conversation. These cultures delight in verbal play, and knowing about this can give you an important insight into those cultures.

Throughout Africa, the spoken word rather than the written word is generally the main means of communication. "As Tanzania's founding father, Julius Nyerere, has written, 'The very origins of African democracy lay in ordinary oral discussion—the elders sat under a tree and talked until they agreed.'"[44] Whatever language they speak, Africans seem to be natural orators. Visitors are expected to be equally gifted. As a visitor, you should plan on being called upon to give extemporaneous speeches, and it will pay for you to be prepared with a few appropriate points illustrated with amusing stories.[45]

Because of their oral tradition, Africans enjoy debate and exchanges of views. Like storytellers, they seek to hold their audiences' attention through the prolific use of proverbs which enrich their speech and provide insights on how they feel about particular issues.[46] Africans make rich use of the proverb as a means of teaching and perpetuating culture as well as a powerful rhetorical device.

> In conversation, as in storytelling, proverbs and parables, which transmit the wisdom of past generations, play an important role. Nothing is closer to the heart of African society and thought than the proverb. More than any other African tradition, it expresses the essence of African wisdom.[47]

Among the Akan, "part of the rhetorical power of the proverb derives from its authoritativeness, or rather its ascription to authoritative sources."[48] To the outsider, this can present a problem because knowledge of a tribe's cultural history and traditions is required to make sense of the proverbs.

Proverbs reveal the power and credibility of words when they are ascribed to elderhood and ancestry. They express universal truths that also have parallels in Western wisdom and experience. To facilitate intercultural communication, Westerners should embellish their speech with their own proverbs which the Africans will surely understand, appreciate, and in many cases, find similar to their own.[49]

Arabs have a deep love of language. They believe that Arabic is "God's language" and as such treat language with great respect and admiration. An ancient Arab proverb notes, "A man's tongue is his sword." The Arabic language can exercise an irresistible influence over the minds of its users. It can be persuasive to the point where the words used to describe events become more significant than the events themselves. Words are used more for their own sake than for what they are understood to mean. Whereas an American can adequately express an idea in ten words, the Arabic speaker may use one hundred. Boasting about the superiority of one's abilities, experiences, or friends is expected. Arabs ordinarily do not publicly admit to personal deficiencies. They will, however, spend hours elaborating on the faults and failures of those who are not members of their clique.

Virtually every Saudi speaks Arabic, and those who engage in international activities are usually fluent in English as well. In social discourse, Arabs value what, by American standards, might appear to be an exaggerated speaking style. Because most intercultural communication between Saudis and Westerners is likely to use English, it is necessary to know about the transference of Arabic communication patterns into English. The most frequently transferred are intonation patterns, a tendency toward over-assertion, repetition, exaggeration, and organizational logic. Certain intonation and stress patterns may make it difficult for the English-speaking listener to comprehend what is being said. If the patterns have unwanted affective meanings for the listener, speech can sound aggressive and threatening, or if the flat Arabic intonation pattern has been transferred, this monotonous tone can be interpreted as a lack of interest. Arabs expect over-assertion and repetition in almost all types of communication. For example, a simple "No" by a guest to the host's request to eat more or drink more will not suffice. To convey the meaning that he (or she) is actually full, the guest must keep repeating "No" several times, coupling it with an oath such as "By God" or "I swear to God."[50]

Greek culture has a long, rich historical tradition that glorifies rhetorical techniques. The Greeks use a variety of key sayings to express much of their culture. In a sense, these sayings are proverbs because they reflect Greek morality and serve as generic forms of expression that convey much meaning in short phrases. For example, Greeks look harshly on lack of gratitude, and a Greek who feels thus slighted might respond, "I taught him how to swim and he tried to drown me." When a Greek is at fault and has no excuse, he or she is liable to say, "I want to become a saint, but the demons won't let me." Greek men have a linguistic tendency toward arrogance and boastfulness. If one succeeds in putting a halt to the bragging of another, he will say, "I cut out his cough." The Greeks' somewhat cavalier attitude toward the truth is expressed in such sayings as "Lies are the salt of life" and "Only from fools and children will you learn the truth."

Insight into the way that the Spanish language is used in Mexico can help you understand the Mexican culture. First, Mexicans love conversation and delight in verbal play. For example, at a party in which Mexican and North American men are introduced to the wives of the guests, the North American man may say, "I am pleased to meet you." In contrast, the Mexican man may say, "I am *enchanted* to meet you." Mexicans make broad use of double-entendres, come up with clever turns of phrases, and insert old quotations at the right moments in an otherwise ordinary conversation.[51] If there are opportunities to engage in talk, the Mexican is ready, even among casual acquaintances. Once an emotional bond is established, he or she is open and generous, willing to confide and be very hospitable.[52]

Our goal in this section has been to convey the fact that language is inseparable from culture. Culture influences language symbols and rules for using those symbols. As we have also seen, meaning is culturally determined.

FOREIGN LANGUAGE AND TRANSLATION

As international contact and interaction continue to increase, the necessity for effective international communication assumes added urgency. In Chapter 8, when we examine cultural differences in the educational setting, we amplify the idea that many cultures insist that their students learn to speak more than just their native language. In fact, it is not uncommon for members of some cultures to speak two or even three languages fluently. In contrast, North Americans have been slower to recognize the importance of acquiring proficiency in more than one language. Because "most Americans speak only one language, they are usually dependent on finding English speakers or translators."[53] Arrangements such as the North American Free Trade Agreement, involving Canada, the United States, and Mexico, as well as continued immigration to the United States, have been great stimulators for North Americans to expand their language proficiency and seek reliable translations.

Federal courts now require certified interpreters. Schools and hospitals print materials in various languages. Employers offer bilingual manuals, and businesses advertise in non-English languages. Small translation companies have turned into thriving businesses with contracts running in the millions of dollars, and some professional translators make up to 40 cents a word.[54] Schulte concisely portrays the role of the interpreter as we move into a global twenty-first century:

> The person who will have to play a major role in regulating the pendulum between global and local communication is the translator. . . . Translators build bridges not only between languages but also between the differences of two cultures. We have established that each language is a way of seeing and reflecting the delicate nuances of cultural perceptions, and it is the translator who not only reconstructs the equivalencies of words across linguistic boundaries but also reflects and transplants the emotional vibrations of another culture.[55]

It is an accepted truism that our globally oriented world necessitates accurate translators. But, effective translations may be elusive because the act of translating is so demanding and complex. People tend to assume that text in one language can be accurately translated into another as long as the translator uses a good bilingual dictionary. Unfortunately, languages are not this simple, and direct translations in many cases are difficult if not impossible. A language may be difficult to translate if the structure of the receptor language is different than the source language, for example, translating German, an Indo-European language into Hungarian, a Finno-Ugrian language. Also the difficulty in translation multiplies when the cultures are extremely different from each other. As Nida states, "a translation may involve not only differences of linguistic affiliation but also highly diverse cultures, e.g., English into Zulu, or Greek into Javanese."[56]

The slightest cultural difference may affect the way in which a text is understood or interpreted. The feeling of joy is experienced differently in various cultures. In most European languages, the heart is where joy is experienced. But, in the Chadic languages of Africa, joy is related to the liver. In Hebrew, the kidneys are said to experience joy while in the Mayan language the abdomen is the site of joy.[57]

Even when messages provide adequate interpretations of original text, there is usually no full equivalence through translation. Word-for-word correspondences do not exist and what may appear to be synonymous messages may not be equivalent. This lack of correspondence may be seen in the translation of biblical references. The Bible idealizes sheep. But, in some cultures, sheep are viewed negatively or do not even exist. Shuttleworth and Cowie relate how the translation of the biblical phrase "Lamb of God" is translated into an Eskimo language using the term "Seal of God." The fact that lambs are unknown in polar regions has led to the substitution of a culturally meaningful item that shares some of the important features of the source language expression.[58] In the following section, we will first briefly explore linguistic equivalence in terms of securing adequate translation. Then we will examine ways to enhance the translation result when working with an interpreter.

Problems of Translation and Equivalence

When the American historian Henry Brooks Adams wrote, "Words are slippery," he must have been referring to the fact that language translation is difficult and subject to countless misinterpretations. There is a case of a missionary who was preaching in the West African Bantu language and who, instead of saying, "The children of Israel crossed the Red Sea and followed Moses," mistakenly said, "The children of Israel crossed the red mosquitoes and swallowed Moses." The examples in this section illustrate the difficulties of foreign-language translation and the serious consequences of the inept translation of words with multiple meanings. These difficulties are referred to as linguistic equivalence, including vocabulary, idiomatic, grammatical-syntactical, experiential-cultural, and conceptual equivalence.

Vocabulary or Lexical Equivalence

One of the goals of translation is to convey the meaning and style of the original language, but dictionary translations rarely reflect common language usage in a culture. Although thorough proficiency in both the source and target languages is important, translators need to translate not only to a target language, but to a target culture as well.[59] Translators also need to deal with nuances and with words that have no equivalents in other languages. In English, there is a distinction between the words *taboo* and *sin*. Among the Senoufo people of Africa, there is only one term for both of these concepts: *kapini taboo*. But, the taboos included in the Senoufo term are such things as a man seeing his wife sewing or a man whistling in a field unless he is resting. The Senoufo emotional attitude toward breaking these taboos is akin to the Christian attitude of sin, but the behaviors are quite different. Among the Senoufo, things considered sinful by Christians such as adultery, lying, or stealing are called *silegebafeebi* or "without-shame-people."[60] Additionally, Reeves points out that there are many terms that appear to be universal, but actually are not. Among these are such things as freedom, equality, democracy, independence, free enterprise, equal opportunity, and justice. He argues that in many cases there is no lexical equivalent to the connotative range implied by these terms.[61]

Idiomatic and Slang Equivalence

Idioms are "a number of words which, when taken together, mean something different from the individual words of the idiom when they stand alone."[62] Many idiomatic phrases come from everyday life or reflect food and cooking and include such expressions as *to make a clean sweep of something, to hit the nail on the head, to eat humble pie*, or *out of the frying pan and into the fire*. Idiomatic expressions are culture-bound; they do not translate well. The English phrase "The spirit is willing but the flesh is weak," for instance has been translated into Russian as "The Vodka is good but the meat is rotten." Also, the English slogan "Things come alive with Pepsi" has been translated into German as "Pepsi can pull you back from your grave." Or, consider this example of an Italian idiom translated into English: *"Giovanni sta memando il cane per l'aia."* Translated literally, this is "John is leading his dog around the threshing floor." A better translation, with greater correspondence of meaning, is "John is beating around the bush."[63] Coming up with the second translation thus requires that the translator be familiar with American idioms. As another example, imagine attempting to translate the sports-influenced statement "I don't want to be a Monday-morning quarterback, but . . ." or "the whole nine yards" into the language of a culture that does not have or understand the sport of American football.

Grammatical-Syntactical Equivalence

Difficulties may also arise when there are no equivalent parts of speech. We discussed many of these earlier in the chapter, but a few more examples will amplify our point. The Urdu language, for instance, has no gerunds, so it is difficult to find an equivalent for one. In the Filipino language, there is no equivalent of the verb *to be*. No relative pronouns in Korean are comparable to the English *who, which, that,* or *what.* "In Japanese, there is no parallel for the distinctions made in English between modifiers of nouns that are 'countable' (such as marbles, days, or flavors), and modifiers of nouns that are 'uncountable' (such as sugar, advice, or money)."[64] As a result, Japanese translations may render statements like "much shoes" or "many patience." In addition the gender of nouns is difficult in translation because the gender may vary by culture or language. *Di sonne* in German is feminine, but *le soleil* in French is masculine. Both words refer to the same object—the sun—but have different gender attachments. And, in English, nouns have no gender designation.[65]

Experiential-Cultural Equivalence

Translators must grapple not only with structural differences between languages but also with cultural differences, which requires precision and the ability to convey the speaker's or author's approach or attitude. As Tymoczko reminds us, "All meaning is relative to the speaker and the situation in which the words are spoken or written."[66] Also, translators need to consider shared experiences. *Peace* and *war* have various meanings for peoples of the world, depending on their conditions, time, and place. The meanings that cultures have for words are based on shared experiences, and the ability of a word to convey or elicit meaning depends on the culturally informed perceptions of both source and receiver.

When we lack cultural equivalents, we lack the words in our vocabulary to represent those experiences. For instance, when the vocabulary of a tribe in a mountainous jungle region has words for rivers and streams but not oceans, how do you translate the notion of an ocean? Or what does a translator do when she or he is faced with the task of translating the biblical verse "Though your sins be as scarlet, they shall be as white as snow" into the language of a tribe that has never experienced snow?

Translations frequently produce misunderstanding or incomprehension because of cultural orientations. For instance, the Quechua language of Peru uses past and future orientations that are the opposite of those used in the English language. Quechua visualizes the past as being in front of or ahead of a person because it can be seen, and it visualizes the future as being behind one because it cannot be seen. Americans instead speak of the past being behind them and the future being ahead. If this difference in cultural orientation were not known or were ignored, translations about time, the past, and the future could be incomprehensible. People could be told to look behind them for what they normally expect to find ahead of them.

Conceptual Equivalence

Another difficulty in translation lies in matching concepts. Some concepts are culture-specific (emic) and others culture-general (etic). By definition, it is impossible to translate perfectly an emic concept.[67] So different, for instance, are Spanish cultural experiences from the English that many words cannot be translated directly. Strong affection is expressed in English with the verb *to love*. In Spanish, there are two verbs, *te amo* and *te quiero*. *Te amo* refers to nurturing love, as between a parent and a child or between two adults. *Te quiero* translates literally as *I want you*, which connotes ownership, a concept not present in the English expression *I love you*. Commonly used to express love between two adults, *te quiero* falls somewhere between the English statements *I love you* and *I like you*.

The Spanish language as spoken in Mexico has at least five terms indicating agreement in varying degrees. These include *me comprometo* (I promise or commit myself), *yo le aseguro* (I assure you), *si, como no, lo hago* (yes, sure, I will do it), *tal vez lo hago* (maybe I will do it), and *tal vez lo haga* (maybe I might do it). The problem, of course, is to understand the differences between *me comprometo* and *tal vez lo haga* in their cultural sense so that one can render a correct translation. Misunderstandings and confusions may arise if we simply translate each of these phrases of agreement as "okay." About the only way in which an emic concept can be translated is to attempt to relate it to an etic one and to tie it to the context in which the concept might be used.[68] Now that we have discussed some of the equivalence problems inherent in language translation, we will consider how to increase understanding when working with a translator

Working with a Translator

Proper use of an interpreter can enhance your ability to communicate with people of other cultures, but misuse can have serious consequences. A good interpreter needs special, highly developed skills. "Translation, as every translator learns quickly, is not just a matter of imitation, or finding our words to imitate their words, but it is also the re-creation of the context of the foreign text."[69] He or she must be able to translate a message so that others hear it as though it were the original message. This means that the interpreter must be skilled in more than vocabulary. A translator is responsible for taking several factors into account. These include culture, context, and audience. Additionally, translators must be sensitive to the nuances of words in both the source and target languages and sensitive to the style, tone, and purpose of the speaker.[70] She or he must also know the word's emotive aspects, as well as the culture's thought processes and communication techniques. In certain situations, interpreters should include and communicate possible meanings of cues such as body posture, gestures, movement, and other devices. Finally, Reeves recommends that if you want to maintain the intention of the sender of the message, you can "attempt by means of commentary, notes and explanatory renderings to reveal those underlying values."[71]

Improving Translation

There are a number of things translators can do to improve the quality of their translations. Clemmens suggests that the starting point is respect for individual cultures and appreciation of what they are, not what we think they should be.[72] Setton recommends that a translator have a wide base of knowledge of a number of things if translation is to be accurate. Among these are current world and local events, the writer or speaker, the audience, the setting in which the communication takes place, and, of course, the subject of discussion.[73]

Among the many factors one should consider when translating are: (1) history of the culture, (2) social and political institutions (3) message genre and accompanying vocabulary, and (4) the intentions of the sender and the translator.[74] The following example makes this point. In a courtroom, an interpreter was interpreting for a Latin American defendant, and the judge asked the defendant his name. He answered "Jose Manuel Gomez Perez-Marin." The judge asked, "Why do you have so many last names? The defendant answered, "They are my first last name and my second last name." Instead of interpreting word for word, the interpreter drew on her background knowledge of Latin culture in which individuals often carry their father's and their mother's last names. She interpreted to the judge, "They are my father's last name and my mother's last name." By accessing her cultural knowledge, the interpreter not only avoided a lengthy interrogation but also avoided creating an impression of the defendant as a criminal who used several aliases to cover his identity.[75]

Effective Use of an Interpreter

The effective use of an interpreter requires the establishment of a three-way rapport: between the speaker and the interpreter, between the speaker and the audience; and between the interpreter and the audience. This is an extremely difficult state to attain because of the complexity of translation in "real time." Consider what an interpreter must do simultaneously. When the speaker says a phrase, the interpreter must listen to that phrase. While the speaker says the next phrase, the interpreter must not only be translating the first phrase, but also listening to the second phrase. Then, while the speaker is saying the third phrase, the interpreter must be storing in his or her memory the first, interpreting the second, and listening to the third. This procedure goes on and on throughout the process of message delivery, but "because the speaker doesn't stop to let the interpreter do all this, the interpreter must listen, process, and store *incoming* information while processing and delivering the *previous* information."[76]

Selecting an Interpreter

If you are selecting an interpreter, you should look for the following qualities or qualifications. The first is compatibility. You need someone with whom you are comfortable, a translator who is neither domineering nor timid. The second is ethnic compatibility. You need a translator who is, or is very close to, the same tribe, religious group, or ethnic background as the people for whom he or she will be translating. The third is knowledge of dialect. Your translator should speak the same dialect as the people for whom he or she will be translating. And the last is specialized knowledge of your field and its terminology.

Facilitating Translation

When using an interpreter, you can do several things to facilitate this complex process. Before the meeting or presentation, brief him or her on its tone, substance, and purpose. Review any technical terms that will be used. Ask the interpreter to brief you on any cultural differences in eye contact or other nonverbal behaviors that may be important to your presentation. Ask about local customs pertinent to your presentation, such as appropriate time of day for the presentation and your audience's concepts of time. Ask about unwritten rules of conversation. In Muslim countries, for instance, it is considered impolite to ask a man about his wife or wives. During the presentation, speak slowly enough for the interpreter to understand and follow you. Speak in relatively short sentences, pause often, and look at the audience while you speak, not at the interpreter. Prepare yourself to give greetings and farewells in the other language, and refrain from using profanity, obscenities, slang, regional dialect, acronyms, jargon, and colloquialisms. At the end of your presentation, recap the major points and clear up any ambiguities.

Because of the increasing mobility of people around the world and because of continued immigration to the United States, there will always be a segment of the population that does not speak English. The need for qualified interpreters continues to rise. When you work with an interpreter, you should remember the complexity involved in translating one language into another as well as things you can do to make the interaction smoother.

LANGUAGE DIVERSITY IN THE UNITED STATES

Language diversity has become a prominent issue in the United States. "At least 38 million people in the United States speak a language other than English at home."[77] And, over 3 million students in the United States speak little or no English. Spanish is the native language of 70 percent of these students followed by Asian languages constituting 15 percent.[78] Such diversity in language has spurred change and adaptation in linguistic usage. There are numerous instances that demonstrate this adaptation process. For example, on the U.S.–Mexico border, Spanish is laced with English-sounding words, yielding a dialect known as "Spanglish." In English, we say *to choose*. In Spanish, the equivalent word is *escoger*, and the Spanglish rendition is *chusar*. Even within the English language itself, there are adaptations and variations between British English and American English. For example, Canada has its own distinct usage that combines both U.S. and British English.

Because of its prominence, language diversity has become a controversial issue in the United States. Politicians at all levels of government continue to propose specific legislation to make English the official language of the United States. While we do not endorse proposals to make English an official language, we do believe, as Brown points out, that knowledge of English and the ability to communicate in English are essential in American society. The "inability to speak the language of the community in which one lives is the first step towards misunderstanding, for prejudice thrives on lack of communication."[79] The obvious solution to this issue is to ensure that all people have access to suitable English language learning and yet be free to preserve their native cultures and languages as they desire.

In the upcoming section, we examine the notion that people living within the same geographic boundaries often use language in ways that differ from those of the dominant culture. Specifically, we explore two facets of this idea. First, we will discuss alternative languages—private languages used by subgroups in the United States. Second, we will discuss co-cultures, specifically African Americans and women, and their language usage in the United States.

Alternative Languages

The use of alternative languages reflects a co-culture's need to have a language that permits individuals to share membership, participate in their social and cultural communities, identify themselves and their place in the universe, and communicate with one another about their own social realities. Because alternative languages are usually limited to a particular co-culture, one way to gain insight into that co-culture is to examine its use of language and vocabulary. The rationale is a simple one: Because "vocabulary is a part of language that is most immediately under the conscious manipulation and control of its users, it provides the most accessible place to begin exploration of shared and disparate experiences."[80] To help you better understand the uses and functions of alternative languages, we will (1) examine the types of alternative languages most commonly found in the United States and (2) discuss the functions alternative languages perform within the larger cultural setting.

Types of Alternative Languages

Alternative languages consist of at least four varieties: *cant*, *jargon*, *argot*, and *slang*. These language forms persist and thrive because they serve useful societal functions.

Cant. This is a specialized vocabulary of some disreputable or underworld co-culture. It is the language of pickpockets, murderers, drug dealers, and prostitutes. It includes such expressions as *college* (meaning prison), *stretch* (meaning a jail sentence), *to mouse* (meaning to escape from prison), and *lifeboat* (a pardon). Prostitutes frequently use the word *gorilla* to indicate someone who beats them up and *outlaw* to designate a prostitute who works without a pimp.

Jargon. Jargon is the technical language of a professional class such as nuclear physicists, physicians, lawyers, economists, and carpenters. Terms such as *gluons*, *quarks*, *inflationary spiral*, *party of the first part*, and *cripple wall* are examples of such professional jargon.

Argot. This is a more or less private vocabulary peculiar to many nonprofessional (usually noncriminal) groups such as taxi drivers, truck drivers, ham radio operators, military personnel, and circus and carnival workers. Argot used by truck drivers might include *smoky* to represent the highway patrol. Ham radio operators use terms such as *QSL* to represent a radio conversation, *old man* and *Y L* (young lady) to represent male and female ham radio operators, and *QRM* to designate static or other radio interference. And, circus and carnival workers frequently use terms such as *dip* for a pickpocket and *monkey* for someone who gets fleeced in a confidence game.

Slang. Slang designates those terms derived from cant and argot that are understood by most people but not often used in normal society or in formal written communication. Slang involves such linguistic terms as *booze* for alcohol, *broad* for woman, *stud* for man, *phat* for good, *random* for completely off the wall, *hoopty* for a car, *joints* for any popular brand of sneakers, and *bytebonding* for computer nerds who are discussing things no one else can understand.[81]

One major difference between an alternative language and a foreign language lies in the relationship between sounds and meanings. In a foreign language, the sounds are different, but the referents are often the same. In English, the sound of the thing we sit at to eat dinner is *table*; in Spanish, it is *mesa*. In other words, the sounds are different, but the table is still a table. In an alternative language, the sounds remain the same, but the meanings change. Simple words may have multiple meanings unique to the co-cultural reality. The word *pot*, for instance, may refer to the pot you smoke, the pot that hangs over your belt, or the pot in which you cook your dinner. The sound remains the same, but the meanings differ significantly. Another major difference between a sublanguage and a mainstream language is the cultural reference. One can assume specific cultural identifications when referring to dominant languages such as English, Spanish, French, German, Chinese, Tagalog, Japanese, and Arabic. Here, the name of the language suggests its culture. But when we examine an alternative language, we find that it does not refer to a specific dominant culture but to specific co-culturess.

Functions of Alternative Languages

Alternative languages reveal another way in which language and behavior are linked together. They can serve a variety of functions for co-cultures. Although we discuss four of the most prominent, keep in mind that the alternative language of a specific co-culture may serve only one or two of these functions, not necessarily all four.

Empowerment. Alternative languages can function as a form of empowerment. *Nushu* is a 3,000-year-old language used exclusively by Chinese women. "Ancient Chinese women were barred from formal education and were treated as illiterate and unthinking by men. So women of this region empowered themselves by creating their own language which uses a different set of characters."[82] *Nushu* empowered women by giving them a way to detail their private lives on a personal basis. It was used as a powerful source of support between women "who were bound as property to their husbands, bound to Draconian cultural roles, and cripplingly bound about their feet."[83]

Self-Defense. Alternative languages help in developing a sense of self-defense by providing a code that helps the co-culture survive in a hostile environment.[84] The use of Yiddish by the European Jews during periods of harsh discrimination is an obvious example. There are, however, even more subtle and contemporary instances. Prostitutes, because they engage in an illegal profession, use language for concealment. They must not only conceal the sexual acts themselves, but camouflage discussion of the acts to avoid arrest. Cant serves this purpose. The following might be a typical comment from a pimp to a prostitute. "I have a steak if you're interested. I tried for some lobster but couldn't get it." A *steak* is a client who will pay $50 to be with the prostitute; a $75 client is often called *roast beef*; someone willing to pay $150 is a *lobster*; and a $300 client is labeled *champagne*.[85] In instances such as these, sub-languages are also a cultural storehouse for the hostility the users feel toward the dominant culture. It permits the expression of frustration and hatred without risk of reprisal.

Solidarity and Cohesiveness. Gangs have become prominent as co-cultures in the past several years because of the violence associated with their drug dealing and territoriality. *Buster* refers to a gang member who does not stand up for his gang, but sells them out. A *claim* is the area that gang members have staked out as their own. If persons are asked what they claim, they are being asked to which gang they belong. A *wannabe* is a person who pretends or wants to be a member of a gang but has not been accepted by it. *Crippin'*, a word that members of the Crips gang use, means to survive any way you can. *Drive-bys* is an abbreviation for drive-by shootings. Gangs frequently use drive-bys to frighten rival gang members or to exact revenge. *Flashing signs* refers to using hand signals to communicate with other gang members. A sign may signify membership in a particular gang or be a signal that some gang activity is in progress. *Gang bangin'* means participating in any kind of gang activity, ranging from hanging out to dealing drugs or being involved in drive-bys. A *homegirl* is a young woman who hangs out with gang members. *Jump in* is the initiation process whereby a claimer fights members of the gang to which he desires to belong. *Pancake* designates a person who has become a homosexual as a result of his experience in jail, and *strawberry* refers to a female who exchanges sexual favors for drugs.

Social Viability. Alternative languages help establish groups as real and viable social entities. During the 1960s, for example, when drug use became a way of life, people gathered at specific locations and immediately developed what became known as *drug language*. As these individuals became more than a group of people simply taking drugs, they developed a rather elaborate glossary of terms that helped transform them into a

A culture's use of language often contributes to group solidarity and cohesiveness.

counterculture. Some of their terms were *Bernice* for cocaine, *hay* for marijuana, *heat* for police, *pipe* for a large vein, *roach* for the butt of a marijuana cigarette, *octagon* for a square person, *lightening* for inducing a drugged state, and *head* for a heavy drug user.

We conclude our examination of alternative languages by issuing two caveats. First, there is a great deal of overlap between sub-languages. This does not negate the notion that sub-languages are a community's unique language. Instead, it means that an individual may be a member of several co-cultures simultaneously. For instance, a person may be a poor, drug-using, gay prostitute who is in prison. Another person might be a convicted white, drug-using armed robber serving a prison term. Second, we must remember that sub-langues change. As the dominant culture learns words or phrases in the code, the co-culture will usually eliminate the word or phrase. Hence, many of the examples we have cited are no longer used by the co-cultures from which they came. It is not a particular word that is significant, but rather the idea that sub-languages offer us valuable insight into the experiences of these groups—experiences to which many of us might not have access.

Co-Cultures and Language Use

When discussing the Sapir-Whorf hypothesis, we indicated that language is a guide to dealing with and understanding social reality. From this notion comes the corollary idea that cultures evolve different languages unique to their own needs. As Nanda and Warms point out:

> All human groups have language and all languages are equally sophisticated and serve the needs of their speakers equally well. A language cannot make its speakers more or less intelligent, sexist, sophisticated, or anything else. Individual knowledge of vocabulary may vary, as may the artfulness with which an individual communicates, but every human speaks with equal grammatical sophistication."[86]

Co-cultures exist within nearly every society, but, as we indicate in Chapter 2, they function both within and outside of the dominant culture. Members of most co-cultures operate in two or more very distinct groups. Hence, their enculturation can be strikingly different from that of the dominant culture. Their process of language evolution tends to be shaped by the dominant culture's attitudes toward them. In many co-cultures, the name given to an experience clearly demonstrates how they perceive and interact with the dominant culture. Through the examination of a co-culture's language, you can learn a great deal about that group's experiences, values, and behaviors. To facilitate this form of understanding, we will examine the unique language behaviors of the African American and women's co-cultures in the United States.

African Americans

There is little question that many African Americans and whites speak differently creating different speech communities. According to Shade,

> These communities employ different varieties of speech, follow different rules for interaction, possess different core cultural elements that influence white and black communication behaviors, and possess different world views which accounts for the differences in communication and the way blacks and whites process and interpret messages.[87]

African Americans have evolved a particular language referred to as African American English Vernacular (AAEV) which allows them to create, maintain, and express their culture and to deal with European America.[88] African American English reflects African roots[89] and the adjustment of the African people to American slavery. It has been passed on from generation to generation through socialization.[90] African American English involves much more than a vocabulary shift or the rhymed and accented lyrics of a rap artist. It is a distinctive language form with a unique syntax, semantic system, grammar, and rhythm. The grammar rules differ in many ways and form a logical system that is independent of mainstream English. African American English contains a variety of terms denoting different ways of talking that depend on the social context. Its own style and function characterize each manner of speaking. But, you must remember as Nanda and Warms suggest, that African American English "is in no way linguistically inferior. Like every other language, it is fully systematic, grammatical, symbolic, and certainly no barrier to abstract thought."[91]

Hecht, Collier, and Ribeau point out that sentence structure and semantics in African American English have been particularly influenced by early African tribal languages.[92] This has led to the development of a language style that has a number of unique identifiable characteristics. Some of these characteristics are outlined below.

1. Shortening of the third-person present tense by dropping the *s:* "He walk," "She go," "He talk."[93, 94]
2. Use of the verb *to be* to indicate continuous action: "He be gone" for He is gone frequently/all the time.[95]
3. Deletion of the verb *to be* in the present indicative: "He tired" for He is tired.[96]
4. Use of *been* to express a meaning of past activity with current relevance: "I been know your name."[97]
5. Use of a stressed *been* to emphasize the duration of something: "He been married" for "He has been married for a long time (and still is)."[98]
6. Use of *done* or *be done* to emphasize an action that has been completed: "She done finished the book," "We be done washed all those cars soon."[99, 100]

7. Use of double and triple negatives: "Won't nobody do nothing about that," "He ain't got no money."[101, 102]
8. Simplification of consonants at the ends of words: "door" becomes "do."[103]
9. The final *ng* sound drops the *g*: "talking" becomes "talkin."[104]
10. The final *th* is sometimes replaced with *f*: "with" becomes "wif."[105]
11. Substitution of the *x* sound for the *s* sound: "ask" becomes "axe."

African American street language also uses several different lexical forms. These include syllabic contractions, as in *supoze* for *suppose*; the fore-stressing of bisyllabic words, as in *po-lice* for *police*; and hypercorrection, as in *pickted* for *picked*.[106] African American English is also very rhythmic. "It flows like African languages in a consonant-vowel-consonant-vowel pattern."[107] This rhythm is often achieved by holding some syllables longer or giving them a stronger accent than in standard American English.

African American English is a vivid and imaginative language that seeks to generate movement and power within its listeners. This is clearly evident in what is referred to as the "call and response." This is an interactive play between the speaker and the listener in which the listener's responses are just as important as the speaker's comments. For example, listeners may respond to a message with encouraging remarks such as *"all right," "make it plain,"* and *"that all right."* These responses make the speaker successful.[108]

Although there is a mixture of cultures and classes in the United States, the most powerful group generally determines what is "proper" English. Thus, mainstream American English is the norm for communication. As with any nonstandard dialect, the dominant culture tends to stigmatize its users and afford them less status. African Americans have developed several strategies or ways of dealing with the stigma attached to African American English by the dominant culture. These include language mobility and code-switching, which is the situational changing between African American English and mainstream American English language groups.[109] Many African Americans prefer style switching and associate the selective adoption of mainstream American English with being educated and professional. In casual settings among other African Americans or with familiar European Americans, African American English and slang may be used to communicate experience and feelings, to create cultural identity and bonds, and even to make a political statement that African Americans have not given up their language.[110] As Garner and Rubin point out, both language systems are important for linguistic competency. Individuals who do not know when and in what context to use mainstream American English rather than slang or street vernacular are held in less regard and viewed as uneducated by both African Americans and European Americans.[111]

Women

In speaking of communication between men and women, Tannen notes, "Different words, different worlds." Communication for women has different purposes and rules than communication for men.[112] "Females put a greater and different emphasis on conversation."[113] In a general sense, it is safe to say that women and men constitute two linguistic groups.

We begin our exploration of female communication by identifying the purpose of communication for women. For most women, communication is a primary way to establish and maintain relationships with others.[114] Wood identified seven features of women's communication that foster connections, support, closeness, and understanding.[115] First, equality is an important feature of female communication. Women achieve symmetry and equality by matching experiences. For instance, a woman may say, "I've done the same thing many times." This establishes equality in the sense that the speaker is not alone in how he or she feels. This creates an interactive pattern in conversations rather than rigid turn taking.

Second, showing support for others is characteristic of women's speech. Phrases like, "Oh, you must feel terrible" and "I think you did the right thing" demonstrate understanding and sympathy.[116]

Third and closely related to the feature of understanding and sympathy is the presence of questions that probe for greater understanding of feelings. Questions such as, "How did you feel when it occurred?" and "Do you think it was deliberate?" address content while paying serious attention to the feelings involved.[117]

Fourth, women's speech is characterized by conversational maintenance work.[118] That is, women engage in efforts to sustain the conversation by prompting others to speak or elaborate, and by initiating topics for others. Phrases like, "Tell me about your day," or "Was your faculty meeting interesting?" serve to initiate and maintain interaction.

Responsiveness is a fifth feature of women's talk. Females are usually socialized to care about others and to make them feel valued. As such, they usually respond to what others have said. A woman might say, "That's interesting," or she might nod to show she is actively engaged in the conversation.[119]

A sixth characteristic of women's talk is a personal and concrete style. Interpersonal closeness is created by the use of "details, personal disclosures, anecdotes, and concrete reasoning."[120] This personal tone in women's conversation cultivates connection and identification so that communicators' feelings are emphasized and clarified.

Finally, tentativeness has been identified as a feature of women's communication. Tentativeness can take a number of forms. Verbal hedges are phrases like *I think, I believe, I feel, I guess, I mean,* and *I wonder.*[121] Qualifying terms include words like *well, you know, kind of, perhaps,* and *possibly.* An example of a qualifying statement is "I am probably not the best judge of this, but . . ." Intonation also indicates tentativeness. For example, when a woman is asked, "What is the organizational plan for the new chapter?" she might respond by saying, "An introduction and then the four basic assignments?" The intonation turns the answer into a question, as if to say, "Is that okay with you?"[122] Tag questions also serve to keep the conversation provisional. "That was a pretty good movie, don't you think?" leaves the door open for further conversation.

Much controversy exists about the purpose of tentativeness in women's speech. Prior research claimed that these tentative communication devices were inferior and represented a lack of confidence, uncertainty, and low self-esteem. Others have called this speech powerless, a reflection of women's socialization into subordinate roles.[123] Although there may be some validity to these assertions, more recent research indicates that there may be several different explanations for women's tentative speech.[124] As evidenced by the seven features identified by Wood, this tentative communication, rather than reflecting powerlessness and inferiority, may instead "express women's desires to keep conversation open and include others."[125] Other researchers have found women's use of tentative communication to be context based. Although some women may use servile, submissive, or polite tentative communication, these traits are often a stereotype of how women talk and not the way they actually do talk. Instead, the way they communicate is heavily influenced by the context. For example, women may use more tentative communication when in the presence of men, but less in the presence of women. A board meeting may be conducive to tentative communication in order to establish camaraderie, but the courtroom may not. One study even found that men were just as likely to use tentative communication as women depending on the context.[126] As a result, it is a good idea to consider the context before stereotypically putting a negative label on women's tentative communication.

These features of female communication stand in sharp contrast to features of male communication. For most men, the primary purpose of communication is to exert control, preserve independence, and enhance status.[127] Wood identified five tenets of masculine speech. First, it focuses on an instrumental activity and does not acknowledge feelings. This usually involves problem-solving efforts, data collection, and solution suggestions. Content, rather than feelings, is emphasized. "Second, it expresses superiority and maintains control."[128] Despite jokes about women's talkativeness, men usually have conversational dominance. They talk more and for longer periods.[129] They reroute conversations for their own benefit and interrupt as a controlling or challenging device.[130] Third, men assert themselves in absolute ways. Their language is usually forceful and direct with infrequent use of tentative communication. Fourth, men tend to speak in abstract terms that are general and removed from personal experiences.[131] Finally, men's conversation tends not to be very responsive. Sympathy, understanding, and self-disclosure are rarely expressed because the rules of men's speech dictate that these responses are condescending and make one vulnerable.[132]

In summary, women are primarily concerned with personal relationships when they communicate, but men are concerned only with getting the job done. Whereas women wish to include everyone, men seek to establish their own status. Women's concrete terminology often clashes with the abstract nature of men's verbiage. Whereas women may engage in tentative speech, men's speech is characteristically assertive. Women's communication is decidedly responsive, while men's communication is distinctly unresponsive. It is easy to see how the different rules and features of women's and men's speech create the potential for misunderstanding and conflict between women and men.

SUMMARY

- Language is important to human activity because it is how we reach out to make contact with others.
- Language permits us to remember the past, deal with the present, and anticipate and plan for the future.
- Language functions to facilitate emotive expression, thought, social interaction, the control of reality, the maintenance of history, and the expression of identity.
- It is impossible to separate our use of language from our culture.
- Language is a set of symbols and the rules for combining those symbols that are used and understood by a large community of people.
- Symbols (words) and sounds for those symbols vary from culture to culture. The rules (phonology, grammar, syntax, and intonation) for using those symbols and sounds also vary.
- Language serves as a guide to how a culture perceives reality.
- The meanings we have for words are determined by the culture in which we have been raised.
- Word usage and meaning are learned, and all cultures and co-cultures have special experiences that frame usage and meaning.

- Each of us learns and uses language as we do because of our cultural background.
- As the world evolves into a global village, the importance of international communication and language translation takes on added significance.
- People tend to assume that text in one language can be accurately translated into another.
- Translation is often problematic because there are difficulties in linguistic equivalence such as vocabulary, idiomatic, grammatical-syntactical, experiential-cultural, and conceptual equivalence.
- Interpreters must be skilled in understanding not only a language's vocabulary, but also emotive aspects, thought processes, and communication techniques.
- Language diversity has become a prominent issue in the United States.
- People living within the same geographical boundaries can also use language in ways that differ from the dominant culture.
- Alternative languages are a private vocabulary that members of a co-culture share.
- Examining alternative languages helps gain insight into a co-culture and its social realities.
- African Americans have a distinct language known as African American English Vernacular, which facilitates the creation, maintenance, and expression of their unique culture.
- Women's communication patterns and practices differ in form and substance from those of men.

INFOTRAC® COLLEGE EDITION EXERCISES

1. This chapter discusses the Sapir-Whorf hypothesis, the theory that a particular language may influence an individual's ways of thinking and seeing. Using the subject search term "linguistic relativity," locate and read the article "A Cross-Cultural Study of English and Setswana Speakers on a Colour Triads Task: A Test of the Sapir-Whorf Hypothesis." According to the experiment reported in the article, what is the influence of language on color perception? (Hint: For more articles on the subject of the Sapir-Whorf hypothesis, use the subject search term "Anthropological Linguistics.")

2. Using the subject search term "Business Letters," locate and read the article "Dear Friend" (?): Culture and Genre in American and Canadian Direct Marketing Letters." According to this article, what are the key ways in which public communication and letter writing differ between Americans and Canadians? What are the key ways in which Canadians need to be viewed as different from American audiences? (You may wish to browse other articles identified by this subject search such as "Foreign Exchange: The Rules for Global Business Writing" or "Korean Business Letters: Strategies for Effective Complaints in Cross-Cultural Communications." If you are interested in reading more on the subject of translation, use the subject search term "Translating and Interpreting".)

ACTIVITIES

1. Ask an informant whose native language is not English for examples of expressions from his or her native language that are difficult to translate into English. Idioms are the most likely category in which to find examples. Try to determine why the difficulty exists. What cultural values might these expressions represent?

2. Try to think of examples where the alternative language of co-cultures reflects their unique experiences, values, and lifestyles.

3. Visit a class in which English is taught as a second language. Try to distinguish what difficulties the students are experiencing and which, if any, are culturally based.

DISCUSSION IDEAS

1. What problems are associated with language diversity in a country? What are some of the solutions that have been proposed to deal with these problems? Draw examples from the United States and Canada, as well as from any other bilingual or trilingual countries with which you are familiar.

2. What is meant by the phrase "language influences our perceptions and our view of the universe"?

3. Why is foreign language translation so difficult? Try and think of ways in which translation difficulty can be minimized.

4. How can men and women in the United States learn to communicate better with one another?

chapter 6

Nonverbal Communication: The Messages of Action, Space, Time, and Silence

Do not the most moving moments of our lives find us all without words?

MARCEL MARCEAU

In human intercourse the tragedy begins not when there is misunderstanding about words, but when silence is not understood.

HENRY DAVID THOREAU

In the United States people greet by shaking hands. Arab men often greet by kissing on both checks. In Japan, men greet by bowing, and in Mexico they often embrace. Touching one's ear is protection against the evil eye in Turkey. In southern Italy, it denotes jeering at effeminacy, and in India, it is a sign of repentance or sincerity. In most Middle and Far Eastern countries, pointing with the index finger is considered impolite. In Thailand, to signal another person to come near, one moves the fingers back and forth with the palm down. In the United States, you beckon someone to come by holding the palm up and moving the fingers toward your body. In Vietnam that same motion is reserved for someone attempting to summon their dog. The Tongans sit down in the presence of superiors; in the West, you stand up. Crossing one's legs in the United States is often a sign of being relaxed; in Korea, it is a social taboo. In Japan, gifts are usually exchanged with both hands. Muslims consider the left hand unclean and do not eat or pass objects with it. Buddha maintained that great insights arrived during moments of silence. In the United States, people talk to arrive at the truth.

The above examples were offered for two reasons. First, we hoped to arouse your interest in nonverbal communication. Second, we wanted to demonstrate that although much of nonverbal communication is universal, many of your nonverbal actions are touched and altered by culture. Hence, this chapter looks at the various ways culture and nonverbal communication work in tandem.

THE IMPORTANCE OF NONVERBAL COMMUNICATION

To appreciate the importance of nonverbal communication to human interaction, reflect for a moment on the countless times in a single day that you send and receive nonverbal messages when in the presence of other people. Barnlund highlights some of the reasons why this form of communication is important to the study of intercultural communication:

> Many, and sometimes most, of the critical meanings generated in human encounters are elicited by touch, glance, vocal nuance, gestures, or facial expression with or without the aid of words. From the moment of recognition until the moment of separation, people observe each other with all their senses, hearing pause and intonation, attending to dress and carriage, observing glance and facial tension, as well as noting word choice and syntax. Every harmony or disharmony of signals guides the interpretation of passing mood or enduring attribute. Out of the evaluation of kinetic, vocal and verbal cues, decisions are made to argue or agree, to laugh or blush, to relax or resist, to continue or cut off conversation.[1]

Judging Internal States

Barnlund is stating that consciously and unconsciously, intentionally and unintentionally, people make important judgments and decisions concerning the internal states of others—states they often express without words. For example, you evaluate the quality of your relationships according to interpretations of these nonverbal messages. Nonverbal communication is a powerful tool for expressing your emotional and relational feelings toward another person.[2] From tone of voice, to the distance between you and your partners, to the amount of touching in which you engage, you can gather clues to the closeness of your relationships. Nonverbal communication is so subtle that a shifting of body zones can also send a message. The first time you move from holding hands with your partner to touching his or her face, you are sending a message, and that message takes on added significance if your touch is returned.

If you observe someone with a clenched fist and a grim expression, you do not need words to tell you that this person is not happy. If you hear someone's voice quaver and see his or her hands tremble, you may infer that the person is fearful or anxious, despite what he or she might say. Your emotions are reflected in your posture, face, and eyes—be it fear, joy, anger, or sadness—so you can express them without ever uttering a word. For this reason, most people rely heavily on what they learn through their eyes. In fact, research indicates that you will believe nonverbal messages instead of verbal messages when the two contradict each other.[3] As Heraclitus remarked over two thousand years ago, "Eyes are more accurate witnesses than ears."

First Impressions

Nonverbal communication is important in human interaction because it is usually responsible for first impressions. In fact, in most instances nonverbal messages arrive before the verbal. Think for a moment of how often your first judgments are based on the color of a person's skin, facial expression, manner of dress, or if he or she is in a wheelchair. More importantly, those initial messages usually influence the perception of everything else that follows. Even how you select friends and sexual partners is grounded in first impressions. You often approach certain people because of how attractive you find them, and of course, avoid others because of some rapid decision you made concerning their appearance.

Subconscious Actions

Nonverbal communication has value in human interaction because many of your nonverbal actions are not easily controlled consciously. Occasionally you may say something for which you are sorry and have to quickly offer an apology, but usually some degree of control is seen in your selection of language. However, with nonverbal behavior your emotions are hard to control. It is difficult to control a blushing face when you are embarrassed, a clenched jaw when you are angry, or stammering speech when you are nervous. These behaviors, and countless others, are usually automatic and unconscious.

Culture-Bound

While much of your nonverbal communication is "part of a universally recognized and understood code,"[4] a great deal of your nonverbal behavior is rooted in your culture. As you shall see throughout this chapter, a culture's nonverbal language can be as unique as its verbal. From your use of eye contact to the amount of volume you employ during interaction, your culture influences the manner in which you send and receive nonverbal symbols. For example, in many cultures, outward signs of emotion are accepted as natural. People from the Middle East and the Mediterranean are generally expressive and animated. For the Japanese, excessive and public displays of emotion are often considered a mark of rudeness, a lack of control, and even an invasion of another person's privacy.[5]

What we have been trying to say in the last few pages is that learning about the alliance between culture and nonverbal behavior is useful to students of intercultural communication. By understanding important cultural differences in this behavior, you will be able to gather clues about underlying attitudes and values. You have already seen that nonverbal communication often reveals basic cultural traits. Smiling and shaking hands tells us that a culture values amiability. Bowing tells you that another values formality and rank and status. It is not by chance that Hindus greet each other by placing their palms together in front of them while slightly tilting their heads down; this salutation reflects the belief that the deity exists in everyone, not in a single form.

The study of nonverbal behaviors can assist you in isolating your own ethnocentrism. You might, for instance, feel less critical about someone's body odor if you realize that the meanings attached to smell are culturally based. As a way of identifying your own cultural patterns and biases, we begin our discussion of each category of nonverbal communication by noting some of the basic behaviors found in the dominant culture of the United States. Knowing what attitudes and behaviors Americans bring to a communication event can help you understand your response to the people you meet. As Anne Morrow Lindberg wrote, "When one is a stranger to oneself then one is estranged from others too."

DEFINING NONVERBAL COMMUNICATION

Because the central concern of this chapter is to examine how and why people communicate nonverbally, and with what consequences in the intercultural setting, we begin with a definition of nonverbal communication. As you discovered in earlier chapters, there is no shortage of definitions for culture and communication. The same proliferation is characteristic of the term *nonverbal behavior*. We shall, therefore, select a definition that is consistent with current thinking in the field and that reflects the cultural orientation of this book.

We propose that *nonverbal communication involves all those nonverbal stimuli in a communication setting that are generated by both the source and his or her use of the environment and that have potential message value for the source or receiver.* It is not by chance that our definition is somewhat lengthy: We wanted to offer a definition that would not only mark the boundaries of nonverbal communication, but would also reflect how the process actually works. Our definition also permits us to include unintentional as well as intentional behavior in the total communication event. This approach is realistic because you send the preponderance of nonverbal messages without ever being aware that they have meaning for other people. In verbal communication, you consciously dip into your vocabulary and decide what words to use. Although you often consciously decide to smile or select a certain piece of jewelry, you also send countless messages that you never intend to be part of the transaction: For example, frowning into the sun and making someone believe you are angry, leaving some shampoo in your hair and having someone think you look silly, and holding someone's hand for an extended period of time and having that person think you are flirting are all examples of how your actions, without your blessing, can send a message to someone else.

The sociologist Goffman describes this fusing of intentional and unintentional behavior:

> The expressiveness of the individual (and therefore his capacity to give impressions) appears to involve two radically different kinds of sign activity: the expression that he gives and the impression that he gives off. The first involves verbal symbols or their substitutes which he uses admittedly and solely to convey the information that he and the other are known to attach to these symbols. This is communication in the traditional and narrow sense. The second involves a wide range of action that others can treat as symptomatic of the actor (communicator), the expectation being that the action was performed for reasons other than the information conveyed in this way.[6]

FUNCTIONS OF NONVERBAL COMMUNICATION

One point should be clear by now: Nonverbal communication is multidimensional. That is to say, it involves a variety of messages that can be sent simultaneously. This multidimensional aspect is also seen in the fact that nonverbal communication often interacts with verbal messages. The interfacing of the verbal with the nonverbal carries over to the many uses and functions of nonverbal behavior.[7] Let us examine five of those uses: (1) repeating, (2) complementing, (3) substituting, (4) regulating, and (5) contradicting. It is important to note that initially we are describing the dominant culture in the United States. Later we discuss cultural differences in the use of nonverbal communication.

Repeating

In the United States, people often use nonverbal messages to repeat a point they are trying to make. If you were trying to tell someone that what they were proposing was a bad idea, you might move your head from side to side while you were also uttering the word "no." We might hold up our hand in the gesture that signifies a person to stop at the same time we actually use the word *stop*. Or we might point in a certain direction after we have just said, "The new library is south of that building." The gestures and words have a similar meaning and reinforce one another.

Complementing

Closely related to repeating is complementing. Although messages that repeat can stand alone, complementing generally adds more information to messages. For example, you can tell someone that you are pleased with his or her performance, but this message takes on extra meaning if you pat the person on the shoulder at the same time. Physical contact places another layer of meaning on what is being said. Many writers in the area of nonverbal communication refer to this as a type of accenting because it accents the idea the speaker is trying to make. You can see how an apology becomes more forceful if your face, as well as your words, is saying, "I'm sorry." You also can accent your anger by speaking in a voice that is much louder than the one you use in normal conversation.

Substituting

In the United States people substitute nonverbal communication when they perform some action instead of speaking. If you see a very special friend, you are apt to enlarge the size of your smile and throw open your arms to greet him or her, which is a substitute for all the words it would take to convey the same feeling. If a group of people is boisterous, you might place your index finger to your lips as an alternative to saying, "Please calm down so that I can speak." Or if you object to someone's behavior you might roll your eyes back as a way of "voicing" your disapproval.

Regulating

You often regulate and manage your communication by using some form of nonverbal behavior: you nod your head in agreement to indicate to your communication partner that you agree and that he or she should continue talking; or you remain silent for a moment and let the silence send the message that you are ready to begin to give the other person a chance to talk. A parent might engage in "stern" and direct eye contact with a child as a way of "telling" him or her to terminate the naughty behavior. In short, your nonverbal behavior helps you control the situation.

Contradicting

On some occasions, your nonverbal actions send signals opposite from the literal meanings contained in your verbal messages. You tell someone you are relaxed and at ease, yet your voice quavers and your hands shake. It also is a contradictory message when you inform your partner that you are glad to see him or her, but at the same time you are sulking and breaking eye contact. Because people rely mostly on nonverbal messages when they receive conflicting data, you need to be aware of the dangers inherent in sending opposing messages. As the German psychiatrist Sigmund Freud noted, "Though we may lie with our lips, betrayal oozes out of us at every pore."

NONVERBAL COMMUNICATION: GUIDELINES AND LIMITATIONS

Because nonverbal communication is complex, multifaceted, and often misunderstood, we need to pause before pursuing the topic of nonverbal communication in any more detail and mention some potential problems associated with this important area of study.

Nonverbal Communication Is Often Ambiguous

We alluded to the first problem in the study of nonverbal communication earlier when we discussed the intentional and unintentional nature of nonverbal communication. Ambiguity, however, and the problems it creates, is worthy of another discussion. Simply stated, *nonverbal communication can be ambiguous*. Wood clearly underscores this point when she writes, "We can never be sure that others understand the meanings we intended to express with our nonverbal behavior."[8] Not only are there cultural differences in what a specific action means (in the United States the number one is communicated with the forefinger, in parts of Europe it is the thumb that carries that message), but nonverbal communication is also contextual. The ambiguity of context is clearly seen if someone brushes your leg on an elevator—was it merely an accident or an aggressive sexual act? Our point should be obvious: When you use nonverbal communication you need to be aware of the ambiguous nature of this form of interaction. Or as Osborn and Motley tell us, "meanings and interpretations of nonverbal behaviors often are on very shaky ground."[9]

We Are More Than Our Culture

The next problem relates to individual differences. Simply stated, not all people engage in the same actions we will discuss in this chapter. You need to keep in mind both in this chapter and when you interact with people of cultures different from your own, that while there are generalizable cultural characteristics, *you are all more than your culture*. You might, for example, note that many Native American children avoid direct eye contact as a sign of respect; yet because of individual differences, there may well be exceptions to this assertion. We noted in Chapter 1 that people are the products of not only their culture, but also their regions, occupations, political affiliations, educational backgrounds, and countless other associations that have shaped their perceptions, values, attitudes, beliefs, *and* nonverbal communication.

Overstating Differences

Another potential hazard in studying nonverbal communication stems from the fact that we often are guilty of *making the differences more important than they really are*. It might make witty and clever cocktail party chatter to know that in the Sung Dynasty, tongue protrusion indicated mock terror and the tongue stretched far out showed surprise, but this idiosyncrasy does help you understand intercultural communication in the twenty-first century.

Nonverbal Communication Seldom Operates in Isolation

Finally, there is the problem of forgetting that *nonverbal behaviors seldom occur in isolation*. Although in the remainder of this chapter we examine individual messages, in reality these messages are but part of the total communication context. As we noted earlier, you usually send many nonverbal cues simultaneously, and these cues are normally linked to both our verbal messages and the setting in which you find yourself.

NONVERBAL COMMUNICATION AND CULTURE

It should be obvious by now that the study of nonverbal behavior is an important component to the study of intercultural communication. Hall highlights this importance:

> I am convinced that much of our difficulty with people in other countries stems from the fact that so little is known about cross-communication. . . . Formal training in the language, history, government, and customs of another nation is only the first step in a comprehensive program. Of equal importance is an introduction to the nonverbal language which exists in every country of the world and among the various groups within each country. Most Americans are only dimly aware of this silent language even though they use it everyday.[10]

The importance of nonverbal communication, and its significance to the study of intercultural communication, is made even more apparent if you recall from Chapter 2 that culture is invisible, omnipresent, and learned. Nonverbal communication has these same qualities. Hall alerts us to the invisible aspect of culture and nonverbal communication by employing phrases such as *silent language* and *hidden dimension*. Andersen makes much the same point by telling you that "Individuals are aware of little of their own nonverbal behavior, which is enacted mindlessly, spontaneously, and unconsciously."[11] Both of these scholars are saying that much of your nonverbal behavior, like culture, tends to be elusive, spontaneous, and frequently beyond your awareness.

We remind you that culture is all-pervasive, multidimensional, and boundless; it is everywhere and in everything. The same is true of nonverbal behavior.[12] Your clothes and jewelry, the countless expressions you can reflect with your face, the hundreds of movements you can make with your body, where and how you touch people, your gaze and eye contact, vocal behaviors such as laughter, and your use of time, space, and silence are just some of the behaviors in which you engage that serve as messages. Hence, as with culture, examples of nonverbal behavior are virtually limitless.

Another parallel between culture and nonverbal behavior is that both need to be learned. Although much of outward behavior is innate (such as smiling, moving, touching, eye contact), you are not born knowing the communication dimensions associated with nonverbal messages. First, a word about some exceptions to this notion before we develop this relationship between learning and nonverbal communication. Research supports the view that because people are all from one species, a general and common genetic inheritance produces universal facial expressions for most of your basic emotions (for example, fear, happiness, anger, surprise, disgust, and sadness).[13] Most scholars would agree however that "cultures formulate display rules that dictate when, how, and with what consequences nonverbal expressions will be exhibited."[14] Macionis summarized this important principle in the following manner:

> People the world over experience the same basic emotions. But what sparks a particular emotion, how and where a person expresses it, and how people define emotions in general vary as matters of culture. In global perspective, therefore, everyday life differs not only in terms of how people think and act, but how they infuse their lives with feelings.[15]

CLASSIFICATIONS OF NONVERBAL COMMUNICATION

Most classifications divide nonverbal messages into two comprehensive categories: those that are primarily produced by the body (appearance, movement, facial expressions, eye contact, touch, smell, and paralanguage); and those that the individual combines with the setting (space, time, and silence).

Body Behavior

General Appearance and Attire

From hair sprays to hairpieces, from reducing diets to twenty-four-hour fitness centers, from false eyelashes to blue contact lenses, people show their concern for how they look—and we support a multibillion-dollar industry in the process. And how do we

Much of the world's people still dress in their traditional attire.

© Robert Fonseca

calculate the price you pay in mental anguish over your personal appearance should you not quite measure up to the ideal the culture demands of you? It seems most of you believe the words of philosopher Thomas Fuller: "By the husk you may judge the nut." For most people in the United States, the husk should be flawless. Very early in life most people realize that outward appearances, as revealed in "our sex, clothing style, race, age, ethnicity, stature, body type, and mood all reveal our physical persona."[16] Reflect for a moment on how you make judgments of other people based on personal appearance, dress, and the objects people carry around or place on their bodies. Studies show that being overweight in the United States reduces income, lowers the chances of getting married, and helps decrease the amount of education one receives.[17] When deciding whether or not to strike up a conversation with a total stranger, you are influenced by the way that person looks. Ruben says we make inferences (often faulty) about a person's "intelligence, gender, age, approachability, financial well-being, class, tastes, values, and cultural background" from attractiveness, dress, and personal artifacts.[18] Your culture's obsession with attractiveness is so deep-seated, and begins so early in life, that, as one study revealed, even very young children select attractive friends over less attractive children.[19]

As we noted, defining racial group membership is also directly related to a person's appearance. By looking at a person you can almost immediately recognize their skin color and make judgments about that color. As Vazquez and others point out, "skin color is the first racial marker children recognize and can be considered the most salient of phenotypic attributes."[20] Skin color "may also be the basis of the allocation of economic and psychological privileges to individuals relative to the degree those privileges are awarded to valued members of the dominant culture."[21]

Appearance. Concern with how one appears is not confined to the United States. It is ancient and universal. As far back as the Upper Paleolithic period (about forty thousand years ago), your ancestors were using bone for necklaces and other bodily ornaments. From that period to the present, historical and archaeological evidence has shown that people are fixated on their bodies. They have painted them, fastened objects to them, dressed them, undressed them, and even deformed and mutilated them in the name of beauty. As the anthropologist Keesing has noted, "The use of the body for decoration appears to be a cultural universal."[22] Face painting is still common in parts of Africa, in South America, and among some Native American tribes—and of course, many women in the United States use lipstick and other means to alter the colors of their features.

In intercultural communication, appearance is important because the standards you apply and the judgments you make are subject to cultural interpretations. In the United States, people tend to value the appearance of tall, slender women, but in many other cultures, the definition of what is attractive calls forth a series of different images.[23] In Japan, diminutive females are deemed the most attractive. In Africa we can see yet another definition of physical attractiveness. Richmond and Gestrin note:

> Ideas of pulchritude in Africa differ from those of Europe and the Americas. In traditional African societies, plumpness is considered a sign of beauty, health and wealth, and slimness is evidence of unhappiness or disease or that a woman is being mistreated by her husband.[24]

Buxom and stout people are also valued in parts of Russia. There is a Russian proverb that states, "One need not worry about being fat, just only about being hungry."

And China has yet another cultural standard for female attractiveness. As Wenzhong and Grove note, "Many women keep their hairstyles simple (often one or two braids) and make little attempt to draw attention to themselves through self-decoration such as colorful scarves, jewelry, or makeup."[25]

Because cultures are dynamic, it might be interesting to observe if perceptions of attractiveness begin to change in Japan, Africa, Russia, and China as these cultures come into greater contact with Western cultures.

Attire. Clothing—how much, how little, and what kind—is also a reflection of a culture's value orientation. For example, modesty is highly valued among Arabs. In most instances, "girls are not allowed to participate in swimming classes because of the prohibitions against exposing their bodies."[26] The link between cultural values and clothing is also seen among Filipinos. Gochenour tells us, "Values relating to status and authority are the root of the Filipino's need to dress correctly."[27] Of the German culture, Hall and Hall write:

> Correct behavior is symbolized by appropriate and very conservative dress. The male business uniform is a freshly pressed, dark suit and tie with a plain shirt and dark shoes and socks. It is important to emulate this conservative approach to both manners and dress. Personal appearance, like the exterior appearance of their homes, is very important to Germans.[28]

The Spanish also link appearance to one's rank, as Ruch notes: "Historically, dress has denoted social status."[29] In Spain, it is not uncommon to see people of high status wearing a suit and tie in very hot weather.

Perhaps nowhere in the world is the merger between attire and a culture's value system more evident than in Japan. McDaniel makes the connection when he writes: "The proclivity for conservative dress styles and colors emphasizes the nation's collectivism and, concomitantly, lessens the potential for social disharmony arising from nonconformist attire."[30]

In much of the world, people still dress in their traditional garments. For Arab men, says Ruch, correct business attire would "include a long loose robe called a *dishdasha* or *thobe* and a headpiece, a white cloth *kaffiya* banded by a black egal to secure it."[31] Arab women cover their hair with scarves and wear floor-length, full-sleeved clothing, often a long black cloak called an *abaya*.[32]

For Muslims clothing is much more than apparel to cover the body. As Torrawa points out, "The connection between recompense and garment is an organic in Arabic."[33] What Torrawa is saying is that as is the case with so many aspects of culture, there is often a "below the surface" reason for our actions. This deep structure, and its tie to attire in the Arab world is eloquently articulated by Torrawa when he writes:

> In all its guises, clothing inscribes ideologies of truth and deception, echoing the words of Scripture, and revealing—and unraveling—that honor can only be attained when every robe donned is a robe of honor and every garment a garment of piety.[34]

Whether it be Sikhs in white turbans, Hasidic Jews in blue yarmulkes, or Africans in white dashikis, you need to learn to be tolerant of external differences so that you do not let these differences impede communication. What you might consider quite a garish costume or excessive formality in dress may very likely be a reflection of a culture's particular set of values. Each culture teaches its members about what is appropriate.

Even co-cultures are defined by nonverbal communication nuances. DeFleur, Kearney, and Plax observe that for many African Americans, "clothing provides not only a functional purpose, but also a 'costume.'"[35] Some writers contend that differences in women's and men's clothing in the United States are due to more than physical differences. They argue that since the Victorian period, the male-dominated culture has encouraged women to wear clothing that restricts their movements, limits their activity, and produces an image of submissiveness and frailty.[36]

Body Movement: Kinesics

People have always known that action communicates. As Benjamin Franklin said, "None preaches better than the ant, and she says nothing." The study of how movement communicates is called *kinesics*. In general, kinesic cues are those visible body shifts and movements that can send messages about (1) your attitude toward the other person (standing face to face with a friend (direct body orientation), or leaning forward may show that you are relaxed), (2) your emotional state (tapping on the table or playing with coins can mean you are nervous), and (3) your desire to control your environment (motioning someone to come closer means you want to talk to him or her).

Because scholars have suggested that people can make as many as 700,000 distinct physical signs, any attempt at cataloging them would be frustrating and fruitless. Our purpose is simply to call your attention to the idea that while all people use movement to communicate, culture teaches you how to use and interpret these movements. In the upcoming sections, we look at a few cultural differences in posture, sitting behavior, and movements of the body that convey specific meanings (gestures). Before we begin, we must point out that in most instances the messages the body generates operate only in combination with other messages. People usually smile and say hello to a friend at the same time. In Mexico, this is illustrated when asking someone to wait for "just a minute" (*Un momento, por favor*): the speaker also makes a fist and then extends the thumb and index finger so that they form a sideways U.

Posture. Posture and sitting habits offer insight into a culture's deep structure. We can see the bond been culture and values by simply looking at the Japanese, Thai, and Indian cultures. In Japan, and other Asian cultures, the bow is much more than a greeting. It signifies that culture's concern with status and rank. In Japan, for example, low posture is an indicator of respect.[37] Although it appears simple to the outsider, the bowing ritual is actually rather complicated. The person who occupies the lower station begins the bow, and his or her bow must be deeper than the other person's. The superior, on the other hand, determines when the bowing is to end. When the participants are of equal rank, they begin the bow in the same manner and end at the same time. The Thai people use a similar movement called the *wai*. The *wai* movement—which is made by pressing both hands close together in front of one's body, with the fingertips reaching to about neck level—is used to show respect. The lower the head comes to the hands, the more respect is shown.[38]

In India the posture when greeting someone is directly linked with the idea that Hindus see God in everything—including other people. The *namaskar* (Indian greeting) is carried out by a slight bow with the palms of both hands together, the fingertips at the chin.[39]

In the United States and Canada, where being casual and friendly is valued, people often fall into chairs or slouch when they stand. In many countries, such as Germany and Sweden, where lifestyles tend to be more formal, slouching is considered a sign of rudeness and poor manners. In Belgium, putting one's hands in one's pockets is a sign of disrespect. Cultures also differ in the body orientations they assume during communication. For example, Arabs use a very direct body orientation when communicating. The Chinese, on the other hand, tend to feel uncomfortable with this style and normally will carry out their business in a less direct stance.

The manner in which you sit also can communicate a message. In Ghana and in Turkey, sitting with one's legs crossed is extremely offensive.[40] People in Thailand believe that because the bottoms of the feet are the lowest part of the body, they should never be pointed in the direction of another person.[41] In fact, for the Thai, the feet take on so much significance that people avoid stomping with them.

Even within the United States, there are differences in how people move, stand, and sit during interaction. Women often hold their arms closer to their bodies than do men. They usually keep their legs closer together and seldom cross them in mixed company. Their posture is also more restricted and less relaxed than the posture of males. Most research in the area of gender communication concludes that these differences are related to issues such as status, power, and affiliation.[42] Posture and stance play an important role in the African American co-culture. This is most evident in the walk employed by many young African Americans. According to Hecht, Collier, and Ribeau, "The general form of the walk is slow and casual with the head elevated and tipped to one side, one arm swinging and the other held limply."[43] The walk, says the *San Diego Union-Tribune*, "shows the dominant culture that you are strong and proud, despite your status in American society."[44]

Gestures. The power of gestures as a form of communication is reflected in the fact that the co-culture of the deaf in the United States has a rich and extensive vocabulary composed of gestures. A grimmer example of the power of gestures can be found in the hand signals used by various urban gangs. The slightest variation in performing a certain gesture can be the catalyst for a violent confrontation.

Andersen offers an excellent introduction to the complex and all pervasive nature of gestures when he writes, "Gestures are both innate and learned. They are used in all cultures, tend to be tied to speech processes, and are usually automatic."[45] We would also add that many gestures, like all the nonverbal behaviors in this chapter, have a strong connection to culture. For example, an Arabic specialist once cataloged 247 separate gestures that Arabs use while speaking.[46] And in a large study involving forty different cultures, Morris and his associates isolated twenty common hand gestures that had a different meaning in each culture.[47]

We now offer a few examples of how gestures can communicate different meanings from culture to culture. We begin with the simple act of *pointing*. In the United States, we point to objects and even at people with the index finger. Germans point with the little finger, and the Japanese point with the entire hand, palms up. In much of Asia, pointing with the index finger is considered rude.[48]

In Argentina, one twists an imaginary mustache to signify that everything is "okay." In the United States, "making a circle with one's thumb and index finger while extending the others is emblematic of the word 'OK'; in Japan (and Korea) it signifies 'money' (okane); and among Arabs this gesture is usually accompanied by a baring of teeth, and together they signify extreme hostility."[49] This same gesture has a vulgar connotation in Mexico and Germany, and to the Tunisian it means "I'll kill you."

The taken-for-granted sign we make for *beckoning* is also culturally based. In the United States, when a person wants to signal a friend to come, he or she makes the gesture with one hand, palm up, fingers more or less together and moving toward his or her body. Koreans express this same idea by cupping "the hand with the palm down and drawing the fingers toward the palm."[50] When seeing this gesture, many Americans think the other person is waving good-bye. In parts of Burma, the summoning gesture is made palm down, with the fingers moving as though playing the piano. Filipinos often summon someone with a quick downward nod of the head. In Germany and much of Scandinavia, a beckoning motion is made by tossing the head back. For many Arabs, nonverbally asking someone to "come here" is performed by holding the right hand out, palm upward, and opening and closing the hand.[51] And in Spain to beckon someone you stretch your arm out, palm downward, and make a scratching motion toward your body with your fingers.

Head movements denoting *acceptance* and *rejection* take opposite forms in Thailand and the United States. Greeks express "yes" with a nod similar to the one used in the United States, but when communicating "no," they jerk their heads back and raise their faces. Lifting one or both hands up to the shoulders strongly emphasizes the "no."

There are also cultural differences regarding the *amount and size* of gestures employed during a communication encounter. Jews, Mexicans, Greeks, Italians, Middle Easterners, and South Americans are quite animated when they interact. Members of many Asian cultures perceive such outward activity quite differently, often equating vigorous action with a lack of manners and restraint.[52] Germans are also made uncomfortable by gestures that are, by their standards, too flamboyant. Ruch offers the following advice to American executives who work with German corporations:

> Hands should be used with calculated dignity. They should never serve as lively instruments to emphasize points in conversation. The entire game plan is to appear calm under pressure.[53]

You can also see the significance of gestures by looking at various co-cultures. For example, as compared to males, women tend to use fewer and smaller gestures.[54] African Americans value a lively and expressive form of communication and hence display a greater variety of movements than whites when interacting.[55]

Facial Expressions

At one time or another, most people have been intrigued by how the looks on other people's faces have influenced their reactions to them. The early Greek playwrights and the Kabuki actors of Japan were keenly aware of the shifts in mood and meaning that facial expressions conveyed. Both forms of drama used masks and extensive makeup to demonstrate differences in each actor's character and attitude. People in every culture have been keenly aware of the manner in which the face offers insight into the character of a person. Whether it be the Mexican adage that "One's face is the mirror of one's soul," or the Yiddish proverb that states "The face tells the secret," people everywhere have been captivated by the face.

The importance of facial expressions in communication is well established; however, the intercultural implications of these expressions are difficult to assess. At the core of a lingering academic debate lies this question: Is there a nearly universal language of facial expressions? One position holds that anatomically similar expressions may occur in everyone, but the meanings people attach to them differ from culture to culture.[56]

The majority opinion, which we introduced earlier in the chapter, is that there are universal facial expressions for which people have similar meanings. Ekman offers this point of view: "The subtle creases of a grimace tell the same story around the world, to preliterate New Guinea tribesmen, to Japanese and American college students alike. Darwin knew it all along, but now here's hard evidence that culture does not control the face."[57] What is being presented is the theory that there are "a basic set of at least six facial expressions that are innate, universal, and carry the same basic meaning throughout the world."[58] These six pancultural and universal facial expressions are happiness, sadness, fear, anger, disgust, and surprise.

Despite the biological-based nature of facial expressions, there seem to be clear cultural expectations as to how cultural norms often dictate when, how, and to whom facial expressions are displayed.[59] As Matsumoto points out, "Different cultures recognize the power of the face and produce many rules to regulate not only what kinds of facial behavior are permitted in social interaction, but also how it may be even to attend to the faces of others during interaction."[60] A few specific examples will illustrate the role of culture in the production and interpretation of facial expressions.

In many Mediterranean cultures, people exaggerate signs of grief or sadness. It is not uncommon in this region of the world to see men crying in public. Yet in the United States, white males suppress the desire to show these emotions. Japanese men even go so far as to hide expressions of anger, sorrow, or disgust by laughing or smiling.[61] In one study, Japanese and American subjects revealed the same facial expressions when viewing a stress-inducing film while they were alone. However, when viewing the film in the presence of others, the Japanese manifested only neutral facial expressions. Min-Sun Kim says that Koreans believe animated facial expressions "are associated with the projection of their emotions."[62] The Chinese also do not readily show emotion for reasons that are rooted deeply in their culture—the Chinese concept of saving face being one of the most important. For the Chinese, displaying too much emotion violates face-saving norms by disrupting harmony and causing conflict.[63]

The smile is yet another emotional display that is rooted in one's culture. The whole world smiles, but the amount of smiling, the stimulus that produces the smile, and even what the smile is communicating often shifts from culture to culture. In America, a smile can be a sign of happiness or friendly affirmation. Although these same meanings are found in the Japanese culture, the smile can also mask an emotion or be used to avoid answering a question.[64] People of lower status in Japan may also use the smile "to denote acceptance of a command or order by a person of higher status when in fact they feel anger or contempt for the order or the person giving the order." [65] In Korean culture, too much smiling is often perceived as the sign of a shallow person. Dresser notes that this "lack of smiling by Koreans has often been misinterpreted as a sign of hostility."[66] Thais, on the other hand, smile much of the time. In fact, Thailand has been called the "Land of Smiles."[67]

Even within a culture, there are groups that use facial expressions differently from the dominant culture. Summarizing the research on gender differences, Pearson, West, and Turner report that, compared to men, women use more facial expressions and are more expressive, smile more, are more apt to return smiles, and are more attracted to others who smile.[68]

Eye Contact and Gaze

In drama, fiction, poetry, and music, eyes have always been a fascinating topic—from Shakespeare's "Thou tell'st me there is murder in mine eye" to Bob Dylan's "Your eyes said more to me that night than your lips would ever say," to the lyric " Your lips tell me no, no, but there's yes, yes in your eyes." Even the "evil eye" is more than just an expression. In one study, Roberts examined 186 cultures throughout the world and found that 67 of them had some belief in the evil eye.[69]

The number of messages we can send with our eyes is almost limitless. We have all heard some of the following words used to describe a person's eyes: *direct, sensual, sardonic, expressive, intelligent, penetrating, sad, cheerful, worldly, hard, trusting, suspicious.* The impact of eye contact and gaze on human interaction is seen in the fact that people use less eye contact when they are depressed, suffer from low self-esteem, and are uncomfortable in a particular situation.[70] According to Leathers, there is ample evidence to conclude that in the United States, eyes serve six important communication functions: they "(1) indicate degrees of attentiveness, interest, and arousal; (2) influence attitude change and persuasion; (3) regulate interaction; (4) communicate emotions; (5) define power and status relationships; and (6) assume a central role in impression management."[71]

Most studies, as well as our personal observations, tell us that culture modifies the amount of eye contact in which we engage and who is the recipient of the eye contact. For the dominant culture in the United States eye contact is highly valued.[72] In fact, most people in Western societies expect the person with whom they are interacting to "look them in the eye." There is even a tendency to be suspicious of someone who does not follow the culturally prescribed rules for eye contact. Direct eye-to-eye contact is not a custom throughout the world. As Chen and Starosta note, "Direct eye contact is a taboo or an insult in many Asian cultures." In Japan, for example, prolonged eye contact is considered rude, threatening, and disrespectful.[73] Dresser points out that "people from Latin American and Caribbean cultures also avoid eye contact as a sign of respect."[74] This same orientation toward eye contact is found in Africa. Richmond and Gestrin tell us, "Making eye contact when communicating with a person who is older or of higher status is considered a sign of disrespect or even aggression in many parts of Africa where respect is shown by lowering the eyes."[75] There is even a Zulu proverb that states that the eye is an organ of aggression.

Problems can arise when Westerners attempt to do business with a group of people who believe it is a sign of impertinence to make prolonged eye contact with their communication partners. Arabs, on the other hand, look directly into the eyes of their communication partner, and do so for long periods. They believe such contact shows interest in the other person and helps them assess the truthfulness of the other person's words.[76]

In America, the prolonged stare is often a part of the nonverbal code that the co-culture of the male homosexual employs. An extended stare, along with other nonverbal messages, at a member of the same sex is often perceived as a signal of interest and sexual suggestion.[77] A few other differences in the use of eye contact in the United States are worthy of our consideration. The Hopi interprets direct eye contact as offensive and usually will avoid any type of staring. The Navajos dislike unbroken eye contact so strongly that they have incorporated it into their creation myth, reports *Psychology Today.* The myth, which tells the story of a "terrible monster called He-Who-Kills-With-His-Eyes," teaches the Navajo child that "a stare is literally an evil eye and implies a sexual and aggressive assault."[78]

Differences in the use of eye contact also characterize communication between African Americans and white Americans. When speaking, African Americans use much more continuous eye contact than do whites, yet the reverse is true when they are listening. That is, whites make more continuous eye contact when they are listening than do African Americans.[79] This difference, say La France and Mayo, is even more pronounced among African American children, who are "socialized into not looking when being spoken to."[80] The same socialization process often has Latino children avoiding eye contact as a sign of attentiveness and respect. It is easy to understand how teachers who have experience only with the dominant white population might well misinterpret the avoidance of direct eye contact as a challenge to authority.

There also are gender variations in how people use their eyes to communicate. A summary of the research on the subject indicates that in most instances, women maintain more eye contact than do men; women look at other women more and hold eye contact longer with one another than do men.[81] We should add that gender characteristics regarding eye contact vary from culture to culture. For example, in cultures where gender segregation is the norm (India, Saudi Arabia, etc.) direct eye contact between men and women is avoided.[82]

As you might imagine, eye contact is also an important consideration when communicating with a member of the deaf community. Without visual contact American Sign Language could not be used. Turning your back to someone who is "signing" is essentially the same as ignoring them. So delicate is the use of eye contact that you seldom realize the modifications you make. For example, the next time you are talking with a disabled person, perhaps someone in a wheelchair, notice how little eye contact you make with him or her as compared with someone who is not disabled.

Touch

Touch, like your words and movements, are messages about what you are thinking and feeling. The meanings you assign to being touched, and your reasons for touching others, help you gain insight into the communication encounter, as the character Holden Caulfield vividly helps illustrate in the American classic *The Catcher in the Rye:*

> I held hands with her all the time. This doesn't sound like much, but she was terrific to hold hands with. Most girls if you hold hands with them their god damn hand dies, or else they think they have to keep moving their hand all the time, as if they were afraid they'd bore you or something.[83]

Touch is the earliest sense to mature; it manifests itself in the final embryonic stage and comes into its own long before eyes, ears, and the higher brain centers begin to work. Soon after birth, infants begin to employ their other senses to interpret reality. During the same period, they are highly involved with touch: they are being nuzzled, cuddled, cleaned, patted, kissed, and in many cases breast-fed. So important is touch to human communication that researchers now know that children who are denied "caregivers' touch" have serious biochemical and emotional problems.[84] The American playwright Tennessee Williams eloquently expressed the power of touch when he wrote, "Devils can be driven out of the heart by the touch of a hand on a hand, or a mouth on a mouth."

As you move from infancy into childhood, you learn the rules of touching. You are taught whom to touch and where they may be touched. A set of cultural regulations and an emphasis on other modes of communication replace childhood desires to touch and be touched. By the time you reach adolescence, your culture has taught you how to

Touch helps convey internal ideas and feelings.

© Larry Samovar

communicate with touch. Consciously and unconsciously, like culture itself, you use touch for sex, consolation, support, and control. In the United States, people learn to shake hands with nearly everyone (making sure it is a firm shake), hug certain people (but not everyone with the same intensity), be intimate with still other people (knowing well in advance the zones of the body that you can touch), and make love to one person (being aware of the sexual regions defined by culture and sex manuals).

You need only watch the news on television or stand at an international airport to know that there are major differences in how cultures use touch, even in the simple act of greeting or saying good-bye. In a study involving touch behavior among culturally diverse couples at an international airport, Andersen offers the following narrative of some of their findings:

> A family leaving for Tonga formed a circle, wove their arms around each other' back, and prayed and chanted together. A tearful man returning to Bosnia repeatedly tried to leave his sobbing wife; each time he turned back to her, they would grip each other by the fingertips and exchange a passionate, tearful kiss and a powerful embrace. Two Korean couples departed without any touch, despite the prolonged separation that lay ahead of them.[85]

Let us look at a few cultural examples so that we might further emphasize the link between culture and touch. As we have said elsewhere, Muslims, because of religious and social traditions, eat and do other things with the right hand, but to greet with the left can be a social insult. For many Asians, the head has religious meaning. Dresser offers the following observation regarding touching the head of Asians: "Many Asian people believe the head houses the soul. Therefore, when another person touches their head, it places them in jeopardy. It is prudent for outsiders to avoid touching the heads and upper torsos of Asians."[86]

Many African Americans are also annoyed if a white person pats them on the top of their head. They believe it carries the same meaning as being told, in a condescending manner, that they are a good little boy or girl.

Men in much of Eastern Europe, Spain, Italy, Portugal, and the Arab world will kiss when they meet their friends. There is also much more same-sex touching in Mexico and Spain. Men will greet each other with an embrace (abrazo). As Condon notes, "Hugs, pats on backs, and other physical contact are an important part of communication in Mexico."[87] As we have said elsewhere, physical contact varies from culture to culture. In much of Southeast Asia, for example, people not only avoid touching when meeting, but also have very little physical contact during the course of the conversation. Describing business practices in Japan, Rowland tells you, "Touching fellow workers and associates is not common in Japan. Patting someone on the back or putting a friendly arm around them is not done."[88]

Even the simple act of kissing has cultural overtones. Although mouth-to-mouth kissing, as a sexual act, is common in most Western cultures, it is not widespread in many parts of Asia. In fact, the Japanese have for centuries rhapsodized about the appeal of the nape of the neck as an erotic zone. The Japanese have no word for kissing, so they have borrowed from the English language for their word kissu.

Why do these and countless other variations exist? In nearly every instance, the manner in which members of a culture communicate is a reflection of that culture's attitudes and values. Cultures that believe in emotional restraint and rigid status distinction (German, English, Scandinavian) do very little touching as compared with cultures that encourage outward signs of affection (Latin American, Middle Eastern, Jewish, Greek, Eastern European). The connection of cultural values to touch can even be seen in how the Hindus of India believe that you show respect to someone of great importance by touching their feet.[89]

There are also gender and ethnic differences in how individuals use and react to touch. Bates notes, "Much research has indicated that men touch women more than women touch men, both in work settings and in general social interaction."[90] From her review of numerous studies, she has also concluded that "women initiate hugs and embraces far more often than men do, to other women, to men, and to children."[91]

African Americans "give skin" and "get skin" when greeting each other, but they do not normally use "skinning" (touching) when greeting white people unless they are close friends. There are a limited number of studies that reveal that African American males touch each other more often than do white males.[92] And, Leathers says, one study has shown that "black females touch each other almost twice as often as white females."[93]

Smell

When the German philosopher Nietzsche wrote "All credibility, all good conscience, all evidence of truth come only from the senses," we are sure he intended to include the sense of smell in his declaration. For although you can grant that you receive most of your messages from the outside world through vision and hearing, the sense of smell can also be a conduit for meaning. From the burning of incense in India, to the aroma of flowers and herbs in China being used for medicinal purposes, cultures have been using odor in a variety of ways. Americans, for example, spend billions of dollars making certain that they, as well as their surroundings, exude the proper fragrance. The reason is obvious: odor communicates. It communicates not only when you are face to face with another person, but even when the other person is not present. Victor Hugo said, "Nothing awakens a reminiscence like an odor."

A number of elements affect the meaning we give to a smell: (1) the strength of the smell in relation to competing fragrances and odors (French perfume versus an inexpensive aftershave lotion), (2) smell's distance from the other person, (3) the perceived relationship between the parties involved, and (4) the context of the encounter.

Culture influences our reaction to each of these four variables. In Bali, when lovers greet one another, they often breathe deeply in a kind of friendly sniffing. Smell plays a big part in "sensory-information gathering among Filipinos."[94] It is not uncommon for young Filipino lovers to trade small pieces of clothing on parting, so that the smell of the other person will evoke their affection for each other. The Filipino culture is so very conscious of the power of smell that after investigating this culture, Gochenour noted, "A not-so-rare complaint against Americans is that they do not bathe enough. . . . Filipinos are scrupulous about personal hygiene and have sensitive noses."[95] In Japan, where smell is an important part of the culture, young girls will often play a game involving the placing of five fragrances in tiny boxes. The girl who identifies the most aromas wins the game. And it is not uncommon in Japan to have various fragrances emitted in the workplace.

Americans represent an example of a culture that tends to be uncomfortable with natural smells. Many other cultures regard natural odors as normal, and most Arabs actually perceive a person's smell as an extension of the person. Hall describes this cultural value:

> Olfaction occupies a prominent place in the Arab life. Not only is it one of the distance-setting mechanisms, but it is a vital part of the complex system of behavior. Arabs consistently breathe on people when they talk. However, this habit is more than a matter of different manners. To the Arab good smells are pleasing and a way of being involved with each other. To smell one's friends is not only desirable, for to deny him your breath is to act ashamed. Americans, on the other hand, trained as they are not to breathe in people's faces, automatically communicate shame in trying to be polite.[96]

As with all of our other categories of nonverbal messages, not knowing cultural variations in attitude toward smells can create uncertainty and even ill feeling. As we move from culture to culture, it is important that we pay attention to the scents around us and the way they influence our communication.

Paralanguage

When the German poet Klopstock wrote "The tones of human voices are mightier than strings or brass to move the soul," he knew that the *sounds* we generate often communicate more than the words that they produce. Most of you have attended, at one time or another, the showing of a foreign film with English subtitles. During those intervals when the subtitles were not on the screen, you heard the actors uttering an unfamiliar language but could essentially understand what was happening just from the sound of the voices. Perhaps you inferred that the performers were expressing anger, sorrow, joy, or any of a number of other emotions. Maybe the sound of the voices could even tell you who the hero was and who was cast in the role of the villain. The rise and fall of voices also may have told you when one person was asking a question and another was making a statement or issuing a command. Whatever the case, certain vocal cues provided you with information with which to make judgments about the characters' personalities, emotional states, ethnic background, and rhetorical activity. To be sure, you could only guess at the exact meaning of the words being spoken, but sound variations still told you a great deal about what was happening. Shakespeare said the same thing with great style when he wrote, "I understand the fury in your words, but not the words."

What we have just been considering is often referred to as *paralanguage*, which involves the linguistic elements of speech, that is, how something is said and not the actual meaning of the spoken words. Most classifications divide paralanguage into three kinds of vocalizations: (1) vocal characterizers (laughing, crying, yelling, moaning, whining, belching, yawning); (2) vocal qualifiers (volume, pitch, rhythm, tempo, resonance, tone); and (3) vocal segregates ("un-huh," "shh," "uh," "oooh," "mmmh," "humm"). It is extraordinary how many inferences about content and character can be made just from the sounds people produce. For example, paralanguage cues assist you in drawing conclusions about an individual's emotional state, socioeconomic status, height, ethnicity, weight, age, intelligence, race, regional background, and educational level.[97] Let's pause for a moment and look at some of the paralanguage messages you receive that help you draw those conclusions.

Volume. As with all other aspects of our nonverbal behavior, culture influences our use of and response to paralanguage. We only have to look at differences in the use of volume to see this. Arabs speak very loudly because loudness for them connotes strength and sincerity, "while softness communicates weakness and deviousness."[98] For Israelis, increased volume reflects strong beliefs toward the issue under discussion. Ruch says the Germans conduct their business with a "commanding tone that projects authority and self-confidence."[99] On the other end of the continuum, there are cultures that have a very different view toward loud and firm voices. For Thai people, "a loud voice is perceived as being impolite."[100] In Japan, raising one's voice often implies a lack of self-control. For them, a gentle and soft voice reflects good manners and helps maintain social harmony—two important values in Japanese culture. When interacting with Americans, people from cultures that speak softly often believe that Americans are angry or upset because of their relatively loud speech.

"Noises." The "noise" people make also carries meaning. The Maasai, for example, use a number of sounds that have special significance, the most common one being the "eh" sound, which the Maasai draw out and which can mean "yes," "I understand," or "continue." In Kenya, the "iya" sound tells the other person that everything is okay; in Jamaica, the "kissing" or "sucking" sound expresses anger, exasperation, or frustration. The Japanese also make ample use of vocalics in their conversations. During interpersonal discussions, say Richmond, McCroskey, and Payne, the "Japanese will often hiss or inhale one's breath while talking to others as a sign of respect."[101] They will also make small utterances (such as *hai* [yes, certainly, all right, very well], *so* [so], or *e* [well. . . ; let me see . . .]) to demonstrate their attentiveness.[102]

Laughing. Laughing and giggling also send different messages, depending on the culture. Although smiling and laughing are signs of joy in all cultures, the Japanese often laugh to hide displeasure, anger, sorrow, and embarrassment.[103]

Accents and Dialects. Accents and dialects are additional components of paralanguage that often influence the communication process. In a rather humorous way, this point was made clear to the famous Norwegian anthropologist Thor Heyerdahl during one of his trips to London to appear on British television. Heyerdahl, because he had a very busy schedule, was assured by the British Broadcasting Company that they would send someone to pick him up and bring him to the television studio. As the minutes ticked by, Heyerdahl became very anxious. Finally, fearing he would miss the broadcast, he approached a man who looked as if he might be a taxi driver. He said to the gentleman, "I'm Thor Heyerdahl. Are you looking for me?" With a very thick British accent, the driver replied, "No sir. I have been sent to pick four Airedales for the BBC."

Although the above example seems trivial, in many instances accents and dialects can cause more serious communication problems. Before we mention some of these problems, let us discuss the thin difference between accents and dialects. *Accent* refers only to distinctive pronunciation, whereas *dialect* refers to grammar and vocabulary as well.[104] The importance of accents and dialects is obvious to those who have found themselves making a judgment about another person based on the person's accent or dialect. Because most people view "standard English" as proper and correct, anyone not using this standard is perceived to be of lower status and/or not speaking correct English.[105] Andersen summarizes the results of these negative responses to accents when interacting with people from various backgrounds:

> Research has shown that regional, ethnic, and blue-collar accents are preferred by members of one's own group but thought of as signs of low intelligence, low education, low status, and low success by the dominant, or "mainstream" culture.[106]

People who hold these attitudes mentioned by Andersen fail to recognize that standard English is as much a dialect as any one of the thousands found throughout the world. That is, in one place or another, what one person speaks is a foreign dialect someplace else. As a Hindustani proverb reminds us, "The tree casts its shade upon all, even the woodcutter." We therefore urge you to guard against reacting negatively when you confront someone with an accent or a dialect different from your own.

Co-cultures also use paralanguage in subtle and unique ways. For example, as part of their unique communication style, many African Americans use more inflection, are more intense and more dynamic, and have a greater emotional range in their use of voice than most white Americans.[107] As was the case with accents, some members of the dominant culture view these characteristics in a negative light.[108] Differences in paralanguage also mark the communication patterns of males and females. In several studies, females evidenced a faster rate of speech than men and also had fewer silent pauses while speaking.[109] After reviewing numerous studies on gender differences in the use of voice, Pearson, West, and Turner concluded that females speak at a higher pitch than men, speak more softly, are more expressive, pronounce the complete "ing" ending to words, and come closer to standard speech norms.[110]

During the first part of the chapter, we focused on nonverbal communication through body behavior. We now explore how people employ space, time, and silence as ways of communicating. Although these variables are external to the communicator, they are nevertheless used and manipulated in ways that send messages. For example, imagine your reaction to someone who stands too close to you, arrives late for an important appointment, or remains silent after you reveal some personal information. In each of these instances, you would find yourself reading meaning into your communication partner's use of (1) space and distance, (2) time, and (3) silence. Knowing the impact of these three factors on communication, and how cultures use them differently, can help you understand your own behavior and that of others.

Space and Distance

The flow and shift of distance between you and the people with whom you interact are as much a part of communication experiences as the words you exchange. Notice how you might allow one person to stand very close to you and keep another at a distance. You use space and distance to convey messages. The study of this message system, called *proximics*, is concerned with such things as your (1) personal space, (2) seating, and (3) furniture arrangement. All three have an influence on intercultural communication.

Personal Space

Your personal space, that piece of the universe you occupy and call your own, is contained within an invisible boundary surrounding your body. As the owner of this area, you usually decide who may enter and who may not. When your space is invaded, you react in a variety of ways. You may back up and retreat, stand your ground as your hands become moist from nervousness, or sometimes even react violently. Your response is a

Cultures that stress individualism demand more space than do communal cultures.

manifestation not only of your unique personality, but also your cultural background. For example, cultures that stress individualism (England, the United States, Germany, Australia) generally demand more space than do collective cultures and "tend to take an active, aggressive stance when their space is violated."[111] This perception and use of space is quite different from the one found in the Mexican and Arab cultures. As Condon tells us, in Mexico the "physical distance between people when engaged in conversation is closer than what is usual north of the border."[112] With regard to Arabs, Ruch writes, "Typical Arab conversations are at close range. Closeness cannot be avoided."[113] According to Richmond and Gestrin "Africans get physically close to complete strangers and stand even closer when conversing."[114]

As is the case with most of your behavior, your use of space is directly linked to the value system of your culture. In some Asian cultures, for example, students do not sit close to their teachers or stand near their bosses; the extended distance demonstrates deference and esteem. Extra interpersonal distance is also part of the cultural experience of the people of Scotland and Sweden, for whom it reflects privacy. And in Germany, Hall and Hall tell us, private space is sacred.[115]

Seating

Culture influences even the manner and meaning in seating arrangements. Notice, for example, that Americans, when in groups, tend to talk with those opposite them rather than those seated or standing beside them. This pattern also influences how they select leaders when in groups: in most instances, the person sitting at the head of the table is chosen (or the leader will move directly to the head table position). In America, leaders usually are accustomed to being somewhat removed physically from the rest of the group and consequently choose chairs at the ends of the table. In China, seating arrangements take on different meanings. The Chinese often experience alienation and uneasiness when they face someone directly or sit on opposite sides of a desk or table from someone. It makes them feel as if they are on trial. In China, meetings often take place with people sitting on couches. In Korea, seating arrangements reflect status and role distinctions. In a car, office, or home, the seat at the right is considered the one of honor.

For the Japanese, "seating arrangements at any formal or semiformal function are also based on hierarchy."[116] The most important person sits at one end of the rectangular table, with those nearest in rank at the right and left of this senior position. The lowest in class is nearest to the door and at the opposite end of the table from the person with the most authority. Seating arrangements are also a way of demonstrating social hierarchy in the culture of Fiji.[117] The seat near the central-house post is the seat of honor. Status in this culture is also reflected in the fact that women sit "below" men in the home and seniors sit above junior members of the household. In China, the traditional philosophy of *feng shui* (the relationship of humans to their environment) is often seen in the way some Chinese arrange themselves at a table.[118] In signing business agreements the Chinese will often want to sit in a seat that they believe allows them to be in consonance with their surroundings.

Furniture Arrangement

Furniture arrangement within the home communicates something about the culture. For example, people from France, Italy, and Mexico who visit the United States are often surprised to see that the furniture in the living room is pointed toward the television set. For them, conversation is important, and facing chairs toward a television screen stifles conversation. In their countries, furniture is positioned to encourage interaction.

Even the arrangement of offices gives us a clue to the character of a people. According to Hall and Hall, "French space is a reflection of French culture and French institutions. Everything is centralized, and spatially the entire country is laid out around centers."[119] In Germany, where privacy is stressed, office furniture is spread throughout the office. In Japan, where group participation is encouraged, many desks are arranged hierarchically in the center of a large, common room absent of walls or partitions.[120] The supervisors and managers are positioned nearest the windows. This organization encourages the exchange of information, facilitates multitask accomplishments, and promotes the Confucian concept of learning through silent observation.

Co-cultures also have their own use of space. Prostitutes, for example, are very possessive of their territory. When they mentally mark an area as their own, even though it may be a public street or hotel lobby, they behave as if it were their private property and attempt to keep other prostitutes away.[121] In prisons, where space is limited, controlled, and at a premium, space and territory are crucial forms of communication. New inmates quickly learn the culture of prison by learning about the use of space. They soon know when to enter another cell, that space reduction is a form of punishment, and that lines form for nearly all activities. Women normally allow both men and other women to stand closer to them than do men. Summarizing other gender differences in the use of space, Leathers has concluded:

> Men use space as a means of asserting their dominance over women, as in the following: (a) they claim more personal space than women; (b) they more actively defend violations of their territories—which are usually much larger than the territories of women; (c) under conditions of high density, they become more aggressive in their attempts to regain a desired measure of privacy; and (d) men more frequently walk in front of their female partner than vice versa.[122]

Spatial distance is also a variable when interacting with members of the deaf culture. For example, when using American Sign Language it is necessary for the person "signing" to be seen. It would not be uncommon for two signers to sit across from one another at a distance that hearing people might perceive as impersonal.[123]

Time

When Shakespeare wrote "The inaudible and noiseless foot of Time," he was putting into words what we all know but often overlook. Although you cannot hold or see time, you respond to it as if it had command over your life. When three centuries ago the Dutch mathematician Christiaan Huygens built the first pendulum clock, which allowed people to keep track of hours and minutes, little did he know that his invention would have such an impact on people's lives. You now strap clocks to your wrists, hang them on your walls, and give them power to control everything from your moods to your relationships. Because time is such a personal phenomenon, all of you perceive and treat it in a manner that expresses your character, and as we shall demonstrate later, your culture. If you arrive thirty minutes late for an important appointment and offer no apology, you send a certain message about yourself. Telling someone how guilty you feel about your belated arrival also sends a message. Studies even point out that one of the hallmarks of a successful and intimate relationship is the amount of time people spend together.[124] What is happening is obvious; how the parties are perceiving and using time is sending a message about how much they care for each other.

A culture's use of time can provide valuable clues to how members of that culture value and respond to time. In America, most members of the dominant culture adhere to the advice of Benjamin Franklin which tells us that "Time is money." We also hear the phrase "He who hesitates is lost." The Chinese know the Confucian saying "Think three times before you act." Reflect for a moment on how differently each of these cultures perceives time. A culture's conception of time can be examined from three different perspectives: (1) informal time; (2) perceptions of past, present, and future; and (3) Hall's monochronic and polychronic classifications.

Informal Time

Most of the rules for informal time, such as pace and tardiness, are not explicitly taught. Like most of culture, these rules usually function below the level of consciousness. Argyle makes much the same point when he compares cultural differences in punctuality standards:

> How late is "late"? This varies greatly. In Britain and America one may be 5 minutes late for a business appointment, but not 15 and certainly not 30 minutes late, which is perfectly normal in Arab countries. On the other hand in Britain it is correct to be 5–15 minutes late for an invitation to dinner. An Italian might arrive 2 hours late, an Ethiopian after, and a Javanese not at all—he had accepted only to prevent his host from losing face.[125]

Our reaction to punctuality is rooted in our cultural experiences. In the United States, we have all learned that the boss can arrive late for a meeting without anyone raising an eyebrow; if the secretary is late, he or she may receive a reprimand in the form of a stern glance. A rock star or a doctor can keep people waiting for long periods of time, but the warm-up band and the nurse had better be on time. In Latin America, one is expected to arrive late to appointments as a sign of respect. And in Africa people often "show up late for appointments, meetings, and social engagements."[126] These two views of tardiness would be perceived as rudeness in Germany. According to Hall and Hall, "Promptness is taken for granted in Germany—in fact, it's almost an obsession."[127]

We can ascertain a culture's attitude toward time by examining the pace at which members of that culture perform specific acts and respond to certain events. Americans, because of the pace of life in the United States, always seem to be in a hurry—for them, there is always one more thing to do. Conveniences—from fast-food restaurants, to one-stop gas stations, to microwave ovens—help most of you get things done quickly. Americans are constantly seeking faster computers and cars. You grow up hearing people say, "Don't waste so much time." You are impatient when things take too long, and you act as if you believe the French proverb "Patience is the virtue of asses." Other cultures see time differently and hence live life at a pace different from that of most people in the United States. The Japanese, Arab, and Chinese cultures, for example, treat time in ways that often appear at cross-purposes with American goals. The Chinese, for example, have a proverb that states, "He who hurries cannot walk with dignity."

Drawing on the Japanese culture for his example, Brislin illustrates how pace is reflected in the negotiation process:

> When negotiating with the Japanese, Americans like to get right down to business. They were socialized to believe that "time is money." They can accept about 15 minutes of "small

talk" about the weather, their trip, and baseball, but more than that becomes unreasonable. The Japanese, on the other hand, want to get to know their business counterparts. They feel that the best way to do this is to have long conversations with Americans about a wide variety of topics. The Japanese are comfortable with hours and hours, and even days and days, of conversation.[128]

Indonesians are yet another group that do not want to be pressured or hurried. They perceive time as a limitless pool. According to Harris and Moran, there is even "a phrase in Indonesia describing this concept that translates as 'rubber time,' so that time stretches or shrinks and is therefore very flexible."[129] In Africa, where a slow pace is the rule, "people who rush are suspected of trying to cheat," says Ruch.[130]

Manifestations of pace take a host of forms. One study, for example, pointed out that even the speed at which people walk reflects a culture's concept of time. People from England and the United States move much faster than people from Taiwan and Indonesia.[131]

Past, Present, and Future

How a culture perceives and uses the concepts of past, present, and future is discussed in Chapter 3. Let us review some of those findings so that you can see how time and non-verbal behavior are linked.

Past-oriented cultures such as the British place much emphasis on tradition and are often perceived as resisting change. A statement one often hears in England when people ask about the monarchy is "We have always done it this way." The Chinese, with their tradition of ancestor worship and strong pride in their culture's persistence for thousands of years, are another culture that uses the past as a guide to how to live in the present. As a Chinese proverb advises, "Consider the past and you will know the present." Native Americans also value tradition and look to the past for guidance when confronting new situations. These cultures—like the Greek, Japanese, French, Chinese, and the Arab—have histories that date back thousands of years, so they find it normal to take a long-range view of events and are less likely to be rushed when they face decisions. Cultures that value the past are also more likely to respect and venerate the elderly than are cultures that value the future.

Filipinos and Latin Americans are *present oriented* and emphasize living in the moment. These cultures tend to be more impulsive and spontaneous than others and have a casual, relaxed lifestyle. The Irish, even with their historical problems with England, have much the same view of life and time. It can be summarized in the Irish proverb that states "Life is a dance not a race." This somewhat cavalier approach to life is often confusing to Westerners, who frequently misinterpret a concern with the present as a sign of indolence and inefficiency.

The third orientation, which puts great faith in the *future*, is the one most Americans have. As a people, Americans are constantly planning for the future, and their children play with toys (dolls, cars, guns, and so on) that prepare them for adulthood. Many of you can hardly wait to finish what you are doing so that you can move on to something else. As we noted during our discussion of pace, having an eye to the future often produces a very low tolerance for extensions and postponements. What you want, you want now, so you can dispose of this moment and move on to the next. In addition, future-oriented cultures welcome innovation and change and "have less regard for past social or organizational customs and traditions."[132]

Monochronic (M-time) and Polychronic (P-time) Classifications

Anthropologist Hall advanced another classification of time as a form of communication. Hall proposed that cultures organize time in one of two ways: either monochronic (M-time) or polychronic (P-time).[133] Although he did not intend these as either/or categories, they do represent two distinct approaches to time.

M-time. *M-time* is characteristic of people from Germany, Austria, Switzerland, and America. As Hall explains, "People of the Western world, particularly Americans, tend to think of time as something fixed in nature, something around us and from which we cannot escape; an ever-present part of the environment, just like the air we breathe."[134] As the word *monochronic* implies, this approach sees time as lineal, segmented, and manageable. Time is something you must not waste; you must be doing something or feel guilty. The English naturalist Charles Darwin echoed this view when he wrote, "A man who dares to waste one hour of time has not discovered the value of life." You behave as if time were tangible: you talk of "saving time," "losing time," or "killing time." The time clock records the hours you must work, the school bell moves you from class to class, and the calendar marks important days and events in your lives. Appointments and schedules are very important to members of monochronic cultures.

P-time. People from cultures on *P-time* live their lives quite differently. P-time cultures, for example, deal with time holistically. They can interact with more than one person or do more than one thing at a time. According to Dresser, this multidimensional approach to the moment "explains why there is more interrupting in conversations carried on by people from Arabic, Asian, and Latin American cultures."[135] Africans are yet another culture that takes great stock in the activity that is occurring at the moment and emphasize people more than schedules. As Richmond and Gestrin note, "Time for Africans is defined by events rather than the clock or calendar."[136] "For Africans, the person they are with is more important than the one who is out of sight."[137] For P-time cultures, time is less tangible; hence, feelings of wasted time are not as prevalent as in M-time cultures. This leads, of course, to a lifestyle that is more spontaneous and unstructured—characteristics that often confuse and frustrate Americans and other Westerners.

In Table 6-1 Hall and Hall summarize the basic aspects of both approaches. Their condensation takes many of the ideas we have mentioned and translates them into specific behaviors.

Within the United States, there are co-cultures that use time differently from the dominant culture. Most Native American Indian languages do not even have a word for second, minute, or hour. Mexican Americans frequently speak of "Latino time" when their timing varies from that of the dominant culture. Burgoon and Saine have observed that the Polynesian culture of Hawaii has "Hawaiian time,"[138] a concept of time that is very relaxed and reflects the informal lifestyle of the Native Hawaiian people. And among Samoans, there is a time perspective referred to as "coconut time," which is derived from the notion that it is not necessary to pick coconuts because they will fall when the time is right. African Americans often use what is referred to as "BPT" (Black People's Time) or "hang-loose time."[139] This concept, which has its roots in the P-time cultures of Africa, maintains that priority belongs to what is happening at that instant. Statements such as "Hey, man, what's happenin'?" reflect the importance of the here and now.

Table 6-1 *Comparison of Monochronic and Polychronic Cultures*

Monochronic Time People	Polychronic Time People
Do one thing at a time.	Do many things at once.
Concentrate on the job.	Are easily distracted and subject to interruptions.
Take time commitments (deadlines, schedules) seriously.	Consider time commitments an objective to be achieved, if possible.
Are low context and need information.	Are high context and already have information.
Are committed to the job.	Are committed to people and human relationships.
Adhere to plans.	Change plans often and easily.
Are concerned about not disturbing others; follow rules of privacy.	Are more concerned with people close to them (family, friends, close business associates) than with privacy.
Show great respect for private property; seldom borrow or lend.	Borrow and lend things often and easily.
Emphasize promptness.	Base promptness on the relationship.
Are accustomed to short-term relationships.	Have strong tendency to build lifetime relationships.

Source: Adapted from Edward T. Hall and Mildred Reed Hall, *Understanding Cultural Differences: Germans, French and Americans* (Yarmouth, ME: Intercultural Press, 1990), 15.

Silence

An African proverb states, "Silence is also speech." We contend that silence sends us nonverbal cues concerning the communication situations in which we participate. Observe the poignant use of silence when the classical composer strategically places intervals of orchestration so that the ensuing silence marks a contrast in expression. Silence can indeed be a powerful message. There is a story of how the American philosopher Ralph Waldo Emerson "talked" in silence for hours to the famous English writer Thomas Carlyle. It seems that Emerson, on a visit to Europe, arranged to meet with Carlyle, who was his idol. Emerson maintains they sat together for hours in perfect silence until it was time for him to go, then parted company cordially, congratulating each other on the fruitful time they had had together.

Silence cues affect interpersonal communication by providing an interval in an ongoing interaction during which the participants have time to think, check or suppress an emotion, encode a lengthy response, or inaugurate another line of thought. Silence also helps provide feedback, informing both sender and receiver about the clarity of an idea or its significance in the overall interpersonal exchange. Silence cues may be interpreted as evidence of agreement, lack of interest, injured feelings, or contempt. Like olfactory and tactile cues, silence cues transcend the verbal channel, often revealing what speech conceals. The intercultural implications of silence are as diverse as those of other nonverbal cues, as Crystal helps to illustrate:

> Cross-cultural differences are common over when to talk and when to remain silent, or what a particular instance of silence means. In response to the question "Will you marry me?", silence in English would be interpreted as uncertainty; in Japanese it would be interpreted as acceptance. In Igbo, it would be considered a denial if the woman were to continue to stand there, and an acceptance if she ran away.[140]

Silence is not a meaningful part of the life of most members of the dominant culture in the United States. Talking, watching television, listening to music, and other sound-producing activities keep us from silence. Numerous studies have pointed out that most Americans believe that talking is an important activity and actually enjoy talking.[141] Americans are not alone in their avoidance of silence. In Jewish, Italian, and Arab cultures, which stress social interaction among friends and family, there is often very little silence. In fact, talking in these cultures is highly valued. A famous Arab proverb states that "A man's tongue is his sword." In Greek culture, there is also a belief that being in the company of other people, and engaging in conversation, is a sign of a good life. There are no references to concepts of solitude and silence; rather, history and literature are replete with allusions to rhetoric and dialogues. A culture that praises Aristotle, Plato, and Socrates is not one that will find silent meditation very appealing. This is in sharp contrast to cultures in which a hushed and still environment is the rule. We now look at a few cultural variations in the use of silence so that you might better understand how a lack of words can influence the outcome of any communication event.

In the Eastern tradition, the view of silence is much different from the Western view. Easterners do not feel uncomfortable with the absence of noise or talk and are not compelled to fill every pause when they are around other people. In fact, there is often a belief among many Eastern traditions that words can contaminate an experience and that inner peace and wisdom come only through silence. Barnlund says of Buddhism: "One of its tenets is that words are deceptive and silent intuition is a truer way to confront the world; mind-to-mind communication through words is less reliable than heart-to-heart communication through an intuitive grasp of things."[142] Further, Buddhism teaches that "what is real is, and when it is spoken it becomes unreal." The Chinese philosopher Confucius had much the same view of silence. Think for a moment about these two pieces of counsel advanced by Confucius: "Believe not others' tales, / Others will lead thee far astray"; "Silence is a friend who will never betray." Many Japanese proverbs, such as the following, also underscore the value of silence over words: "It is the duck that squawks that gets shot," "Numerous words show scanty wares," "Out of the mouth comes all evil," "A flower does not speak," and "The mouth is to eat with not to speak with." Compare these perceptions of silence with the American saying "The squeaky wheel gets the grease." You can easily imagine how the use of silence might create communication problems when people representing these two divergent styles come together. For example, Adler says that during business negotiations between Japanese and Americans each has a different rendering of the same silent period. The Japanese use the silence to "consider the Americans offer, the Americans interpret the silence as rejection." [143]

Silence can also play a dominant role in the Indian culture. The Hindu believes that "self-realization, salvation, truth, wisdom, peace, and bliss are all achieved in a state of meditation and introspection when the individual is communicating with himself or herself in silence."[144]

Some co-cultures living in the United States also differ from the dominant American culture in the use of silence. Many Native Americans, for example, believe that silence, not speaking, is a sign of a great person. The famous Indian leader Chief Joseph is quoted as saying "It does not require many words to speak the truth." Johannesen, in discussing the function of silence among Native Americans, noted that for this co-culture "one derives from silence the cornerstone of character, the virtues of self-control, courage, patience and dignity."[145] Native Americans use silence as a gesture of respect to persons of authority, age, or wisdom. Because of the way they have been socialized, women are often silenced intellectually and creatively. In mixed-gender conversations, women are quieter than males.[146]

Two points should be obvious from our discussion. First, you must be careful not to assume that people are communicating only when they talk. As the American composer John Cage declared, "There is no such thing as empty space or an empty time. There is always something to see, something to hear. In fact, try as we may to make silence, we cannot." Second, because of cultural variations in this form of communication, it behooves you to know cultural attitudes toward talk, noise, and silence. This knowledge can save you from both anxiety and ethnocentrism in intercultural communication.

SUMMARY

- We make important judgments and decisions about others based on their nonverbal behavior.
- We use the actions of others to learn about their emotional states.
- Nonverbal communication is culture-bound.
- Nonverbal communication involves all nonverbal stimuli in a communication setting that are generated by both the source and his or her use of the environment and that have potential message value for the source or receiver.
- Nonverbal messages may be both intentional and unintentional.
- Nonverbal communication has five basic functions: to repeat, complement, substitute for a verbal action, regulate, and contradict a communication event.
- It is important to remember that we are all more than our culture.
- In nonverbal communication, we often make differences more important than they should be.
- Nonverbal actions seldom occur in isolation.
- Nonverbal communication and culture are similar in that both are learned, both are passed on from generation to generation, and both involve shared understandings.
- Studying nonverbal behavior can lead to the discovery of a culture's underlying attitudes and values.
- Studying nonverbal behavior can also assist us in isolating our own ethnocentrism.
- Our body is a major source of nonverbal messages. These messages are communicated by means of general appearance and attire, body movements (kinesics), facial expressions, eye contact, touch, smell, and paralanguage.
- Cultures differ in their perception and use of personal space, seating, and furniture arrangement.
- We can understand a culture's sense of time by learning about how members of that culture view informal time, the past, present, and future, and whether or not their orientation toward time is monochronic or polychronic.
- The use of silence varies from culture to culture.

INFOTRAC® COLLEGE EDITION EXERCISES

1. Using the subject search term "nonverbal communication," locate the article "Interpersonal Distance, Body Orientation, and Touch: Effects of Culture, Gender, and Age." According to the research reported in this article, what are the differences in nonverbal communication norms between Dutch, English, and the French individuals? Conduct your own informal research and observe nonverbal communications occurring in your own culture. Prepare for class discussion a prediction of how your own culture's nonverbal communications would compare with the nonverbal communcations analyzed in this article.

2. Using the search term "nonverbal communcation," locate the article "Beliefs About Female and Male Nonverbal Communication." Before reading the arti-cle, note your own stereotypical predictions about the differences between male and female nonverbal communication. After reading the article, how accurate were your own beliefs about the different ways in which men and women in American culture use nonverbal communication?

3. Using the subject search term "somatotypes" (body types), locate the article "Body Type Preferences and Body Characteristics Associated with Attractive and Unattractive Bodies by African Americans and Anglo Americans." According to the research reported in this article, what cultural differences affect the ways in which appearances are judged by African Americans and Anglo Americans? What are other ways in which you believe your own culture judges attractiveness?

ACTIVITIES

1. Ask your informant (from a culture different from your own) to demonstrate examples of his or her culture's use of communicative body movements (kinesics). What similarities are there between yours and your informant's? What differences are there? What are the potential areas for misunderstandings?

2. In small groups, produce an inventory of common American gestures. An example of one is the "OK" gesture: the thumb and forefinger of one hand form an O, and the rest of the fingers on that hand arch above the O. What other gestures can you think of? Compare your findings with those of the rest of the class and make a master list.

3. Watch a foreign film and look for examples of differences in proxemics, touch, and facial expressions. Compare these differences to the dominant culture of North America.

4. In a small group, read the following paragraph and explain what went wrong.

    Jan was in Brazil on business. Ciro, a Brazilian associate, invited her to a dinner party he and his wife were giving. The invitation was for "around 8, this Friday night." Jan arrived at Ciro's house at exactly 8:00. Ciro and his wife were still dressing and had not even begun to prepare the food.

5. Select an airport, supermarket, or shopping mall where people from different cultural backgrounds might be interacting. Observe the interactions in light of some of the items listed below:

    a. What are the average distances between the people you observed? Were there differences related to culture?

    b. What differences did you observe in touching behavior?

DISCUSSION IDEAS

1. In what situations might you need to interpret the nonverbal behavior of someone from another culture? What problems could arise from not understanding differences in nonverbal behavior?

2. Give your culture's interpretation of the following nonverbal actions:

- Two people are speaking loudly, waving their arms, and using a lot of gestures.
- A customer in a restaurant waves his hand over his head and snaps his fingers loudly.
- An elderly woman dresses entirely in black.
- A young man dresses entirely in black.

- An adult pats a child's head.
- Two men kiss in public.

3. How can studying the intercultural aspects of nonverbal behavior assist you in discovering your own ethnocentrism? Give personal examples.

4. How late can you be for the following: a class? work? a job interview? a dinner party? a date with a friend? Now ask these same questions of members of Latin American and Asian cultures.

5. What is meant by the phrase, "Nonverbal communication is rule governed"?

chapter 7

Cultural Influences on Context: The Business Setting

Live together like brothers and do business like strangers.

ARAB PROVERB

There are two fools in every market: one asks too little, one asks too much.

RUSSIAN PROVERB

There is a well-known saying that everyone has to be someplace. This chapter is about those places—the settings where communication events occur. Communication is not devoid of external influence: All human interaction is influenced to some degree by the social, physical, and cultural settings in which it occurs. This is known as the communication context.

When you communicate with members of your own culture, you have pretty well internalized the cultural rules that prescribe the behavior within that context, and are able to communicate without giving much thought about those rules. But when you are engaged in intercultural communication, you must be aware of how culture influences the communication context; otherwise, you may encounter a variety of surprises. In this chapter and the next two, we consider the influence culture has on the communication setting. We start here first by discussing the relationship between communication and context, and then we examine how it functions in the business setting. In Chapter 8, we consider the context of the educational setting, and in Chapter 9, we explore the context of health care. We have selected these three arenas because they are the places where you are most likely to encounter people from cultures different from your own.

CONTEXT AND COMMUNICATION

In order for you to see the importance of context to intercultural communication, we need to review three basic assumptions about human communication: (1) *communication is rule governed*, (2) *context specifies communication rules*, and (3) *communication rules are culturally diverse*.

Communication Is Rule Governed

People, both consciously and unconsciously, expect their interactions will follow culturally determined rules or forms of behavior. Communication rules prescribe appropriate behavior by establishing appropriate responses to communication stimuli for the various social contexts found within the larger culture. Social settings usually stipulate which rules govern a particular situation, but it is culture that makes the rules. In Iraq, for instance, a contextual rule prohibits women from having unfamiliar male guests visit them in their homes. In the United States, however, this is not socially inappropriate. Communication rules cover both nonverbal and verbal behaviors and determine not only what should be said but also *how* it should be said. Nonverbal rules, as we saw in Chapter 6, apply to touch (who gets touched and where), facial expressions, (where and when to reveal a smile), eye contact (the appropriateness and inappropriateness of staring), and paralanguage (when to whisper, when to shout).

Verbal rules govern such things as turn taking, voice volume, and formality of language. Obviously, the rules differ depending on the context. In an employment interview, you might frequently use the respectful words *sir* or *ma'am* when responding to your potential employer. At a basketball game, your language would be less formal, incorporating slang phrases and quite possibly negative or derogatory remarks about the opposing team or the officials. For a job interview, you might wear what Americans call a "power suit," whereas at a basketball game, jeans or shorts and a T-shirt could be appropriate. Your nonverbal behavior would also be different. At an interview, you would probably shake hands with your prospective employer, but at the basketball game, you might hug your friends, slap them on the back, or hit a "high-five" (a hand gesture) as a form of greeting.

Context Specifies Communication Rules

The second assumption about communication is that the context specifies the appropriate rules. Think for a moment about how such diverse contexts as a classroom, bank, church, hospital, courtroom, wedding, or funeral determine which communication rules apply. Also, imagine the responses of others if your behavior departs from accepted norms. Extreme deviations can lead to social sanctions such as being ignored, being asked to leave a theater, or even being cited for contempt of court.

Communication Rules Are Culturally Diverse

The third assumption is that rules are culturally diverse. Although cultures have many of the same social settings or contexts, they frequently abide by different rules. Consequently, concepts of dress, time, language, manners, nonverbal behavior, and control of

© Greg Mancuso/Stock Boston

the communication ebb and flow can differ significantly among cultures. When doing business in Turkey, for example, your Turkish colleagues will insist on paying for all the entertainment. Turkish hospitality is legendary and you will not be allowed to pay for even part of the meal. In the United States, the rules for business entertaining are very different. The cost of the meal or entertainment is often shared. Different cultures, different rules.

To be successful in intercultural communication, it is essential that you know not only your own culture's rules but also the cultural rules of the person with whom you are interacting. If you know the rules, the other person's behavior will make greater sense to you and you will be able to control and modify your behavior to conform to his or her expectations.

Having considered context and communication in general, we now look at cultural diversity and communication in the context of business. We begin by looking at the international business context and cross-cultural views of management. Next, we examine the conduct of business, including protocol and negotiation in a variety of cultures. Finally, we survey the workforce in the United States in order to see how cultural diversity affects the workplace.

CULTURE AND THE BUSINESS CONTEXT

As you saw in Chapter 1, many countries are tied directly to an international system of economic interdependence, and most countries have at least one asset within their borders that is needed by another country. The United States alone exports over $650 billion in goods and services to its major trading partners. In 1996, service exports totaled $237 billion accounted for primarily by American movies and television programs, professional and technical advice, and foreign use of U.S. hospitals and schools. Trade, however, is reciprocal. During the first six months of 1996, for example, the United States imported over $122 billion from China and Japan alone.[1] And, in 1998, according to the U.S. Department of Commerce, the United States imported over $719 billion in foreign goods.[2]

No country is completely self-sufficient. Foreign competition and the need to trade more effectively overseas have forced most corporations to become more culturally sensitive and globally minded.[3] Consequently, never before in history has the business arena portrayed such global qualities and a need for effective intercultural communication.

The increase in globalization is a result of growth in U.S. and foreign multinational industries since the 1960s. Trade agreements like GATT and NAFTA that lower tariffs, tap larger markets, and improve standards of living in the world have become commonplace. Multinational corporations increasingly participate in various international business arrangements involving joint ventures between two or more organizations that share in the ownership of a business undertaking.

Globalization also requires new approaches to doing business. Business models and practices that sufficed within a country are usually inadequate for international markets. According to Rogers and Steinfatt:

> Companies in many industries today operate in a global marketplace. They must design products to fit a wide diversity of cultures, advertise them in numerous languages, and meet the demands of very different consumers. The global marketplace means that these companies are vitally involved in intercultural communication.[4]

One approach to globalization has been the uniting of national businesses to form multinational organizations. Through acquisitions and mergers, many long-familiar U.S. companies have been absorbed into other companies or gained new names. For instance, the recent merger of Daimler-Benz and Chrysler has created the new Daimler-Chrysler Company. The British Beecham Group purchase of the U.S. Smith Kline Beckman Company and the acquisition of Columbia Pictures by Sony represent other recent mergers or acquisitions.

Another approach to globalization has been through partnerships among two or more companies. One such partnership—involving three global corporations, Asahi Glass of Japan, the Samsung Group of Korea, and Corning International of the United States—recently joined in a venture called Video Monitores de Mexico, which will make the glass tubes that are a key component of televisions and computer monitors. The plant will be located in the El Florido industrial park on the eastern edge of the city of Tijuana.[5]

Subcontracting has also become commonplace in the global economy. Subcontracts are arrangements in which a company pays another company to perform part of the production process in manufacturing a product. An example of subcontracting that has seen rapid growth is found in the *maquiladora* plants along the U.S. and Mexican border where Mexican labor is used to assemble parts shipped from the United States and other nations. In 1998, more than 975 *maquiladoras* were operating in Baja, California, alone involving nations of origin ranging from the United States to Mexico, Japan, South Korea, Taiwan, Canada, and numerous European countries.[6]

Finally, management contracts have also increased dramatically over the last decade. In management contracts, one company provides another company with managerial expertise, production, technical, and marketing advice for a fee.

Cultures often have different rules for conducting business.

These international business arrangements usually result in individuals from one culture working not only with, but also *for* individuals from another culture. This situation often proves to be difficult because, as Harris and Moran reveal,

> . . . there are many problems when working or living in a foreign environment. Communication across cultural boundaries is difficult. Differences in customs, behavior, and values result in problems that can be managed only through effective cross-cultural communication and interaction.[7]

In the final analysis, the most successful firms in the global arena will be those companies

> whose managers not only understand world economics and global competitiveness but who also are "sensitive to the broader implication of his or her actions and decisions upon organizational and world cultures."[8]

This challenge exists because even a seemingly universal concept like "management" can be viewed differently from culture to culture. We now turn our attention toward the views various cultures hold regarding management and managers.

THE INTERNATIONAL BUSINESS CONTEXT

Cultural Views Toward Management and Managers

North American Management Culture

It is imperative that you understand the dynamics of management behavior in other cultures if you are to interact successfully with businesspeople from diverse cultures. But, we believe you first need to have an appreciation of North American management culture before examining other cultural systems. From a business and management perspective, Harris and Moran describe Americans as being goal and achievement oriented, believing they can accomplish almost anything given sufficient resources. Americans tend to resent governmental or external interference in their affairs and possess a strong work ethic. They tend toward friendliness and informality, yet in greeting behavior they tend to be a noncontact culture in public. In both play and business, Americans tend to be competitive and aggressive because of their drives to achieve and succeed.[9]

Hofstede provides an insightful view of management that is consistent with the American culture:

> [Management] refers not only to the process but also to the managers as a class of people. This class (1) does not own a business but sells its skills to act on behalf of the owners and (2) does not produce personally but is responsible for making others produce, through motivation. Members of this class carry a high status and many American boys and girls aspire to the role. In the United States, the manager is a cultural hero.[10]

This set of values and orientations is not cross-culturally consistent. In fact, the American management culture is quite different from those of much of the rest of the world.

European Management Cultures

While there are similarities between American and German cultures, German management styles differ considerably. In Germany, for instance, the manager is not a cultural hero. Like Americans, Germans belong to a data-oriented, low-context culture. They "like receiving detailed information and instruction to guide them in the performance of tasks at which they wish to excel."[11] Germans believe in a world governed by *Ordnung*—order. Everyone and everything has a place in a grand design calculated to produce maximum efficiency. *Ordnung* is "inherently a German concept that goes further than even the pragmatic and orderly intent of Americans, British, Dutch, and Scandinavians."[12] The highly skilled and responsible German workers do not necessarily need an American style manager to motivate them. "They expect their boss or *Meister* to assign their tasks and to be the expert in resolving technical problems."[13] German values include a strong sense of professional calling and pride in work, a tendency toward an authoritarian leadership style, and paternalistic commitment to the country's welfare. From a German perspective, effective managers are self-confident, energetic, open-minded, and particularly competitive. Most Latins and many Anglo-Saxons experience difficulty in working or dealing with Germans because of the seemingly rigid framework within which many German firms operate.[14]

French business practices, in many respects, follow from the philosophy of René Descartes and are based on a tendency toward logic and clarity. Humans are considered reasonable beings with a good mind and able to cope and solve their own problems. This suggests that people can use their wits to achieve their goals by means of craftiness, cunningness, and tricksterism. Rules, regulations, and principles that constitute a body of authoritative ideas govern proper forms of business. This leads to the French management style being more autocratic than the German.[15] The French language supports this management style because it is rational, precise, ruthless in clarity, and argues its points with a logical urgency leaving little room for ambiguity or ambivalence.[16]

The French are high on the power distance scale. Hofstede provides this insight into French management practices:

[The] French do not think in terms of managers versus nonmanagers but in terms of cadres versus non cadres; one becomes a cadre by attending the proper schools and one remains in it forever; regardless of their actual task, cadres have the privileges of a higher social class, and it is very rare for a non-cadre to cross the ranks.[17]

Obviously, the French value this high power differential. Additional values include individualism and authority based on absolutism. Because French managers or cadres are well paid, have attended the best schools (*grand écoles*), and come from well-established families, they tend to have an elitist approach to management.[18]

In a vein similar to the French, the British tend toward elitism in their management practices. Unlike the French, however, their views do not follow from a Cartesian perspective but rather from feudal and imperial origins. "The class system still persists in the UK and status is still derived, in some degree, from pedigree, title and family name."[19] British managers can be described as diplomatic, tactful, laid back, casual, reasonable, helpful, and willing to seek compromise and to be fair.[20] British English differs significantly from American English because it does not employ the exaggeration and tough talk of the American version. British managers manipulate their subordinates with friendly small talk, reserved statements of objectives, and a casual approach to work.[21]

Asian Management Cultures

The management cultures found in Asia differ considerably from those based on European elitism. Asian cultures stress collectivism and harmony, and these characteristics are reflected in their organizational cultures.

Chinese business values have been strongly influenced by Confucianism. Hofstede summarizes the Chinese view:

> Overseas Chinese American enterprises lack almost all characteristics of modern management. They tend to be small, cooperating for essential functions with other small organizations through networks based on personal relations. They are family owned, without the separation between ownership and management typical in the West, or even in Japan and Korea . . . . Decision making is centralized in the hands of one dominant family member, but other family members may be given new ventures to try their skill on. They are low-profile and extremely cost-conscious, applying Confucian virtues of thrift and persistence. Their size is kept small by the assumed lack of loyalty of non-family employees, who, if they are any good, will just wait and save until they can start their own family business.[22]

To the Chinese, harmony is the ultimate goal of human interaction.[23] Harmony is the axis of social interaction; it is seen as the end goal of all human communication. Additionally, kinship, interpersonal connections, face, and power are major factors dominating Chinese management practices.[24] Power is the ultimate determinant influencing Chinese social interaction. In Confucian-influenced cultures, seniority is the main source of power. In China, as well as most Asian nations, seniority derives from age and length of service in an organization. Seniority not only commands respect, it disarms criticism in the Chinese society.[25]

The Japanese, as was the case with the Germans, do not share a strong sense of management. A characteristic feature of Japanese management style is the high value that it places on the harmonious integration of all members of the organization into the corporate structure. Japanese managers typically view their organization as a large extended family.[26] Managers—section chiefs or department heads—value "groupism, harmony, acceptance of hierarchy in work relationships, sense of obligation, and debt of lower level personnel to superiors, and consensual decision making."[27] "While American managers emphasize supervisory style, decision making, and control mechanism, the Japanese are more concerned with communication processes, interdepartmental relations, and a paternalistic approach."[28]

The Japanese language is capable of delicate nuances of states of mind and relationships. Indirect and vague communication is more acceptable than direct and specific orders. Sentences are frequently left unfinished so that the other person may reach the desired conclusion.[29] Japanese dress and appearance are neat, orderly, and conservative for managers. Workers and students frequently wear a distinctive uniform and frequently a company pin.[30]

Latin American Management Cultures

We see yet another difference in managerial approaches when we look at Latin America. You should recognize that Latin America contains a "rich number of cultures"[31] that exist in a widespread area that includes Mexico as well as the regions of Central and South America. Global managers have discovered that all countries south of the U.S. border are not the same. The languages (Spanish, Portuguese, and Native Indian), food, music, and ethnicity (European, Indian, African, and Mestizo) vary among countries and even within countries. For the most part, however, the power, politics, economics, and business continue to be dominated by people living in a culture that has evolved from earlier Spanish and Portuguese colonial cultures.[32]

The Mexican and Latin American managerial styles generally follow that of France, being characterized as autocratic and paternalistic.[33] In middle-sized companies, the CEO is often the owner, and even in very large firms a family name or family connections may dominate the structure.[34] Task orientation is directed from above; strategies and success are dependent largely on social and ministerial connections as well as cooperation between dominant families.[35]

Managerial style in Mexico differs considerably from that in the United States. Mariah de Forest summarizes this notion as it applies to Mexico:

> As in any authoritarian order, Mexicans value status and its observance. Americans regard status as "undemocratic" and try to minimize the differences by dressing casually, calling [someone] by his/her first name (and insisting that we be called by our first name). Americans try to train Mexican supervisors to do the same. But the Mexicans accept the hierarchy and their "stations" in life. To them the issue is honor, not equality. Rather than resent their "rank," workers expect respectful recognition of their roles within the hierarchy. Even the janitor expects respect.[36]

As a result of this authoritarian but honorable business system, there is a delicate balance between maintaining formal respect in the hierarchy and portraying informal sensitivity toward workers' dignity. Although Mexican management may appear autocratic and paternalistic, this style no longer functions as in the past. Contemporary managers and professionals, in particular, do not respond well to directives and commands although they may have done so in the past.[37] As Stephens and Greer note:

> Mexicans are far less tolerant of abrasiveness and insensitivity in managerial styles than are Americans. . . . You can hurt the feelings of Mexican workers very easily. . . . This "soft culture" reflects the informal side of the formal/informal duality of the Mexican management style.[38]

Management style in Mexico is also affected by a company's ownership. Mexican managers who work for large multinational corporations in Mexico, such as Ford and Johnson & Johnson, generally seem more similar to U.S. managers than those who work for Mexican firms.[39] Mexican decision-making authority tends to be centralized, seemingly undemocratic, and retained by a few top-level executives.[40]

From this examination of various cultural views regarding management styles and managers, you can appreciate how a business procedure, often thought of as universal, can differ from culture to culture. Because of the cultural diversity in the global economy, you may soon find yourself employed by an organization that transacts business with people from many different cultures. You may find yourself managing, being managed by, or co-managing with members of other cultures. Your ability to succeed in these situations will very much depend on your skills as an intercultural business communicator. With this in mind, we now move from broad cultural views of management to cultural-based differences in business protocol and negotiation.

Culture-Specific Business Practices

Business Protocol

A popular bumper sticker in the United States reads "Rules Are for Fools." While this may be expressive of the high value Americans place on individualism and independence, we urge you not to follow that admonition when doing business with people from other cultures. In most parts of the world, culturally correct protocol is both expected and respected. To introduce you to some of the variations in protocol, we start with the elements that help initiate business relationships: *initial contacts, greeting behavior*, and *gift giving*.

Initial Contacts. The protocol for orchestrating an initial contact and appointment to conduct business can range from making a brief telephone call to writing a formal letter of request to the use of a "go-between" or an emissary. The manner in which the initial business contact is made and the amount of advance notice between the contact and appointment are key factors that you must consider when doing business with another culture. A few examples will clarify this point. In El Salvador and much of Latin America, including Mexico, appointments must be made at least a month in advance by mail or telephone and then verified one week before the meeting. In Latin American culture, you should establish your contacts as high up in the organization as possible. It is also very helpful to "use a local *persona bien colocada* (well-connected person) to make introductions and contacts for you."[41]

To obtain an appointment in Egypt, sending a letter of introduction to the Egyptian contact can facilitate appointment seeking. Because a significant majority of Egyptians have ambivalent or negative perceptions of Americans and the rest of the Western world,[42] the use of an intermediary who is willing to set up appointments with all the right people is essential in the Egyptian business world. "Business by 'who you know' has always been an influential force in doing business in Egypt."[43]

In Africa, the use of an intermediary is essential. There is a Congo proverb that states: "The friends of our friends are our friends." Intermediaries can open doors, ensure a warm reception for your upcoming visit, and assess the prospects for the proposal you plan to present. An intermediary is an absolute must in Africa when approaching someone of a higher status.[44]

When doing business in China, it is important to establish contacts *before* you invest in a trip. "The United States Department of Commerce/East Asia and Pacific Office can assist in arranging appointments with local Chinese businesses and government officials, and can identify importers, buyers, agents, distributors, and joint venture partners."[45] To do business in Saudi Arabia, you must have a sponsor act as an intermediary, make appointments, and arrange meetings. In Italy as well, strong contacts who can represent you and make appropriate introductions are preferred. Even with such a representative, it is important that your initial contact be written and in Italian.

The date you plan your business trip is also of major importance when dealing with another culture. For example, in China, many businesses close the week before and the week after the Chinese New Year. In Saudi Arabia, no business is conducted during *Aid-al-Fitr*—the three-day festival of breaking fast at the end of the month of Ramadan—and *Aid-al-Adha*—the three-day feast of sacrifice.[46] In Japan, business is not conducted during New Year's holidays, Golden Week, April 29 to May 5, and Obon, in mid-August, because many people travel to the graves of their ancestors. In Israel, the Jewish holy day—the Sabbath—begins at sunset on Friday and ends at sunset on Saturday. The business week, therefore, runs from Sunday through Thursday. Attempting to conduct business on the Sabbath would be highly inappropriate.

Greeting Behaviors. Once a meeting has been arranged, it is important that the greeting protocol of the host culture be observed. Americans tend to be informal and friendly. Both men and women shake hands on meeting and leaving. A small kiss on the cheek or a hug is appropriate between women or between men and women who have known each other for a sufficient time. First names generally are used with the exception of senior persons or formal situations. Business cards are exchanged in business settings but not in social settings. These greeting behaviors, typical to North Americans, are uncommon in many cultures. For instance, in Saudi Arabia, greetings involve numerous handshakes and tend to be expressive and elaborate. Saudi men often embrace and kiss on both cheeks. Saudi women are rarely present for business meetings, but when they are, an introduction is unlikely. Titles are very important for Saudis and are always used. Business cards are routinely exchanged and are printed in both Arabic and English.

China offers a contrasting example. Communicating a good impression to the Chinese businessperson starts with punctuality. The Chinese have a low tolerance for ambiguity, and they do not like surprises. It is therefore necessary to communicate the details of the meeting agenda as well as any other issues to them prior to the meeting.[47] Chinese do not like to be touched or slapped on the back or even to shake hands. A slight bow and a brief shake of the hands is most appropriate.[48] When being introduced you should stand and remain standing for the duration of the introductions. Seating and order of entrance into the meeting room are important in China since rank is honored. You should allow others to seat you and walk ahead of you to ensure that you are seated in the right position for the meeting.[49] Business cards are routinely exchanged. They should be translated into standard Chinese and include the name of your company, your position plus titles, for example Ph.D., MBA, vice president, or general manager. It is important to clearly indicate your position in the company so the Chinese can treat you accordingly. When presenting business cards, be sure to use both hands as a sign of politeness. When receiving a business card spend a few seconds looking it over.[50] In China, the family name is always mentioned first.[51] Consequently, when addressing someone with the name Li Chen, the proper form of address would be Mr. or Mrs. Chen Li.[52]

Greeting behaviors are influenced by culture.

© Owen Franken/Stock Boston

In Finland, firm handshakes are the normal greeting for men and women. In Finland, it is customary for women to be greeted first. So important is a firm handshake to the Finnish that even children are encouraged to shake hands. However, hugs and kisses are reserved for greetings with close friends and family. Introductions include first and last names or a title and a last name.[53] As a final example of cultural variations in greeting behavior, in Nepal "the traditional greeting is the *namaste*, formed by pressing the palms together, fingers up, below the chin. A slight bow may be added to show respect."[54]

Gift Giving. An old adage in the United States says "Beware of Greeks bearing gifts." Most Americans view gift giving in the business setting akin to bribery, but in many cultures, gift giving is a standard part of business protocol. As such, it is important to know not only the views concerning gift giving, but also what gifts are appropriate for the culture in which you will be doing business. Examples of gift giving in Japan can illustrate this point effectively. Gifts are very common in the Japanese culture. "Business gifts absolutely must be given at midyear (July 15) and at year end (January 1). They are often given at first business meetings."[55] It is also a standard practice to bring flowers, cakes, or candy when invited to a Japanese home. The ceremony of gift giving is more important to the Japanese than the gift itself, although both modest and elaborate gifts are prevalent. It is appropriate to allow your Japanese business colleagues to present gifts first, then match your gift with the same quality as theirs. Do not expect gifts to be opened directly in front of you because this may be construed as a sign of greed. In the rare instances where gifts are opened in front of you, expect restrained appreciation regardless of what they think of the gift. You should not open gifts in front of your Japanese business colleagues, but instead open them when you are alone and thank them later. The paper the gift is wrapped in is also very important to the Japanese. Rice paper is ideal; paper that Americans consider appropriate is distasteful to the Japanese. Although items made by well-known manufacturers are usually good gifts, you should avoid giving knives and scissors because these items symbolize the severance of the relationship. A clock also is an inappropriate gift because it reminds the recipient that time is running out. "To give a clock as a gift is equivalent to saying, 'I wish you were dead.'"[56] Gifts with even numbers of components are also highly inappropriate in Japan, particularly in numbers of four, which could be considered the equivalent of the inauspicious number 13 in the United States.

As the preceding example indicates, the rules for gift giving in Japan are very different from the rules for gift giving in the United States. If gifts are given at all in the United States, they usually conform to the $25 tax deductible gift allowed by law. Even when visiting a home in the United States, it is not customary to bring a gift, although a small token of flowers, a plant, or a bottle of wine is appreciated.[57] Instead of gifts, letters of thanks are standard in the United States.

We have covered only a few elements of business protocol to make the point that business practices differ from culture to culture. This introduction to variations in protocol should amplify the importance of knowing and utilizing the business practices that are acceptable in the culture in which you will be doing business. As with protocol, there is cultural diversity in negotiation strategies and the communication surrounding negotiation. We now turn our attention to this important matter.

Negotiation

In the normal conduct of business, most agreements are achieved through the practice of negotiation. Harris and Moran suggest that "Negotiation is a process in which two or more entities discuss common and conflicting interests in order to reach an agreement of mutual benefit."[58] This is true whether the business goals are to arrange the purchase of products or services, agree to marketing protocols, reach licensing agreements, or to achieve a merger or acquisition. Consequently, people of many different cultures are busily engaged in negotiations worldwide, and the approach taken by each side is strongly affected by their culture.[59] Cultural diversity in negotiation behaviors involves *pacing, negotiating styles*, notions of what constitutes *evidence and truth*, and *social trust*.[60]

Pacing. The pace at which negotiations take place is a culturally diverse characteristic of the negotiation process. Foster relates the following witticism that clearly illustrates this major difference in cross-cultural negotiation:

> There's a joke about an American and a Japanese sitting on a park bench in Tokyo. Both are businessmen. The American says, "Well, you know I've been in Japan for my company for

forty years. Forty years! And now they are sending me back home to the States in just a few days." The Japanese replies, "That's the problem with you Americans: here today and gone tomorrow."[61]

To better understand the negotiation practices of other cultures, it is important for you to first be aware of the standard negotiation practices in the United States. Americans grow up believing in the motto "He who hesitates is lost." Therefore, most Americans conduct business at lightning speed. It is not uncommon for contracts to be signed during the first business meeting. These rapid contracts are facilitated by the fact that middle managers have the authority to make quick decisions without consulting the "boss" or conferring with the group. Sales forces are taught to "close the deal" as rapidly as possible. Brief small talk often precedes the business interaction, but the "bottom-line," short-term rewards, and financial arrangements quickly become the focus.

In much of Latin America, business negotiations are conducted at a much slower pace than in the United States. There is even a proverb that states, "To a hurried demand, a leisurely reply." In Argentina, it may take several trips to accomplish your goal, partly because it takes several people to approve each decision that is made. In some cultures, personal relationships take priority over the product or service, and therefore business does not begin until friendships are established. Personal relationships are so important that if you do not have a contact or intermediary, you may well never get an appointment. For this same reason, Argentines prefer to deal with the same representative for each transaction, or the whole negotiation process begins again from scratch.[62]

In Mexico, too, relationships are important, and a great deal of time is spent building rapport before business proceeds. Mexicans are verbally expressive, and interactions often involve loud exchanges. These exchanges should not be taken personally, since embarrassing one's counterpart is generally avoided.[63] Brazilians, like Argentines and Mexicans, enjoy bargaining and tend to make concessions slowly. In written agreements, there is the general assumption that unless each item of the contract is approved, it is open to continual renegotiations. Success in much of Latin America is tied to appearances. Business executives dress fashionably and expect their counterparts to embody this same aura of success.

In Western Europe, negotiations also progress in a different manner. The French view the negotiation setting as both a social occasion and a forum for their own cleverness. Their sense of history provides them with the desire to fulfill their traditional role of international mediator.[64] French negotiators are often reserved. But, the French team leader will be a highly skilled speaker whose Cartesian logic will reduce less skilled speakers to temporary incoherence.[65]

Negotiation in Eastern Europe is also different from that in the United States. In Poland, Hungary, and Russia, the time it takes to negotiate business usually depends on whether or not the government is involved. When it is, negotiations proceed at an unhurried pace. When you deal with entrepreneurs, however, transactions can progress rapidly. Prior contacts are helpful but not necessary because a person's last successes are deemed more important. Communication is usually indirect, informal, competitive, and at times argumentative.

Negotiation Styles. The manner in which people engage in negotiations is referred to as their negotiation style. It is yet another cultural variable that affects international business communication. Americans tend to have a negotiation style that emphasizes efficiency and directness. They want to get directly to the point, reach an agreement, and sign the accords as rapidly as possible. Their communication tends to be direct and at times argumentative. Other cultures, however, have different negotiating styles that are frequently at odds with American experiences and expectations.

In Germany, business is also conducted very formally with great attention to order, planning, and schedules. Because of this slow methodical process, it is virtually impossible to speed up a business transaction. Humor, compliments, and personal questions are not a part of German negotiations. Instead, business may begin immediately after an introduction.[66] It is important to be well prepared when conducting business in Germany. "Proposals and presentations should be detailed, logical, and filled with appropriate technical data. Be thoroughly knowledgeable in product and contract details."[67] Germans tend to be direct, blunt, and up front. They will ask you all the difficult questions from the start. You must convince them of your efficiency, quality of goods, and promptness of services.[68] It is better to be silent rather than offer an uneducated opinion.

Finns and Swedes expect modernity, efficiency, and new ideas. They believe themselves to be up to date and sophisticated. They will expect your company to have the latest in office computers and streamlined factories.[69] Swedes show little emotion during negotiation and expect the same from you. Consensus is important to Swedish negotiators, and they tend to avoid confrontation. They may cut off a discussion abruptly if they think it will lead to an argument over a sensitive topic. In conversations, Swedes do not appreciate exaggeration or superficiality. However, silence is a part of their language pattern, so expect interactions to be filled with long pauses. In Switzerland, "business is a serious and somber undertaking" as well.[70]

Direct, factual communication is important to Russians. "Russians regard compromise as a sign of weakness; it is morally incorrect."[71] As such, they usually try to "out-sit" the other negotiators for more concessions. Negotiations are often spirited and dramatic, with the Russian negotiator insisting the deal is over and storming out of the room, only to return to the negotiation table a short time later. Formalized contracts take time to construct, but until the process is complete, Russians rely on a signed *protokol* after each meeting to keep track of what occurred. The *protokol* is a "joint statement that delineates what was discussed. It is not a formal agreement."[72] Because business laws in eastern Europe are in a state of flux, it is often a good idea to have a legal representative present when negotiating with the Russians.

In the Middle East, business transactions have a different flavor as well. In Israel, a strong sense of fatalism pervades the business environment. This possibly is due to the fact that neighboring countries have been hostile to Israel and have frequently attempted to destroy it. Futuristic plans are of little importance if there is no assurance of life in a year. As a result, "successful business deals in Israel must promise an immediate return. Long-term guarantees and warranties are rarely selling points."[73] Most Israelis, at least by American standards, are confrontational and emotional in their negotiating style. Interactions are conducted at very close distances, and physical contact is common among men, but not with women.

Egyptians love to bargain. In Egypt there are two bargaining styles: *suk* and *Bedouin*. Suk bargaining is of the marketplace; it is less formal and usually begins with outrageous first quotes. Based on a process of give-and-take, suk bargaining eventually leads to a mutually acceptable price. The Bedouin bargaining style revolves around "face" and is based upon uncompromising principles. It may involve third-party mediators because the reputation of the individual in the eyes of his or her group is at stake.[74]

Negotiating in Mexico is usually a long and complex procedure. Before Mexican managers will engage in business discussions, they need to determine if a working relationship is possible between the individuals or organizations involved. Courtesy, dignity, tact, and diplomacy dominate Mexican culture. Protocol is important and social competence is as critical as technical competence.[75] The establishment of a warm working relationship with one's counterparts is essential to the process and facilitates negotiation.[76] Initially, Mexicans are more formal than Americans and are not accustomed to establishing a first-name basis as quickly.[77] They will, however spend time over coffee, meals, or drinks in order to get know a potential associate and his or her intonations. They put as much stock in an individual's character as in their resources and expertise. Contracts may go to a friend rather than to the lowest bidder.[78]

As a final example of cultural diversity in negotiation styles, we examine some cultures in the Pacific Rim. There are many commonalties in negotiation issues in Pacific Rim countries. You can expect negotiation and decision-making processes to last longer than in the United States. Trust, respect, and long-term relationships are valued above contracts. Face-saving and status are crucial issues; as a result, many Pacific Rim countries prefer to conduct business with an intermediary in order to avoid conflict. Concessions tend to be in an escalating pattern, with minor ones coming first. For many of these cultures, age is equal to status, so the most respect as well as the conversation should be directed to the eldest person present. Communication tends to be very indirect, and silence is prominent in all interactions. As we have already shown, "yes" can mean "no" as well as a host of other things. Consequently, in China, Japan, and some African nations, negotiators will avoid saying "no." They may use such terms as "inconvenient," "under consideration," or "being discussed" to mean "no."[79] Smiles may hide embarrassment, shyness, bitterness, discord, or loss of face. When a negotiator from one of these countries draws air in through the teeth, there usually is a problem.

Despite many commonalities among Pacific Rim nations, each culture has unique negotiation styles. For example, in South Korea, you may be asked the same question repeatedly because Koreans are trying to make sure they are correct in their decisions. "Consistently repeated answers will help you more than fresh creative ideas."[80] In Japan, big decisions take time. The Japanese dislike making decisions and prefer to let decisions be made for them by gradually building up a weighty consensus. In their case, a decision might involve months of negotiations.[81] In Indonesia, there is such a great deference to superiors that subordinates will tell them exactly what they want to hear rather than the truth. The purpose of this practice is to shield the superior from bad news in public. The superior will then be told the truth later in private by means of informal channels. In China, doing business is not about "doing business"; it is about building relationships.[82] Newcomers and new business organizations will have to adapt to the Chinese style of negotiations and contract making.[83] The Chinese, however, are genuinely interested in finding common ground and learning from those with whom they do business.[84] They generally give preference to companies with long-standing relationships with state trading companies. Hong Kong negotiators, perhaps because of their Western exposure, tend to be more direct and quick-paced than negotiators from other Pacific Rim cultures. In Hong Kong, negotiations always occur over tea, and the tea cups commonly are used as visual aids. "One cup may be used to represent your company, another cup to represent the Hong Kong company, and the position of the cups will be changed to indicate how far apart the companies are on the terms of agreement."[85]

Evidence and Truth. Cultures can differ greatly about what they consider to be evidence and truth. North American cultures tend to rely on objective observations to establish facts. Truth is that which is verifiable. Statistics and empirical knowledge are utmost. In other cultures, however, you will find other approaches to what constitutes acceptable evidence and the truth.

The French have a saying: "Only truth is beautiful." It is also relative, for an important part of the negotiation process is determining what form of truth is acceptable and/or believable. That is, there are many different kinds of truth in the world, and the source of "truth" for a culture can heavily influence business transactions. Whereas many cultures, including the United States, rely on the accumulation of objective facts, other cultures may trust subjective opinions, religious beliefs, and/or mysticism. For successful business negotiations to occur, it is important to understand the form of evidence or truth the culture you are doing business with prefers. For example, in much of Latin America, decisions are often based on subjective data that are usually influenced by the Catholic Church or political affiliations. Facts are accepted only if they support subjective feelings.[86] Faith in the Catholic Church as a source of truth often results in a strong sense of fatalism among people in Latin America. This sense of fatalism extends into business transactions. Proverbs such as "If your trouble has some remedy, why worry? And if it has no cure, again why worry?" and "Tomorrow is another day" reflect this outlook. In short, many Latin Americans are far more impressed with affect and emotion than logic.

In eastern Europe, countries are shifting from subjective faith in a communistic ideology to a reliance on more objective facts and reasoning. Western Europe has traditionally relied heavily on analytical, objective facts as the focus of evidence. As early as 43 B.C., Cicero, one of the great Roman orators, said, "Reason is the ruler and queen of all things." The locus of these facts is based in ideologies of democracy in Germany and the social welfare state in Sweden. However, in Switzerland, the segments of the population that are not German or French rely on subjective feelings based on faith in nationalism and utopian ideas.[87]

Middle Eastern countries tend to value their religious faith as the primary source of evidence and truth. For instance, in Israel, subjective faith in Judaism and the success and security of the nation are prominent influences. Objective facts may supplement these feelings, but the strong sense of fatalism pervading Israel is clear in a proverb that states, "Life is too short to keep arguing; let's make a deal and be done with it."[88] In Egypt and Saudi Arabia, faith in Islamic ideas forms the basis of all truth. Objective facts may support Islamic ideologies for many Egyptians, but for most Saudis, objective facts seldom overrule their faith.

Pacific Rim countries generally rely on subjective interpretations as the source of evidence or truth. In South Korea, decisions are often based on nationalistic ideologies, but reliance on some objective facts is becoming common. In Hong Kong, one's feelings are supported by the ideology of the group and wholeness. In China, a faith in the governmental party is the source of truth. Chinese philosophy, which is founded in ideologies of universal order and harmony, has an impact on business. That is, ancient beliefs and religious practices are very much a part of Chinese business dealings today. Two such ritualistic practices are reliance on the lunar calendar and the use of "diviners" or a *feng shui* man to determine auspicious dates and arrangements for meetings, opening new offices, moving, and so forth. For example, "A restaurant column in the *Los Angeles Times* mentions that the chef-owner of an elegant Chinese restaurant was having a piece of property evaluated by a *feng shui* master before purchasing it for a second location."[89] Respecting your counterpart's belief in the *feng shui*'s prophecies is important when conducting business with the Chinese. It should be clear by now that criteria for defining truth are culture-bound, and the source of evidence and truth in one culture may not be the source of evidence and truth in another.[90]

Social Trust. Another variable that confounds cross-cultural business negotiation is the issue of trust. Eventually, negotiators have to trust their counterparts. This trust can be based on written laws of a particular country or it can be based on friendship and mutual respect and esteem.[91] Among the Chinese, for example, trust derives from perceptions of personal character, honesty, sincerity, and being true to your word.[92] We have alluded to the fact that establishing trust before conducting business is very important in several cultures, but it is also necessary to consider the trust level of the society as a whole in determining the potential for successful business negotiations. Fukuyama labels this trust variable *social capital* and defines it as:

> a capability that arises from the prevalence of trust in a society or in certain parts of it. It can be embodied in the smallest and most basic social group, the family, as well as the largest of all groups, the nation, and in all the other groups in between. Social capital differs from other forms of capital insofar as it is usually created and transmitted through cultural mechanisms like religion, tradition, or historical habit.[93]

Trust or social capital has a profound impact on business from the transaction itself to the entire culture's economic growth. As with the other values mentioned in Chapter 3, cultures can be placed on a continuum of high trust to low trust. For example, cultures such as Germany, Japan, and the United States are high-trust oriented in their business dealings. They have a marked proclivity toward association with other cultures. Their trust in dealing with other cultures has allowed them to create large, private business organizations. "It is no accident that the world's best-known brand names—Kodak, Ford, Siemens, AEG, Mitsubishi, Hitachi—come from countries that are also good at creating large organizations."[94] In contrast, in low-trust societies like China, Taiwan, Hong Kong, France, and Italy, the reluctance to trust non-kin has resulted in many small family businesses.

As we mentioned earlier, the cultures of the world are becoming increasingly dependent on one another. As a result, "the most useful kind of social capital is often not the ability to work under the authority of a traditional community or group, but the capacity to form new associations and to cooperate within the terms of reference they establish."[95] Success in cross-cultural business negotiations requires that you factor social capital or trust intercultural business communication.

THE DOMESTIC BUSINESS CONTEXT

As we note throughout this book, through birthrates and immigration, the United States is becoming a nation of increasing cultural diversity. With the U.S. minority population now exceeding 75 million, about a quarter of the workforce is now composed of minorities.[96] Demographers predict that by the year 2015, because of the move toward a multiracial, multiethnic society, minorities will make up more than one-third of the U.S. population.[97] Because the cultural diversity in the United States is so widespread, many of the issues that we discussed under the international context also apply to the domestic business context. Monterey, California, is a vivid example of domestic diversity within the United States. "On Alvarado Street, a paisley-shirted tourist over-hears two students speaking in Mandarin Chinese to an Iranian jewelry vendor. In quick succession, pairs of strollers are heard kibitzing in Urdu, Arabic, Farsi, and Korean."[98] In this section, we briefly discuss two areas of concern to our multicultural domestic business context: (1) the importance of diversity in advertising and (2) conflicts in the workplace caused by cultural diversity.

The Importance of Diversity in Advertising

The driving force behind marketing as we approach the twenty-first century is diversity and culture. Groups of people in the United States can be identified on the basis of ethnicity, gender, nationality, age, class, physical ability, and sexual orientation. Advertisers must encourage these group alliances as well as individual uniqueness to maintain a business edge.[99] The following look at the purchasing power of several groups illustrates the importance of this marketing balance. The Selig Center for Economic Growth at the University of Georgia estimated the purchasing power of ethnic markets as follows: $400 billion for African Americans, $235 billion for Latino Americans, and $150 billion for Asian Americans.[100] With a combined $785 billion and rising ethnic market, many companies like Procter & Gamble, Colgate-Palmolive, IBM, Avon, Levi-Strauss, Kraft Foods, NYNEX, and Nordstrom are reaching out to these diverse markets.[101] Two specific examples illustrate this point. Nordstrom, which is considered a pacesetter for diversity in advertising, has been presenting persons of color as models for over a decade; today over one-third of the models in their catalogs display diverse characteristics. Nordstrom also routinely features persons with disabilities in their advertisements. They were the first "upscale retailer to advertise in *Ebony*, a magazine that targets African Americans. Now it advertises in several other ethnic magazines including *Essence*, *Hispanic Magazine*, and *Latina Style Magazine*."[102] Macy's is yet another retailer that has begun to pay particular attention to its multicultural market. The San Francisco Macy's recognized the large Asian American population that lived in the area, as well as the large percentage of Asian American visitors. In response, they created a "special boutique that stocks a large inventory of women's clothing in petite sizes" to serve the smaller Asian woman.[103]

Diversity consulting and market analysis firms are appearing throughout the United States. Many of these businesses are owned and operated by ethnic group members. They promise strategy development, cultural assessment, implementation, training and measurement, and, of course, results. One such company is Hispanic Market Connections, Inc., a full-service market and research firm that is bilingual and bicultural. One of its advertisements states, "Understanding Hispanics' lifestyles, values and culture can mean the difference between Hispanic marketing success and failure." Another advertisement from a different advertising agency encourages marketers to tap into the gay market. Part of its advertisement reads, "Why are more companies targeting the GAY market? We'll be STRAIGHT with you. It's a simple fact: gay men and women are a lucrative niche market."

Cultural Conflicts in the Workforce

As we have shown throughout this book, cultures differ in their value orientations, and these value differences are manifested in the workforce. It is not hard to imagine how differences in such values as individualism versus collectivism, differences in uncertainty avoidance and power distance, and differences in views of masculinity and femininity can be reflected in a diverse workforce. There are, however, more subtle values with the potential for conflict: *discrimination* and *sexual harassment*.

Discrimination

Discrimination in the workplace impacts intercultural communication, because effective intercultural communication demands the ethical and equal treatment of all cocultures in the workforce. Discrimination is not only morally wrong, it makes the working environment a tense and stressful place. And as such, everyone suffers, including the businesses and organizations that are the settings for these discriminatory practices. Workplace discrimination is manifest in many forms including *racial, ethnic, gender, religious*, and *language* discrimination.

Racial/Ethnic Discrimination. Racial and/or ethnic discrimination occurs when an employee is treated differently because of his or her racial or ethnic membership. A recent example of racial discrimination involved hiring and promotion practices by the Washington-Amtrak passenger railroad. African American managers alleged that they were denied promotions and pay raises because of their race and that African American job applicants were the victims of racial discrimination as well. In a court settlement, Washington-Amtrak agreed to pay $8 million to current and former African American managers.[104] In another situation now before the federal courts, Coca-Cola is accused by four current and former employees of discriminating against African American workers in pay, promotions, and performance evaluations.[105]

Because of real and perceived racial and ethnic discrimination in the workplace, many African Americans report they are steering away from corporate America because they believe they will not fit into the corporate environment. Some believe they are not ready to face the kind of challenge they think corporate America represents. While racial discrimination does persist, diversity is helping change American corporate culture to recognize the strengths and potential contributions people can make regardless of race, gender, age, physical ability, ethnicity, sexual orientation, or any other differences.[106]

Gender Discrimination. This form of discrimination is usually practiced against women—although men are not immune—and involves treating employees differently because of their gender. In one recent situation, Mazda motors agreed to promote two or three women to management roles and raise the pay of about 500 female employees in an attempt to eliminate gender discrimination.[107] In Spokane, Washington, two women alleged that senior male executives of the Tidyman supermarket chain discriminated against them and did not promote them because of their gender. In April 1999, a federal court jury agreed with the women's claim and awarded them damages.[108] In a gender discrimination case involving a male, an art teacher was passed over for a tenured teaching position at the University of Wisconsin and the position was offered to a woman. Under terms of a tentative agreement, the teacher could receive $150,000 and a position at the university.[109]

Religious Discrimination. Religious practices are another area in which employers frequently discriminate against employees. Doris Karimnadir is an example of what can happen when unfamiliar religious practices become a part of the workplace. Doris, who practices the Islamic tradition of wearing a *hijab* (a traditional scarf), was sent home from a new assignment as a security guard when she refused to remove her headdress. The company, after realizing its mistake, apologized, reinstated her in a new post, and paid her for lost time at work.[110]

In many workplaces, Muslim employees are finding difficulty reconciling their religious needs with production requirements. The main cause seems to stem from misunderstanding by both employers and employees (both Muslim and non-Muslim) of the religion, particularly with respect to the division between its compulsory, recommended, and optional elements. Additionally, some employers fear that allowing a proportion of the workforce to take time off to follow certain religious practices might jeopardize production. And some employers are concerned that catering to the needs of Muslim employees entails religious favoritism and discriminates against non-Muslims.[111]

Language Discrimination. Language problems also plague work environments. For instance, because many workers are new to the United States, they may have an inadequate knowledge and command of the English language. This language deficiency can easily result in misunderstood instructions. Other consequences of multilingualism in the workplace are the suspicion and feelings of uneasiness that frequently develop when some members of the workforce speak a language that is difficult to understand. Unfortunately, employers sometimes display a lack of respect for other people's language and engage in discriminatory practices. In a recent situation, for instance, a Nigerian bank employee of the Rhode Island Hospital Trust National Bank was denied promotion after three years of good evaluations from his supervisors because of his accent. The Rhode Island Commission for Human Rights ruled in the employee's favor and ordered the bank to pay him $50,000 plus back pay.[112]

Sexual Harassment

As we note in Chapter 1, women are a significant factor in the workforce. The number of women in the workforce has doubled to over 60 million since 1976. Women now account for 46 percent of the labor force and have climbed the management ranks and are making decisions about workplace policies.[113] Of the twenty million businesses in the United States, more than one-third are owned by women. These businesses employed over 13.2 million in 1997, and in sales they generated over $3.1 trillion in 1997.[114]

Despite this progress, women often and men sometimes encounter sexual discrimination and harassment in the workplace that is cause for concern about the proper and effective communication between the sexes. It must be emphasized that the workplace is not an appropriate surrounding to express feelings, desires, or attractions.[115]

Gender discrimination and sexual harassment have resulted in numerous legislative actions and court decisions. In one recent sexual harassment case, the U.S. Equal Employment Opportunity Commission filed a civil rights lawsuit against MBNA Corporation alleging that the company allowed a two-year pattern of sexual harassment against a woman by a male coworker.[116] In another case of sexual harassment, the Ford Motor Company agreed to pay $7.75 million to as many as 900 women to settle complaints that they were groped and subjected to crude comments and graffiti at two Chicago-area plants. In addition, the settlement called for sensitivity training at Ford plants across the nation.[117] Even in the realm of education, sexual harassment is too frequently present. In St. Tammany Parish, Louisiana, for example, a junior high school teacher believed to be involved with a 12-year old student and a band teacher accused of fondling and kissing a sixth-grade girl were recently arrested.[118]

Granting there are many areas of conflict in the domestic workforce, we have not intended to create a profile of American business that is deeply embedded with problems that can never be resolved. As we discuss in Chapter 10, people have the ability to change. An awareness of the important influence culture has on the conduct of business is the first step toward change. As our awareness has increased, there has been progress in the integration of a culturally diverse workforce. For example, many companies appear to be working to promote cultural diversity among their workers. At Silicon Graphics, respect for diversity is so much a part of the organizational culture that "in the middle of lunch in the cafeteria, you will see *hijabs*, Jewish yarmulkes, and Hasidic headwear, and people will not bat an eye."[119] Major companies such as Apple Computer, AT&T, Avon, Coca-Cola, Corning, Gannett, General Motors, Goodyear, IBM, Xerox, Digital Equipment Corporation, Dupont, Hughs, Motorola, and Procter & Gamble have incorporated diversity management programs into their businesses.[120] Kellogg, the world's largest cereal maker, conducts diversity training programs and evaluates its vice presidents in part on their progress in minority hiring and promotion.[121] Prudential Insurance has sent more than seven thousand members of its middle and executive managers to diversity training in the last few years.[122]

We conclude this section by urging you to be aware of the important influence culture has on the conduct of business. Part of that awareness is realizing that you may be uninformed of significant aspects of the business context as it relates to culture. Therefore, we implore you to heed the words of former president John F. Kennedy: "The greater our knowledge increases, the greater our ignorance unfolds."

SUMMARY

- Culturally derived rules specify how communication is to take place by prescribing the appropriate behaviors in given contexts.
- Most nations and many multinational business organizations have international facilities and do business on a global basis.
- The most successful companies will be those who understand world economics and global competitiveness, and who have the ability to communicate effectively with their international counterparts.
- The concept of management can be viewed differently from culture to culture.
- The procedures for seeking business appointments, the ways in which people greet one another, and gift-giving practices differ from one culture to another.
- Strategies for negotiation differ from culture to culture.
- There are many different kinds of evidence and truth in the world, and the source of "truth" for a culture can influence business transactions.
- Trust, on a global scale, should be factored into cross-cultural business issues.
- The American workforce is undergoing rapid cultural changes.
- Major forces behind marketing as we approach the twenty-first century are diversity and culture.
- Cultures differ in their value orientations, and these differences sometimes cause conflict in the workplace.
- Issues such as religious practices, human rights, language diversity, sexual harassment, and sexual and racial discrimination present potential areas of conflict in the workplace.

INFOTRAC® COLLEGE EDITION EXERCISES

1. Americans are often skeptical about rules and protocol and view "etiquette" as concerned with trivial matters of soup spoons and napkin folding. When dealing in an international environment, however, it is very important to be informed about norms and protocols that may differ widely from what one is accustomed to. Using the subject search terms "Business Etiquette," locate and read at least one article that describes cultural differences and examines cross-cultural business communications. Come to class with notes that you would use in preparing for international business communications.

2. Using the PowerTrac option, locate the article "A Cross-National Study of Managerial Values" by William J. Bigoness and Gerald L. Blakely. According to the research reported in this article, what similarities in values exist across nations' managers? What do you perceive to be the key differences reported in the article?

ACTIVITIES

1. In a small group, discuss the various negotiation strategies used by countries in North America, Latin America, eastern Europe, western Europe, the Middle East, and the Pacific Rim.

2. In your local community, seek out various businesses and determine the degree to which the workforce is multicultural.

3. In a small group, discuss how the workplace in the United States can adapt to the increasingly diverse workforce.

DISCUSSION IDEAS

1. Why is effective intercultural communication crucial for cross-cultural business success?

2. How do business protocols differ among cultures?

3. How can businesses do a better job of meeting the needs of a diverse population?

4. How can American society best adapt to the racial/ethnic and gender diversity found in today's workforce?

chapter 8

Cultural Influences on Context: The Educational Setting

There is only one curriculum, no matter what the method of education: what is basic and universal in human experience and practice, the underlying structure of the culture.

WILLIAM HAZLITT

The schools of a country are its future in miniature.

TEHYI HSIEH

CULTURE AND EDUCATION

The Chinese have a saying; "By nature all men are alike, but by education widely different." This chapter is about the relationship between culture and education. We believe it is important to examine the educational setting for three reasons. First, you can gain valuable insight into a culture by studying its perception of and approach to education. For example, the simple proverb "learning is a treasure which follows its owner everywhere" tells us the importance of education to the Chinese. Second, because education is one of the largest professions in the United States, many of you will be encountering members of diverse cultures in your classrooms. An awareness of the cultural diversity in education can help your understanding of specific communication behaviors in multicultural classrooms. Finally, as parents, or potential parents, it behooves you to know the dynamics of a culturally diverse classroom.

In essence all cultures teach the same thing: the perpetuation of the culture passing their history and traditions from generation to generation. Each culture's system of formal and informal education seeks to meet the perceived needs of its society. Thus, in every culture, schools serve a multitude of functions. First, *they help fashion the individual*. As children grow, what they learn and the ways in which they learn influence their thinking and behavior. From a child's view, education provides a way to certainty. It

好好学习天天向...

Schools are a primary means by which a culture's history and traditions are passed from generation to generation.

offers to every child a set of guidelines and values. The English philosopher Herbert Spencer wrote, "Education has for its object the formation of character." Children are also shaped by their schools as they become aware of what they need to know in order to lead productive, successful, and satisfying lives.[1]

Second, *schools are a primary means by which a culture's history and traditions are passed from generation to generation.* Or as historian Will Durant said, "Education is the transmission of civilization." To transmit civilization, schools teach the formal knowledge a culture deems necessary: language, history, government, science, art, music, and how to survive in society. This is true whether you are considering a country as large and complex as the United States or a small tribal society in the midst of a South American rain forest. For instance, the basis of survival in the United States, as is presented in our educational system, is to obtain the knowledge and skills necessary to secure employment that provides income sufficient to live comfortably. In the forest, survival skills may include how to set an animal snare, how to fashion a functional bow and arrow, how to make a fire, or how to recognize which plants are edible and which toxic.

Third, the function of an educational system is to *teach the informal knowledge of a culture.* By the time children attend school, they have already been exposed to and internalized many of the basic values and beliefs of their culture. They have learned the rules of behavior that are considered appropriate for their role in the community and have begun to be socialized into that community.[2] In school, children continue this process and learn the rules of correct conduct, a hierarchy of cultural values, how to treat one another, gender-role expectations, respect, and all of the other informal matters of culture.

Cultural Differences in Education

Cultures with formal educational systems tend to teach much the same thing—literacy, mathematics, history, and so forth—but diversity is found in *what cultures emphasize* and *how it is taught*. We will look closely at both of these issues.

What Cultures Teach

In order for you to understand how culture influences education, we will begin with an examination of what cultures teach. In earlier chapters we emphasized that cultures impress upon each generation their world view, values, and perceptual filters. This task is in part a function of the formal educational systems within a culture. What is taught, therefore, becomes crucial to the maintenance and perpetuation of a culture

Although the teaching of history is common to all cultures, the history the culture emphasizes is its own. For the United States, the history of the Industrial Revolution might be taught. In Mexico, the focus could be on the impact of Spanish colonization of that country. Likewise, the teaching of language is common to all cultures, but the language emphasized is its own. By teaching a culture's history and language to school-children, a society is reinforcing its values, beliefs, and prejudices. Each culture, whether consciously or unconsciously, tends to glorify its historical, scientific, and artis-tic accomplishments and frequently to minimize the accomplishments of other cultures. In this way, schools in all cultures, whether they intend to or not, teach ethnocentrism. For instance, the next time you look at a world map, notice that the United States is prominently located in the center—unless, of course, you are looking at a Chinese or Russian map. Many students in the United States, if asked to identify the great books of the world, would likely produce a list of books by Western, white, male authors. This attitude of subtle ethnocentrism, or the reinforcing of the values, beliefs, and prejudices of the culture, is not a uniquely American phenomenon. Studying only the Koran in Iranian schools or only the Old Testament in Israeli classrooms is also a quiet form of ethnocentrism.

What a culture emphasizes in its curriculum can give you some insight into the char-acter of that culture. Spanish students, for instance, are taught the basic skills of read-ing, writing, and arithmetic. In addition to these basics, Spanish students are also instructed in "formative" skills, "national spirit," and "complementary" skills. Formative skills are taught through religious education. For the Spanish, their culture is a matter of great pride. This pride is partially instilled by the teaching of national spirit as a part of the educational process. Consequently, instruction in history, geography, language, and physical training are an important part of their education process. Complementary skills are those topics the Spanish include because they believe they will be of benefit to their students. English, for instance, has been recently introduced into some Spanish classrooms because the Spanish understand that knowing English can have economic benefits in a global marketplace.

Because Chinese culture is distinctively collectivist, Chinese education emphasizes the goals of the group of society, fosters in-group belonging, demands cooperation and interdependence, and pursues harmony. The Chinese always stress moral education over intellectual and physical education. Confucian tradition holds that teachers should not only teach knowledge but also cultivate in students a strong sense of moral and righteous conduct. Chinese teachers, consequently, hold a position of moral authority and instruct students in the culture's moral rules of conduct.[3]

The Japanese educational system is characterized by a high degree of uniformity. The *Monbusho*, a centralized ministry of education, science, and culture, controls Japanese education. Curriculum standards are specified in a national course of study. Generally speaking, students throughout Japan in the same grade study essentially the same material in virtually the same kind of classroom at approximately the same time and pace.

The Japanese curriculum "emphasizes social studies, democratic political processes, and religious tolerance."[4] The Japanese are highly collectivist. This strong collective value is aptly expressed in the Japanese proverb that states "A single arrow is easily broken, but not in a bunch." Like the Chinese, Japanese students are taught cooperation, harmony, and interdependence. The Japanese strongly believe that proper social behavior is absolutely essential to social harmony; it is considered the bedrock of Japanese morality. Proper social behavior, therefore, is something that all students can and must attain and is paramount in the Japanese educational system.[5]

Although reading, writing, and mathematics are emphasized in Japan, unlike the United States, oral language is not.

> Educators in Japanese schools do not overtly concern themselves with "oral language development" in the curriculum. . . . Reticence is valued in the presence of elders and superiors in Japanese culture, and the school complements the home in imbuing this value in youngsters. Furthermore, even when it is one's prerogative to speak, simple and brief remarks are valued over lengthy or pointed statements. . . . Traditional fairy tales concerning "The Monkey and the Crab" show the smooth-talking crab to be quite a disreputable character. Japanese will point out that their nation has never produced a great orator or even a notable historical speech.[6]

This lack of practice in oral skills often causes Japanese students to experience serious problems if they attend school in the United States.

In Korea, all schools follow the same program of study. The Ministry of Education determines the curriculum content. There are few electives in middle schools and high schools, and variations are tailored to the type of school a student attends. Schools take a variety of forms. There are general schools, vocational schools, or specialized schools, and assignment is based on regional examination and lottery.[7] Reading and writing are highly emphasized, and children learn both Korean and Chinese in elementary school. Although children must learn approximately 1,600 Chinese characters to be able to comprehend a daily newspaper, Koreans believe that it is a sign of a well-educated person to be able to use Chinese characters. English, as well as an additional foreign language, is required in middle school and high school. Writing emphasizes penmanship rather than composition, and students are encouraged to imitate classical works rather than initiate their own original creations. In addition to standard subjects, Korean schools also emphasize moral education. Thus, "social values, civic awareness and duty, and academic preparation are all integral parts of the educational program."[8]

Mexico presents us with yet another insight of what a culture deems important in the education of its people. Knowledge of Mexican educational practices is also important because so many students from Mexico now attend school in the United States.

Education in Mexico differs in a number of ways from the educational systems found in the United States, China, Japan, Korea, or other countries. Mexico's educational system mandates that students complete the twelfth grade. The severe economic climate in parts of Mexico often precludes students from doing this. Some Mexican classrooms appear similar to those in North America. In rural schools, however, students seldom have the luxury of individual textbooks or the use of videos and computers. Rural schoolteachers frequently may have to read from a single textbook while students recite after them or write down what is said in a notebook.[9]

As is the case with most educational systems, history is emphasized. The arts, trades, vocational skills, and Mexican cultural values also are firmly emphasized. As Mexican children grow up within cooperative environments that emphasize strong family ties, the schools reinforce this primary value. Students are taught the value of cooperation over competition and to obtain rewards for others. So strong is the value of cooperation that "the Mexican student will tend to look down on overt competition because of his or her fear of arousing the envy and destructiveness of peers."[10]

Each year, Mexican students must take a battery of tests and pass every one of them before they are allowed to continue their education. Schools attempt to direct students into fields where they have proven inclinations as indicated from the scores on the tests. At the university level, there are few required classes; instead, a student is encouraged to focus on his or her specialty.

As you can see from the examples we have discussed, cultures tend to teach what is deemed essential for it to continue from generation to generation. In many cases—particularly within industrialized cultures—there are close similarities in the areas of science and mathematics. But, in other areas such as history and philosophy, and social values, there may be extensive differences in what is taught because of diverse cultural perspectives.

How Cultures Teach

As we have seen, being familiar with what a culture teaches can give you knowledge about that culture. But, knowing how the culture teaches is just as important because it (1) provides you with an insight into the nature of the culture, (2) helps you understand interpersonal relationships between students and between students and teachers, and (3) gives you a familiarity with the importance a culture places on education.

Inasmuch as cultures vary in what they emphasize, you should not be surprised to learn that there is cultural diversity in how students participate in the learning process. How education proceeds in a culture is tied directly to the values and characteristics of the culture. In some cultures, teachers talk or lecture a great deal of the time, whereas in others students do most of the talking. Silence and minimal vocal participation characterize some classrooms, whereas others tend to be noisy and active. In many cultures, students recite and then write down what their teacher has said rather than using individual textbooks. This is particularly true in countries where the economy does not permit the luxury of textbooks. Also, as we shall see in the next few pages, the authority vested in the teacher varies from culture to culture. Even nonverbal aspects such as space, distance, time, and dress codes are cultural variables in the classroom.

The Spanish classroom is characterized by a lack of competition. Unlike American students, Spanish students do not compete for grades. Because Spanish schools do not emphasize extracurricular activities, Spanish students tend to spend about twice as much time studying academic subjects than do American students. Because the Spanish culture has a high level of uncertainty, the classroom tends to be structured so that students feel comfortable. Teachers outline specific objectives for the day, enforce rules of conduct, and explain assignments clearly. Spanish teachers tend toward traditional styles of instruction such as lectures and drills.

Since the Spanish place a high value on loyalty and group consensus, disagreement may disrupt the cohesiveness of the learning environment. In the Spanish classroom, teachers are considered to be experts. Students, therefore, are expected to agree with their teachers at all times or be viewed as disloyal. On examinations and written assignments, students are expected to repeat the teacher's ideas rather than provide their own thoughts or creative answers. Students are rewarded for their ability to solve problems accurately rather than for their ability to think creatively.

Reward for student achievement is delayed in the Spanish classroom. Students are expected to complete their homework assignments and other projects on time, but they must wait until their final examination to receive a grade. The evaluation of student work does not emphasize how well the student did, but rather what needs to be improved.

In Japan, prestige is determined almost entirely by education. This has led to the development of a teaching system that is intensely competitive yet nourishes group solidarity and collaboration. The Japanese have a school year of 243 days compared to 180 days in the United States.[11] Over the course of nine years of education, this can add up to an extra two full years of schooling. Despite the collective emphasis of the culture, the Japanese educational system makes distinctions in individual ability very early in the academic process. Only the most academically advanced students gain entrance into the most prestigious college-preparatory junior and senior high schools. Many students often attend additional private schools called *juku*. Classes meet every day after school, on Saturdays, and during school vacations.

Korean educational processes are similar to those of Japan. Teachers assume leadership roles in the areas of social values, civic awareness and duty, and academic preparation. Parents hold teachers responsible for disciplining their children, and children are often told that their teachers will be notified if they misbehave at home.

For most subjects, Korean students remain in their homerooms and teachers rotate among classes. This permits the homeroom teacher to be both the social and academic counselor who can easily deal with discipline problems. As group solidarity and conformity are important goals in the Korean educational system, having students take all of their classes together and wear badges and uniforms leads to the achievement of these goals. These goals are further achieved through rules governing appearance, such as hair length for boys and no makeup for girls, which are strictly enforced even on the way to and from school.

As with what is taught in Mexico, how it is taught is also quite different from the other cultures you have just examined. Teachers are expected to be the autocratic head of the classroom, but they are also expected to be sensitive and nonabrasive toward their students. Because there are fewer teachers in the Mexican school system, classes tend to be very large. This leads to an expectation that students will obey class rules. Mexican teachers hold the authority to permanently expel a student from class for unruly behavior. Yet, rather than being cold and aloof, Mexican teachers are usually involved in their students' personal lives. In short, as well as being academic instructors, Mexican teachers are *friends* with their students.[12]

In the Mexican classroom, the school reinforces the primary cultural value of cooperation. As a result, Mexican students may allow others to share their homework or answers in order to display group solidarity, generosity, and helpfulness.[13] In the Mexican classroom, group interaction is the primary learning mode, yet there are times when the teacher will talk and students will sit quietly at their desks. Because Mexican culture values conversation, when students are engaged in group interaction, they will participate enthusiastically in classroom discussion. It is not considered impolite for more than one person to speak at the same time. Multiple conversations may be carried out simultaneously. Teachers move about the classroom during these periods, interact at very close distances, and offer pats on the back or touches as a means of praise or reinforcement.

Finally, as we have said elsewhere in this book, Mexicans value the present. As the famous Latino writer Octavio Paz said, "Reality is a staircase going neither up nor down; we don't move, today is today, always is today." This focus on the present pervades the Mexican classroom. Rather than moving from one subject area to another simply because the clock tells them it is time to change topics, Mexican students work at a relaxed pace even if it means taking longer to finish. Mexican students are more concerned with doing a job well, regardless of the amount of time required.[14]

From our discussion of these representative educational systems, it should be clear that culture dramatically affects the learning process. What the culture teaches exemplifies the culture's unique history and traditions. Cultures also differ in how they teach—lecture versus interaction, cooperation versus competition, silence versus noise, active versus passive, textbook versus recitation, and the like. Even the status of teachers and the esteem in which education is held are reflections of a culture's values, beliefs, and prejudices. We now turn our attention to the complex issue of multicultural education in the United States and the challenges inherent in meeting the educational needs of many diverse students in the same classroom.

MULTICULTURAL EDUCATION IN THE UNITED STATES

As we indicated in Chapter 1, the world is experiencing a major population explosion. The projected world population in 2025 is 8.3 billion people. The United States is not immune to the effects of this population explosion. Immigration policies have made it possible for many people of diverse cultures to call the United States "home." "According to the Census Bureau, 8.7 percent of Americans were born in other countries, the highest percentage since before W.W.II."[15] In addition, four in five legal immigrants now residing in the United States are of non-European ancestry.

The 1990 census indicates that the racial and ethnic composition of the American population is changing dramatically. This trend has continued, and currently nearly one in three Americans identify themselves as African American, Latino, Asian and Pacific Islander, or American Indian. The California Department of Finance estimates that "by the year 2040, the state will be comprised of 49.7 percent Latinos, 32.4 percent non-Hispanic whites, 11.8 percent Asian and 5.9 percent black."[16] An indication of this trend is reflected in the ethnic breakdown of students in San Diego County in California: White, 46%; Latino, 23%; African American, 9%; Filipino, 5%; Asian, 5%; Native American, 1%; and Pacific Islander, 1%.[17]

The schools in the United States have been greatly affected by the combination of population and immigration increases. "In California public schools 1 out of 6 students was born outside the United States, and 1 in 3 speaks a language other than English at home. The Los Angeles school system now absorbs 30,000 new immigrant children each year."[18] In this section, we examine how schools in the United States have attempted to respond to the diversity now found in most classrooms. First, the goals of multicultural education are examined. Second, various approaches to multicultural education are discussed, and third, the impact of language diversity in the American classroom is discussed.

Goals of Multicultural Education

Regardless of culture, educational systems must prepare people to become useful, functioning members of society. This, of course, is an evolutionary process: As society changes, so must the educational systems. One of the difficulties facing the United States today is the fact that the educational system is not adequately preparing children for today's information-age economy.[19] Recently, a semiconductor company was searching for a manager who understood why computer chips are designed in India, water-etched in Japan, diced and mounted in Korea, assembled in Thailand, encapsulated in Singapore, and distributed everywhere in the world.[20]

To help satisfy this type of need, educational systems must continually adapt to the ever-changing needs of the global marketplace and develop students to fulfill the needs of society. Chen and Starosta eloquently point out the value of a multicultural education in preparing students to meet societal needs:

> Academic exposure to the multicultural environment will provide students with the skills to excel in the real world. As the business world adjusts its views to fit a changing society, the academic environment must do the same. Because students ultimately return to the world outside the school, the more fully they learn to recognize and to respect differences in the beliefs, values, and worldviews of people of varying cultural extraction, the more effectively will they promote a multicultural society beyond the classroom.[21]

This requires that attention be given to the characteristics of the students that the system intends to educate.

The challenge of education in the United States is complicated by two factors. First, the American educational system is based on the idea that as many people as possible should have access to as much education as possible.[22] This, of course, means that the educational system must be designed to accommodate all levels of student ability and all areas of interest. The second factor is increasing student cultural diversity. Historically, the classroom culture has been an extension of mainstream American culture. Its values were those of independence, individualism, and concern for relevance and application. Many students whose backgrounds are different from the dominant culture experience a difficult time adjusting to this classroom culture.[23]

Fortunately, schools are adapting to the increase in student diversity. Teachers, administrators, and parents are coming to recognize that "As classrooms in the United States become more diverse culturally, it is important for both teachers and students to understand some of the cultural factors that affect learning."[24] Many schools now routinely teach the experiences and values of many ethnic cultures. Current textbooks incorporate a variety of ethnic individuals who have achieved success. Struggles for equality are vividly depicted, and past racism is bluntly acknowledged. Cultural pluralism is now generally recognized as the organizing principle of education, and children in American schools learn that variety and cultural diversity are assets.[25]

Concrete examples of teaching cultural diversity can be found at every grade level. For young children, who tend to be egocentric, culture is taught most effectively when they study the culture of their peers, rather than that of entire groups of people such as "Native Americans." Learning about topics such as their peers' native languages, birth places, families, and ethnicity will help students learn about culture. Cultural awareness may be enhanced when students are taught to find the similarities in cultures among the differences.[26] Elementary school students learn not only about the traditional Thanksgiving celebration in the United States, but also about other harvest holidays around the world. They learn that African tribal farmers observe harvest festivals to thank their ancestors for keeping them well and sending rain. The moon's birthday is the start of the Chinese harvest festival called *Chung Ch'ui*, in which the Chinese give thanks and remember a victory over an invading army. In India, Hindu women honor Gauri, the goddess of the harvest and the protector of women. In Japan, thanksgiving is a national holiday and a time to give thanks for blessings. Koreans offer prayers for good harvests on Tano Day, and in Switzerland and Sweden, children carry lanterns made from vegetables to celebrate their harvest holiday.[27] Middle schools and high schools include literature from around the world offering alternative perspectives on social problems and significant historical events. Ethnic studies departments can be found in high schools and colleges. Many schools further require that students take courses in cultural diversity.[28]

Multicultural education teaches that human communication is often dependent on one's knowledge of culture. In this approach, teachers and students gain cultural knowledge and this information can enhance appreciation and sensitivity of students' own as well as others' cultures. This enhanced view of culture can help change misconceptions of culture that at one time may have caused miscommunication between members of diverse cultures. A successful multicultural classroom is one in which students and teachers understand each other in their communicative interactions.

There is some evidence that attempts at multicultural education are working. In the United States, for example, "graduation rates are up. The share of high school students taking a core of academic subjects increased from 13 percent to 47 percent in the past decade. The gap between whites' and minorities' test scores has narrowed."[29] These accomplishments may well be attributed to educators who daily confront diversity in their classrooms and have identified the central issues in educating a culturally diverse population. Those issues deal with (1) learning style differences and (2) language diversity. Let us look at these topics so that you can appreciate the link between culture and the educational process.

Approaches to Multicultural Education

Multicultural education must recognize the cultural diversity of students and the effect that diversity has on the learning process. In the classroom setting, both *learning styles* and *language diversity* affect how students learn and participate in the educational process.

Learning Styles

Aristotle once wrote, "To learn is a natural pleasure, not confined to philosophers, but common to all men." Although learning may be natural to humankind, all people do not learn in the same way. There are diverse styles of learning that affect the way in which a learner learns and processes information.[30] Preferred learning styles differ among people and from culture to culture. "The way students in one culture learn may not be the way students of a different culture learn."[31] The strong link between culture and learning is evidenced by research indicating that culture and ethnicity have a greater influence on cognitive style than does social class.[32] It is important for you to note at this juncture that no learning style is better or worse than another.[33] Additionally, research has shown that "When students are permitted to learn difficult academic information or skills through their identified learning style preferences, they tend to achieve statistically higher test and aptitude scores than when instruction is dissonant with their preferences."[34] In this section we will examine four dimensions of learning styles subject to cultural variations: (1) *cognitive*, (2) *communication*, (3) *relational*, and (4) *motivational* styles.

Cognitive Styles. In Chapter 5, we discussed the Sapir-Whorf hypothesis and the influence culture has on language and thought. This impact carries over into the education context because people from different cultures may perceive their environments and process information differently. These different ways of perceiving and processing information are known as cognitive styles. Although there are several recognized cognitive styles, culture plays a large role in determining individual preferences. Understanding the different ways people think and process information is essential to developing learning systems appropriate to a multicultural society. Hence, we will look at four common cognitive styles as they apply to the multicultural classroom.

Field independence versus field sensitivity refers to the manner in which people tend to perceive their environment and the emphasis they place on the field (the whole concept) or on the parts of the field. This is sometimes casually referred to as whether one tends to see the forest or the trees. "Field-sensitive individuals have a more global perspective of their surroundings; they are more sensitive to the social field. Field-independent individuals tend to be more analytical and more comfortably focused on impersonal, abstract aspects of stimuli in the environment."[35] Field-sensitive students prefer to work with others, seek guidance from the teacher, and receive rewards based on group relations. In contrast, field-independent students prefer to work independently, are task oriented, and prefer rewards based on individual competition. Low-context, highly industrialized, individualistic societies such as the United States are predominantly field independent, whereas high-context, traditional, collectivistic societies like Mexico and Japan are field sensitive. Leung examined a significant amount of research conducted by ethnic minority investigators and found that African Americans, Asian Americans, Hispanic Americans, Native Americans, and Hmong students tend to be field-sensitive, holistic learners.[36] Kush has found growing evidence that children raised in traditional Mexican settings develop a more field-dependent cognitive style than do children raised in Mexican American families that have been assimilated to the Anglo culture.[37] Many educators believe that "teachers should begin to function bicognitively in the classroom and teach students to operate bicognitively" as well.[38]

Cooperation versus competition describes a cognitive style denoting whether learners prefer to work together in a cooperative environment or to work independently in competition with one another. Latino cultures, for instance, teach their children cooperation and to work collectively in groups. North Americans, on the other hand, teach their young to work individually and to compete with each other.[39] Cultures vary in the degree to which they stress cooperation or competition. In addition to the Latino culture, African Americans, Asian and Pacific Rim Americans, Filipino Americans, and

Hawaiian Americans tend to raise their children cooperatively. Students working together on class assignments manifest this emphasis in the classroom. For example, in Hawaiian families, multiple caretakers, particularly older siblings, bring up children. This behavior extends to the classroom and is evidenced by "high rates of peer interaction, frequently offering help to peers or requesting assistance from them."[40] Cleary and Peacock indicate that Native Americans also tend to thrive in cooperative rather than competitive learning environments.[41] Teachers who understand which of their students respond to cooperative learning and which students prefer more competitive situations can provide classroom opportunities to accommodate both.

Trial and error versus "watch then do" refers to people's preference to learn by engaging themselves in a task and learning to do it by trial and error or whether they prefer to observe first and then attempt the task. Students from the mainstream American culture usually prefer to solve problems and reach conclusions by trial and error. They practice over and over, expecting and accepting mistakes, until they become skilled.[42] "In other cultures, individuals are expected to continue to watch how something is done as many times and for as long as necessary until they feel they can do it."[43] Many Native American students, for example, prefer to watch until they feel competent to engage in an educational activity.[44]

Tolerance versus intolerance for ambiguity indicates how well people deal with ambiguous situations. Some cultures are open-minded about contradictions, differences, and uncertainty. Other cultures prefer a structured, predictable environment with little change. American culture has a low tolerance for ambiguity in the classroom. As such, the school day is highly structured and students move from subject to subject based on the clock. The level of tolerance or intolerance for ambiguity also affects what is taught in the classroom. For example, American culture emphasizes right/wrong, correct/incorrect, yes/no answers. Native American cultures, on the other hand, have a high tolerance for ambiguity and give little regard to truth in absolute terms.

Communication Styles. In the classroom, communication is probably the most vital activity because it is the mechanism by which learning occurs. Communication involves speaking, listening, and critical thinking. There are, however, various manners in which people engage in these activities. The preferred way in which people interact with one another is called communication style. In this section we will look at four styles of communication most relevant to the classroom.

Direct versus indirect communication reflects the degree to which culture influences whether people prefer to engage in direct or indirect communication. The communication style of Americans tends to be frank and blunt.[45] This level of openness, however, is often shunned by Asian Americans, particularly first-generation immigrants, because such behavior often causes a loss of face. These cultures also view directness as a lack of intelligence. As a Chinese proverb addressing this issue states, "Loud thunder brings little rain." Also, Native American children do not like to speak in front of the class; they feel put on the spot and become uncomfortable. Teachers who are not familiar with cultural preferences for direct or indirect forms of communication may perceive students who prefer indirect communication as stupid, unmotivated, or learning disabled.[46]

Formal versus informal communication reflects the degree of formality expected in communication situations. Cultural differences regarding formality and informality can cause serious communication problems in the classroom. Many foreign students are accustomed to quite formal relationships and sometimes have difficulty bringing them-

In many cultures, the classroom is a very formal setting.

selves to speak to their teachers at all, let alone address them by their given names.[47] For example, in Egypt, Turkey, and Iran, teacher/student relationships are extremely formal and respectful. An Egyptian proverb exemplifies this formal respect: "Whoever teaches me a letter, I should become a slave to him forever." In cultures that value formal communication, students are expected to rise when the teacher enters the room, and teachers are addressed with their appropriate titles and last names, or referred to honorably as "teacher." In Taiwan, for example:

> students rise when the teacher enters the room, and in chorus they say, "Good morning, teacher." They remain standing until the teacher gives them permission to be seated. When students hand papers to teachers, they use both hands, avoid looking them in the eye and bow.[48]

Contrast this with the relaxed, informal student/teacher relationships in American colleges. "'My adviser wants me to call him by his first name,' many foreign students have said. 'I just can't do it! It doesn't seem right. I have to show my respect'"[49] On the other hand, professors have said of foreign students, "They keep bowing and saying 'yes sir, yes, sir.' I can hardly stand it! I wish they'd stop being so polite and just say what they have on their minds."[50]

Nonverbal communication is too varied to categorize into particular styles. It is important to note that this subtle form of communication is heavily influenced by culture and often misinterpreted in the classroom. A few examples will amplify the notion that teachers need to become familiar with the nonverbal behaviors associated with their students' cultures. Puerto Rican students use a nonverbal wrinkling of the nose to indicate "What do you mean?" or "I don't understand." "In Alaskan Native cultures . . . raised eyebrows are often used to signify yes and a wrinkled nose means no."[51] In

Jamaica, students snap their fingers when they know the answer to a question, but in the United States, students raise their hands. In most Asian and Native American cultures, direct eye contact with the teacher is perceived as rude, whereas in the United States a lack of direct eye contact is considered rude. Even the color of ink used by the teacher can have nonverbal communicative effects. Teachers in the United States often use red ink to grade papers. However, in many cultures, such as Korea and parts of Mexico and China, red ink is a sign of death, and a person's name is written in red only at the time of death or the anniversary of a death. To see the names of their children written in red ink may be horrifying to parents and students from these cultures.[52] A familiarity with the nonverbal behaviors of each student's culture will help to reduce miscommunication and improve learning.

Topic-centered communication versus topic-associating communication addresses the manner in which students examine and study a topic. This also is influenced by culture. European American students tend to be topic centered in their approach. That is, their "accounts [are] focused on a single topic or closely related topics, [are] ordered in a linear fashion, and [lead] to a resolution."[53] For example, a topic-centered approach might include a rendition of a day at camp when candles were made. It would begin with the selection of different colored wax and progress to heating the wax, dipping the string in the wax, and finally cooling the wax in water to set the candle. In contrast, African American students often use a topic-associating approach. Their accounts often "present a series of episodes linked to some person or theme. These links are implicit in the account and are generally left unstated."[54] For instance, a topic-associating approach might include a rendition of the purchase of a new coat. The story might include the following information: It was summer when the coat was purchased, the plastic bag had to be kept away from baby sister, cousin began to cry because he wanted to wear the new coat outside to play, and mother was not at home that day. When instructors are not familiar with the topic-associating approach, they may not allow the student to finish his or her thought.

Relational Styles. The manner in which people relate to each other is called their relational style. As with other aspects of human behavior, relational style is yet another activity that is subject to cultural diversity and culturally learned preferences. Individual response styles carry over into the classroom context and can affect the way in which interaction occurs within the culturally diverse classroom. Of the various relational styles, we will examine five that have the greatest impact on multicultural education.

Dependent versus independent learning reflects the degree to which students rely on the support, help, and opinions of their teachers. "Compared to European American students, many but not all non-European American students, especially Hispanic Americans, Native Americans, Filipino Americans, and Southeast Asian Americans, tend to be more interested in obtaining their teachers' direction and feedback."[55] When teachers are aware of this issue, they can develop an effective support strategy in the classroom for students who show little initiative or independence.

Participatory versus passive learning describes how students prefer to participate in the learning process. In some cultures, students are taught to participate actively in the learning process by asking questions and engaging in discussion. In other cultures, the teacher holds all the information and disseminates it to the students, who passively listen and take notes. Many Hispanic, Asian, and Pacific Rim cultures expect their students to learn by listening, watching (observing), and imitating. In the American school system, however, critical thinking, judgmental questioning, and active initiation of discussion are expected of students. Here, again, there is an opportunity for teachers who are not familiar with cultural differences in how students participate in the learning process to make inappropriate judgments about a student's interest, motivation, and intelligence if they do not participate actively in the classroom.

Reflectivity versus impulsivity is indicative of how long students think about a question or problem before arriving at a conclusion. In the United States, students are taught to make quick responses to questions. "Impulsive students respond rapidly to tasks; they are the first ones to raise their hands to answer the teacher's question and the first ones to complete a test."[56] In other cultures, students are reflective and seek answers slowly. In cultures that emphasize reflectivity, if one guesses or errs, it is an admission of not having taken enough time to find the correct answer. This can result in a painful loss of face. Asian and Native Americans are examples of students who are taught to examine all sides of an issue and all possible implications before answering.[57] In the reflectivity and impulsivity dimension, Mexican and North American cultures are the most similar. Both cultures teach their children to think on their feet and make quick responses or guesses to questions. The major difference between the two cultures is in their motivation to respond. Latino students respond quickly because they wish to please their teachers and make the moment pleasant. North American students respond rapidly because individual success and achievement motivate them.[58]

Aural, visual, and verbal learning is concerned with the degree to which students are primarily aural, visual, or verbal learners. For example, Native Americans tend to be both visual and oral learners and tend to use a combination of visual and oral learning styles although they lean toward visual learning.[59] This means that they learn better through observation and images. Yet, because of the strong oral tradition of Native American cultures, Indians are also oral learners. As Cleary and Peacock point out:

> the strong oral tradition of American Indian tribal groups remains a potent influence on the ways many of the students learn, despite the fact that many of these students are first language English speakers or the fact that many have not been directly influenced by traditional storytellers.[60]

As a result of their cultural tradition, listening is highly valued in Native American cultures. This may seem like an advantage for Indian students, but because they listen with little feedback, teachers may perceive them as not paying attention or not being involved in learning. In contrast, "many students, including African Americans, Hispanic Americans, Haitian Americans and Hmong Americans tend to be aural learners."[61] "Haitians usually have a highly developed auditory ability as evidenced by the oral traditions and rote learning methods."[62] Because the Hmong do not have a written language, they have highly developed aural skills.[63] When the classroom contains aural, visual, and verbal learners, a multisensory approach to teaching is often effective.

Energetic learning versus calm learning describes whether students function better in highly active and animated classrooms or calm and placid environments. African American students are used to more stimulation than is found in many schools.

> Many African American children are exposed to high-energy, fast-paced home environments, where there is simultaneous variable stimulation (e.g., televisions and music playing simultaneously and people talking and moving in and about the home freely). Hence,

Culture influences a student's level of motivation in the classroom.

low-energy, monolithic environments (as seen in many traditional school environments) are less stimulating. . . . Variety in instruction provides the spirit and enthusiasm for learning.[64]

Motivation Styles. Cultures provide diverse reasons why it is important and desirable to learn. These reasons are the motivational bases that prompt students to participate and excel in the educational process. Here, we will discuss two types of motivational style that impact on the multicultural classroom.

Intrinsic versus extrinsic motivation is concerned with the source of motivation. We have seen how cultures vary in their orientation to education. As such, motivation is a primary concern for the multicultural teacher who must employ a variety of motivational techniques that coincide with the students' cultural backgrounds. Intrinsic motivation implies that the locus of motivation is found within. Extrinsic motivation reflects outside forces that impact upon the learner. Some students are motivated intrinsically to succeed, whereas others are motivated extrinsically. European American students generally are motivated to learn for intrinsic reasons. For example, many European American students desire to succeed academically so that they can secure a good position and earn a great deal of money. In contrast, Asian students are often motivated extrinsically. "Asian children are often found to be motivated extrinsically by their parents and relatives. They study hard because they want to please their parents and impress their relatives."[65] Native American students are often motivated to learn so that they can please others rather than offend or hurt them.[66]

Learning on demand versus learning what is relevant or interesting describes whether learning proceeds best based on a set curriculum or whether students should be permitted to learn about what is of interest and immediately relevant to them. "All cultures require children to learn many things whether they want to or not."[67] Some cultures, however, emphasize learning what is useful and interesting rather than learning information for the sake of learning. The Japanese culture, for example, requires that all students memorize information such as dates, complex sequences, and lengthy formulas in mathematics, science, and social studies. Each student is also required to learn how to play a musical instrument, regardless of his or her musical ability, and instruction often begins in first grade.[68] In contrast, the Hispanic and Native American cultures stress the importance of learning what is relevant and useful. Native American students:

> prefer to learn information that is personally interesting to them; therefore, interest is a key factor in their learning. When these students are not interested in a subject, they do not control their attention and orient themselves to learning an uninteresting task. Rather, they allocate their attention to other ideas that are more personally interesting, thus appearing detached from the learning situation.[69]

In light of the numerous examples we have examined, it should be clear that multicultural educators have a complex matrix of learning styles to attend to in the classroom. It may be impossible to accommodate all of these learning styles simultaneously. When teachers are aware of these various learning styles, however, they can better choose which styles are most appropriate for their particular classroom.

Language Diversity

Language holds particular significance both in and out of the classroom. As we noted in Chapter 5, language is a system of symbolic substitution that enables us to share our experiences and internal states with others. A common language assumes mutual understanding. It facilitates shared meaning and allows us to communicate on a similar level.

Functions. Language also performs another vital function that affects the educational setting: it provides the individual with his or her ethnic identity. As Dicker notes, "It is not surprising that our native language is often referred to as our 'mother tongue,' a term which recalls our earliest memories and influences."[70] A person's native language has a deep significance because it is the seed of identity that blossoms as children grow.[71] This language passes on the cultural tradition of the group and thereby gives the individual an identity that ties him or her to the in-group and at the same time sets him or her apart from other possible groups of reference.[72] When non- or limited-English-speaking students enter the American school system, they are encouraged to assimilate into the English-speaking culture. This very activity acts as a wedge between their existing identity and the social system into which they are entering.

Degree of Diversity. Language diversity in the American classroom has confounded the educational process. The lack of a common language is often a major reality in many urban American schools. The U.S. Census has determined that of the estimated 45 million school-aged students in the nation's public schools, about 9.9 million, or approximately 22 percent, lived in households in which languages other than English were spoken.[73] By 2040, if existing trends continue, one-half of the U.S. population will speak Spanish as a first language.[74] In many urban schools, diversity has already eliminated the concept of an ethnic majority. Nationally, one-third of all students attending urban public schools speak a foreign language first.[75] In New York City public schools, children are taught in ten different languages; in Dade County, Florida, students speak no fewer than fifty-six tongues; and in California, one in three students speaks a language other than English at home.[76] As a result, some children come to school barely speaking English, some students are limited in their English usage, and other students are bilingual.

Problems. In response to the growing concern about the effectiveness of current LEP programs, Secretary of Education Richard Riley in April 1998 announced a major shift in national educational policy calling for a goal of English language proficiency in three years for virtually all English language learners.[77] This position has achieved support from educators both inside and outside the field of bilingual education who believe that children spend too much time in native language instruction.[78] Many educators believe that in its current form "bilingual education seems to be hurting" Latino students especially—"the one group it was initially designed to help."[79]

These reconsidered views stand in sharp contrast to the current position that English language learners should be taught all academic subjects in their native language for not fewer than five and preferably seven years. Advocates of this position hold that extensive academic instruction in the native language is necessary for students to benefit from mainstream classrooms.[80] What changes will result from the policy change announced by Secretary Riley remains yet to be seen. Some recent events, however, indicate that some large school districts such as New York and Denver and states such as California are seriously rethinking how they will educate English language learners. Both parents and teachers have begun to question the small amount of time devoted to English language development in many bilingual education programs in the primary grades.[81]

Limited English Proficiency Students. Limited English Proficiency, or LEP, students are the fastest growing student population in the United States. These limited English students have an exceptionally difficult time in school because of both cognitive and linguistic problems. McKeon identified four such problems. First, LEP students must be concerned with both the cognitive aspects of learning and with the linguistic problems of learning English. LEP students "must decipher the many structures and functions of the language before any content will make sense."[82] They not only must grasp the content, but also must make the new language express what they have learned. This requires LEP students to perform at a much higher cognitive and linguistic level than their English-speaking peers who need only to deal with the cognitive aspects of learning.

Higher cognitive and linguistic levels are often difficult to attain because of a second problem that plagues LEP students—academic delays. Many students who enter American schools are academically delayed in their first language. As a result, it is virtually impossible for them to function at the prescribed grade levels, much less higher cognitive and linguistic levels.[83]

Another problem for LEP students is that they enroll in U.S. schools at various points in their academic career—kindergarten, second grade, eleventh grade, and so on. "The higher the grade level, the more limited-English-proficiency is likely to weigh on students because at higher levels of schooling, the cognitive and linguistic loads are heavier."[84]

A final complication for LEP students is that they arrive from countries that may emphasize special curricular sequences, content objectives, and instructional methodologies. For example, Asian students use different rules and formulas for algebra. A deductive instructional approach generally is used in the United States, but Asian cultures use an inductive approach. American schools emphasize written education, whereas African and Middle Eastern schools emphasize oral education. As we noted in Chapter 3, the North American culture values argumentation and debate, whereas many other cultures emphasize harmony and cooperation. Hence, students from these cultures may not possess argumentative skills that are often found in North American classrooms.

IMPROVING COMMUNICATION IN THE MULTICULTURAL CLASSROOM

Classroom teachers must quickly acquire a comprehensive understanding of the ethnic, cultural, and social-class diversity present in today's schools. They must discover that culture creates expectations about appropriate behaviors for teachers and students and describes the "best" way to learn. Culture also determines how classroom activities are structured, dictates how classroom behavior is regulated and controlled, prescribes how teachers should teach, and affects perceptions about the importance of education.[85] Without this perspective, teachers will face the difficulty of instructing effectively in classrooms made up of 51 percent minority students.[86] Additionally, teachers must obtain a more coherent view of knowledge and life that will provide not only personal empowerment but a social perspective truly reflective of the social reality in the larger world.[87]

We have highlighted several key issues in multicultural education. By so doing, it has not been our intent to generate an image of an educational system that is helplessly mired in problems. Instead, by identifying the impact of culture in educating a diverse society, illuminating the problematic issues, and considering the concerns of all those involved, we hope to extend the dialogue of multicultural education. Because the schools contain such diversity, educators, students, and parents must learn to communicate with one another and work together to find workable solutions to the problems. With this optimistic outlook in mind, let us consider some perspectives and competencies teachers can acquire to facilitate communication and improve learning within their diverse classrooms. Perspectives refer to a philosophical orientation toward multicultural education. Competencies, on the other hand, refer to demonstrable characteristic behaviors of a competent multicultural teacher. Although there is an overlap between perspectives and competencies, we have chosen to discuss them separately because they represent different aspects of the same goal: improving communication in the multicultural educational environment.

Multicultural Teaching Perspectives

Although teachers may neither be of the same culture nor speak the native languages of their students, they should adopt the concept of creating a socially sensitive multicultural classroom setting that will assist the learning of their students. According to Hollins, King, and Haymen,

> Culturally responsible pedagogy involves providing the best possible education for children that preserves their own cultural heritage, prepares them for meaningful relationships with other people, and for living productive lives in the present society without sacrificing their own cultural perspective.[88]

There are a number of perspectives teachers can employ to assist them in the creation of a socially sensitive classroom. These include *community in the classroom, structure in the classroom, involving the outside community,* and *grouping.*

Community in the Classroom

Teachers can begin this approach by creating a sense of community in the classroom. "Real learning does not happen until students are brought into a relationship with the teacher, with each other, and with the subject."[89] According to Orbe,[90] there are six characteristics of a "true community" that may be applied to the multicultural classroom.

First, a community must be inclusive. It must generate a general acceptance and appreciation of differences. A community must stress that differences are necessarily neither positive nor negative, but just different.

Second, the members of a community must have a strong sense of commitment. Such a commitment will allow them to "persevere through both positive and negative experiences."[91]

Third, a community must recognize the necessity of consensus. A true classroom community must possess the ability to acknowledge and process cultural differences until a consensus is reached.

Fourth, members of a community must have an awareness of both themselves and others. This recognition will lead them to develop knowledge of how "these two entities interact with the larger external surroundings."[92]

Fifth, members of the community must feel secure enough to be vulnerable to one another. This is accomplished through the creation of a safe classroom "where students are accepted for who they are."[93]

And, sixth, the community must be able to resolve differences. In such a community the members must address problems using productive conflict-reduction strategies instead of avoiding or minimizing or disregarding differences.

Structure in the Classroom

Another approach to the development of a socially sensitive pedagogy is the maintenance of structure in the classroom. Commonalties in day-to-day routines help integrate meaning even with minimal linguistic forms. For example, elementary students learn that the roll is taken first every day, followed by mathematics and then a break. Students in higher grades may learn that class begins with a discussion of a recent current event, then proceeds to a lecture, and culminates with an activity. These standard classroom scripts help students to learn the intended information and respond appropriately.[94]

Involving the Outside Community

Another strategy teachers can employ to assist their students in learning is to seek out culturally diverse members of the community. The larger community often has a vested interest in ensuring children receive the best education possible. Individuals in churches or businesses from the same culture as the students may be able to provide invaluable information about the culture and its language. In some cases, community individuals may be able to help with translations of key assignments or classroom rules.

Grouping

Although many teachers believe that grouping students by ability can lower the self-esteem of the less academically advanced and LEP students, a strategy of using selected assignments or activities based on this grouping may be helpful. These groupings allow students to work as quickly or slowly as they are capable. Thus, children who previously were not academically challenged can move ahead, and children who need to focus longer on a concept have that opportunity. Those who previously were bored can expand their curiosity, and those who were struggling may be relieved not to be with students who always know the answers.[95]

Finally, it is important to remember that children have the capacity to make rapid adaptations across vastly different cultural and linguistic systems.[96] When teachers and students work together, learning is facilitated. As Malcolm notes, "We are underestimating teachers when we consider them to be captives to the invisible culture of the classroom and we are underestimating pupils when we consider them to be captives to their own cultural patterns which contradict it."[97]

Multicultural Teaching Competencies

In addition to the adoption of the teaching perspectives discussed above, multicultural classroom teachers must develop several important competencies appropriate for the multicultural education process. These competencies include *understanding diversity, understanding the self, assessing acculturation, building dialog,* and *empathy.*

Understanding Diversity

First, *it is important to know as much about the cultural backgrounds of the students as possible.* This includes a familiarity with the educational structure of the students' cultural heritages, as well as their particular learning style preferences, linguistic rules, nonverbal behaviors, and gender role expectations. Although this knowledge acquisition places an initial burden on the instructor, such knowledge will facilitate understanding and learning in the classroom.

Understanding the Self

The American writer Thoreau once wrote, "Explore thyself." This is excellent advice for anyone who is going to teach in a multicultural classroom. Put into practical terms, *teachers should be aware of what they "bring" to the classroom.* An honest, straightforward evaluation can be very helpful in promoting the learning of all students. Teachers might ask themselves questions such as, What are my strengths? What are my weaknesses? How can I enhance my strengths and compensate for my weaknesses? Do I have any ethnic or gender biases? How do these biases manifest themselves in the classroom? Does my own ethnic or gender identification affect the classroom? Am I prepared to handle attacks on my racial background or those of my students? What new knowledge or experiences can I seek to assist in these issues?[98]

Assessing Acculturation

Development of the ability of *assessing students' acculturation levels will help teachers determine how much their students are involved in their own culture as well as the Anglo-American culture.* Educators can choose from a wide selection of formal assessment procedures for evaluating students' acculturation levels. The Acculturation Scale for Mexican-Americans by Cueller, Harris, and Jasso (1980),[99] the Acculturation Scale for Mexican-American children by Franco (1983),[100] and the Asian Self-Identity Acculturation Scale are three such instruments.[101] Teachers also can determine acculturation levels by observing students' behavior—which students they socialize with, the language they prefer, how they identify themselves, how they dress, their reaction to ethnic holidays, and the like. Teachers can further interview students or consult with colleagues who are familiar with students' backgrounds.[102]

Building Dialogue

Teachers must maintain an open dialogue with their students. This is not to imply that the students should be in charge of the learning environment. Instead, it means that teachers and students need to discuss and negotiate learning styles, communication patterns, and expectations. This requires students to make connections between course content and their preferred method of learning. Students' voices should be routinely honored in the classroom through open discussion or teacher/ student dialogues.[103] In this way, teachers and students can achieve shared understanding and common communication codes.

Empathy

Finally, *a key characteristic of the competent teacher is empathy.* The empathic teacher must be able to infer the feelings and needs of his or her students. He or she must be able to imagine what it might be like to try and adapt to a classroom where surroundings, language, and behavior are often different and unfamiliar. Additionally, teachers must use cultural knowledge and acculturation assessment information to determine appropriate cultural responses to their students' needs. From observing the teacher's empathy and actions, students too will learn empathy and tolerance. As the American author Helen Keller wrote, "The highest result of education is tolerance."

It is our hope at this point that you understand and appreciate the impact cultural diversity has on the American classroom. And we want you to acknowledge that an educational system that fails to understand cultural diversity will lose the richness of values, world views, lifestyles, and perspectives of the diverse American co-cultures.

SUMMARY

- Education is an important social context in which cultural influences are much in evidence.
- Systems of formal and informal education seek to meet the perceived needs of societies.
- Schools help to fashion the individual.
- Schools are a primary means by which a culture's history and traditions are passed from generation to generation.
- Schools teach the informal knowledge of a culture.
- Schools are a primary vehicle for teaching cultural values.
- Schools in the United States are becoming increasingly more diverse.
- Schools no longer teach only Eurocentric cultural values; instead, today schools routinely teach the experiences and values of many cultures.
- Despite improvements in multicultural education, there is still much controversy about approaches to teaching multiculturally.
- Learning styles are particular ways that individuals receive or process information.
- Cognitive, communication, relational, and motivational learning styles have a profound impact on classroom learning.
- Language diversity is an important issue in the multicultural classroom.
- Students who are limited in their English proficiency face various obstacles in the classroom.
- Teachers should develop a socially sensitive multicultural classroom setting.
- Teachers should know as much about students' cultural backgrounds as possible.
- Teachers should be aware of what they bring to the classroom.
- Assessing the acculturation levels of the students in the classroom will help teachers determine how much their students are involved in their own culture as well as the Anglo American culture.
- A key characteristic of the competent multicultural teacher is empathy.

 INFOTRAC® COLLEGE EDITION EXERCISES

1. Using the subject search term "Education—International Aspects," locate the article "A Study of Three Cultures: Germany, Japan, and the United States—An Overview of the TIMSS Case Study Project." According to the research reported in this article, what are the key differences between these three cultures in national standards, teacher training, differing student abilities, and the place of school in adolescents' lives? (Hint: if you're interested in learning more about educational comparisons between countries, locate the article "The Public Doesn't Believe It" by Gerald W. Bracey. Bracey discusses the ways in which countries vary in their assessments of the effectiveness of high school education systems.)

2. Using the subject search term "Bilingual Education," locate the following two articles:

   (a) "A Babel of Tongues: Bilingual Education in US History"
   (b) "Bilingual Education Si o No?"

   After reading both articles, describe the ways in which the United States has changed in its views of bilingual education. What do you think accounts for these changes? What future changes regarding bilingual education are probable in the United States? What are your views of bilingual education?

3. Home schooling has become an increasingly popular and accepted educational option in the United States. Use the search term "Home Schooling" to learn more about this educational choice. (Hint: A good overview article is "Home Schooling Comes of Age.") After reading about home schooling, what educational values and attitudes does this trend seem to reflect?

ACTIVITIES

1. Drawing upon your school experiences, develop a list that indicates the impact of culture on the classroom.
2. Develop a plan for how you would approach a sixth-grade classroom with the following student clientele: six Latinos, eight European Americans, five African Americans, four Japanese, two Lebanese, and one Iranian.
3. Given the classroom described above, what kinds of communication problems would you anticipate at the beginning of the school year?

DISCUSSION IDEAS

1. In what ways does your current classroom setting embody American cultural values?
2. What problems might students from various cultural backgrounds encounter in a classroom setting that does not foster a variety of approaches to learning?
3. How can multicultural education be effective if it must deal with a large variety of learning styles and language differences?

chapter 9

Cultural Influences on Context: The Health Care Setting

If you are not in tune with the universe,

there is sickness in the heart and mind.

NAVAJO SAYING

He who has health, has hope; and he who has hope, has everything.

ARABIAN SAYING

HEALTH CARE AND COMMUNICATION

The goal of any health care system is to provide optimal care for all of its clients. This, however, can be difficult in a multicultural society. As we have shown throughout this book, cultural diversity is a vital concern in virtually all sectors of society. This becomes especially true in the realm of health care because diverse cultural experiences produce different expectations and forms of communication.

It is important to examine the health care setting for many reasons. First, the promotion of health and the prevention of disease constitute an urgent need for studying this context. Thousands of people die daily from lack of immunization and from diseases and viruses such as AIDS, tuberculosis, cholera, and dysentery.[1] In addition, many of these diseases are highly contagious, and if immigrants with these disorders are not brought into the health care system, they can transmit these diseases to other people.

Second, misunderstandings from ineffective communication cause many people to suffer needlessly. Misdiagnosis, risky procedures, and unnecessary treatments are the result of this miscommunication.[2] Finally, in one way or another, you may be part of an intercultural health care interaction. The health care industry is one of the fastest-growing industries in the United States, and as such, you may someday become a health care professional.

Communication between health care professionals and clients is complex even when the two are from the same culture. When the factor of cultural and language diversity is added, it can create a seemingly impossible situation. How, for instance, does a young woman from Mexico, who speaks no English explain to a medical team in an emergency ward in Los Angeles that the liquid drops she put into her baby's mouth (which the doctors intended for the baby's ears) have made her child worse? Why does a young Japanese woman on her way to surgery begin to cry when she notices that she is being wheeled into operating room number four? Why might an East Indian Hindu woman refuse to answer personal questions about her health in the presence of her husband? Or, why might some hospitalized Japanese Americans politely decline offers of food or water?

As the nexus of thought and relationships, communication is the means by which people connect. When people do not share the same language or the same culture, their attempts to communicate may fail to establish the necessary connection that facilitates healing. "Human communication is the singularly most important tool health professionals have to provide health care to their clients."[3] But, "when there is a conflict between the provider's and the client's belief system, the provider is typically unable to understand the conflict, and hence, usually finds ways of minimizing it."[4] Health care providers, therefore, must learn ways of caring for their clients that match the clients' perceptions of particular health problems and their treatment.[5] Communication becomes the tool by which health care providers can understand the folk beliefs and cultural pressures that are common to various cultures and co-cultures. Understanding the belief systems, however, may not mean the health professional can change them. "Calls for 'culturally competent care' ignore the dynamic nature of culture."[6]

As children grow up, they learn about appropriate health care behaviors from their parents, families, and schools. They learn from medical workers and from many others with whom they interact. Culture teaches children what makes people sick or causes injury. It also teaches them the language or words they should use to describe body parts and illness sensations, how they should behave when they are ill or injured, and what they need to say or do to feel better.[7] People who have grown up in diverse cultures have acquired very different sets of knowledge, beliefs, values, and attitudes about health.

Effective communication is necessary to resolve health issues. This chapter explores some of those issues. We begin by considering cultural diversity in causes of illness, how illness is treated, and how it can be prevented. Second, we explore some specific issues concerning religion, spirituality, and health care. Third, we examine communication patterns in the multicultural health care setting of the United States. And, finally, we offer some suggestions for improving cross-cultural health care communication.

CAUSES, TREATMENT, AND PREVENTION OF ILLNESS

Health Belief Systems

Cultures differ in their understanding of the causes, treatment, and prevention of illness. Despite these differences, all health belief systems can be divided into three categories: *biomedical*, *personalistic*, and *naturalistic*.[8]

Cultures differ in the way they explain, treat, and prevent illness.

Biomedical System

The biomedical system is the dominant belief system in the United States and focuses on the objective system of diagnosis and scientific explanation of disease.[9] In this view, illness is the result of abnormalities in the body's functioning or structure. Agents such as bacteria and viruses or a physical condition such as an injury or aging generally cause these. Treatment destroys or removes the causative agent, repairs the affected body part, or controls the affected body system. "Prevention of disease involves avoiding pathogens, agents, or activities known to cause abnormalities."[10]

Personalistic System

In the personalistic system, according to Angelucci:

> Disease is the result of active intervention by a supernatural being (deity or god), a non-human being (ghost or evil spirit) or a human (witch or sorcerer). The person is a victim of punishment and is rendered ill by the agent. Treatment involves assuring positive association with spirits, deities, etc.[11]

Hmong culture provides a vivid illustration of the personalistic system. In Fresno, California, the courts were asked to decide if a young immigrant boy from Laos should be forced to have surgery on his clubfoot against the wishes of his parents. The parents believed that the surgery would arouse angry spirits who have punished the boy for a wrong deed committed by an ancestor. In this case, the family believed that the evil spirit could be appeased only if the boy suffered for the entire family.

Naturalistic System

Finally, in the naturalistic system, disease is a result of disequilibrium between the hot and cold elements of the body. "All foods, medicines, conditions and emotions are ascribed hot and cold qualities."[12] Treatment involves restoring the balance by prescribing hot remedies for cold illnesses and cold remedies for hot illnesses. "Prevention of illness involves maintaining balance of the hot and cold forces within the mind, body, and environment."[13] Now that you have an understanding of the three major categories of health belief systems, we will consider some cultural manifestations of those beliefs.

Cultural Diversity in the Causes of Illness

Biomedical Causes

Most health care practitioners in Western cultures subscribe to the biomedical model of health and illness. This approach emphasizes biological concerns and is primarily interested in abnormalities in the structure and function of body systems and in the treatment of disease. Adherents of this approach view this model as "real" and significant in contrast to psychological and sociological explanations of illness.[14] Disease is diagnosed when a person's condition is seen as a deviation from clearly established norms based on biomedical science. Treatment through surgery, medicine, or therapy is designed to return the person to the scientifically established "norm."

Personalistic Causes

The Hmong believe an individual's spirit is the guardian of the person's well-being. If the spirit is happy, then the person is happy—and well. A severe shock or scare may cause the individual's spirit to leave, resulting in unhappiness and ill health.[15] In a similar manner, for the Laotian, "*Phi* (the spirits of nature) control people's lives and can cause illness."[16] Illness also may be caused by losing one of the body's thirty-two souls or by a sorcerer who can cast a spell by projecting foreign objects into a person's body. Often, examining the yolk of a freshly broken egg will tell the Laotian the exact cause of illness. In a similar manner, many Vietnamese subscribe to personalistic causes of illness.[17]

Naturalistic Causes

Many people of Asian origin (Chinese, Filipinos, Koreans, Japanese, and Southeast Asians) do not believe they have control over nature. They possess a fatalistic perspective in which people adjust to the physical world rather than controlling or changing the environment.[18] Traditional Asian teaching stresses a harmonious relationship with nature in which the forces of *yin* and *yang* are kept in balance. *Yin* represents a negative, inactive, feminine principle while *yang* represents a positive, active, masculine force.[19] *Yin* and *yang* combine to produce every occurrence in life. Consequently, many Asians believe that an imbalance in this combination causes illness.[20]

Traditional Mexican and Puerto Rican medical beliefs are based on the Hippocratic humoral theory that specifies four humors of the body.[21] These body humors are "blood—hot and wet; yellow bile—hot and dry; phlegm—cold and wet; and black bile—cold and dry."[22] An imbalance of one of the four body humors is seen as a cause of illness.

People of African, Haitian, Jamaican, or Native American origin often view illness as a result of disharmony with nature.[23] Haitians, for instance, believe that both natural and unnatural events such as spells, curses, magic, and evil people can cause others to become ill.[24] In Native American cultures, where people hold strong beliefs about fate, reasons for becoming ill often are not even questioned. For them, ill health and even death itself are accepted as part of the process of birth and rebirth. An Indian proverb summarizes this view: "That which blossoms must also decay."

Many cultures rely on herbs and other natural ingredients to treat illnesses.

Cultural Diversity in the Treatment of Illness

The English satirist Jonathan Swift once wrote, "We are so fond of one another, because our ailments are the same." Notice he did not say that the *treatments* for ailments were the same. Just as cultures differ in their beliefs of what causes illness, so too do they differ in views of what constitutes proper treatment of illness. As with health belief systems and causes of illness, cultural diversity in the treatment of illness may be approached from the biomedical, personalistic, and naturalistic perspectives.

Biomedical Treatments

As the cause of illness from a biomedical perspective is an abnormality in the body's function or structure, the treatment is to return the body to normal through medical intervention where treatment destroys or removes the cause of illness. In this sense, antibiotics are used to destroy illness-causing bacteria. Surgery and radiation are employed to destroy cancers. And nutritional supplements such as vitamins and minerals are used to return the body to its normal state.

Biomedical treatments are the dominant form of treatment in the United States and in many Western countries. In the United States, however, members of co-cultures may subscribe to a combination of beliefs about treatment and seek biomedical treatment for some illnesses and personalistic or naturalistic treatments for others. Many Chinese Americans, for example, use both Western and Chinese medical services.[25]

Personalistic Treatments

For many Asians—including Laotians, Hmong, and Vietnamese, as well as many people from Cuba, Puerto Rico, and Brazil—the belief that illness is in part caused by evil winds or spirits leads to treatments that are meant to induce the evil influence to leave the afflicted person.

In this vein, many Asian groups use "cupping" to cure illness. "Cupping" involves placing a heated glass upside down on the chest or back of the sick person and pulling it off after it has cooled. Another common practice among Asian cultures is "spooning" or "coining." In the spooning treatment, a spoon is rubbed vigorously back and forth across the patient's body, most often on the back and the back of the neck. Coining involves the use of a coin about the size of a quarter, which one rubs on the back of the neck, the stomach, the chest, the upper arms, and even along the forehead and temples. These practices are believed to "rub out" evil winds and spirits, but often leave marks that the unaware Western practitioner may interpret as a form of physical abuse. The Hmong use folk healers to cure illness. These shamans enter the spiritual world by chanting, which summons good spirits who then diagnose illness and prescribe treatment through the shamans. For the Mein, treatment involves elaborate healing ceremonies that require the offering of an animal, which the family cooks and eats.[26]

Naturalistic Treatments

In Chinese medicine, the restoration of balance between the *yin* and *yang* forces is of primary importance. As Dresser notes:

> To restore the balance of *yin* and *yang*, specialists may use acupuncture (metal needles inserted into skin at precise points) and moxibustion (heating crushed wormwood or other herbs directly on the skin). Herbalists, easily found in Chinatown shops, act as health consultants, prescribing and creating herbal remedies.[27]

The Chinese may also rely on fortune-tellers to determine auspicious times to perform scheduled surgeries or other medical procedures.

In Mexico, folk medicine is a common form of treating illness. Folk medicine can be traced back to sixteenth-century Spain. It looks beyond illness symptoms and seeks an imbalance in an individual's relationship with the environment; emotional states; and social, spiritual, and physical factors. When one becomes ill, folk healers use foods and herbs to restore the desired balance. A hot disease is treated with cold or cool foods. A cold disease is treated by hot foods. Hot and cold does not refer to the temperature of the foods but to their intrinsic nature. Hot foods include chocolate, garlic, cinnamon, mint, and cheese. Cold foods include avocados, bananas, fruit juice, lima beans, and sugar cane.[28]

Among the common folk healers in Mexico are *Curanderos*, *Yerberos*, and *Sobadors*.

> *Curanderos* (healers), believed to be chosen and empowered by God, are the most respected folk healers. . . . *Yerberos* (herbalists) specialize in the use of herbs and spices to treat and prevent illness. . . . *Sobadors* (masseuses) attempt to correct musculoskeletal imbalances through massage or manipulation.[29]

Many people from Cuba, Puerto Rico, and Brazil believe in *Santeria* (a type of religion). Whenever someone becomes sick, a *santero* is contacted who consults an *Orisha* (saintlike deity) to assist in the cure.[30] It is not uncommon for Haitians to consult voodoo priests and priestesses for treatment that can involve candles, baths, charms, and spirit visits. Within the United States, some groups, particularly African Americans, rely on *pica*—a craving for nonfood substances—to treat illness. For example, an individual may eat laundry starch to "build up the blood" after an auto accident.[31]

Not everyone subscribes to a specific approach in the treatment of illness. In Africa, for instance, there is no typical approach to seeking medical treatment. The effects of colonialism, spirituality, and ancestral traditions affect the varying perceptions toward health care. Many Africans differentiate health care into modern and traditional. Modern medicine follows the active biomedical model of Western medicine. Traditional medicine follows the folk healer tradition. Dependent on the type of illness, patients will choose the most effective treatment.[32]

Although some of these treatments may seem unusual or even bizarre from a Western perspective, medical practitioners in other cultures have been treating their patients with these methods for centuries.

Cultural Diversity in the Prevention of Illness

Cultures also differ in their beliefs and practices about what can be done to prevent illness. Unlike the causes and treatment of illness, where the approaches were rather systematic, in the prevention of illness, people from many cultures employ a combination of biomedical, personalistic, and naturalistic approaches. In the United States and other highly technological cultures, for instance, good health is based on annual physicals, immunizations at specified times, exercise, and good nutrition. Yet, many people also follow health regimens that may include stress-reducing meditation, the ingestion of a variety of "natural" herbs to stimulate sexual performance, prevent or reduce memory loss, and promote energy. In addition, they may seek treatment from chiropractors, acupuncturists, or colon irrigationists as preventive measures.

In sharp contrast, many Muslim Afghanis rely on the Koran to protect them from illness. In a practice called *ta' wiz*, Koran verses are written on paper, wrapped in cloth, and worn by babies and the sickly.

> *Shuist* are Koran verses written on paper, then soaked in water that is drunk. *Dudi* are Koran verses written on paper and burned with rue close to the patient so the smoke will kill germs and ward off evil spirits.[33]

Many members of Mexican and Puerto Rican cultures believe that good health is the result of good luck or a reward from God for good behavior.[34] Consequently, they frequently depend on a variety of items for protection. Amulets or charms, often inscribed with a magic symbol or saying, are common to protect the wearer from disease or evil. Candles, herbs, crystals, statues of saints, shells, and teas also provide protection.

In many Asian cultures, a *Baci* ceremony is a common practice. During pregnancy, birth, marriage, a change of location, illness, or surgery, the family hosts a ceremony. Family members, including a community elder, gather around an altar of "candles, incense, rice, holy water, flowers, and strings."[35] Because some Asians believe that the spirit might depart from the body on these occasions, the body spirits are contacted by the chanting of the elder, and then strings are tied around the patient's wrist to bind the spirits to the body. These strings are usually worn for three days.

Many other cultures avoid violating cultural taboos for protection from illness or in an attempt to avoid exacerbating the illness. For example, several Native American cultures believe it is taboo to cut a child's hair because the child will become sicker and die. This belief can even extend to procedures on the child's head, such as stitches that require removal of the hair. The only way to avoid the death of the child is to counteract the violation of the taboo by attaching a medicine bundle to the child's chest.[36] In a similar manner, Hmong women who become pregnant ensure the health of their children by paying close attention to food cravings. It is their belief, for example, that if a woman craves ginger and fails to eat it, her child will be born with an extra finger or toe.[37]

Although many cultures practice preventive measures, for others prevention is a totally new concept. Many Haitians, for example, do not believe in preventive strategies and rarely engage in immunization. They may bring their ailing to the hospital only when death is imminent. Some cultures believe that the cure for our illnesses can often be found within us. A Yugoslavian proverb says, "Good thoughts are half of health."

Our examination of explanations, treatments, and prevention of illness clearly indicates that what a patient believes can profoundly affect the treatment process. We must also point out that Western medicine, like the Western media, is reaching more people worldwide. As a consequence, many of the cultures we have discussed, while still adhering to their traditional medical practices, are becoming aware of and adapting Western biomedical approaches either alone or in conjunction with traditional cultural practices in the treatment of some illnesses.

Throughout this discussion, we have alluded to the impact of religion and spirituality. Because these deep structural issues have such a profound effect on health care, they warrant further consideration.

RELIGION, SPIRITUALITY, AND HEALTH CARE

What has been long known in several cultures around the world is now becoming recognized in Western societies—a person's mental attitude and spirituality can help in the prevention and healing of illness. In many cultures religion, spirituality, and health care are intertwined, and religion provides solutions and solace when one is in ill health. "It [religion] dictates social, moral, and dietary practices that are designed to keep a person in balance and healthy and plays a vital role in a person's perception of the prevention of illness."[38]

In Mexico, which is predominantly Catholic, fatalism saturates Mexicans' existence. They even have a saying that illustrates this view perfectly: "We submit to pain because it is inevitable, to bereavement because it is irreparable, and to death because it is our destiny."

In many Eastern religions, people are portrayed as spiritual, and a sense of wellness or good health influences a person's spiritual journey.[39] In these cases, health and spirituality are reciprocal. Bhayana highlights this balance:

> Quiet acceptance of one's fate, also pervasive in some Eastern philosophies, is difficult to reconcile with a commitment to preventive methods. Symptoms may be ignored because the fear of dying is lessened. Extraordinary efforts to preserve life may be hard to accept when a deep-rooted belief in reincarnation exists.[40]

Buddhism and Hinduism both offer examples of how religion influences health care practices. Although it is not a common practice, some Buddhists do not accept responsibility for illness because they believe that illness is caused by spirits.[41] There are also some Hindu sects that are not concerned about ill health because they believe that it is a result of misdeeds committed in a past life. They also believe that praying for health is the lowest form of prayer because medical treatment, although useful, is transitory.[42]

Most Western religions are accepting of modern medicine, although there is a great deal of diversity in religious practice. Christian beliefs, for the most part, are very much in line with modern medical practices and good health is highly valued. One exception that can pose difficulty to physicians is the Jehovah's Witnesses' refusal to accept blood transfusions.[43] Jehovah's Witnesses base their philosophy of refusal to accept blood transfusions on biblical injunctions against "eating blood." They believe that the blood of individuals contains both the moral and physical characteristics of that person and accepting a transfusion would result in pollution and the loss of holiness.[44]

By now, it should be obvious that religion and spirituality have a strong influence on the way people define illness and choose to prevent it. In the United States, modern medicine and technology have often outweighed spiritual faith and alternative-healing methods. As medical practices in other cultures become better known, some health care personnel are becoming more open to the influence of spiritual healing and acknowledging it as an effective form of recovery and prevention. The Harvard Medical School, for instance, recently conducted a course entitled "Spirituality and Healing Medicine" attended by 800 scholars, doctors, clinicians, chaplains, and nurses from around the United States. The course consisted of presentations about the healing traditions of various faiths, including Islam, Roman Catholicism, Christian Science, Seventh Day Adventist, and Hinduism.[45]

Western medical practitioners, quite naturally, are requiring research data and experience before wholeheartedly advocating these positions. Evidence supporting the health–spirituality connection is fairly straightforward. For example, "In 212 clinical studies conducted since the mid-1980's, 160 showed positive effects of religious commitment on health, while only 15 showed negative effects."[46] As a consequence, many medical institutions are incorporating mind–body components into their programs.

HEALTH CARE FOR A DIVERSE POPULATION

The delivery of health care in the United States presents a unique challenge. Part of this challenge is an economic and logistic problem. But, more importantly, it is a cultural problem. "With the rising cultural diversity of individuals entering the United States comes increasing diversity in the health care beliefs and practices of those seeking health care."[47] In dealing with this diversity, satisfying ways of caring for all members of society must be discovered and practiced. As Spector suggests:

> In many situations, this is not difficult; in other situations, it seems impossible. . . . the needs most difficult to meet are those of people whose belief systems are most different from the "mainstream" health-care provider culture.[48]

Transcultural medicine thus becomes a major aspect of American society. In health care, culture intervenes at every step of the way.[49] As should be evident by now, the opportunities for miscommunication constitute a major problem in the health care setting. If optimal health care is to be a goal in the multicultural United States, then health care providers must be aware of potential problems related to cultural differences. As Qureshi points out:

> Ignorance of culture can lead to false diagnosis. Only by taking a full history and being sensitive to a patient's culture can a doctor make an accurate diagnosis, understand the patterns of illness in various ethnic groups, and isolate diseases which may or may not be specific to a particular ethnic group.[50]

In this next section, we focus on the cultural and communication problems related to *family roles*, *self-disclosure*, *language*, *nonverbal messages*, and *formality*.

Family Roles

Culture assigns different roles to various members of a family. Culture also contributes guidelines that tell family members how to perceive and communicate regarding health care issues. In this section, we examine some of those guidelines as they affect communication in the health care setting. To this end we will consider *male dominance, modesty and female purity*, and cultural differences in *pregnancy and childbirth*.

Male Dominance

In much of the world male and female roles are not as fluid as they are in the United States; many cultures make sharp distinctions between what is appropriate behavior for men and for women. In the Middle East, Asia, Latin America, Mexico, and Africa, for instance, men are in positions of authority both in and out of the home. This cultural characteristic can become a source of misunderstanding and conflict in the health care setting.

Earlier in this chapter, we posed the question: "Why might an East Indian Hindu woman refuse to answer personal questions about her health in the presence of her husband?" The answer lies in the assignment of family roles within this culture. Traditionally, the role of East Indian Hindu women is faithfulness and servility to the husband.[51] The husband is regarded as the head of the family and is the primary spokesperson regarding family matters including the health care of the individual members.[52] As with the East Indian Hindu culture, in the Saudi Arabian culture, men believe it is their duty to act as an intermediary between the world and their wives. When men from this country and others like it bring in their wives for emergency room or doctor visits, they usually answer all the questions directed to their wives. Even if the wife can speak English, the Saudi male will speak for her.

When dealing with patients from these and similar cultures, health care practitioners should expect the wife to be deferring all questions to her husband. He may consult with his wife about her health status before he answers the question. The practitioner who ignores the husband and seeks information directly from the wife runs the risk of raising feelings of personal humiliation and disrespect of the husband in the eyes of the family.[53]

Such misunderstanding may have severe consequences. At one extreme, routine procedures may be delayed, and at the other extreme, the life of the patient may be endangered. The case of Rosa Gutierrez and her two-month-old son demonstrates this. Rosa had brought her son to the emergency room because he was having diarrhea and had not been nursing.

> The staff discovered that he was also suffering from sepsis, dehydration, and high fever. The physician wanted to perform a routine spinal tap, but Rosa refused to allow it. When asked why, she said she needed her husband's permission before anything could be done to the baby. The staff tried to convince her that this was a routine procedure, but Rosa was adamant. Nothing could be done until her husband arrived.[54]

In most traditional Mexican households, the man makes all the major decisions. Rosa could have legally signed the spinal tap consent form, but from her cultural perspective, she did not hold the authority to do so.

An additional issue of male dominance of concern for health care practitioners is that men from cultures with strong masculine values often give little credibility to female physicians and nurses. In the extreme, they may refuse to be treated or have their family treated by women.

Modesty and Female Purity

The English essayist Joseph Addison wrote, "Modesty is not only an ornament, but also a guard to virtue." Modesty and female purity are also issues that can affect the health care setting. Modesty plays a strong role in Somali culture; men and women cannot be treated together. In addition, men must be treated by males and women by females. In an instance where flu shots were being administered to immigrant Somalis, the shots had to be given to males and females in separate rooms. Male nurses had to give shots to men and female nurses had to give shots to women.[55]

In many male-dominated cultures, modesty and female purity are of paramount importance. Males are charged with protecting female honor. Females are expected to be virgins until they are married. Only their husbands are allowed to see them naked. If these rules are broken, it brings dishonor to the family. The only way honor can be restored to a family in which a female's purity and modesty have been compromised is to punish the girl.

A female from such a culture may be reluctant to seek medical attention, follow medical advice, or undress for a medical examination because of these values. Western practitioners often do not understand the possible consequences of violating one of these cultural norms, particularly if the woman is from an extremely traditional background.

Galanti, a medical anthropologist, reported a story that clearly illustrates the importance of female purity and family honor. Fatima was an eighteen-year-old Saudi Arabian who had been brought to an Air Force hospital with a gunshot wound in her pelvis. Her cousin to whom she was betrothed had shot her. As was customary, her parents had arranged the marriage. Fatima, however, was in love with someone else and did not wish to marry her cousin. An argument followed in which her drunk cousin shot her, paralyzing her from the waist down. At the hospital, X-rays to examine the bullet revealed that Fatima was pregnant. One of the doctors in the case had lived in the Middle East for ten years and realized the potentially explosive situation facing him—and the girl. Girls with out-of-wedlock pregnancies typically were stoned to death. The doctor swore the X-ray technician to secrecy and arranged to have Fatima flown to London for a secret abortion and to remove the bullet. The internist involved was reluctant to go along with the plan, but finally agreed. Unfortunately, as Fatima was being wheeled to the waiting plane, the internist could not live with his conscience and told Fatima's father about the pregnancy. Galanti continues the story:

> The father did not say a word. He simply grabbed his daughter off the gurney, threw her into the car, and drove away. Two weeks later, the obstetrician saw one of Fatima's brothers. He asked him how Fatima was. The boy looked down at the ground and mumbled, "She died." Family honor had been restored.[56]

Pregnancy and Childbirth

Much of the world embraces the Irish saying "Bricks and mortar make a house, but children make a home." We can say with some degree of accuracy that in every culture, childbearing and the gift of life are treated with celebration. All cultures have specific attitudes, practices, gender-related roles, and normative behaviors with regard to pregnancy and childbirth.[57] For these reasons, childbearing is another crucial issue in the health care setting. Although childbearing is a deeply felt emotional experience, the meaning and significance of the experience are often dictated by culture. Childbearing is valued for distinct reasons in different cultures. In the Mexican culture, a woman's status is often derived from the number of children she has borne. In Asian cultures, children, especially males, are valued because they carry on the family name and care for their parents in old age. For Orthodox Jews, childbirth is valued because it is in obedience to biblical law to multiply and replenish the earth. In some cultures, children are valued because of the labor and support they can contribute to the family.

Whereas birth might be a private experience in one culture, it is a societal event in another. For North Americans, the birth experience is normally a private affair involving only the nuclear family. In many non-Anglo cultures, the birth experience is anticipated and shared by a large extended family. Often, Asian, Mexican, and Gypsy families crowd outside delivery rooms awaiting the event. Attendance of the actual birth itself varies from culture to culture as well. In North America, it is standard for the woman's husband to assist her in the labor and delivery of their child, but for many cultures this is not the case. Orthodox Jewish men rarely participate in childbirth because a man is forbidden to touch a woman during "unclean" times—when blood is present during menstruation or childbirth. Many Arab men feel that birthing is a female's job. Many Mexicans feel this way as well, so the woman's mother usually accompanies her during birth, and the husband does not see his wife or child until delivery is over and they have both been cleaned and dressed. In Asian families, because couples generally reside with the husband's parents, the mother-in-law is often the birth attendant.[58]

In some cultures, the pain of childbirth is responded to with self-restraint and silence; yet in other cultures, pain is openly and freely expressed. As we noted earlier in this book, culture dictates the expression of emotion. In many Asian cultures, pain and discomfort are expected to be a part of labor and delivery, but to express the pain brings shame. As a result, many Asian women are stoic, and only white knuckles and looks of intense concentration evidence pain.[59] In Middle Eastern and Mexican cultures, women are not expected to be inhibited in their expression of pain. In the Iranian culture, women are compensated for their suffering during childbirth with gifts. Larger, more expensive gifts are given for greater suffering.[60]

As this discussion shows, family roles can have a profound impact on communication in the health care setting. Communication, assessment, and identification of the various family role beliefs, values, attitudes, and behaviors held by patients are essential to providing efficient, optimal health care. With our recognition of the impact various health care beliefs can have, we now examine health care in the diverse population of the United States.

Self-Disclosure

Closely related to cultural diversity in family roles are the cultural norms that govern self-disclosure. Proper health care demands that the patient trust the health care professional so that both parties can exchange essential medical information. Cultural norms about openness and self-disclosure, however, can often impede the communication process. Although Americans tend to have few qualms about disclosing personal information, in other cultures information of a personal nature is less forthcoming.

Cultural rules may strongly influence patient self-disclosure and communication. Additionally, culture often dictates who can discuss what with whom. Some women from Mexico and Latin America, for instance, may feel embarrassed or shy when talking about "female problems." Frequently, they will refrain from talking about birth control or childbirth with American physicians. When a Latina, who spoke no English, had to sign an informed consent form for a hysterectomy, she relied upon her son to act as a translator. When the son explained the procedure to his mother, he seemed to be translating accurately and indicating the proper body parts. The next day, however, his mother was very angry when she learned that her uterus had been removed and she could no longer bear children. Because of the cultural prohibition against the son discussing his mother's private parts, the embarrassed son had explained that a tumor would be removed from her abdomen and pointed to the general area where the surgery would be performed. Even speaking the same language may be insufficient. It is best to use same-sex interpreters when translating matters of a sexual or private nature.

Asian cultures are generally high-context. For the Asian American, therefore, the problems associated with self-disclosure are somewhat different. Among the Chinese, for instance, too much talk about personal matters is often considered in poor taste. Asian women, as a consequence, tend not to talk about or discuss female problems. In this collective culture, self-importance is a violation of a cultural norm.

The Germans, because they value proper decorum, are also reluctant to disclose highly personal information in most settings. The German proverb "A friend to everyone is a friend to no one" clearly underscores their view of superficial relationships. This reticent and reserved attitude often transfers to the health care context.

Communication characteristics among Russians and Russian immigrants have been fashioned by traditions and experiences over centuries of historical context. The culture remains unique from that of other Europeans as well as Americans. Many Russians fear nurses and physicians for treatment. They do not trust doctors. This leads to a lower reliance on health care professionals and a reluctance to talk about or disclose personal information.[61]

The above examples demonstrate that not all patients are willing to talk to health care providers with the same degree of openness. Being familiar with these cultural variations regarding communication styles and self-disclosure can help the professional extract important and valuable information concerning the patient's health.

Language Barriers

Many of the problems we discussed in Chapter 5 concerning language diversity apply to the health care context as well. Obvious problems such as language differences and the use of interpreters complicate medical interactions. As noted earlier, literal translations often do not convey the true meaning of a communicated message. Think for a moment about the potential for confusion if a Western doctor speaks of a woman's "period" to someone whose culture does not use this euphemism. Also, a literal translation of the phrase "have your tubes tied" may render an understanding that they can just as easily be "untied." Medical implications resulting from such miscommunication can be detrimental to the patient.

Subtle forms of communication behavior can have just as great an impact. From the following example, we can see how the use of idioms can cause misunderstandings.

A Chinese-born physician called the night nurse one evening to check on a patient scheduled for surgery the next day. The nurse advised the physician that she noticed a new hesitancy in the patient's attitude. "To tell you the truth, doctor, I think Mrs. Colby is getting cold feet." The physician was not familiar with this idiom, suspected circulation problems, and ordered vascular tests.[62]

The use of medical jargon may also complicate health care interaction. For example, the use of words like *rhinitis* rather than *hay fever*, *anosmia* instead of *a loss of taste*, and *dementia* rather than *memory loss* can be confusing to native language speakers and even more so for individuals who speak a different language. In addition, "It is sometimes difficult for members of diverse cultures to articulate their symptoms and feelings in the nonnative language."[63] As a result, vague symptoms and generalized descriptions of health may be conveyed. Finally, members of some cultures may be reluctant to reveal personal or private problems, particularly if their children are used as interpreters. For instance, a Mexican woman whose son usually interpreted for her suffered a great deal before the doctor discovered her actual problem—a fistula in her rectum. She was so embarrassed about her condition that she was reluctant to reveal her symptoms through her son. Only when a cultural interpreter was called did she reveal her true symptoms.[64]

Latinos are one of the most medically underserved co-cultures in the United States. Variation in language performance is a crucial determinant of health service utilization where not speaking English will deter Latinos from using health care services.[65] "Compared with non-Hispanic whites in the United States, Hispanics, especially Mexican-Americans, underutilize preventive health services. They tend to forgo such routine procedures as physical checkups, dental and eye examinations, and prenatal care."[66] Within the Mexican American community, the most obvious barrier to health care is language. In spite of the fact that Spanish-speaking people constitute one of the largest minority groups in this country, very few health care deliverers speak Spanish.[67]

Nonverbal Messages

Cultural diversity in nonverbal behavior can affect health care communication. Beliefs, feelings, and attitudes about illness and treatment are frequently expressed nonverbally by both health care practitioners and recipients. While it would be ideal if health care providers were knowledgeable about the nonverbal behavior of all cultures, it does not seem unreasonable to ask that they do learn more about the meaning and use of nonverbal behavior across cultures.[68] There are four areas of nonverbal communication that are especially salient in health care communication: *eye contact, facial expressions, touch,* and *time.* Although these were discussed extensively in Chapter 6, we will look at these again briefly in the specific context of health care.

Eye Contact

Eye contact can be a nonverbal source of confusion. Eye contact is valued in the dominant American culture, and lack of eye contact may be interpreted as a sign of rudeness or an indication of a lack of attention.[69] Many other cultures and co-cultures, however, avoid direct eye contact because they believe direct eye contact is a sign of disrespect, especially when conversing with authority figures such as physicians and other medical professionals. Central Americans, for instance, feel uncomfortable making immediate eye contact with strangers.[70] For the Japanese, avoidance of eye contact traditionally denotes respect, and direct or sustained eye contact with relative strangers may be interpreted as a sign of hostility.[71] Native Americans often stare at the floor during conversations to indicate that they are paying close attention to the speaker.[72] And Vietnamese people are sometimes uncomfortable with steady or direct eye contact and prefer fleeting glances.[73]

Facial Expressions

Facial expressions are commonly perceived as being a guide to a person's feelings. Many cultures and co-cultures such as Italians, Jews, African Americans, and Spanish-speaking people smile readily and use a wide variety of facial expressions. In other cultures, such as in England and Ireland as well as in many northern European countries, fewer facial expressions are used.[74]

Smiling and laughing are indicative of happiness in the dominant American culture. In other cultures, however, smiles may reflect a variety of other emotions including confusion, embarrassment, or politeness. Facial expressions can be used to express feelings that are opposite those being felt. In many Asian cultures, negative emotions are often concealed with a smile. The Vietnamese have a tendency toward impassive facial expressions that make it difficult to understand what the individual is communicating or thinking.[75] In some cases, members of cultural groups such as Native Americans may not use facial expressions to display emotion unless the observer has a deep understanding of the person and the cultural norms.[76]

Touch

Tactile behavior is yet another form of nonverbal behavior that can affect the health care context. Although members of the dominant American culture are usually accustomed to being touched by their physicians and nurses, individuals from many other cultures are not. Vietnamese patients, for instance, prefer touching of the body be kept to a minimum.[77]

Cultural modesty can affect feelings toward touching in the health care context. Members of the Latino cultures seem to engage in high levels of touching behavior. Yet, females are reluctant to expose their bodies to men or other women and can become especially embarrassed during pelvic examinations.[78] Many Latino men may also feel threatened during physical examinations because of strong feelings about modesty.[79]

In some cultures, touch has overtones of magic. Among some Latinos and Native Americans, touch is a symbol for undoing an evil spell; it is seen as a means of preventing harm and of healing.[80] Some Vietnamese, on the other hand, believe they may leave the body through physical contact, which can result in health problems.[81] Additionally, the Vietnamese perceive the human head to be the seat of life, and any procedure that invades the surface or orifice of the head may cause strong feelings of fear.[82]

Time

A patient's orientation to time may affect when or whether he or she shows up for appointments. Time orientation may also affect how consistently a patient will take medicine according to a particular schedule or whether he or she will return for follow-up visits. Differences in time orientations can also influence the amount of time health care professionals spend with patients. Members of the dominant American culture tend to follow a monochronic time orientation, and they do not expect to spend much time with physicians establishing rapport or discussing the causes and cures of illness. Members of other cultures with a polychronic time orientation may have different expectations. They expect a physician or nurse to spend sufficient time to build an appropriate interpersonal relationship and to explain all of the details of their illness and its cure.

Formality

The degree of formality or informality in communication can affect the health care environment. Members from Asian, Mexican, and European cultures, as well as others who value formality in language use, may be disturbed by the North American practice of addressing each other by first names. A physician who addresses an Asian by his or her first name rather than by title and first and last name may inadvertently diminish his or her credibility.

Formality is also reflected in varying degrees of politeness. For example, "Chinese politeness calls for three refusals before one accepts an offer."[83] In North America, however, "no" means "no" the first time. Imagine the confusion and misunderstanding experienced by a Chinese patient politely declining the first offer of pain medication from a North American nurse and then politely suffering while waiting for the second and third offer, which are not forthcoming.

Formal politeness is also reflected in face-saving communication. In many cultures, authority figures are not to be disagreed with or challenged. Even if the patient does not concur or understand the physician's advice, he or she may agree to comply because of politeness norms. Many Mexican Americans, for example, believe that directly contradicting a physician is rude and disrespectful. They may indicate compliance in order not to embarrass the physician, but in actuality, they have no intention of following the instructions. The physician who then perceives agreement erroneously believes that a plan of action has been agreed upon.[84]

As these examples suggest, many misunderstandings in the health care setting can be traced to miscommunications in language or nonverbal patterns. Although being sensitive to cultural differences is important, health care professionals also need to have excellent intercultural communication skills to be able to handle cultural issues. This need for sensitivity and effective communication skills is clearly evident, for instance, when a folk illness represents a real medical emergency. In the Mexican culture, *caida de mollera* is a folk illness in which a baby has a fever, irritability, vomiting, and diarrhea. This illness is often treated with folk remedies. But these symptoms can also indicate a far more serious illness in an infant for which prompt medical attention is needed.[85] In situations like this, the health care provider needs to be sensitive to the patient's beliefs while educating him or her (or the parents in this case) about the negative consequences of relying on folk remedies. Conveying this information in a respectful manner requires excellent communication skills so that the patient is not humiliated or insulted, which would prevent compliance with the medical advice. This often is not as easy as it might sound. Many health care professionals as well as researchers have sought strategies to facilitate the unique interactions necessary in the medical environment. In the final section of this chapter, we share some tactics for improving the multicultural health care interaction.

IMPROVING MULTICULTURAL HEALTH CARE INTERACTION

The communication problems frequently associated with multicultural health care interaction are *not* necessarily caused by a lack of shared cultural knowledge but rather from the failure to use that knowledge. When awareness, acknowledgment, and action characterize the multicultural health care context, greater empathy is achieved. Health care professionals can better understand the problem from the patient's perspective, and solutions that are satisfactory to all can be the result. In this way, optimal health care for all patients can be accomplished.

It is important that you do not presume that the suggestions offered here are mutually exclusive or exhaustive. We likewise recommend that you do not assume that the information contained in this chapter applies to all people associated with a particular culture. For you to do so fails to acknowledge individuality. Additionally, acculturation

*Health care profes-
sionals need excellent
intercultural commu-
nication skills.*

and assimilation levels will affect a patient's response to illness and treatment. Despite these caveats, the suggestions provided should be helpful in facilitating communication in the cross-cultural health care encounter.

First, *it is important to recognize that many cultures may have several medical systems on which they rely.* Even in the United States, many alternative medical systems exist, including the mind–body and spiritual connections discussed earlier. Chiropractic, naturopathy, herbalism, and the laying on of hands can also be considered alternative medical systems.[86] In many instances, Western biomedicine is combined with an alternative method with great success.

Second, *"even in cases where Western scientific medicine is superior, if the patient believes it is insufficient for treating the problem, it probably will be."*[87] As a result, successful treatment of patients requires that their beliefs concerning the causes of illness, how illness should be treated, and how it can be prevented in the future must be acknowledged. This concept is clearly illustrated in the following story. An eighty-three-year-old Cherokee Indian woman was brought to a hospital emergency room after she passed out at home. X rays revealed a bowel obstruction that required surgery. The woman refused to sign the consent form because she wanted to see the medicine man on the reservation. At the request of the social worker, the woman's grandson drove to the reservation and returned with the medicine man in full traditional dress. He conducted a healing ceremony complete with bells, rattles, chanting, and singing for forty-five minutes. At the end of the ceremony, the medicine man indicated that the woman was ready to sign the consent form. She did, and her immediate surgery was uneventful and without complications.[88]

Recognizing various medical systems and being sensitive to patients' beliefs require a great deal of information. In addition to cultural knowledge and an awareness of communication patterns, particular knowledge of the individual is necessary. Fitzgerald offers a series of questions that may provide basic information about an individual's health care beliefs. These questions have cultural implications in that they illuminate cultural diversity in the manner in which the questions are answered.

1. What do you think has caused your problem?
2. Why do you think it started when it did?
3. What do you think your sickness (or injury) does to you? How does it work?
4. How severe is your sickness (or injury)? Will it have a long or short course?
5. What kind of treatment do you think you should receive?
6. What are the most important results you hope to achieve from this treatment?
7. What are the chief problems your sickness (or injury) has caused for you?
8. What do you fear most about your sickness or injury?[89]

As we conclude, we again remind you of the primary motivation behind this chapter. Simply stated, an understanding of different cultural medical systems, communication patterns, and individual beliefs should assist health care providers in becoming more attuned to the culturally based health care expectations held by people whose cultural background is different from their own.

SUMMARY

- Cultures differ in the way they explain, treat, and prevent illness.
- All health belief systems can be divided into three categories: biomedical, personalistic, and naturalistic.
- There is cultural diversity in beliefs about the causes of illness.
- There is cultural diversity in beliefs about the appropriate treatment of illness.
- There is cultural diversity in the approaches to the prevention of illness.
- Religion, spirituality, and health care are often intertwined.
- For many cultures, religion and prayer often provide solutions and solace when one is in ill health.
- Health care practices must accommodate a culturally diverse population.
- Culturally determined family roles can affect communication in the health care setting.
- In much of the world, male dominance affects communication patterns in the health care setting.
- In many cultures, women fulfill roles that are subservient to men. These subservient roles may affect communication in the health care setting.
- In many cultures, modesty and female purity are of paramount importance.
- In all cultures of the world, childbearing and the gift of life are treated with celebration.
- If optimal health care is to be provided in a multiethnic society such as the United States, an awareness of culturally diverse patterns of communication is essential.
- Language barriers, nonverbal messages, and formality and politeness can cause miscommunication in the health care setting.

- Often it is not a lack of shared cultural knowledge that causes the breakdown of communication in the multicultural health care interaction. Instead, failure to act on that knowledge tends to cause problems.

 INFOTRAC® COLLEGE EDITION EXERCISES

1. Using the subject search term "Transcultural Medical Care," locate the article "Cross Cultural Geriatric Ethics: Negotiating Our Difference." According to this article, what are some of the ethical dilemmas in treating older people that are raised by cultural and ethnic differences? After reading the article, review the opening case study of Mrs. Chu. Imagining yourself as a member of Mrs. Chu's health care team, how should the team proceed in caring for Mrs. Chu?
2. How has the influence of Western culture changed Russian health care? How are cultural beliefs and customs about pregnancy and childbirth relevant to developing public health policies in Hawaii? How can psychiatrists treat patients who believe in ghost possession? These are some of the topics addressed in *InfoTrac College Edition* articles examining the connections between health care and culture. Use the subject search term "Transcultural Medical Care" to locate an article that you believe presents an intriguing look at the interaction between culture and health care. Come to class prepared to summarize the article and to discuss the implications of the ideas presented in the article.

ACTIVITIES

1. Approach a member of a culture different from your own and determine what differences may exist between you and your informant's beliefs about the explanation, treatment, and prevention of illness.
2. In a small group, discuss the impact of spirituality on the health care setting.
3. Interview members of your local health care community in order to determine the challenges of providing optimal health care to all patients in a multicultural society.

DISCUSSION IDEAS

1. What is necessary to achieve effective intercultural communication in the multicultural health care setting?
2. How does cultural diversity in language usage complicate the multicultural health care setting?
3. Why might it be important to incorporate more than one medical belief system in the treatment of patients in a multicultural health care setting?

part 4

Knowledge into Action

© Elizabeth Crews/Stock Boston

chapter 10

Accepting and Appreciating Similarities: A Point of View

We should do more than tolerate our diversity; we should honor and celebrate it.
William Jefferson Clinton,
State of the Union Address, January 17, 2000

Not unless we fill our existence with an aim do we make it a life.

REICHEL

There is an English proverb that tells us a good beginning makes a good ending. Believing this idea to have merit, we approach the final chapter of the book in much the same way we opened the first chapter: with two interrelated manifestos regarding intercultural communication. First, shifting demographics and changes in transportation, information systems, political dynamics, and economics have brought people from diverse backgrounds into contact with each other with a regularity that is unique to this period of history. As we enter the new century you will find that your next-door neighbor speaks a different language, your boss and office mate are from another culture, and your Internet "chat-room" partner is thousands of miles away. Second, it behooves you to learn how to become more effective communicators when you are confronted with the people who are part of these changes. The manner in which you face and respond to these intercultural contacts influences your life in subtle and profound ways. These contacts may have positive results as you make new friends whose cultural experiences you find exhilarating. You might also see manifestations of cultural values that you are quick to denounce without understanding the cultural roots of those values. As Schneider and Silverman point out, "In today's global world, condemning other societies leads to misunderstanding and violence. The world's peoples need to learn about each other."[1] This book has been about that learning process. In this final chapter we continue our "instruction" by pursuing five interrelated goals. First, *we will offer a personal philosophy* that reflects our optimism about your ability to improve the manner in which you engage in intercultural communication. Second, *we will examine some potential problems* in attempting to communicate with someone from a cultural background different from your own. Third, *we will explore the resolution of these problems* and offer some advice for improvement. Fourth, because communication is an activity that has consequence, *we will propose some ethical guidelines* that must be taken into consideration when engaging in intercultural communication. Finally, we conclude the chapter, and the book, by *looking at the future of intercultural communication.*

A PHILOSOPHY OF CHANGE

When the Greek philosopher Heraclitus wrote "Everything flows, nothing stays still," he was not only talking about nature and the universe changing, but he was also referring to how people change. This spirit of change is at the heart of our approach to intercultural communication. We believe that improving intercultural communication is not only expedient, but also *possible*. This optimistic view is based on three interrelated assumptions about human communication: (1) the brain is an open system, (2) we have free choice, and (3) our communication behavior influences other people. If these three axioms seem familiar, it is because we introduced them in Chapter 2. Because they serve as the force behind this entire chapter, we now scrutinize them further.

The Brain Is an Open System

This characteristic of communication has its roots in a very special feature of the human brain: our ability to learn and never stop learning. That is to say, *there is not a "top end" to how much new information a person can acquire*. We present the following two examples to make our point. The first word in our dictionary is *aal*, and it is an East Indian shrub; the root of which yields a red dye. We also want to tell you that Buddha was the son of a rich king born into the Shakyan clan. If these two facts were new information for you, your brain would be adding to your fund of knowledge. This is why we describe the brain as an open system. Being able to take in new data as long as we live— and some world views would claim even after—has implications for anyone interested in the study of intercultural communication.

First, this concept of the brain alerts you that although each of *you can learn new ideas throughout life*, your response at any one instant is a product of your genes and what your brain has experienced. Because many of your experiences are directly linked to culture, not all brains have gathered the same information. Put rather simply, at the moment of birth, depending where that birth takes place, you can turn out to be one kind of individual or another. A Maasai child born in Africa will receive information that might be very different from the experiences that confront a baby born in Beverly Hills. This concept, although elementary, is often overlooked by people who fail to understand why cultures often have different ways of perceiving the world and interacting in that world. In short, an awareness that there are different funds of knowledge is important to anyone who seeks cross-cultural understanding.

Second, the notion of the brain as an open system reminds you that *you can learn from each other*. One culture's special skill for treating heart disease can be transmitted to a culture lacking that information. A culture that uses acupuncture to cure ailments can teach this art to groups of people who lack it in their culture. Yet another culture

We are able to learn new ideas throughout our lives.

may transmit the rewards of patience to a culture whose members are always dashing from event to event. In short, the best that you have as a people can be shared.

Third, because you can always continue to learn, *you are capable of learning new information about other people*. You can use those insights to change your own behavior. A strong belief in change is at the very core of this book. We hope that by learning new information about intercultural communication, you will be able to make alterations to your own communication behavior. What is required of you in this time of increased intercultural contact is information, tolerance, and a willingness to change when such change is beneficial to you and society.

We Have Free Choice

Having just developed the idea that learning and change are inescapable, we now offer another truism about human behavior that extends the concept one step further and also adds support to our belief that improvement is possible. This supposition, although intricate in how it is acted out, is uncomplicated in its wording: *you have free choice*. Most of what you do in life, from selecting a single word when you speak to deciding if you should drive over the posted speed limit, you do of your own free will. Although many cultures have a strong belief in fate, and others limit the choices available to their members, in most instances people choose what to do and what not to do. Reflect on the two examples we just used: selecting words and driving fast. We said that each word we choose is under our jurisdiction. We could, for example, have used the word *control* instead of *jurisdiction* in the last line, but we selected the word we wanted—it was our choice. The same idea applies to the influence you have over your nonverbal actions. Even though many actions are habitual, when you greet a stranger, you can still decide to smile, frown, look the person in the eye, or glance down.

Our second example, that of driving fast, also underscores the degree of freedom you enjoy in conducting your life. When you decide how to spend your time, or whom to select as a friend or a mate, you are reflecting free choice. Although selecting a lover might be harder than selecting what words to use, the principle is the same—you have free will. The degree of choice is a function of your cultural background. For example, Americans have a great deal of choice in nearly everything from the selection of clothing to careers. In many parts of the world, however, people have much less freedom. In Japan, China, and India, it is not uncommon for parents to help select marriage partners for their children. Yet even with these cultural differences, everyone must make decisions. As the Irish novelist George Moore wrote, "The difficulty in life is the choice." This final chapter urges you to choose strategies that improve how you communicate with people from different cultures.

Communication Has a Consequence

Our final introductory edict concerning improvement is yet another one of those ideas that first appeared in Chapter 2. In that chapter we discussed how each of our actions produces a response. Some of the responses are obvious and others are subtle. But they all produce a result. Much like the Arab proverb that notes "If you strike mud against the wall, even though it does not stick, it will leave a mark," when you communicate your actions you "leave a mark." Part of improving your communication behavior demands that you take control of your actions.

We now begin talking about improving intercultural communication by asking you to see the interconnective nature of the three points we developed in the last few pages: the brain is an open system (you can learn), you have choices (you can communicate one way or another), and your actions produce a response (you do something to other people). Remembering these ideas should convince you that you have a great deal of power over whether or not you improve your communication behavior.

POTENTIAL PROBLEMS IN INTERCULTURAL COMMUNICATION

Before we begin our analysis of potential communication problems we need to remind you of two important points. First, common sense tells you that the complex nature of human behavior produces many more communication problems than the seven we have isolated in this section of the book. We have trimmed our list based on space constraints and a careful review of the existing literature. Second, although our discussion of potential problems and solutions has a strong theory base, it nevertheless is colored by our personal and cultural backgrounds. We are two white college professors born and raised in America, and although we have visited many countries and studied countless cultures, we have done so from our culture's perspective. Therefore, the "hidden grip" of culture has undoubtedly influenced the way we perceive and interact with the world. Although we have tried to assume a global orientation, we want to alert you to the Western bias that may occasionally, and we hope only accidentally, creep into our commentary.

Seeking Similarities

Think for a moment about the meaning of the following proverb, which, in one form or another, is found in nearly every culture: "Birds of a feather flock together." The meaning is clear—most people seek to be near others with whom they share common outlooks, habits, and traits. Now ask yourself the following two questions: What group of people do you choose to be around, and how do you select those people? If you are consistent with the research in interpersonal communication, you gravitate toward *people who are similar to you*. Although this observation is not profound, it is nevertheless true. For decades, the research in initial attraction and the development of friendships has revealed an overwhelming tendency among everyone to seek out people whom they perceive to be much like themselves.[2] It is a very natural inclination when meeting someone to talk about a topic that both parties might enjoy; and should those talks prove interesting, it is equally natural for friendships to form and evolve. The more points of contact you can establish, the more comfortable you feel.[3]

The connection between intercultural communication and your inclination to solicit friends and acquaintances who mirror your personality should be obvious. As we have said throughout this book, a culture offers its members specialized patterns of communication—patterns that are often dissimilar to those of people from other cultures. The seriousness of this problem is seen globally as well as interpersonally. As the world gets more complex, and people feel overwhelmed by events, you find that "many millions of people believe that their best haven of certainty and security is a group based on ethnic similarity, common faith, economic interest or political like-mindedness."[4] We are not suggesting that there is anything basically wrong with seeking ethnic or cultural similarity, in fact we already mentioned how common it is to seek out the familiar. The problem arises when the pull of similarities is at the exclusion or even the elimination of those who are different. You can see extreme examples of this tendency in all parts of the world. Cleveland offers us two vivid instances of valuing likenesses at the expense of those you deem ethnically or culturally different:

> In Africa ethnicity took over as an exclusive value, resulting in mass murder by machete.
> In ex-Yugoslavia (and too many other places), gunpowder and rape accomplished the same purpose, trampling on human rights and erasing human futures.[5]

What we have been suggesting in this first problem is that culture often separates you from people with a history different from your own. The poet Emily Dickinson vividly described this separation when she wrote, "The Soul selects her own Society- / Then shuts the Door- / To her divine Majority- / Present no more." Her message is crystalline: Most people prefer their "own kind" and "shut the door" on the unfamiliar. This tendency is the very reason the bias of similarity can be a potential communication problem. Later in the chapter, we suggest some ways to keep this characteristic of perception in check, but for now we simply remind you that to banish the unfamiliar can often deny you many exciting and challenging experiences.

Uncertainty Reduction

Our second potential problem is directly related to our first and stems from the theory of *uncertainty reduction*.[6] The communication axioms this theory has generated are clear and directly related to intercultural communication. Berger and Calabrese summarize this theory: "Central to the present theory is the assumption that when strangers meet, their primary concern is one of uncertainty reduction or increasing predictability about the behavior of both themselves and others in the interaction."[7] According to the theory, all of you have a need to understand both the self and the other in interpersonal situations. Simply put, you have a desire to reduce the uncertainty built into every new meeting. As your ability "to predict which alternative or alternatives are likely to occur next decreases, uncertainty increases."[8] In addition, as Gudykunst notes, "There is greater uncertainty in our initial interactions with strangers than with people from our ingroup."[9] Gudykunst links this problem to intercultural communication when he adds, "If the amount of uncertainty present in initial interactions is not reduced, further communication between the people will, in all likelihood, not take place."[10]

Uncertainty can take a number of forms, all of which can interfere with intercultural communication. First, there are behavioral questions that deal with how you should act during a particular situation and with specific people. Should you shake hands or bow? Should you speak English or try your broken French? Should you offer a business card or wait for him or her to offer you a card? Should you ask questions about the person's family or avoid personal topics? In each of these instances, the uncertainty can cause stress. Second, there are a series of cognitive questions that can also bring about feelings of uncertainty and hamper predictability. How does the other person view time? How does the other person perceive women? How does the other person define status?

One point that should emerge from our brief discussion of uncertainty avoidance is that communication is the central tool we use to reduce uncertainty and gain insight into our communication partner. As we have already indicated, however, making accurate predictions and gathering information to reduce uncertainty is difficult when you are confronted with people from other cultures. As you have learned in this book, the information you seek is often unfamiliar or even strange. If you fail to understand what a certain action means, how can you use that action to define the situation and reduce uncertainty? When this happens, you can become frustrated. This frustration, coupled with your need for closure, is at the core of many communication problems. Later in the chapter, we advocate that you learn the technique of suspending judgment and discover the practice of being patient when trying to reduce uncertainty. You might be rewarded. As the Chinese proverb notes, "With time and patience, the mulberry leaf becomes silk."

Stereotyping

Stereotyping represents yet another problem that is often easier to talk about than to arrest, for it, like culture, often lies below the level of awareness. Stereotyping is rooted in your compulsion to make in-group and out-group distinctions.

Defining Stereotypes

Stereotyping is a complex form of categorization that mentally organizes your experiences and guides your behavior toward a particular group of people. Lippmann, who called attention to this concept as early as 1922, indicated that stereotypes were a means of organizing your images into fixed and simple categories that you use to stand for the entire collection of people.[11] Stereotyping is found in nearly every intercultural situation. The reason for the pervasive nature of stereotypes is that human beings have a psychological need to categorize and classify. The world you confront is too big, too complex, and too transitory for you to know it in all its detail. Hence, you want to classify and pigeonhole. Stereotypes, because they tend to be convenient and expeditious, help you with your classifications.

Developing Stereotypes

How do you acquire stereotypes? You are not born with them. Stereotypes, like culture itself, are learned in a variety of ways. First, people learn stereotypes from their parents, relatives, and friends. Individuals who hear their parents say "It is too bad that all those Jews are in control of the film industry" are learning stereotypes. Second, stereotypes develop through limited personal contact. If you meet a person from Brazil who is very wealthy, and from this meeting you conclude that all people from Brazil are wealthy, you are acquiring a stereotype from limited data. Finally, many stereotypes are provided by the mass media. Television has been guilty of providing distorted images of many ethnic groups. The problem is that for many people, these false facsimiles often become their private reality.

Problems in Stereotyping

As we have indicated, in most instances, stereotypes are the products of limited, lazy, and misguided perceptions. Their harmful effect on intercultural communication is clearly described by Adler:

> Stereotypes become counterproductive when we place people in the wrong groups, when we incorrectly describe the group norm, when we inappropriately evaluate the group or category, when we confuse the stereotype with the description of a particular individual, and when we fail to modify the stereotype based on our actual observations and experience.[12]

Let us look at a few additional reasons why stereotypes, as a form of negative classification, hamper intercultural communication. *First, it is not the act of classifying that creates intercultural problems, rather, it is assuming that all culture-specific information applies to all individuals from the cultural group.*[13] That is to say, stereotypes assume that all members of a group have exactly the same traits. As Atkinson, Morten, and Sue note, "They are rigid preconceptions which are applied to all members of a group or to an individual over a period of time, regardless of individual variations."[14] This problem of assuming similarities at the expense of exceptions is the main reason we have, throughout this book, reminded you that culture is one of the characteristics that determine attitudes, values, beliefs, and ways of behaving.

Second, stereotypes also keep us from being successful as communicators because they are oversimplified, overgeneralized, and/or exaggerated. They are based on half-truths, distortions, and often untrue premises. Therefore, they create inaccurate pictures of the people with whom we are interacting.

Third, stereotypes tend to impede intercultural communication in that they repeat and reinforce beliefs until they often become taken for "truth". For years, women were stereotyped as a rather one-dimensional group. The stereotype of women as "homemakers" often keeps women from advancing in the workplace.

Finally, stereotypes can serve as a "self-fulfilling prophecies." Once the stereotype is in place there is a tendency to perceive the stereotyped person engaging in behavior that corroborates our stereotype—even when the behavior is not present. That is to say, negative stereotypes confirm your expectations whether they are valid or not.

Prejudice

The French philosopher and essayist Voltaire knew of the dangers associated with prejudice when he wrote that "Prejudices are what fools use for reason." His rationale for this observation was simple—deep felt prejudices cause serious problems. Let us examine the nature of prejudice and some of the problems associated with this destructive activity.

Defining Prejudice

Macionis offers a detailed definition of prejudice while explaining its damaging effect on intercultural communication:

> Prejudice amounts to a rigid and irrational generalization about a category of people. Prejudice is irrational to the extent that people hold inflexible attitudes supported by little or no direct evidence. Prejudice may target people of a particular social class, sex, sexual orientation, age, political affiliation, race or ethnicity.[15]

When applied to the interpersonal and intercultural setting, prejudice often includes various levels of hostility. This hostility dimension is explained by Levin, who believes that prejudice deals with "negative feelings, beliefs, and action-tendencies, or discriminatory acts, that arise against human beings by virtue of the status they occupy or are perceived to occupy as members of a minority group."[16]

Expressions of Prejudice

Prejudices, like stereotypes, are learned. For some people, prejudices offer rewards ranging from feelings of superiority to feelings of power. Prejudice is expressed in a variety of ways—at times subtle and on other occasions overt. Five of those expressions were discussed by Allport.[17] Although Allport's analysis was presented over forty years ago, it is still relevant today. In fact, many contemporary social scientists base their current theories on the work of Allport.[18] Knowing how prejudice is manifested will help you identify your own prejudices and in so doing will greatly improve the manner in which you perceive, approach, and interact with other people.

First, prejudice can be expressed through what Allport refers to as *antilocution*. This level of prejudice involves talking about a member of the target group in negative and stereotypic terms. Someone would be engaging in this form of prejudice if he or she told a friend, "Those Germans did it once, so we can never trust any of them ever again." Another example of antilocution prejudice is the statement "Don't pay the Mexicans very much. They don't have any education and will work for almost nothing."

People act out prejudice when they *avoid and/or withdraw* from contact with the disliked group. The problems associated with this form of prejudice are obvious. How do you interact, solve problems, and resolve serious conflicts when you are separated from other people? You can no longer learn from, support, or persuade people if you avoid them and close all of the channels of communication. On both the international and domestic levels, avoidance and withdrawal often have marked the intercultural exchange. History is full of examples of how one nation or group of people refused to attend (withdrew from) an important peace conference. For decades, the political leaders of the United States and the Soviet Union, East and West Germany, and Israel and its Arab neighbors rebuffed each other, only to discover decades later that talking benefited both parties. What is true with regard to governments is also characteristic of individual behavior. Have there been occasions when you, like governments, withdrew from communication because a person was a different color or spoke a different language? When this happens, there can be little communication. In an age when each cultural group has some sway over another, prejudice that produces retreat can harm everyone. As the philosopher Flewelling once wrote, "Neither province, parish, nor nation; neighborhood, family, nor individual, can live profitably in exclusion from the rest of the world."

Third, when *discrimination* is the expression of prejudice, the prejudiced person undertakes to exclude all members of the group in question from certain types of employment, residential housing, political rights, educational and recreational opportunities, churches, hospitals, or some other type of social institution. Often in cases of discrimination, we observe ethnocentrism, stereotyping, and prejudice coming together in a type of fanaticism that completely obstructs any form of successful intercultural communication. When discrimination replaces communication, we see overt and covert expressions of anger and hate that restrict one group's opportunity or access to opportunities that rightly belong to everyone. When a real-estate agent will not show certain homes to African Americans, we have discrimination. When businesses promote less qualified males instead of competent women, we have discrimination.

Fourth, when prejudice moves to the next level of expression, we often see *physical attacks*. This form of prejudice often accelerates in hostility and intensity if it is left unchecked. From the burning of churches to the writing of anti-Semitic slogans in Jewish cemeteries, physical acts occur when minorities are the target of prejudiced activity.

The fifth, and most alarming, form of prejudice is *extermination*. This expression of prejudice leads to acts of physical violence against the out-group. History is replete with examples of lynching, massacres, and programs of genocide. In such cases as Hitler's "master plan," the former Serbian "ethnic cleansing," and the current situation in Rwanda, an attempt is made to destroy an entire racial or ethnic group.

To this point, we have talked only about the problems associated with stereotyping, prejudice, and discrimination. Later in the chapter, we provide some practical and philosophical guidelines for identifying and dealing with these three serious impediments to intercultural communication. But for now, it is important to remember that deep prejudice and hatred not only hurt the out-group but can destroy the prejudiced person and culture. The Spanish philosopher Jose Ortega y Gasset advanced much the some observation when he wrote, "Hatred is a feeling which leads to the extinction of values."

Racism

As we start this new century it appears that for most people of color Martin Luther King's "dream" that children "will not be judged by the color of their skin but by the content of their character" is still only a dream. For as Dana points out, "Both subtle and overt racism still permeates mainstream American society."[19] What is sad but true about racism is that it has existed for centuries and is found throughout the world—not only in the United States. Let us examine this harmful and insidious characteristic so that you can work to eliminate it in your professional and private lives.

Defining Racism

Racism, in many ways, is an extension of prejudice in that "racism refers to the belief that one racial category is innately superior to another."[20] A more detailed explanation of racism, and some of the basic and false suppositions behind those who support racism, is offered by Nanda and Warms:

> There are biological fixed races; different races have different moral, intellectual, and physical characteristics; an individual's aptitudes are determined primarily by his or her race; races can be ranked on a single hierarchy; and political action should be taken to order society so that it reflects this hierarchy.[21]

The folly of the racist thinking described above is that it is not only unethical and cruel, but it is also constructed on false premises. It is now common knowledge, for those who are willing to be receptive to the knowledge, that "the big differences among human groups are the result of culture, not biological inheritance or race. All human beings belong to the same species and the biological features essential to human life are common to us all."[22] Yet in spite of the truth and wisdom contained in the last paragraph, racism remains a major hindrance to successful intercultural communication. Perhaps you can work to overcome this obstacle if you understand some of the forms racism takes. For throughout this book we have maintained that knowledge, insight, and ethical behavior are the best ways to reduce ignorance and improve the human condition.

Forms of Racism

Racism ranges from forms that are almost impossible to detect and to signs that are blatant and transparent. Four of the most common forms are identified by Brislin and are worthy of our consideration.

Intense Racism. In this form of racism "some people believe that virtually all members of certain outgroups are inferior in various ways and are not able to benefit fully from society's offerings such as education, good jobs, and participation in community affairs."[23] This form of racism begins with the belief that certain people (those of a race different from the person making and drawing the conclusion) are inferior, and hence are perceived as being of low worth.

Symbolic Racism. Some people hold racist views because "they feel that the outgroup is interfering with important aspects of the culture."[24] This "interference," reflected in racism, can be in the form of "causing trouble" to "getting more economically than they deserve."[25]

Tokenism. Tokenism, whether it be in the form of prejudice or racism, is difficult to detect. In this case the person does not want to admit that he or she harbors negative or racist views. People will even engage in "token" activities to "prove" they are even-handed in the treatment of other races.

Arm's-Length Prejudice. Brislin describes this negative behavior in the following manner: Some people engage in friendly, positive behaviors toward out-group members in some social settings but treat those same out-group members with noticeably less warmth and friendliness in other settings.[26] We see this kind of subtle racism when the "friendly" real-estate agent will not show certain homes that are for sale to African Americans.

One reason racism is so pervasive is that it is often learned early in life, and like much of culture, becomes part of our world view without our realization. In a somewhat poetic manner the African American author Maya Angelou makes the same point when she writes, "The plague of racism is insidious, entering into our minds as smoothly and quietly and invisibly as floating airborne microbes enter into our bodies to find life-long purchase in our bloodstreams."

Power

Much of what we have been taking about the last few pages, be it prejudice or racism, has its roots in issues related to power. Power has been a consideration among people and cultures for a long time. Groups have employed guns, bombs, language, space, money, and even history as devices for gaining and keeping power over others. We would suggest that understanding power—how it can be misused and its effect on communication—is an important part of understanding intercultural communication.

Defining Power

Why do humans seek out power whenever they can? The answer to this question can be found in the very definition of power: Power is the ability to control what happens, to cause things you want to happen and to block things you don't want to happen.[27] What makes power an important dimension in intercultural communication, and a potential problem, is that power usually means not only controlling your own life, but also the lives of others. As Nanda and Warms tell us, "Power is thus the ability to make and carry out decisions affecting one's own life, control the behavior of other human beings, and transform objects and resources."[28] In many cultures this often means that the people in power can "follow their own interests at the expense of the goals of others."[29]

Power and Intercultural Communication

What is so very interesting about power is that the methods of power are as diverse as they are widespread. Power can get acted out from a historical or an interpersonal perspective. That is to say, power is present in nearly every human experience, from global politics to face-to-face interactions between the dominant culture and co-cultures. Therefore, the dynamics of power greatly influence all phases of intercultural communication. Martin and Nakayama offer an excellent summary of this point when they note, "We are not equal in intercultural encounters, nor can we ever be equal. Long histories of imperialism, colonialism, exploitation, wars, genocide campaigns, and more leave cultural groups out of balance when they communicate."[30]

The reason power is such an important consideration in the study of intercultural communication is that it can show itself in a variety of ways. In interpersonal communication the amount of power you have, or do not have, influences who you talk to, what you talk about, and how much control you have when you talk. Folb adds to the list when she tells us that the people in power have a major impact on what people "believe and do," and also influence the "rules of appropriate and inappropriate behavior, thought, speech, and action."[31] Carried to an extreme, and it often is, we find in many cultures that the following expression is true: "All men (perhaps even women) are created equal—some are just more equal than others."[32]

Your degree of power is contingent on the person(s) with whom you are interacting and the resources that you control. In intercultural communication, these two factors take on added significance, for the sources of power are culturally based. What one culture deems as a source of power, another culture may not consider a power variable. For example, in England, one's language is often a sign of potential power because it signals one's class and station. There also are instances when one culture believes that power is derived from simply being a member of that particular culture. African Americans have long expressed feelings of being controlled and manipulated by white males.[33] Many women in the United States have expressed this same view. It is easy to see how this use, or misuse, of power, when employed to control and determine another's behavior, can restrict openness and communication. As Smith notes, "To allow customary subservience or power a place in human interaction is to introduce an inevitable obstruction."[34]

We again remind you that there are vast cultural differences in both the perception and use of power. In North America, there is a strong cultural message that one should not be powerless. People grow up hearing that they should be "captains of their ships" and "masters of their own fate." Not only do they want power, and think they deserve it, they do not want other people to have power over them. They often leave home at an early age so their parents will not have power over them, and they make teachers, police, and bosses the brunt of jokes because they often are annoyed over the amount of power these people have over them. In America there are cries of black power, gray power, and gay power. Women and minority groups ask for power so that they can have freedom from internal and external restraints. In short, people are taught in North America not to be powerless.

Although all cultures abhor the abuse of power, much of the world is composed of cultures that do not seek individual power. They believe that power resides outside of them and that fate, nature, or God has all the power. Power is not something they want, need, or have. Muslims use the phrase "It is God's will. " For the Hindu, power is the acting out of individual karma, and in much of Mexico and Latin America, a strong belief in fatalism often replaces power. These cultures hold the view that, in most instances, the legitimacy of power is irrelevant.[35]

As an intercultural communicator, it is important that you become aware of each culture's approach to power. However, regardless of the culture you are interacting with, an adherence to the following philosophy advanced by Blubaugh and Pennington could greatly improve most intercultural transactions:

> The ideal power relationship . . . is not concerned with the idea of control. . . . Rather, the desire is to attribute to all groups the credibility that allows them positive influence in communication.[36]

Culture Shock

An old English saying states, "That song is best esteemed with which our ears are most acquainted." Everyone likes the familiar. As we noted in Chapter 2, culture, by repeating experiences, makes them known to the members of the culture. This familiarity helps you reduce stress, for, in most instances, you know what you can expect from your environment and from those around you. However, you are now, by either chance or design, leaving these comfortable surroundings and journeying into new areas and confronting people who are often unlike yourself. As we have pointed out throughout this book, these "excursions" take a variety of forms. Millions of Americans are now overseas attending school, conducting business, or performing government service.[37] For many of these individuals the experience is often confusing and overwhelming. When you are thrust into another culture, by either chance or design, and experience psychological and physical discomfort from this contact, you have become a victim of *culture shock*.[38]

Defining Culture Shock

The term *culture shock* was first introduced by the anthropologist Oberg. In the following paragraph, he offers a detailed definition and account of this phenomenon:

> Culture shock is precipitated by the anxiety that results from losing all our familiar signs and symbols of social intercourse. These signs or cues include the thousand and one ways in which we orient ourselves to the situation of daily life: how to give orders, how to make purchases, when and when not to respond. Now these cues which may be words, gestures, facial expressions, customs, or norms are acquired by all of us in the course of growing up and are as much a part of our culture as the language we speak or the beliefs we accept. All of us depend for our peace of mind and efficiency on hundreds of these cues, most of which we are not consciously aware.[39]

As we indicated at the beginning of this section, culture shock is often discussed as it applies to businesspersons, students, or government employees. However, the feelings associated with culture shock (having basic values, beliefs, and patterns of behavior challenged) can, as Brislin notes, "be experienced by individuals who have face-to-face contact with out-group members within their own culture."[40]

Understanding Culture Shock

The reactions associated with culture shock vary from individual to individual. For the person who is constantly encountering other cultures, the anxiety period might be mild and brief. However, for many people, culture shock can be characterized by depression, serious physical reactions (such as headaches or body pains), anger, irritability, aggression toward the new culture, and even total withdrawal. All of these reactions would obviously hamper intercultural communication. Therefore, we agree with Lynch and Hanson when they say "understanding the concept of culture shock and its characteristics and stages provides a framework that enable individuals to recognize their feelings, analyze the cause, alter their approach, consciously manage their own behavior, and regain emotional equilibrium."[41] Having already mentioned the characteristics of culture shock, let us now turn to a brief discussion of the most common stages of culture shock.

The Stages of Culture Shock (The U-Curve)

Although there might be great variations in how people respond to culture shock, and the amount of time needed for that adjustment, most of the literature in the area of culture shock and adaptation suggests that people normally go through four stages. We should first mention that the seam separating the stages is almost impossible to see. That is to say, the transition from stage to stage is not as clear-cut as our description might imply. It might be helpful if you were to view the stages as a U-shaped curve.[42]

The *initial phase*, at the top of the U, is usually filled with excitement, optimism, and a sense of euphoria as the individual anticipates being exposed to a new culture. This phase is followed by feeling disappointed and even let down. It is the *crisis period* of culture shock. As we indicated, the person becomes confused and baffled by his or her new surroundings. This frustration can make them easily irritated and hostile. The *third phase* sees the person gradually making some adjustments and modifications in how he or she is coping with the new culture. Events and people now seem much more predictable and less stressful. In *the final phase*, the top of the U, the person now understands the key elements of the new culture (values, special customs, beliefs, communication patterns, etc.) and can function with some degree of success. This ability to "live within two" cultures is often accompanied by feelings of enjoyment and satisfaction.

Some researchers suggest that there is also a kind of reverse culture shock that takes place when people return "home." As Harris and Moran note, "Having objectively perceived his or her culture from abroad, one can have a severe and sustained jolt through reentry shock."[43] These expatriates often arrive home missing the new friends they made while overseas. Some bemoan the loss of prestige associated with foreign assignments. One common sign of reentry shock is being highly critical of one's own culture. Regardless of the manifestations of reentry shock, it is yet another hindrance to effective human interaction.

Learning from Culture Shock

Although we have placed the topic of culture shock under the category of "problems," we would be remiss if we did not emphasize the idea that culture shock can be an explicit learning experience. For example, as Adler notes, "Severe culture shock is often a positive sign indicating that the expatriate is becoming deeply involved in the new culture instead of remaining isolated in an expatriate ghetto."[44] This involvement normally helps people learn about themselves and, at the same time, other cultures. In a study examining culture shock, Kawano concluded that culture shock "gives the sojourners a chance to learn about themselves. In this sense experiencing culture shock has a strong potential to make people be multicultural or bicultural."[45]

Later in the chapter, we examine specific ways of coping with the problems and anxieties associated with culture shock while looking at specific adaptation strategies. However, it might be useful to conclude our discussion of culture shock by sharing with you the words of the American writer Helen Keller: "Doubt and mistrust are the mere panic of timid imagination, which the steadfast heart will conquer, and the large mind transcend."

Ethnocentrism

Defining Ethnocentrism

One culture views the eating of animals as barbarous and abnormal; the people with such habits are apt to consider the custom of confining the elderly to convalescent homes just as cruel and unnatural—this is *ethnocentrism*. Ethnocentrism might well be the characteristic that most directly relates to intercultural communication. Its important tie with communication can be seen in its formal definition. Sumner, generally credited with introducing the term to the study of culture, defined ethnocentrism as "the technical name for the view of things in which one's own group is the center of everything, and all others are scaled and rated with reference to it."[46] A more contemporary explanation is offered by Nanda and Warms:

> Ethnocentrism is the notion that one's own culture is superior to any other. It is the idea that other cultures should be measured by the degree to which they live up to our cultural standards. We are ethnocentric when we view other cultures through the narrow lens of our own culture or social position.[47]

Anthropologists generally agree that ethnocentrism is found in every culture in that "most peoples in the world regard their own culture as superior."[48] And like culture, ethnocentrism is usually learned at the unconscious level. For example, schools that teach mainly American history, geography, literature, and government are also, without realizing it, teaching ethnocentrism. When you study only the accomplishments of white males, you are quietly learning ethnocentrism. Students exposed to limited orientations develop the belief that America is the center of the world, and they learn to judge the world by American standards. What is true about American ethnocentrism is true about other cultures. As children in Iran learn about the wisdom of Allah, they are learning to judge all religious truths by this singular standard. And when China, for thousands of years, "place themselves in the center of the world, referring to their nation using a Chinese character that literally means central state," they are teaching ethnocentrism.[49] Even the stories and folktales that each culture tells their young people contribute to ethnocentrism. Keesing described this subtle learning when he writes "Nearly always the folklore of a people includes myths of origin which give priority to themselves, and place the stamp of supernatural approval upon their particular customs."[50]

Consequences of Ethnocentrism

Ethnocentrism takes on a negative condition and becomes "destructive when it is used to shut others out, provide the bases for derogatory evaluations, and rebuff change."[51] These feelings that you are right and they are wrong pervade every aspect of a culture's existence. Examples range from the insignificant ("Earrings should be placed on the ears, not on the nose") to the significant ("We need to build up our defenses to protect ourselves from those religious fanatics"). In more subtle ways, ethnocentrism can cause the alienation of co-cultures from the dominant culture, or one group from another. For example, we often find white-collar workers isolated from blue-collar workers, African Americans living apart from whites, and those with disabilities removed from our sight.

The negative impact of ethnocentrism on intercultural communication is clearly highlighted by Stewart and Bennett:

> First, ethnocentric beliefs about one's own culture shape a social sense of identity which is narrow and defensive. Second, ethnocentrism normally involves the perception of members of other cultures in terms of stereotypes. Third, the dynamic of ethnocentrism is such that comparative judgments are made between one's own culture and other cultures under the assumption that one's own is normal and natural. As a consequence, ethnocentric judgments usually involve invidious comparisons that ennoble one's culture while degrading those of others.[52]

To fully appreciate the significance of ethnocentrism as a potential problem, you need only recall one of the major themes of this book: *culture, by selecting and evaluating certain experiences, helps determine our perspective on reality*. For example, if males in the dominant culture value women who are thin, young, and blonde, then they will perceive women who are stout, older, and dark-haired in a less favorable light. If you perceive openness as a positive trait while another culture values privacy, we again have perceptual differences. If you value directness in speech and another culture values vagueness, we might misinterpret what is being said. These three cases—and there are countless others—are examples of how perception influences communication.

As you can see, when your perceptions are narrow and your subsequent behaviors rigid, you are easily susceptible to ethnocentrism. When that ethnocentrism is excessive, serious communication problems can arise. As Jandt points out:

Extreme ethnocentrism leads to a rejection of the richness and knowledge of other cultures. It impedes communication and blocks the exchange of ideas and skills among peoples. Because it excludes other points of view, an ethnocentrism orientation is restrictive and limiting.[53]

Although in the next section of this chapter we discuss methods to overcome ethnocentrism, we conclude our analysis of some of the problems associated with intercultural communication by asking you to think about the following questions. Jews cover their heads when they pray, but Protestants do not—Is one more correct than the other? The Catholic speaks to God, the Buddhist has no god, and the Hindu has many gods—Is one more correct than the others? In parts of Turkey and Saudi Arabia, women cover their faces with veils, whereas women in the United States do not—Is one more correct than the other? These sorts of rhetorical questions are never-ending. We urge you to remember, however, that it is not the questions that are important, but rather the dogmatic manner in which people often answer them. We must be attentive to the ease with which we judge the actions of others. The danger of ethnocentrism is that it is strongest in political, moral, and religious settings. In these contexts, it is easy to let culturally restricted views overshadow rationality. Hence, we again urge you to be alert to narrowness and intolerance in any form. St. Thomas Aquinas said much the same thing hundreds of years ago: "Beware of the man of one book."

BECOMING COMPETENT

Before we submit specific techniques for improving your intercultural skills, we need to offer a few definitions related to the issue of intercultural communication competence.

Defining Intercultural Competence

In its most unadorned form we would agree with Spitzberg when he suggests that intercultural communication competence is engaging in "behavior that is appropriate and effective in a given context."[54] Kim offers a more detailed definition when she notes that intercultural communication competence is "the overall internal capability of an individual to manage key challenging features of intercultural communication: namely, cultural differences and unfamiliarity, intergroup posture, and the accompanying experience of stress."[55] What these two definitions, one general and one specific, are telling us is that being a competent communicator means analyzing the situation (context) and selecting the correct mode of behavior. Most of the research in the area of intercultural competence maintains that in selecting the most appropriate course of action (exercising free choice) effective communicators are those that are (1) motivated, (2) have a fund of knowledge to draw upon, and (3) possess certain communication skills.[56] As we offer explicit recommendations on improvement we will return to these three components throughout the remainder of the chapter.

Approaches to the Study of Intercultural Competence

Our second set of definitions deals with questions related to an issue often characterized by the terms *culture-specific*, *context-specific*, and *culture-general*. These terms refer to various ways of approaching improvement in intercultural communication settings. Let's briefly look at these methods of learning so that we might appreciate some of the alternatives available to anyone who is interested in improving intercultural communication.

Culture-Specific

The culture-specific method assumes that the most effective way to improve intercultural communication is to study one culture at a time and learn all the distinct and specific communication features of that culture. This approach assumes that the person is preparing to work or visit a specific culture for a period of time, and hence necessitates an in-depth culture-specific orientation. For example, to interact with an Arab, you should know his or her values regarding gender, hospitality, pride, honor, and rivalry. You should also know that Islam is a regulator of behavior as well as a religion and that Arab males engage in very direct eye contact. You should even learn about the Arabic language because your communication with Arabs will improve if you know that "Arab language abounds with forms of assertion. Metaphors, similes, long arrays of adjectives, and repetition of words are frequently used by the Arabs in communicating their ideas. Repetition of words is especially common in extending or rejecting invitations for coffee, dinner, and the like."[57] If you were going to Japan, you might benefit from advice about gift giving, the use of first names, greeting behavior, indirect speech, politeness, the use of business cards, the importance of group harmony, social stability, the use of "yes" and "no," and the like.[58]

Context-Specific

In recent years scholars have begun to not only talk about specific cultures, but also the context or setting of the intercultural encounter. In Chapters 7, 8, and 9, for example, we explored the business, educational, and health care settings as a way of assessing the impact of the environment on communication. There are now numerous books, journals, training manuals, and the like that look at improving intercultural competence when working with very young children in an early education environment.[59] Scholars have also offered specific suggestions to psychologist service providers so they can more effectively deal with their culturally diverse clients.[60]

Culture-General

As you have learned by now, the approach of this book is *culture-general*. Although we have offered many specific examples, we primarily have looked at *cultural traits and behaviors that are common to all cultures*. In this chapter, we treat the subject of improvement in the same manner; we look at universal skills that can be used in all cultures. Although there might be slight variations in how each culture manifests the skills we will discuss, the attributes we have selected tend to cut across cultures. For example, in one study Zhong looked at intercultural communication competence as found in the Chinese and American cultures. She concluded that there were no significant differences between the groups in their perceptions of what constituted competent intercultural communication.[61] What we are suggesting is that regardless of the culture you are encountering, it is important to have knowledge of the person's culture and try to adapt whenever possible. These are but two traits we shall be discussing that are not culture-specific, but rather are found in most intercultural experiences. This is what we mean by culture-general. As was the case when we discussed potential problems, the discussion that follows combines our personal advice and the research of others in the area of intercultural communication.

IMPROVING INTERCULTURAL COMMUNICATION

Although this entire book is aimed at improving intercultural communication, our suggestions, admonitions, counsel, and proposals in previous chapters have been only tangentially related to improvement. Our recommendations in this chapter, however, are very direct. And more importantly, all of our suggestions for improvement enable you to exercise your ability to make choices—an issue that was discussed in detail at the beginning of this chapter. Our propositions place *you* in the center of the activity. Whether we are asking you to learn more about a culture's view toward the elderly or appealing to you to develop some new skills, the power is all yours. What is being said here should be quite clear—you must act on your knowledge. The Persian poet Sa'di said much the same thing over seven thousand years ago: "Whoever acquires knowledge and does not practice it resembles him who ploughs his land and leaves it unsown."

Before we offer our first bit of advice we want to acknowledge *a major danger in offering anyone personal advice*. Whenever you tell another individual how to think or act, you run the risk, particularly if he or she listens to you, of making matters worse. The person may have been better off without your advice. For example, we believe that many of you already know a great deal about intercultural communication and, in fact, are very good practitioners of the art. In these cases, we run the risk of spoiling what it took you years to develop. What we are saying is somewhat analogous to the following Chinese fable. In this fable, a monkey and a fish were very good friends. One day, however, they were separated by a dreadful flood. Because the monkey could climb trees, he was able to scramble up a limb and escape the rising waters. As he glanced into the raging river, he saw his friend the fish swimming past. With the best of intentions, he scooped his paw into the water, snatched his friend from the river, and lifted him into the tree. The result was obvious. From this modest story, you can see the dilemma we face; so please remember as we offer advice that, like the monkey, we have the best of intentions.

Know Yourself

In light of what we discussed in the last paragraph, it seems only fitting that we ask you to begin with *yourself*. For as simplistic as it sounds, what *you* bring to the communication event greatly influences the success or failure of that event. Although the idea of knowing yourself is common, it is nevertheless crucial to improving intercultural communication. The novelist James Baldwin said it best when he wrote, "The questions which one asks oneself begin, at last, to illuminate the world, and become one's key to the experience of others." Baldwin's remarks serve as an ideal introduction for the portion of this book that urges you to begin your path to improvement with some self-analysis. As with many of the suggestions we offer in this section, it is easier to state the advice than to practice it. We can write the words "know yourself" with just a few strokes on our keyboard, but it will take a great deal of effort for you to translate this assignment into practice. We believe that the application of introspection should take three directions: first, know your culture; second, know your perceptions; and third, know how you act on those perceptions. Although these three concepts work in tandem, it might be useful to examine them separately.

Know Your Culture

Your first step toward introspection should begin with your own culture, regardless of what that culture might be. Remember, one of the major themes of this book has been that everyone is the product of their culture—and that culture helps control communication. Stewart and Bennett, while speaking about the American culture, made a similar observation when they wrote: "An awareness of American culture along with examples of contrasting cultures contribute to the individual's understanding of her- or himself as a cultural being."[62] In short, you are "cultural beings" and must be ever vigilant as to the impact of your cultural "membership" on perception and communication.

Know Your Attitudes

By exhorting you to examine your attitudes and perceptions, we are not referring to any mystical notions involving another reality, nor are we suggesting you engage in any deep psychological soul searching. Rather, we are asking you to identify those attitudes, prejudices, and opinions that you carry around and that bias the way the world appears to you. If you hold a certain attitude toward gay men, and a man who is gay talks to you, your precommunication attitude will color your response to what he says. Knowing your likes, dislikes, and degrees of personal ethnocentrism enables you to place them out in the open so that you can detect the ways in which these attitudes influence communication. Hidden personal premises, be they directed at ideas, people, or entire cultures, are often the cause of many of your difficulties.

Know Your Communication Style

The third step in knowing yourself is somewhat more difficult than simply identifying your prejudices and predispositions. It involves discovering the kind of image you portray to the rest of the world. Ask yourself, "How do I communicate and how do others perceive me?" If you perceive yourself in one way, and the people with whom you interact perceive you in another way, serious problems can arise. You have all heard stories of

It is important to understand how you present yourself to others.

© Bruce Davidson

how foreigners view Americans traveling abroad. The "Ugly American" example might be old and trite, but your experiences should continue to reinforce its truth. If you are to improve your communication, you must, therefore, have some idea of how you present yourself. If, for instance, you see yourself as patient and calm, but you appear rushed and anxious, you will have a hard time understanding why people respond to you as they do. As we have noted elsewhere, your most taken-for-granted behaviors often are hidden from your consciousness.

As a starting point, we suggest that you *learn to recognize your communication style— the manner in which you present yourself to others.* Many communication scholars have attempted to isolate the characteristics that compose a communication personality. One such inventory, which Norton has proposed, has nine characteristics.[63] In Table 10-1, we offer a summary of each of these so that you can begin to evaluate your own communication style. Remember, awareness is the first step to meaningful action.

Barnlund offers yet another insightful interpretation of what our individual styles often include. Here again, asking yourself how you manifest Barnlund's characteristics can help you understand the manner in which you present yourself to your communication partner.

> By communication style is meant the topics people prefer to discuss, their favorite forms of interaction —ritual, repartee, argument, self-disclosure—and the depth of involvement they demand of each other. It includes the extent to which communicants rely upon the same channels—vocal, verbal, physical—for conveying information, and the extent to which they are tuned to the same level of meaning, that is, to the factual or emotional content of messages.[64]

What should emerge from the last few paragraphs is that all of you have unique ways of interacting. Discovering how you communicate is not always an easy task. It is awkward and highly irregular for you to walk around asking people if they think you are relaxed, argumentative, friendly, animated, and the like. You must, therefore, be

Table 10-1 *Communication Characteristics*

Trait	Communication Characteristics
Dominant	Speaks frequently; interrupts and controls conversations.
Dramatic	Very expressive language. Often exaggerates and embellishes.
Contentious	Argumentative and often hostile.
Animated	Energetic and expressive gestures and facial expressions.
Impression-Leaving	States ideas and feelings in an indelible fashion.
Relaxed	Calm, comfortable, and seldom nervous around others.
Attentive	Good listener. Offers verbal and nonverbal encouragement to the speaker.
Open	Discloses personal information. Shows emotions and feelings.
Friendly	Offers positive feedback and encouragement.

sensitive to the feedback you receive and candid in the reading of that feedback. You must learn to ask yourself questions such as those suggested by Norton and Barnlund. In addition to the challenges inherent in Norton's and Barnlund's descriptions, we also urge you to ask yourself some of the following questions:

- Do I seem at ease or tense?
- Do I often change the subject without taking the other person into consideration?
- Do I deprecate the statements of others?
- Do I smile often?
- Do I interrupt repeatedly?
- Do I show sympathy when someone has a problem?
- Do my actions tend to lower the other person's self-esteem?
- Do I employ a pleasant tone of voice when I talk to people?
- Do I tend to pick the topics for discussion or do I share topic selection?
- What does my tone of voice suggest?
- How do I react to being touched by a stranger?

Frequently overlooked, the subtleties of how we act are often the most important variables in human interaction. Therefore, gaining honest and candid insight into your cultural and individual patterns of communication is an assignment that once accomplished can greatly improve your intercultural skills. Shakespeare said it far more eloquently when he penned the often quoted line from *Hamlet*, "This above all: to thine own self be true, / And it must follow, as the night the day, / Thou canst not then be false to any man." And we would add, "thou canst not then be false to yourself."

Consider the Physical and Human Settings

As we stressed in Chapters 7, 8, and 9, even setting carries meaning. Three attributes of the setting that can influence the encounter are timing, physical setting, and customs.

Timing

Being aware of timing can often make the difference between a successful engagement and one that produces ill feelings, antagonism, and misunderstandings. The effective communicator knows the importance of timing and has developed the skill to determine the appropriate time to talk about a subject. You know from your own experiences that there are right and wrong times to ask your parents for a loan or to ask an acquaintance for a date. Few professors will sympathize with the student who waits until the last week of the semester to announce, "I would like to come to your office and talk about the midterm examination I missed a few months ago." This indeed is poor timing!

Your use of timing is also influenced by culture. For example, as we noted in Chapter 8, students use different views of timing when they are asked to respond to questions from the teacher. And in Chapter 7 we pointed out that considering the "correct time" is a crucial aspect of doing business with other cultures. In the United States, people learn to "get down to business" quickly. However, in Japan, other Asian countries, and Mexico, the most fitting time to talk about business matters is not at the start of a business session. Ruch, discussing Mexico, highlights cultural differences in timing: "Business contacts are often made during the two- or three-hour lunch break. These are social meetings for the most part, with business being conducted in the last few minutes."[65] Notice the words "the last few minutes." This is a vivid example of what we mean by the phrase "consider the timing."

Physical Setting

We believe that physical and social context is important enough to justify three chapters in this book. The basic assumptions behind Chapters 7, 8, and 9 are that communication is rule governed and different cultures have different rules as they move from setting to setting. In the United States, during business negotiations, the two negotiation teams usually sit facing each other. However, for much of the world, this arrangement maximizes competition, not cooperation.[66] In many Arab countries, people often conduct business while sitting on the floor. And in Finland, there are major corporations that use the sauna bath as a setting for meetings. Clutterbuck describes that setting: "In the warm, informal atmosphere both sides are more open to frank discussion. The trappings of rank tend to disappear when no one has any clothes on."[67] In America, one would not, of course, find himself or herself sitting on the floor or conducting business in a sauna.

As we noted in Chapter 8, teachers facing culturally diverse students must also be aware of the role culture plays in the education setting. For example, "the U.S. educational system tends to favor a more interactive classroom."[68] In this setting students will often move about the classroom and interact with the teacher and fellow students. This is not a physical setting that is found throughout the world. In Japan and China, there is far less student activity in the classroom.[69] In short, the setting reflects culture. Being aware of the physical setting, and adapting to it, is often the hallmark of a successful intercultural communicator.

Customs

Your ability to adapt to the customs of each culture will, to a large extent, determine the success of your intercultural encounters. Your experience will not be fruitful if custom calls for you to remain standing when you enter a room, but you take a seat. When, if at all, do you bow? And what is the appropriate bow? When, if at all, do you touch members of the opposite sex? And where do you touch them? What are the customs that prevail with regard to age? These and other questions need to be asked and answered so that you can fashion your behavior to meet the needs of each culture. While there are countless customs in each culture that must be considered, let us mention but four "rules" that will help illustrate our point.

First, we turn to an important business custom in Japan—the exchanging of business cards. Adler tells us, "The Japanese must know the other person's company and position before being able to select the grammatically correct form of address. For this reason, the Japanese always exchange business cards—*meishe*—before a conversation begins."[70]

Second, there are also subtle yet important cultural customs in the perception and manifestation of rank and status. Protocol in Germany has the junior executive walking on the left side of the senior manager. The customs of class are even more elaborate in the Middle East, as Ruch notes:

> Both class and rank are quite important to Arabs despite the Muslim concept of all being equal before God. This becomes rather clear at doorways as they sort themselves out by status, the senior man going through first, being followed by the next and then the next in hierarchy.[71]

Third, there are social customs in each culture concerning the importance of family and friends in the workplace. In the United States, people, because they do not want to be accused of nepotism, seldom show preferential treatment to family members. However, in much of the Arab world, and in Latin America, custom and tradition produce a very different response to the same issue. For example, "In Mexico, family and friends are often favored as employees because they are seen as being trustworthy."[72]

Finally, you can avoid serious communication problems if you know that the number three and sequences that contain three items have significance in the Thai culture.[73] In religious practices you hear repeatedly *Buddha* (the man), the *Dharma* (the teachings of Buddha), and *Sangha* (the monastic order)—a set of three. In many ceremonies, from childbirth to birthdays, the number three is very evident. Knowing about this custom can enable you to adapt your behavior (giving three small gifts before a business meeting) to Thai culture.

As we conclude this section on physical and human settings, we again urge you to be aware of your surroundings and the cultural customs that influence communication. Because you all have free choice, you can make the necessary concessions to custom, but first you must know the custom.

Seek to Understand Diverse Message Systems

The American poet Ezra Pound offers you an excellent introduction to this section when he reminds you that "The sum of human knowledge is not contained in any one language." This is yet another way of saying that while all cultures have verbal and nonverbal codes, these codes evoke meanings that reflect the experiences and ideas of each particular culture. Therefore, as you would suspect, it is difficult to arrive at a common code if you and your communication partner speak different languages. To overcome this problem, let us offer some advice regarding the use of both verbal and nonverbal codes.

Try to Learn the Language of Other Cultures

Our first piece of advice is rather obvious. If you plan to spend time around people from other cultures, try to learn their language. You would be far more effective if you could speak Spanish when doing business in Mexico. Because much of the world speaks English, many Americans have a tendency to assume they need not learn a foreign language. The very fact that others have made an attempt to learn your language should motivate you to reciprocate.

Understand Cultural Variations in the Use of Language

If you do not speak the foreign language of your communication partner, there still are things you can do to facilitate understanding. Try to keep in mind that language is more than a vehicle of communication; it teaches one a culture's lifestyle, ways of thinking, and different patterns of interacting. Much of Jewish culture is reflected in the wide use of stories, parables, and allegories. People, events, and circumstances are talked about in vivid narratives. For many Jews, the story is as important as the point being made by the story. And if you are interacting with Arabs, it would be useful to understand some unique characteristics of their language code. As Nydell points out:

> There are many situations in which verbal statements are required by etiquette. Meeting someone's small child calls for praise, carefully mixed with blessings; the most common are "May God keep him" or "This is what God wills." Such statements reassure the parents that there is no envy (you certainly would not add, "I wish I had a child like this!").[74]

Knowing the characteristics of language we just mentioned for the Jewish and Arab cultures would help you communicate with people from both of these cultures.

The Chinese are yet another culture that perceives and uses language in a manner different than most Americans. As Geo and Ting-Toomey note, "Speech in Chinese culture is constantly exercised with caution and, consequently, perceived as less important."[75] This lack of emphasis on the spoken word means that the Chinese "believe that talk has limitations and that meanings reside beyond mere words."[76] Knowing about this way of utilizing, perhaps we should say underutilizing, language could help you in two ways. First, you could understand why "the ability to surmise and decipher hidden meanings is highly desirable in the Chinese culture."[77] Second, knowing the Chinese view of language could influence the manner in which you send and receive messages from members of the Chinese culture and also how you deal with silence.

Remember Words Are "Culture Bound"

When you are speaking English with someone who is not completely familiar with your language code, there are also some things you can do to facilitate understanding. For example, remembering that most words are culture-bound, you might be extremely careful when using idioms. By definition, idioms are not capable of literal translations. Try to imagine finding meanings for the following sentences in other languages:

It's not surprising the guy couldn't get to first base with his new business: he started with two strikes against him.
Let's put this plan to the acid test by looking at the nuts and bolts of the deal.
If we stop beating our heads against a brick wall, we would not appear to be such wimps.
We need to be careful that the tail doesn't wag the dog.
Do not listen to John—he's got an ax to grind.
She's not the least bit funny—in fact, she's laid an egg.
John dropped the ball on this one, and he's sure ticked off.
If you think we're on the same wavelength, just give me a buzz, or we can play it by ear.
We need to stop dilly-dallying and get off the dime.

Confusion can be caused by a single word as well by idioms. Reflect on the literal translations of the following terms: *affirmative action, jazzed, awesome, interfacing, pro-life, networking, uptight, stoked,* and *sexual harassment.*

Be Aware of Subcodes

In Chapter 5, we pointed out that the English language contains countless subcodes. Although it might be highly improper for you to use these codes if you are not a member of the co-culture, understanding them can offer you insight into both the word and the experiences behind the word. In addition, you also learn some of the differences that exist between various speech styles. For African Americans, Black English is a highly rule-governed speech style that is shared by and reflects the norms of their co-culture.[78] Communication can be impeded when, according to Walters, someone who is speaking mainstream American English feels uncomfortable with the linguistic dissimilarity.[79] We recommend that you realize there are different styles of "talk." One is not right and the others wrong—they are only different.

Be Aware of Nonverbal Codes

As you learned in Chapter 6, nonverbal behaviors also shift from culture to culture. For example, in Japan, a female may cover her mouth out of shyness, but in America, we often associate this same action with fear. In China, blinking eyes at someone is impolite.[80] And in many Buddhist traditions, it is highly improper to sit with the soles of one's feet pointed at the image of the Buddha. These differences should remind us of the two points we made with regard to verbal codes. First, the initial step in discovering a common code is learning how to read existing codes. Second, cultural differences should not keep us from looking for a common code. For example, although there are cultural variations in what makes people smile, and even in to whom they smile, one does not have to speak a foreign language to know that a smile carries nearly the same meaning throughout the world. Those of you who have visited other countries know the power of pointing and laughing as ways of talking.

Be Sensitive to Diverse Coding Systems

Being sensitive to your surroundings and to other people is one of the hallmarks of a competent intercultural communicator. According to Chen and Starosta, intercultural sensitivity is "an individual's ability to develop a positive emotion towards understanding and appreciating cultural differences in or to promote appropriate and effective behavior in intercultural communication."[81] We would suggest that part of the sensitivity means learning about diverse coding systems and developing a code sensitivity toward the message systems used by other cultures. We have already alluded to the inappropriateness of using African American argot if you are white. If you interact with disabled people, you need to learn a list of what are called the "no-no words." *Crippled, gimp, deaf and dumb, deaf mute, victim, abnormal, unfortunate,* or *victim* are examples of words that exhibit a lack of cultural awareness.[82]

It is also employing an improper verbal code and displaying insensitivity when you use words to refer to a co-culture that are not the ones preferred by it. It would reflect respect if you used *Asians* for *Orientals, Gays* for *homosexuals, Native Americans* for *Indians,* and *African Americans* for *Negroes.* However, as we pointed out in Chapter 1 when we noted that all people are more than their culture, that there might be members of the groups mentioned in the last sentence that seek yet another term for their ethnic identification.

Develop Empathy

A well-known Native American proverb tells us "We should not judge another person until we have walked two moons in his moccasins." Our next suggestion for improvement is about "wearing those moccasins." Actually what we should say is that it is about your trying to *imagine* wearing those moccasins. We used the word *imagine* because it is physically and psychologically impossible to ever really know what another person is actually experiencing. As noted in Chapter 2, the envelope of our skin separates us from every other individual. Hence, this is why we said your goal might best be described as trying to *imagine* things from the point of view of others. Ting-Toomey makes the same point about imagining when she describes the process of empathy in the following manner: "[T]hrough empathy we are willing to imaginatively place ourselves in the dissimilar other's cultural world and to experience what she or he is experiencing."[83]

The importance of empathy to the study of interpersonal and intercultural competence cannot be overstated. After reviewing the literature on the topic of empathy, Broome concluded, "Empathy has been recognized as important to both general communication competence and as a central characteristic of competent and effective intercultural communication."[84] Calloway-Thomas, Cooper, and Blake echo Broome's commentary when they write, "[E]mpathy is the bedrock of intercultural communication."[85]

Understanding Empathy

Before we begin our discussion of empathy we need to mention three ideas that will aid you in understanding the role of empathy in intercultural communication. First, as with so much of our counsel, you are again faced with *a skill that is easier to talk about than to put into practice*. The fact remains that however similar you may appear to be, there is something distinctive and unique about each of you. As the English poet John Lyly wrote over five hundred years ago, "Though all men be made of one metal, yet they be not cast all in one mold." Not only are you different one from another, but your internal thoughts are elusive and fleeting, and you know yourself only as a distorted shadow. When you add trying to know the other person to the mix you can see why predicting his or her reactions and needs is a difficult and troublesome activity. And now when you add culture to the formula, you can compound the difficulty of the assignment.

Second, although we have focused primarily on culture, *we also are concerned with the "interpersonal aspects" of intercultural communication*. Perhaps the interpersonal dimension of communication is most evident in the area of empathy. As Miller and Steinberg noted, "To communicate interpersonally, one must leave the cultural and sociological levels of predications and psychically travel to the psychological level."[86] Simply put, empathy, while using knowledge about another's culture to make predications, also demands that the point of analysis be the individual personality.

Finally, it is best to view empathy as a complex activity that is composed of many variables. It involves a cognitive component (thinking), an affective (emotional identification) dimension, and a communication element (activity). Bell explains these three variables, and how they interact with each other, in the following paragraph:

> Cognitively, the empathic person takes the perspective of another person, and in so doing strives to see the world from the other's point of view. Affectively, the empathic person experiences the emotions of another; he or she *feels* the other's experiences. Communicatively, the empathic individual signals understanding and concern through verbal and nonverbal cues.[87]

Before we look at some of the ways to improve our role-taking skills, it might be helpful to examine a few characteristics that can impede empathy.

Hindrances to Empathy

Constant Self-Focus. Perhaps the most common of all barriers to empathy is a *constant self-focus*. It is difficult to gather information about the other person, and to reflect on that information, if you are consumed with thoughts of yourself. Attending to your own thoughts, as if they were the only ones that mattered, uses much of the energy that you should direct toward your communication partner. At times everyone is guilty of behaving according to the German proverb "Everyone thinks that all the bells echo his own thoughts."

The Tendency to Note Only Some Features to the Exclusion of Others. Focusing on only a small portion of the individual often causes you to misuse the data you gather about another person. If, for example, you notice only a person's skin color or that his or her surname is Lopez, and from this limited information assume you know all there is to know about the person, you are apt to do a poor job of empathizing. Admittedly, color and names offer you some information about the other person, but you must add to this type of data. Although it is an overused analogy, you should remember that most outward features represent only the tip of the iceberg.

Stereotyped Notions Concerning Gender, Race, and Culture. We have already talked about the destructive nature of stereotypes, so we now only need to add that they also serve as potential stumbling blocks to empathy. If you believe that "all English people dislike the Irish," you might allow this stereotype to influence your view of an English person. Stereotyped notions are so much a part of your personality that you must be careful not to allow these unsupported generalizations to serve as your models of other people.

Defensive Behavior. People often engage in *defensive behavior* that keeps others from wanting to reveal information about themselves—information you need if you are going to engage in empathetic behavior. If people feel rebuffed by your actions, they are not likely to disclose very much to you. Because defensive behaviors are so common, it would be useful for you to examine how some of these actions inhibit your ability to empathize.

When you appear to be *evaluating other people*, whether by what you say or what you do, you are likely to make them feel defensive toward you. If you believe others are judging and evaluating you, you will hesitate to offer information that will foster empathy. Think about how awkward you feel when, after sharing some personal information, the other person quickly lectures you on the foolhardiness of your act. After a few minutes of criticism and ridicule, you probably would decide not to disclose any other information to that person. In the intercultural situation, you would discourage communication if you referred to a person's cultural habit of meditating as "a complete waste of time."

Manifesting a lack of interest often makes people feel defensive. Empathy is best when it is reciprocal; hence, most of you have an aversion to revealing very much to a person who seems uninterested in you and your ideas. Empathy cannot take place when one of the individuals becomes defensive over the other person's lack of interest. Again, you must answer this question: How much do I enjoy talking to a person who shows no interest in me and what I am saying?

An attitude of superiority, which produces defensive behavior, seldom elicits the kind of information you need for empathizing. Imagine how defensive you would become if someone from France told you that Americans used language in a very dull and unimaginative manner.

Dogmatism is yet another attitude that keeps you from developing empathy. If someone behaved as if he or she had doubted everything you said and had all the answers, even to questions you had not even asked, you probably would become defensive. With a dogmatic person, your defensiveness may take the form of silence or of dogmatism of your own. In either case, this defensive behavior will not be conducive to empathy. Be cautious of dogmatism on your part and on the part of others.

A Lack of Motivation. Many of the hindrances to empathy can be traced to a lack of *motivation*. This problem might well be the most difficult to conquer. You are most motivated to respond to people who are close to you both physically and emotionally. You are primarily concerned about your family. As your personal circle widens, it includes relatives and friends. Interest in other people then moves to neighbors and other members of the community. As you get further and further away from people in your immediate circle, you tend to find it hard to empathize. Think for a moment about your reaction to the news that someone you know had been seriously injured in an automobile accident versus your response to reading that 700,000 people were suffering from severe famine in the Sudan. In most instances you would be more motivated to learn about your friend than about the people thousands of miles away in Africa. Although this is a normal reaction, it often keeps you from trying to understand the experiences of people far removed from our personal sphere. For intercultural communication to be successful, you must all learn to go beyond personal boundaries and try to learn about the experiences of people who are not part of your daily lives. You must avoid following the Russian proverb that states, "When you live next to the cemetery you cannot weep for everyone." Instead, you must realize that you live in an interconnected world, and you must therefore be motivated to understand everyone—regardless of how much you seem separated from them by either distance or culture.

Improving Empathy

Up to this point, we have painted a rather dark picture of empathy and the problems related to it. Although it is nearly impossible to know another person completely and accurately, you can, with practice, develop the skills necessary to overcome the problems we have mentioned.

Pay Attention. Our first bit of advice grows out of a problem we mentioned earlier in this section; however, this time we will put a positive face on the topic of "paying attention." Or as Trenholm and Jensen tell us: "The single most important thing you do is remind yourself to pay attention to the spontaneous emotional expressions of others."[88] As you know from personal experience, staying focused and concentrating on one idea or one person is difficult. This high level of attention is even more strenuous when applied to empathy, for it, like our attention span, is dynamic. Barnlund underscored this idea when he wrote, "Empathy tends to be a fleeting phenomenon, fluctuating from moment to moment and from situation to situation."[89] Thus, problems associated with concentration can be overcome if you work on staying focused on both the other person and the situation.

Communication Empathy. Because empathy is a reciprocal act, you and your communication partner must be expressive (unless you are interacting with someone from a culture that values interpersonal restraint). You cannot expect individuals from other cultures to offer you verbal and nonverbal messages about their internal states if your behavior is not in tandem with their efforts. Trenholm and Jensen say much the same thing: "If your own expressive behavior promotes others to be more expressive and we pay attention to the wider range of nonverbal cues they display, we should be more accurate in reading others' emotional state."[90]

Use Culturally Accepted Behaviors. Empathy can be enhanced through awareness of specific behaviors that members of a particular culture or co-culture might find impertinent or insulting. For example, according to Rich, many African Americans find it offensive when they hear stereotypic statements ("All African Americans have good voices"), when they are called "boy" or "son," or when they are referred to as being "a culturally deprived minority."[91] And you would not receive vital information to use for empathy if you refused the hospitality offered by an Arab. In both these examples, we have made the same point: to be successful as an intercultural communicator, you must develop empathy, and that can be cultivated only if you become sensitive to the values and customs of the culture with which you are interacting.

Avoid Ethnocentristic Responses. Our final proposal is perhaps the one that most closely parallels the main mission of this book. Again we remind you that empathy can be increased if you resist the tendency to interpret the other's verbal and nonverbal actions from your culture's orientation. Learn to suspend, or at least keep in check, the cultural perspective that is unique to your experiences. Knowing how the frame of reference of other cultures differs from your own will assist you in more accurately reading what meaning lies behind words and actions. For example, in the Chinese culture, as a means of "saving face," people will often say one thing when they mean something else; knowing this can help you understand what is actually being expressed.[92]

Encourage Feedback

The interactive nature of communication brings us to our next suggestion: *encourage feedback*. Feedback is the information generated by the person who receives the message—information that is "fed back" to the person who sent the original message. This information may be a smile, the words "No thank you," or even complete silence void of any outward expression. As Wood points out, "Feedback may be verbal, nonverbal, or both, and it may be intentional or unintentional."[93] Regardless of the form of the feedback, it allows you the opportunity to make qualitative judgments about the communication event while it is taking place. These judgments offer useful data that enable you to correct and adjust your next message. Being able to invite feedback, even from members of those cultures that are reluctant to offer such data, is an effective communication skill. In this sense, a competent communicator uses feedback both to monitor the communication process and to exercise some control over it. Feedback clearly manifests the axioms with which we began this chapter: you can learn and adapt. Put another way, with feedback you see or hear what is happening (learn) and alter your actions (exercise free choice).

Granting that feedback is critical, you must learn to create an atmosphere that encourages other people to offer you feedback—feedback you need in order to adjust your own behavior. Therefore, we will review a number of communication skills that encourage other people to send us messages about the current situation.

Nonverbal Feedback

You can use *nonverbal actions* as a way of inspiring others to respond to you honestly. The first step in improving your nonverbal feedback is recognizing that it takes many forms. Think for a moment of all the positive attitudes and images you associate with smiling, head nodding, leaning forward, and laughing. Although these behaviors seem very Western, they often produce positive reactions in other cultures. Each of these actions, separately or in combination with verbal messages, creates an atmosphere that tells other people you are interested in them and want to hear what they have to say.

Verbal Feedback

Positive verbal behavior can also encourage feedback. Like your nonverbal messages, your use of words also takes a variety of forms. In cultures that value conversation and openness, asking questions is an excellent method of encouraging feedback about the quality of your messages. You can ask questions such as, "Perhaps we should start the meeting by introducing ourselves. Is that agreeable?" Or "How do you think we should start the meeting?" Further, questions can be used to seek additional clarification. If asked in an unthreatening manner, even the question "Do you understand?" assists in monitoring the level of comprehension. We should remind you before we leave this point that in some Asian cultures, the word *no* is seldom used. In Japan, for example, instead of responding negatively to your question, "they may simply apologize, keep quiet, become vague, or answer with a euphemism for no."[94]

Your use of words also encourages feedback if you relate them directly to what the other person has just said. You know from your own experience that it is very disconcerting if you tell a friend that you do not feel well, and your friend responds that she or he just received an "A" on an examination.

Silence as Feedback

Sometimes *silence* instead of words will inspire feedback. You have repeatedly seen that every culture has a unique communication style. Some cultural styles call for periods of silence and/or long pauses, and you must learn to respect these phases in the encounter. Giving the person this quiet period creates an atmosphere that promotes feedback once the silence is broken. There are even occasions when the silence itself is a form of feedback. As we noted elsewhere in the book, many Asian cultures do not enjoy being hurried when they are negotiating and/or solving problems. If you learn to remain silent, you will be sending them some positive feedback about the meeting.

It is important to remember that when using feedback you need to *take time*. Rather than leaping to conclusions about what your communication partner is saying, you need to give the other person time to finish his or her thoughts. Although this notion of suspending judgments is not new, it underscores the need to avoid premature evaluations. In face-to-face interactions you often complete the thought or idea before the other person has even finished talking. If you do not cut a person off with your words or actions, you often do it in your mind, and this prevents you from making effective use of feedback. There is no positive compensation for a quick decision, particularly if you made that decision without sufficient feedback. Remember the French proverb: "Patience is bitter but its fruit is sweet."

Develop Communication Flexibility

Our next bit of advice asks you to be flexible when deciding on how to present yourself to another person—particularly if that person is from a culture different than your own. Many experts in communication competence actually believe that one definition of competence is having the ability to adjust and fashion your communication behavior to fit the *setting*, the *other person*, and *yourself*.[95] What is being said is that a competent intercultural communicator "must . . . develop a repertoire of interpersonal tactics."[96] Brislin calls this "a willingness to use various ways to communicate."[97] When speaking to the issue of how communication flexibility applies to international negotiations, Foster used an analogy:

> The better [international] negotiators are ultimately pragmatic. They are not oaks; rather, they are more like willows. Unable to predict every situation, every twist and turn, even in a domestic situation, they know that it is nearly impossible to do so in a cross-cultural one.[98]

All of you have learned a host of communication tactics as part of the socialization process. You know what communication strategies to employ when you buy a new automobile or when you want to make a good impression. Shakespeare wrote, "One man in his time plays many parts." And, of course, we would add the same applies to women.

Regardless of the parts you play or the techniques you employ, you must learn to be flexible. You need to acquire the skills that will allow you to respond to various conditions, people, and situations. Having the skills to play these multiple roles means being able to be reflective instead of impulsive when interacting with a culture that moves at a slower pace. It means behaving in a formal manner when encountering a culture that employs a formal style. It means speaking softly instead of loudly when talking with people who use a subdued communication pattern. It means remembering the Spanish proverb "I dance to the tune that is played."

Your efforts at being flexible when deciding how respond to a person or event will be greatly facilitated if you learn how to *tolerate a degree of ambiguity* while trying to analyze what role to play. As you have learned by now, the intercultural encounter is full of potential ambiguity. For example, if your culture values competition and aggressive action, and you are around someone from a culture that values cooperation and interpersonal harmony, you might find his or her behavior ambiguous and confusing; yet coping with ambiguity is a key element in intercultural competence. As Ruben and Kealey noted, "The ability to react to new and ambiguous situations with minimal discomfort has long been thought to be an important asset when adjusting to a new culture."[99] If you are self-conscious, tense, and anxious when confronted with the unknown, you are apt to use your energy to alleviate your frustration instead of trying to decide how best to communicate to the person and situation.

Learn About Cultural Adaptation

The issue of cultural adaptation is directly linked to the skill of communication flexibility. Except now we are talking about people who must adapt to all aspects of a new culture—and for a long period of time—perhaps permanently. Before we begin a more detailed analysis of the adaptation process, we should point out that the word *adaptation* is but one of a number of words the field of intercultural communication has used to represent this concept. Kim further develops this idea when she writes, "Cross-cultural adaptation embraces other similar but narrow terms, from assimilation . . . and acculturation . . . to coping and adjustment . . . as well as integration."[100] Because adaptation does "embrace" all the other concepts, and because in the final analysis the people involved are having to learn to "adapt," we shall use the term "adaptation" in our discussion.

We begin with these two questions: What problems hamper the adaptation process? What is the best why to adapt to a new culture if your exposure to that culture will take place for an extended period of time? The answer to these questions is at the heart of the adaptation process. As we have already indicated, in this section we discuss cultural contacts that are not transitory, but rather are sustained and ongoing. Immigrants, refugees, international businesspeople with overseas assignments, military personnel, government workers, and exchange students are just a few of the people who need to adapt to a new culture for a long period of time. These people need to cope with the cultural changes brought about by continuous firsthand contact with another culture.

To better understand this important skill, let us (1) examine some challenges that face anyone who is attempting to adapt to a new culture and than conclude by (2) offering a number of the behaviors that can make the adaptation process a successful and rewarding experience.

Challenges of Adaptation

Coping with Ethnocentrism. What is interesting about the role of ethnocentrism in adapting to a new culture is the fact that ethnocentrism is often found in both cultures. That is to say, ethnocentrism moves in both directions. As we pointed out earlier, ethnocentrism is that cultural bias that leads people to judge another culture by the standards and practices that they are most familiar with—their own. Because the person trying to adapt cannot, and usually does not want to, expunge their "home" culture, they bring some ethnocentrism to the "host culture." Anderson makes this point very clear when he notes that "one of the chief characteristics of the adaptation process is that elements of the original culture can never be completely erased."[101] The key to effective adaptation is, of course, for both parties to recognize the strong pull of ethnocentrism and attempt to keep it in check.

Coping with Language Problems. It is obvious that someone living in a new culture will usually face problems associated with having to learn and use a second language. When we speak of problems associated with being exposed to a new language we are talking about both language acquisition and ways of speaking unique to the new culture; both of these can delay the adaptation process. Harper summarizes this view when she notes "Lack of language skills is a strong barrier to effective cultural adjustment and communication whereas lack of knowledge concerning the ways of speaking of a particular group will reduce the level of understanding that we can achieve with our counterparts."[102] In addition, there is ample research that supports the notion that insufficient language skills may result in negative consequences in that it reduces "interpersonal interactions."[103] Therefore, for a variety of reasons the person trying to adapt to a new culture, if they want to interact with that culture, must not only face challenges associated with learning a second language but also the special and unique patterns found within every language. As we mentioned in Chapter 5, cultural variations in the use of language can mean everything from the use of idioms to different rules for turn-taking, to linguistic ways of showing respect.

Improving the Adaptation Process

Now let us turn our attention to a few strategies that will expedite and facilitate the adaptation process.

Acquire Knowledge About the Host Culture. Adaptation is greatly advanced if you are aware of the characteristics of the culture with which you will be interacting. For someone coming to the United States, this means much more than learning how to order a Big Mac and working a VCR. It means learning about the values, beliefs, and modes of behavior unique to each culture. Chen and Starosta note: "Culture awareness refers to an understanding of one's own and others' cultures that affect how people think and behave. This includes understanding commonalties of human behavior and differences in cultural patterns."[104]

As you have learned throughout this book, gathering a fund of knowledge about another culture takes a variety of forms, ranging from the apparent to the subtle. For example, as we just indicated, it is rather clear that learning the language of the host culture produces positive results. If you cannot learn the language of the host culture, you can at least try to master some of the basics of language such as exchanging greetings, polite responses, methods for ordering food, and words that deal with public transportation and shopping.

Learning about a culture is a highly selective process. That is to say, what should you learn? There is, of course, not a simple answer to this question. In some places, such as India and much of the Arab world, it would be important to learn about the religions of those cultures. On a more indirect level, cultural awareness might be as simple as becoming aware of cultural differences as they apply to the use of "yes" and "no." For instance, in the Chinese and Japanese cultures, as we have noted elsewhere, the blunt "no" is seldom used. Hence, the proper answer to the question "Do you want some more rice?" would not be "No thank you." Instead, you would be demonstrating your ability to adapt if you responded by saying, "The food is very delicious. You are such a good cook. I am very full."

Increase Contact with the Host Culture. As you would suspect, direct contact with the host culture promotes successful adaptation to a new culture. Begley accentuates the importance of direct contact when she notes, "Although insight and knowledge can be gained through prior intercultural study, additional practical wisdom is attained through everyday conversations with people from other cultures."[105] Hence, you should try to take the advice of Harris and Moran when they say "Immerse yourself in the host culture. Join in, whenever feasible, the artistic and community functions, the carnivals, the rites, the international and fraternal or professional organizations."[106]

Although there are no substitutes for face-to-face interactions with host nationals, mediated communication such as radio, film, television, and even the Internet can still moderately influence cross-cultural adaptation. Kim has pointed out that a host culture's mass communication "serves as an important source of cultural language learning, particularly during the early phases of the adaptation."[107] In addition to assisting in the language learning, exposure to a culture's mass media can also aid in discovering some cultural values—at least those that are portrayed on television.

When listening, watching, and interacting with people from the host culture it is important to learn about what Althen calls "ritual social actions."[108] Althen offers a list of some of the "rituals" that contribute to understanding interaction in the host culture:

> Notice what people say (and how they say it) and what they do (and how they do it) when they greet an acquaintance, take leave of an acquaintance, are introduced to a new person, and take leave of a person they have just met. Watch for variations according to the age, sex, and apparent social status of the people involved.[109]

We end this section on improvement by reminding you that successful intercultural communication should always begin with gaining a fund of knowledge about another culture. Once you acquire this knowledge, you can then decide what is appropriate and inappropriate behavior. Confucius said it far more eloquently: "The essence of knowledge is, having it, to apply it." We suggest you do both: have accurate knowledge and apply it.

ETHICAL CONSIDERATIONS

One basic theme in this book has been the idea that communication is an instrumental act; and whether it is used to sell cars, secure a mate, get elected to public office, teach children a foreign language, or secure directions, it will always have an impact, either good or bad, desirable or undesirable, significant or insignificant. Most cultures recognize the ethical dimensions of communication on both a legal and interpersonal level. Legally, in the United States, ethical communication is manifested in our libel, slander, truth-in-advertising, and campaign-practice laws. But just because most of our communication does not involve mass media or attorneys does not relieve us of considering the effects of our actions in the interpersonal setting. Whether the consequences of our messages be simple or profound, we cannot hide from the fact that our actions affect other people. As Shakespeare told us in *The Comedy of Errors,* "Every why hath a wherefore." We now ask you to think about "why" and "wherefore"—to think about your actions and the results they produce. In this section, we suggest an interpersonal ethic that will have beneficial consequences for you, for your interpersonal partners, and, because of the symbiotic relationship now existing in the world, for all humanity.

A Definition of Ethics

Ethics refers to judgments that focus "on degrees of rightness and wrongness, virtue and vice, and obligation in human behavior."[110] Religious thinkers, philosophers, and ordinary people have been struggling with the issues surrounding the consequences of our acts for thousands of years. From Epicurus's justification of egotistical behavior, to Martin Buber's "ethics with a heart," people have been trying to decide what their ethical obligations are to others and how they should treat them. As we have indicated, answers range from simplistic and selfish observations ("It is a dog eat dog world"), to philosophical mandates that focus on our moral obligation to other people. This view is eloquently articulated by the great humanitarian Albert Schweitzer: "Just as the wave cannot exist for itself, but is ever a part of the heaving surface of the ocean, so must I never live my life for itself, but always in the experience which is going on around me."

You can see by the last paragraph that ethics is an elusive topic. As Griffin reminds us, "Ethics has to do with the gray areas of our lives. When moral decisions are black and white, knowing what we should do is easy."[111] But what about those countless occasions when the decision is not easy? Where do you turn when you need ethical guidance? To God, to family, to friends, to philosophers, to yourselves? What you find in many instances when seeking ethical advice is a multitude of approaches representing a variety of orientations. Let's briefly pause and look at two of these approaches—*relativism* and *universalism*, and discuss their application to intercultural communication.

Relativism

Ting-Toomey offers an excellent summary of relativism when she notes, "Under the *ethical-relativism approach*, right and wrong are determined predominantly by the culture of the individual. Ethical relativists try to understand each cultural group 'in its own terms, with a minimum of contamination' by outside influence."[112] This ethical philosophy holds to the view that there is no one correct moral code for all times and people, that each group has its own morality relative to its wants and values, and that all moral ideas are necessarily relative to a particular group of people. Wilson underscored this issue of multiple perspectives: "Anthropologists believe that morality has no meaning outside the culture that defines it, philosophers argue that morality depends on a person's motives or the results he achieves, and ordinary people claim that personal freedom is supreme and that its exercise should be uninhibited unless it harms others."[113]

As you can see, by adding the issue of culture to the topic of ethics, we append yet another dimension to this already troublesome subject. Howell clearly summarizes the *relativism (culture-specific)* orientation to ethics when he writes:

> The fundamental connection between culture and ethics is this: Ethical standards are products of particular cultures. So it is not surprising that basic appropriate and inappropriate behavior important to a group varies from place to place. Consequently, we should not be surprised that one way of behaving has a high moral value—rightness—in one culture, has no ethical significance in a second culture, and in a third culture may be negatively moral, that is, considered by the majority of the population to be ethically wrong.[114]

Universalism

Cultural universalism takes the stance that regardless of the context or the culture, there are fixed and universal ethical precepts that apply to all cultures. This generalist approach to ethics can be found in the writings of the German philosopher Immanuel Kant. It was Kant's conviction that for action to be ethically correct, one must be able to will one's words or actions to be a universal law, that is, be willing to have everyone act in the same way.[115] This view toward ethics is perhaps best summarized by Kant's single sentence: "Act only on that maxim whereby you can at the same time will that should become a universal law."

By now, it is clear that the study of ethics is complex and complicated. However, we cannot let the difficulty of the questions keep us from searching for possible answers. Let us spend the remainder of the chapter considering some personal guidelines that you should consider when interacting with people from different cultures. As you read the next few pages, our personal view regarding ethics will become quite clear. Simply stated, we believe that although there are cultural differences regarding *specific* ethical behaviors, there are also universal codes of conduct that apply to all people and all cultures. Let us now look at those common codes.

GUIDELINES FOR AN INTERCULTURAL ETHIC

Be Mindful That Communication Produces a Response

From Chapter 1 to these final few pages we have continued to stress the notion that the messages you send to others produce a response. As you would suspect, in the intercultural environment, because of the diversity of backgrounds, it is much more difficult to assess and predict the type of response your messages and actions will produce. For example, in the United States, people have learned, as part of their cultural endowment, how to thank someone for a compliment or a gift. They can predict, with some degree of accuracy, what others expect from them and how they will respond to their signs of veneration and appreciation. As we indicated earlier in the chapter, forecasting the responses of other cultures is a far more difficult task. Let us stay with our simple example of thanking someone. In Arab cultures, one is expected to be profuse in offering thanks, whereas in England, one is expected to offer restrained thanks because too much exuberance is considered offensive.

Because of the potential power of messages, you must continue to do two things: first, always be aware of this power; and second, always ask yourself what the effect of your message is on other people. This focus on your actions and the results of those actions is called, in the Buddhist tradition, being *mindful*. "Mindfulness is the aware, balanced acceptance of the present experience. It isn't more complicated than that. It is opening to and receiving the present moment."[116] When practicing mindfulness during communication, you are giving your *full attention to what is transpiring right now*. This awareness of the here and now enables you to avoid letting habit instead of insight dictate your actions. By being mindful, you can adjust your messages to both the context and the person. You can, in short, be aware of what you are doing to another person. The need for mindfulness is articulated by Tead:

> Without indulging in too great refinements, let us remind ourselves that communication also has at bottom a moral aspect. It does, when all is said, anticipate a change in the conduct of the recipient. If the change has any large significance it means an interposing or interference with the autonomy of the other person or persons. And the tampering with personal drives and desires is a moral act even if its upshot is not a far-reaching one, or is a beneficial result. To seek to persuade behavior into a new direction may be wholly justifiable and the result in terms of behavior consequences may be salutary. But the judgment of benefit or detriment is not for the communicator safely to reach by himself. He is assuming a moral responsibility. And he had better be aware of the area with which he concerns himself and the responsibility he assumes. He should be willing to assert as to any given policy, "I stand behind this as having good personal consequences for the individuals whom it will affect." That judgment speaks a moral concern and desired moral outcome.[117]

Again, we remind you to reflect on your requests and your messages when you interact with another person or another culture.

Respect the Worth of the Individual

We begin this next ethical precept with this simple question: How do you feel when someone "puts you down" or acts like you are insignificant? The answer is obvious. You do not like being diminished. Everyone wants some level of respect, dignity, and a feeling of worth. It is our contention that an ethical stance gives this respect to *every human being*. We, of course, are not alone in this conviction. Johannesen in his book on ethics uses words such as "devalues," "ridicule," and "excluding" when he speaks of ethical guidelines.[118] On a more universal scale we can turn to Article 1 of the United Nations Universal Declaration of Human Rights. Among other ethical principles it states that "All human beings are born free and equal in dignity and rights." And yet another Article eludes to "degrading treatment." What all of these proclamations are saying is something you know but often have difficulty acting out. For the ethical communicator showing respect demands that all parties protect each other both physically and emotionally. Confucius said much the same thing when he told us "Without feelings of respect, what is there to distinguish men from beasts?"

Although there are cultural variations in what make people smile, it is nevertheless still true that a smile carries the same meaning throughout the world.

© Robert Fonseca

Seek Commonalties Among People and Cultures

We have spent much time in this book talking about differences that make a difference in the intercultural setting. However, we are going to argue that it is often our similarities, not our differences, that contribute to successful communication, and that serve as part of an intercultural ethic. The photographer Edward Steichen had some guidance that we might be able to use as a starting point for this suggestion: "I believe that in all things that are important, in all of these we are alike." This creed of similarity is important to the study of ethics in that it helps you look for common ground as a way of deciding how to treat other people regardless of their culture. It might be intriguing to know that "an American child sticks out his tongue to show defiance, a Tibetan to show courtesy to a stranger, and a Chinese to express wonderment,"[119] but it is more important to know that they share a series of more crucial characteristics that link them together. The similarities that unite people, and in a very real sense make everyone part of a single "community," range from the obvious to the subtle. For example, it is apparent that all 6 billion people share the same planet for a rather short period. And there are thousands of other glaring similarities that bond everyone. Reflect for a moment on just a few universal characteristics. As we noted in Chapter 2, all people share the same emotion and desire to be free from external restraint: the craving for freedom is basic. There is also a universal link between children and family: people all share the same thrill and excitement at a new birth. Mating and wanting good friends tie everyone together. All people must eventually face old age and the potential suffering that often goes with it; and, of course, all people are joined in knowing that death, like birth, is part of life's process. All cultures love music and art, play and have sports, tell jokes, believe in being civil to one another, and search for ways to be happy. And there is nothing religious or metaphysical in the fact that all people seek to avoid physiological and psychological pain while searching for some degree of tranquillity in life.

As a species, you not only have similarities in feelings and experiences, but there are values that are common to all cultures. Even something as simple as the children's television program *Sesame Street* highlights your matching value system. As was pointed out in *U.S. News & World Report*, children in 130 countries view and respond to "universal values, such as racial harmony, peaceful dispute resolution, respect for the environment."[120]

There are also countless religious and philosophical values that bind people together. All religious traditions offer the *same instructions* to their members with regard to killing, stealing, bearing false witness, and adultery. One of the most important of the common values is one we mentioned earlier when we spoke of the need to respect other people. In slightly different language, Kale refers to this as "the dignity of the human spirit."[121] As intercultural communicators, granting this value would demand that you try to adopt an interpersonal "Golden Rule." Or, as Kale counsels us, "Ethical communicators address people of other cultures with the same respect that they would like to receive themselves."[122] The ethical notion of the Golden Rule is found in every culture. Although the words are different, the wisdom contained within the words is universal.[123]

Buddhism: "Hurt not others in ways that you yourself would find hurtful." *Udana-Virga,* 5:8

Christianity: "All things whatsoever ye would that men should do to you, do ye even so to them." *Matthew, 7:12*

Confucianism: "Do not do unto others what you would not have them do unto you." *Analect, 15:23*

Hinduism: "This is the sum of duty: do naught unto others which would cause you pain if done to you." *Mahabharata, 5:1517*

Islam: "No one of you is a believer until he desires for his brother that which he desires for himself." *Sunnah*

Jainism: "In happiness and suffering, in joy and grief, we should regard all creatures as we regard our own self." *Lord Mahavira, 24th Tirthankara*

Judaism: "What is hateful to you, do not to your fellow man. That is the law: all the rest is commentary." *Talmud, Shabbat, 31 a*

Native American: "Respect for all life is the foundation." *The Great Law of Peace*

If it were not for space constraints, we could have included an even longer list of those cultures that exhort their members to the "oneness of the human family." We believe, however, that from this brief sample you can begin to see that Steichen, whom we quoted earlier, was correct—in all those things that are important, we are all alike.

Recognize the Validity of Differences

Former Israeli prime minister Shimon Peres offers us a wonderful introduction to our next ethical canon when he tells us that "All people have the right to be equal and the equal right to be different." Therefore, in this guideline we recommend that you become aware of and tolerant of cultural differences as a way of establishing an intercultural ethic. Put in slightly different terms, keep in mind our theme from Chapter 2 that we are both alike and different. Barnlund wrote of this double-sided nature:

> Outwardly there is little to distinguish what one sees on the streets of Osaka and Chicago— hurrying people, trolleys and buses, huge department stores, blatant billboards, skyscraper hotels, public monuments—beneath the surface there remains great distinctiveness. There is a different organization of industry, a different approach to education, a different role for labor unions, a contrasting pattern of family life, unique law enforcement and penal practices, contrasting forms of political activity, different sex and age roles. Indeed, most of what is thought of as culture shows as many differences as similarities.[124]

Thus, a complete and honest intercultural ethic grants similarities and recognizes differences. By accepting and appreciating both, you can better assess the potential consequences of your acts and be more tolerant of those of others. Wood discusses the need to recognize differences in male and female communication styles:

> In cross-gender communication, we need to remind ourselves there is logic and validity to both feminine and masculine communication styles. Feminine emphases on relationships, feelings, and responsiveness don't reflect inability to adhere to masculine rules for competing any more than masculine stress on instrumental outcomes is a failure to follow feminine rules for sensitivity to others. It is inappropriate to apply a single criterion—either masculine or feminine—to both genders' communication. Instead we need to realize different goals, priorities, and standards pertain to each.[125]

Thomas Jefferson said much the same thing about accepting differences when he wrote, "It does me no injury for my neighbor to say there are twenty gods, or no God."

TAKE INDIVIDUAL RESPONSIBILITY FOR YOUR ACTIONS

We started this chapter with an axiom regarding free choice. We also mentioned that you should be aware (mindful) of what those choices do to other people. Our final ethical consideration places those two ideas into an intercultural context. We advocate a three-point declaration that grants individual uniqueness, the ability to exercise free choice, and the interdependent nature of the world. You need to take individual responsibility for all you do. All your decisions, actions, and even your failures to act have consequences for yourself and countless other people. The obvious ethical consequence of this fact leads us to what the Dalai Lama called "our universal responsibility." Gomez-Ibanez spoke to that responsibility when he wrote:

> If I am linked in some way to all this is, however tenuous the links may seem, then, I am in some respect responsible for the welfare of all this is, also, I am responsible for the common good. That realization, it seemed to me, might be the foundation for all ethics.[126]

The central message is that if you are going to live in this crowded, interconnected world, and if that planet and you, its "temporary residences" are to survive, you must accept your *individual* roles within that world. For as we have shown throughout this book, people and cultures are inextricably linked. As the English anthropologist Gregory Batson noted, "What pattern connects the crab to the lobster and the orchid to the primrose and all four of them to me? And me to you?"

THE FUTURE OF INTERCULTURAL COMMUNICATION

The future is going to see a significant growth in the intercultural "connections" that Batson referred to. Some of these connections shall be obvious as the world's population has reached 6 billion by the year 2000 and will reach nearly 8 billion by 2020—a population that attempts to interact economically, share natural resources, and avoid conflicts. In the United States intercultural contacts come from the continuing growth of immigration, a growth that even now sees nearly 1 in 10 "Americans" born outside of the country.[127] There are already signs of how this increase is forcing Americans to think about intercultural communication in new terms. As Booth points out, "Today, the United States is experiencing its second great wave of immigration, a movement of people that has profound implications for a society."[128] Trying to chart the implications and the course of future events is a very perplexing assignment. For who among you can say, with any degree of accuracy, what tomorrow will be like. One thing, however, does seem certain: There are indications of how cultures, regardless of the cost, are behaving as if their comfort and security can be found in homogeneity and cultural pluralism. The problem is, as philosopher Krishnamurti points out, "For safety and comfort we are willing to kill others who have the same kind of desire to be safe, to feel protected, to belong to something."[129] We would therefore agree with Cleveland when he says, "Ethnic and religious diversity is creating painful conflicts around the world. Finding ways to become unified despite diversity may be the world's most urgent problem in the years ahead."[130]

Ethnic discord is not confined to distant locations. As Ling-Ling tells us, there are "disturbing signs of rising racial and ethic tension at home."[131] This, of course, makes the need for cultural understanding and an overarching intercultural ethic even more demanding. People, whether by choice or necessity, are finding it essential to agree with anthropologist Laura Nader when she says, "Diversity is rich."[132] We must all begin to realize that diversity can be rich without being threatening, for in the end, people of all cultures long for the same things: a place to raise their children, ply their trades, and express themselves aesthetically and socially. When those forms of expression differ from our own, we must respect the rights of people from other cultures. John Comenius articulated this same idea over three hundred years ago:

> To hate a man because he was born in another country, because he speaks a different language, or because he takes a different view of this subject or that, is a great folly. Desist, I implore you, for we are all equally human. . . . Let us have but one end in view, the welfare of humanity.

We would ask those who would say that such a view is simplistic and fanciful to provide alternatives. In a world that can now destroy itself with powerful bombs, toxic gases, or global pollution, we do not consider it romantic or idealistic to issue an appeal for greater understanding—an understanding that will eradicate "ethnic cleansing," prejudice, and racism. Only by understanding other cultures and reflecting an intercultural ethic can we shape a future that is fit for our generation and the ones following. Exercising our free choice, power, and influence over other people does not end when we walk away from them. In a very real sense, our actions and deeds often outlive us. Bishop Albert Pike reminded us of the longevity of our communication behavior when he wrote, "What we have done for ourselves alone dies with us; what we have for others, and for the world remains and is immortal."

SUMMARY

- The belief that improvement in intercultural communication is possible is based on three assumptions: (1) the brain is an open system, (2) we have free choice, and (3) communication has a consequence.
- Avoidance of the unfamiliar, the desire to reduce uncertainty, diversity in communication purposes, stereotyping, prejudice, racism, misuse of power, culture shock, and ethnocentrism are major barriers to intercultural communication.
- Following some basic guidelines such as knowing yourself, considering the physical and human setting, seeking a shared code, developing empathy, encouraging feedback, developing communication flexibility, and learning about cultural adaptation can help improve intercultural communication.
- Because communication is an activity that has a consequence, we must develop a communication ethic.
- An intercultural ethic asks you to be mindful of the power of communication, respect the worth of all individuals, seek commonalties among people and cultures, recognize the validity of differences, and take individual responsibility for your actions.
- The future of intercultural communication will see an ever increasing amount of contact between people from different cultures—contact that has the potential to create serious problems if we do not learn to share the planet in a peaceful way.

INFOTRAC® COLLEGE EDITION EXERCISES

1. This chapter asks you to consider the future of intercultural communications, both for yourself personally, and for our world. Using the PowerTrac option, locate the article "Myths of the Global Information Village" by Claude Moisy. According to the author, what are the optimistic hopes for intercultural communications, and how do the realities of current intercultural communications measure up? Imagine yourself in conversation with Claude Moisy; what observation made in the article most catches your attention? How would you continue the conversation on this subject?

2. Many of the ideas discussed in Chapter 10 can be related to listening: listening to others, listening to yourself, and listening to the ways in which you listen to others. Using the subject search term "Communication and Culture," locate the article "Cultural Differences in Listening Style Preferences: A Comparison of Young Adults in Germany, Israel, and the United States." What claims does this article make about the importance of listening skills? According to the article, what are the stereotypical listening preferences of young adults in the United States? How do your own listening preferences compare with this stereotype? After reading the research reported in this article, identify at least three ways in which you could work to improve your own listening and cross-cultural communication skills.

ACTIVITIES

1. Pick a foreign country in which you would like to study, do business, or visit. Find out as much as you can about that country's culture with regard to your purpose. For example, if you are going as a tourist, you might want to find out about table manners, medical emergencies, tipping, and so on.
2. Bring to class news articles you have collected over a week's time that directly or indirectly have to do with problems in intercultural communication. Then, in small groups, discuss what may have caused the problems (for example, diverse purposes or ethnocentrism) and how the situations might have been improved.
3. With other members of your intercultural communication class, make a rank-ordered list of the five most common communication problems encountered by American students in their interactions with students from different cultures or co-cultures. Discuss these problems to find the most useful and practical solutions.
4. Interview four religious leaders representing four different religious orientations. During the course of the interview ask the leaders some of the following questions:
   a. What are the five worst things a person can do?
   b. What are the five best things a person can do?
5. In small groups discuss the following proposition: What should be an intercultural ethic?

DISCUSSION IDEAS

1. Find examples in the media (especially television and movies) of subtle stereotyping. Explain how the stereotypes may have developed as a result of ethnocentrism.
2. Define your communication style to the best of your ability by answering these questions:
   Do I give people my full attention?
   Do I seem at ease or tense?
   Do I often change the subject without taking the other person into consideration?
   Do I deprecate the statements of others?
   Do I smile often?
   Do I interrupt repeatedly?
   Do I show sympathy when someone has a problem?
   Do my actions tend to lower the other person's self-esteem?

   It may help you to record yourself in conversation with another person or, if you have the means, to videotape yourself.
3. Discuss the pros and cons of the following proposition: There should be a constitutional amendment that English be declared the official language of the United States.
4. Do you see a future where people of different cultures become closer together or one where they become increasingly isolated from each other?
5. Granting the notion of individual and cultural differences, can we ever truly empathize with another person? How do cultural differences compound the problem?
6. Can you think of some ways to improve intercultural communication that were not discussed in this chapter?

Notes

Notes for Chapter 1

1. *Sacramento Bee*, 23 April 1999, A-27.

2. *Discover*, May 1999, 19.

3. *U.S. News & World Report*, 1 June 1998, 38.

4. *San Diego Union-Tribune*, 2 February 1997, A-1.

5. *Time*, 16 December 1996, 22.

6. *Parade Magazine*, 13 April 1997, 20.

7. J. K. Mahbubani, "The Pacific Way," *Foreign Affairs*, Vol. 74, No. 1, January/February, 1995, 106–107.

8. U.S. Bureau of Economic Analysis, February 1999 Survey of Current Business (http://www.fedstats.gov/index20.html).

9. *Newsweek*, 6 April 1998, 17.

10. A. G. Higgins, "Multimedia Readiness of U.S. Ranked No. 1," *San Diego Union-Tribune*, 19 October 1995.

11. *Time*, 19 May 1997, 68.

12. *Newsweek*, 27 February 1995, 39.

13. D. Mutch, "Business Is Booming on the Net and Business Has Control," *Christian Science Monitor*, 3 November 1995, 8.

14. *Time Digital*, 12 April 1999, 7.

15. M. Miller, "Computer Education for Children on the Rise in Asia," *Computerlink*, 11 October 1995, 5.

16. *San Diego Union-Tribune*, 22 July 1998, E-1.

17. U.S. Census Bureau, World Population Clock (http://www.census.gov/cgi-bin/ipc/popclockw).

18. M. Weiner, "Nations Without Borders," *Foreign Affairs*, March/April 1996, 128.

19. H. H. Cooper, "Global Water Shortages," *CQ Researcher*, 5 (December 1995), 1115.

20. *U.S. News & World Report*, 21 October 1996, 59.

21. E. Linden, *Foreign Affairs*, 75 (February 1996), 64.

22. *San Diego Union-Tribune*, 1 December 1997, A-1.

23. E. Linden, 1996, 64.

24. *San Diego Union-Tribune*, 3 December 1998, B-4.

25. *San Diego Union-Tribune*, 28 June 1997, A-15.

26. *Newsweek*, 9 December 1997, 63.

27. *U.S. News & World Report*, 17 May 1996.

28. *U.S. News & World Report*, 12 May 1997, 34.

29. *San Diego Union-Tribune*, 10 January 1999, G-6.

30. *Newsweek*, 25 May 1998, 30–31.

31. A. Schlesinger, Jr. *The Disuniting of America: Reflections on a Multicultural Society* (New York: W.W. Norton, 1992), 10.

32. Schlesinger, 1992, 10.

33. *U.S. News & World Report*, 15 June 1998, 30.

34. *U.S. News & World Report*, 10 February 1997, 55.

35. *San Diego Union-Tribune*, 28 August 1998, C-1.

36. J. Bates & T. Petruno, "Asian Stocks Respond in Kind to Dow Slide," *Los Angeles Times*, 7 February 1994, D-1, D-2.

37. M. Miller, "Pipeline of Controversy," *San Diego Union-Tribune*, 10 November 1995, I-5.

38. S. D. McLemore, *Racial and Ethnic Relations in America* (Boston: Allyn & Bacon, 1994), 60.

39. E. A. Folb, "Who's Got Room at the Top? Issues of Dominance and Nondominance in Intracultural Communication," in *Intercultural Communication: A Reader*, 8th ed., L. A. Samovar and R. E. Porter, Eds. (Belmont, CA: Wadsworth, 1997), 140.

40. Folb, 1997, 140. *U.S. News & World Report*, 20 April 1998, 35.

41. *Newsweek*, 15 July 1996, 43.

42. *Time*, Fall 1993, 3.

43. *U.S. News & World Report*, 20 April 1998, 35.

44. *U.S. News & World Report*, November 1998, 24.

45. *Newsweek*, 4 August 1997, 41.

46. *Time*, 5 May 1997, 33.

47. *U.S. News & World Report*, 21 October 1996.

48. P. Leppert, *Doing Business with Mexico* (Jain Publishing Co., Fremont, CA: 1996), 13.

49. Leppert, 1996, 13.

50. *Sacramento Bee*, 16 July 1998, A-2, A-3.

51. *Sacramento Bee*, 18 July 1999, A-1, A-18.

52. *Newsweek*, 16 March 1998, 35.

53. *San Diego Union-Tribune*, 13 July 1996, B-10.

54. *San Diego Union-Tribune*, 7 December 1997, A-29.

55. H. Beech, "Don't You Dare List Them as Other," *U.S. News & World Report*, 8 April 1996, 56.

56. *San Diego Union-Tribune*, 7 December 1997, A-29.

57. *U.S. News & World Report*, 14 July 1997, 22.

58. M. Weinberg, "Defining Multicultural Education," *Multicultural Newsletter* (California State University, Long Beach), December 1992, 2.

59. "America's New Ambassador to South Africa," *Ebony*, August 1996, 82.

Notes for Chapter 2

1. A. G. Smith, Ed., *Communication and Culture: Readings in the Codes of Human Interaction* (New York: Holt, Rinehart, & Winston, 1966), v.

2. F. E. X. Dance & C. E. Larson, *Speech Communication: Concepts and Behavior* (New York: Holt, Rinehart, & Winston, 1972).

3. B. D. Rubin & L. P. Stewart, *Communication and Human Behavior*, 4th ed. (Boston: Allyn and Bacon, 1998), 16.

4. J. Mascara, *Dhammapada* (New York: Penguin, 1973), 40.

5. W. B. Gudykunst & Y. Y. Kim, *Communicating with Strangers: An Approach to Intercultural Communication*, 3d ed. (New York: McGraw-Hill, 1997), 6.

6. S. Trenholm & A. Jensen, *Interpersonal Communication*, 2d ed. (Belmont, CA: Wadsworth, 1992), 152.

7. S. W. Littlejohn, *Theories of Human Communication*, 3d ed. (Belmont, CA: Wadsworth, 1989), 152.

8. S. Shimanoff, *Communication Rules: Theory and Research* (Beverly Hills: Sage, 1980), 57.

9. E. T. Hall & M. R. Hall, *Understanding Cultural Differences: Germans, French and Americans* (Yarmouth, ME: Intercultural Press, 1990), 18.

10. J. T. Wood, *Gendered Lives: Communication, Gender, and Culture* (Belmont, CA: Wadsworth, 1994), 29.

11. B. D. Ruben, *Communication and Human Behavior*, 3d ed. (New York: Macmillan, 1988), 107.

12. Smith, 1966, v.

13. K. S. Sitaram & R. T. Cogdell, *Foundations of Intercultural Communication* (Columbus, OH: Charles E. Merrill, 1976), 50.

14. E. T. Hall, *Beyond Culture* (Garden City, NY: Anchor Doubleday, 1977), 14.

15. E. T. Hall, *The Silent Language* (New York: Doubleday, 1959), 169.

16. Smith, 1966, 1.

17. M. J. Hanson, "Ethnic, Cultural, and Language Diversity in Intervention Settings," in *Developing Cross-Cultural Competence: A Guide for Working with Young Children and Their Families*, E. W. Lynch & M. J. Hanson, Eds. (Baltimore: Paul H. Brooks Publishing Company, 1992), 3.

18. W. A. Haviland, *Cultural Anthropology*, 7th ed. (Fort Worth, TX: Harcourt Brace Jovanovich College Publishers, 1993), 29.

19. S. Nanda & R. L. Warms, *Cultural Anthroplogy*, 6th ed. (Belmont, CA: West/Wadsworth, 1998), 3.

20. H. L. Shapiro, *Aspect of Culture* (New Brunswick, NJ: Rutgers University Press, 1956), 21.

21. M. Harris, *Cows, Pigs, Wars, and Witches: The Riddles of Culture* (New York: Random House, 1974), 84.

22. S. Nanda, *Cultural Anthropology*, 5th ed. (Belmont, CA: Wadsworth, 1994), 50.

23. A. L. Kroeber & C. Kluckhohn, "Culture: A Critical Review of Concepts and Definitions," *Harvard University Peabody Museum of American Archaeology and Ethnology Papers*, 47 (1952), 181.

24. A. J. Marsella, "The Measurement of Emotional Reactions to Work: Methodological and Research Issues," *Work and Stress*, 8 (1994), 166–167.

25. S. P. Huntington, "The West Unique, Not Universal," *Foreign Affairs*, November/December 1996, 28.

26. Shapiro, 1956, 54.

27. C. Kluckholn, *Mirror for Men* (New York: McGraw-Hill, 1944), 24–25.

28. D. G. Bates & F. Plog, *Cultural Anthropology*, 3d ed. (New York: McGraw-Hill, 1990), 19.

29. E. A. Hoebel & E. L. Frost, *Culture and Social Anthropology* (New York: McGraw-Hill, 1976), 58.

30. F. M. Keesing, *Cultural Anthropology: The Science of Custom* (New York: Holt, Rinehart, & Winston, 1965), 18.

31. Ruben, 1988, 384.

32. J. M. Sellers, *Folk Wisdom of Mexico* (San Francisco: Chronicle Books, 1994), 7.

33. E. G. Seidensticker, in *Even Monkeys Fall from Trees, and Other Japanese Proverbs*, David Galef, Ed. (Rutland, VT: Charles E. Tuttle, 1987), 8.

34. Seidensticker, 1987, 8.

35. W. Wolfgang Mieder, *Encyclopedia of World Proverbs: A Treasury of Wit and Wisdom Through the Ages* (New Jersey: Prentice-Hall, Inc. 1986), xi.

36. Mieder, 1986, x.

37. Nanda & Warms, 1998, 92.

38. C. Tomlinson, "Myth of Invincibility Draws Children to Battles in Zaire," *San Diego Union-Tribune*, 17 December 1996, A-21.

39. R. Erdoes & A. Ortiz, Eds. *American Indian Myths and Legends* (New York: Pantheon, 1984), xv.

40. Erdoes & Ortiz, 1984, xv.

41. Joseph Campbell, *The Power of Myth* (New York: Doubleday, 1988), 5.

42. Campbell, 1988, 6.

43. E. H. Gombrich, *The Story of Art* (New York: Phaidon Publishers, 1955), 102.

44. Nanda, 1994, 403.

45. J. Campbell, *Myths to Live By* (New York: Penguin, 1972), 106.

46. Campbell, 1972, 106.

47. Keesing, 1965, 279.

48. Haviland, 1993, 392.

49. J. Thompson, "Mass Communication and Modern Culture: Contribution to a Critical Theory of Ideology," *Sociology*, 22 (1988), 359.

50. F. Williams, *The New Communications*, 2d ed. (Belmont, CA: Wadsworth, 1989), 269.

51. F. P. Delgado, "The Nature of Power Across Communicative and Cultural Borders" (paper presented at the Annual Convention of the Speech Communication Association, Miami Beach, FL, November 1993), 12.

52. L. P. Stewart, A. D. Stewart, S. A. Friedly, & P. J. Cooper, *Communication Between the Sexes: Sex Differences and Sex-Role Stereotypes* (Scottsdale, AZ: Gorsuch Scarisbrick, 1990), 84–85.

53. H. Smith, *The Religion of Man* (New York: Harper & Row, 1986), 1–2.

54. Nanda & Warms, 1998, 47.

55. R. Brislin, *Understanding Culture's Influence on Behavior* (Fort Worth, TX: Harcourt Brace Jovanovich College Publishers, 1993), 6.

56. Keesing, 1965, 28.

57. J. J. Macionis, *Society: The Basics*, 4th ed. (Saddle River, NJ: Prentice-Hall, 1998), 33.

58. Kluchhohn, 1944, 26.

59. H. L. Weinberg, *Levels of Knowing and Existence* (New York: Harper & Row, 1959), 157.

60. W. H. Goodenough, "Evolution of the Human Capacity for Beliefs," *American Anthropologist*, 92 (1990), 605.

61. Bates & Plog, 1990, 20.

62. P. Ethington, "Toward Some Borderlands Schools for American Urban Ethnic Studies?" *American Quarterly*, 48 (1996), 348.

63. Nanda, 1994, 62.

64. Nanda, 1994, 63.

65. Hoebel & Frost, 48.

66. W. B. Gudykunst & Y. Y. Kim, *Communicating with Strangers: An Approach to Intercultural Communication*, 2d ed. (New York: McGraw-Hill, 1992), 215.

67. Bates & Plog, 1990, 437.

68. D. C. Barnlund, *Communicative Styles of Japanese and Americans: Images and Realities* (Belmont, CA: Wadsworth, 1989), 192.

69. Nanda & Warms, 1998, 57

70. E. T. Hall, *Beyond Culture* (New York: Doubleday, 1976), 13–14.

71. R. Benedict, *Patterns of Culture*, 2d ed. (New York: Mentor, 1948), 2.

72. R. Benedict, *Patterns of Culture* (Boston, MA: Houghton Mifflin, 1934), 21–22.

73. Barnlund, 1989, vii.

74. Macionis, 1998, 214.

75. Nanda & Warms, 1998, 264.

76. M. L. Hecht, M. J. Collier, & Sidney A. Ribeau, *African American Communication: Ethnic Identity and Cultural Interpretation* (Newbury Park, CA: Sage, 1993), 19.

77. Nanda, 1994, 62.

78. S. Lane, "Deafness Shouldn't Be Called Handicap," *Dallas Morning News*, 5 March 1995, 6–J.

79. J. Goodwin, "Sexuality as Culture," in *Handbook of Intercultural Training*," 2nd ed., D. Lanis & R. S. Bhagat, Eds. (Thousand Oaks, CA: Sage Publications, 1996), 417.

80. J. T. Wood, "Gender, Communication, and Culture," *Intercultural Communication: A Reader*, 7th ed., L. A. Samovar & R. E. Porter, Eds. (Belmont, CA: Wadsworth, 1994), 157.

81. A. L. Smith, *Transracial Communication* (Englewood Cliffs, NJ: Prentice-Hall, 1973), 26. See also T. Kochman, *Black and White Styles in Conflict* (Chicago, IL: University of Chicago Press, 1981), 8–9; Hecht, Collier, & Ribeau, 1993.

82. M. L. Hecht, S. Ribeau, & M. Sedano, "A Mexican American Perspective on Interethnic Communication," *International Journal of Intercultural Relations*, 14 (1990), 33.

83. J. T. Wood, *Communication Mosaics: A New Introduction to the Field of Communication* (Belmont, CA: Wadsworth Publishing, 1998), 205.

84. B. Bate, *Communication and the Sexes* (New York: Harper & Row, 1988), 35.

85. Wood, *Gendered Lives*, 1994, 27.

86. Wood, 1998, 205.

87. Wood, "Gender, Communication, and Culture," 1994, 158–159.

88. *Time*, 17 June 1996, 83.

Notes for Chapter 3

1. N. Dresser, *Multicultural Manners* (New York: Wiley & Sons, 1996), 89–90.

2. M. Singer, *Intercultural Communication: A Perceptual Approach* (Englewood Cliffs, NJ: Prentice-Hall, 1987), 9.

3. T. K. Gamble & M. Gamble, *Communication Works*, 5th ed. (New York: McGraw-Hill, 1996), 77.

4. M. Singer, *Intercultural Communication: A Perceptual Approach* (Englewood Cliffs, NJ: Prentice-Hall, 1987), 9.

5. J. W. Bagby, "A Cross-Cultural Study of Perceptual Predominance in Binocular Rivalry," *The Journal of Abnormal and Social Psychology*, 54 (1957), 331–334.

6. G. Guilmet, "Maternal Perceptions of Urban Navajo and Caucasian Children's Classroom Behavior," *Human Organization*, 38 (1979), 87–91.

7. S. W. King, Y. Minami, & L. A. Samovar, "A Comparison of Japanese and American Perceptions of Source Credibility," *Communication Research Reports*, 2 (1985), 76–79.

8. R. B. Adler & G. Rodman, *Understanding Human Communication*, 5th ed. (Fort Worth, TX: Harcourt Brace Jovanovich College Publishers, 1994), 37.

9. W. B. Gudykunst, *Bridging Differences: Effective Intergroup Communication*, 2d ed. (Thousand Oaks, CA: Sage, 1994), 67.

10. P. R. Harris & R. T. Moran, *Managing Cultural Differences: Leadership Strategies for a New World of Business* (Houston, TX: Gulf, 1996), 274.

11. H. C. Triandis, "Cultural Influences upon Perception," in *Intercultural Communication: A Reader*, 2nd ed., L. A. Samovar & R. E. Porter, Eds. (Belmont, CA: Wadsworth, 1976), 119.

12. N. J. Adler, *International Dimensions of Organizational Behavior*, 3rd ed. (Cincinnati, OH: South-Western College Publishing, 1997), 71.

13. N. J. Adler, 1997, 72.

14. E. M. Rogers & T. M. Steinfatt, *Intercultural Communication* (Prospect Heights, IL: Waveland Press, 1999), 81.

15. S. Osborn & M. T. Motley, *Improving Communication* (Boston, MA: Houghton Mifflin, 1999), 206.

16. M. Rokeach, *The Nature of Human Values* (New York: Free Press, 1973), 161.

17. S. Nanda & R. L. Warms, *Cultural Anthropology*, 6th ed. (Belmont, CA: Wadsworth, 1998), 49.

18. E. Albert, "Value System," in *The International Encyclopedia of the Social Sciences*, vol. 16 (New York: Macmillan, 1968), 32.

19. Rokeach, 1973, 5.

20. G. Gao & S. Ting-Toomey, *Communicating Effectively with the Chinese* (Thousand Oaks, CA: Sage Publications, 1998), 39.

21. L. Damen, *Culture-Learning: The Fifth Dimension in the Language Classroom* (Reading, MA: Addison-Wesley, 1987), 110.

22. P. A. Andersen, M. W. Lustig, & J. Andersen, "Regional Patterns of Communication in the United States," *Communication Monographs*, 54 (1987), 128–144.

23. Rokeach, 1973, 3.

24. "Women Are Degrees Ahead," *San Diego Union-Tribune*, 10 May, 1999, C-2.

25. For a more detailed discussion of American values see Adler & Rodman, 1994, 388–389; J. J. Berman, Ed., *Cross-Cultural Perspectives* (Lincoln: University of Nebraska Press, 1990), 112–113; J. L. Nelson, *Values and Society* (Rochelle, NJ: Hayden, 1975), 90–95; E. C. Stewart & M. J. Bennett, *American Cultural Patterns: A Cross-Cultural Perspective* (Yarmouth, ME: Intercultural Press, 1991); Trenholm & Jensen, 1992, 156–158; R. M. Williams, *American Society: A Sociological Interpretation*, 3rd ed. (New York: Alfred A. Knopf, 1970).

26. Stewart & Bennett, 1991, 133.

27. S. P. Huntington, "The West Unique, Not Universal," *Foriegn Affairs*, November/December 1996, 33.

28. *Time*, 27 May 1996, 56.

29. J. J. Macionis, *Society: The Basics*, 4th ed. (Saddle River, NJ: Prentice Hall, 1998), 37.

30. Macionis, 1998, 37.

31. Stewart & Bennett, 1992, 119.

32. Macionis, 1998, 36.

33. G. Althen, *American Ways* (Yarmouth, ME: Intercultural Press, 1988), 11.

34. Althen, 1988, 11.

35. Harris & Moran, 1996, 316.

36. G. Hofstede, *Culture's Consequences: International Differences in Work-Related Values* (Beverly Hills: Sage, 1980). See also G. Hofstede, *Cultures and Organizations: Software of the Mind* (London: McGraw-Hill, 1991).

37. J. O. Yum, "The Impact of Confucianism on Interpersonal Relationships and Communication Patterns," in *Intercultural Communication: A Reader*, 8th ed., L. A. Samovar & R. E. Porter, Eds. (Belmont, CA: Wadsworth, 1997), 78.

38. S. Ting-Toomey, *Communicating Across Cultures* (New York: Guilford Press, 1999), 67.

39. H. C. Triandis, *Individualism and Collectivism* (Boulder, CO: Westview Press, 1995). See also H. C. Triandis, "Cross-Cultural Studies of Individualism and Collectivism," in *Cross-Cultural Perspectives*, J. J. Berman, Ed. (Lincoln: University of Nebraska Press, 1990), 41–133.

40. Triandis, 1995.

41. D. Goleman, "The Group and Self: New Focus on a Cultural Rift," *New York Times*, 22 December 1990, 40.

42. D. A. Foster, *Bargaining Across Borders* (New York: McGraw-Hill, 1992), 267.

43. Triandis, 1990, 52.

44. M. Meyer, *China* (Totowa, NJ: Rowman & Littlefield, 1994), 54.

45. Y. Richmond & P. Gestrin, *Into Africa* (Yarmouth, ME: Intercultural Press, Inc., 1998), 2.

46. M. Kim, W. F. Sharkey, & T. Singelis, "Explaining Individualist and Collective Communication—Focusing on the Perceived Importance of Interactive Constraints" (paper presented at the Annual Convention of the Speech Communication Association, Chicago, October 1992).

47. G. Hofstede, "Cultural Differences in Teaching and Learning," *International Journal of Intercultural Relations*, 10 (1986), 301–319.

48. L. Schneider & A. Silverman, *Global Sociology: Introducing Five Contempory Societies* (New York: McGraw-Hill, 1997), 48.

49. M. L. Hecht, M. J. Collier, & S. A. Ribeau, *African American Communication: Ethnic Identity and Interpretation* (Newbury Park, CA: Sage, 1993), 97.

50. Triandis, 1990, 48.

51. Hofstede, 1984, 308.

52. Hofstede, 1986, 301–319.

53. Harris & Moran, 1996, 217.

54. Foster, 1992, 265.

55. Adler, 1997, 51.

56. C. Calloway-Thomas, P. J. Cooper, & C. Blake, *Intercultural Communication: Roots and Routes* (Boston, MA: Allyn & Bacon, 1999), 196.

57. H. Meguro, *Address to the World Affairs Council*, San Diego, CA, 16 June 1988.

58. "Women in the House," *Time*, 16 June 1997, 20.

59. J. G. Draguns, "Normal and Abnormal Behavior," in *Cross-Cultural Perspectives*, J. J. Berman, Ed. (Lincoln: University of Nebraska Press, 1990), 368.

60. Chinese Culture Connection, "Chinese Values and the Search for Culture-Free Dimensions of Culture," *Journal of Cross-Cultural Psychology*, 18 (1987), 143–164. See also G. Hofstede & M. H. Bond, "Confucius and Economic Growth: New Trends in Culture's Consequence," *Organizational Dynamics*, 16 (1988), 4–21.

61. Ting-Toomey, 1999, 74.

62. F. R. Kluckhohn & F. L. Strodtbeck, *Variations in Value Orientations* (New York: Row & Peterson), 1960.

63. Stewart & Bennett, 1991.

64. R. L. Kohls, *Survival Kit for Overseas Living* (Chicago: Intercultural Network/SYSTRAN, 1979), 22.

65. Kohls, 1979, 23.

66. L. Stevenson & D. L. Haberman, *Ten Theories of Human Nature*, 3rd ed. (New York: Oxford University Press, 1998), 4.

67. Stevenson & Haberman, 1998, 74–75.

68. Stevenson & Haberman, 1998, 28.

69. N. C. Jain & E. D. Kussman, "Dominant Cultural Patterns of Hindus in India," in *Intercultural Communication: A Reader*, 9th ed., L. A. Samovar & R. E. Porter, Eds. (Belmont, CA: Wadsworth, 2000), 89.

70. *Newsweek*, 5 June 1989, 71.

71. N. J. Adler, *International Dimensions of Organizational Behavior* (Boston: MA: PWS-KENT, 1991), 24–25.

72. Adler, 1991, 32.

73. E. R. Curtius, *The Civilization of France* (New York: Random House, 1962), 221.

74. Curtius, 1962, 222.

75. A. C. Wilson, "American Indian History or Non-Indian Perceptions of American History?" in *Natives and Academics: Researching and Writing About American Indians*, D. A. Mihesuah, Ed. (Lincoln, NE: University of Nebraska Press, 1998), 24.

76. Ting-Toomey, 1999, 62.

77. Hecht, Collier & Ribeau, 1993, 102–103.

78. R. Newman, "The Virtues of Silence," *Time*, 2 June 1997, 15.

79. L. Skow & L. A. Samovar, "Cultural Patterns of the Maasai," in *Intercultural Communication: A Reader*, 8th ed., L. A. Samovar & R. E. Porter, Eds. (Belmont, CA: Wadsworth, 1997), 110.

80. E. T. Hall, *Beyond Culture* (Garden City, NY: Doubleday, 1976), 7.

81. Hall, 1976, 74.

82. E. T. Hall & M. R. Hall, *Understanding Cultural Differences: Germans, French and Americans* (Yarmouth, ME: Intercultural Press, 1990), 6.

83. Hall & Hall, 1990.

84. Hall & Hall, 1990.

85. P. Andersen, "Cues of Culture: The Basis of Intercultural Differences in Nonverbal Communication," in *Intercultural*

Communication: A Reader, 8th ed., L. A. Samovar & R. E. Porter, Eds. (Belmont, CA: Wadsworth, 1997), 253.

86. Foster, 1992, 280.

87. Hall & Hall, 1990.

88. Althen, 1988, 27.

89. S. Ting-Toomey, "Managing Intercultural Conflicts Effectively," in *Intercultural Communication: A Reader,* 8th ed., L. A. Samovar & R. E. Porter, Eds. (Belmont, CA: Wadsworth, 1997), 394.

90. Harris & Moran, 1996, 25.

91. A. Javidi & M. Javidi, "Cross-Cultural Analysis of Interpersonal Bonding: A Look at East and West," in *Intercultural Communication: A Reader,* 8th ed., L. A. Samovar & R. E. Porter, Eds. (Belmont, CA: Wadsworth, 1997), 89.

92. Althen, 1988, 10.

93. Dresser, 1996, 151.

94. Stewart & Bennett, 1991, 160.

95. Hall & Hall, 1990, 48.

96. Hall & Hall, 1990, 49.

97. Schneider & Silverman, 1997, 70.

98. E. Gareis, *Intercultural Friendships: A Qualitative Study* (New York: University Press of America, 1995), 27.

99. D. C. Barnlund, *Communication Styles of Japanese and Americans* (Belmont, CA: Wadsworth, 1989), 101–108.

100. Barnlund, 1989, 117.

101. *U.S. News & World Report,* 22 April 1996, 66–67.

102. L. B. Nadler, M. K. Nadler, & B. Broome, "Culture and the Management of Conflict Situations," in *Communication, Culture and Organizational Processes,* W. B. Gudykunst, L. P. Stewart, & S. Ting-Toomey, Eds. (Beverly Hills: Sage, 1985), 109.

103. Barnlund, 1989, 157.

104. H. Wenzhong & C. L. Grove, *Encountering the Chinese: A Guide to Americans* (Yarmouth, ME: Intercultural Press, 1990), 23.

105. R. Cooper & N. Cooper, *Culture Shock: Thailand* (Portland, OR: Graphic Arts Center Publishing Company, 1994), 86.

106. T. Gochenour, *Considering Filipinos* (Yarmouth, ME: Intercultural Press, 1990), 23.

107. Gochenour, 1990, 25.

108. Gochenour, 1990, 24.

109. B. Moeran, "Individual, Group and *Seishin:* Japan's Internal Cultural Debate, " in *Japanese Culture and Behavior,* rev. ed., T. S. Lebra & W. P. Lebra, Eds. (Honolulu: University of Hawaii Press, 1968), 75.

110. J. Hendry, *Understanding Japanese Society* (New York: Routledge, 1987), 194.

111. Hendry, 1987, 43.

112. P. R. Harris & R. T. Moran, *Managing Cultural Differences* (Houston, TX: Gulf, 1979), 296.

113. W. V. Ruch, *International Handbook of Corporate Communication* (Jefferson, NC: McFarland, 1989), 273.

114. Schneider & Silverman, 1997, 9.

115. Gao & Ting-Toomey, 1998, 61.

116. G. Chen & X. Xiao, "The Impact of Harmony on Chinese Negotiations" (paper presented at the Annual Convention of the Speech Communication Association, Miami Beach, FL, November 1993), 4.

117. G. Chen, "A Chinese Perspective of Communication Competence" (paper presented at the Annual Convention of the Speech Communication Association, Miami Beach, FL, November 1993), 6.

118. A. Abdullah, "Understanding the Asian Workforce: The Malaysian Experience" (paper presented at the Twentieth Annual Conference of the Asian Regional Training and Development Organization, Jakarta, Indonesia, November 1993), 7.

119. J. Condon, *Good Neighbors: Communicating with the Mexicans* (Yarmouth, ME: Intercultural Press, 1986), 46.

120. Ruch, 1989, 75.

121. F. M. Moghaddam, D. M. Taylor, & S. C. Wright, *Social Psychology in Cross-Cultural Perspective* (New York: W. H. Freeman, 1993), 124.

122. S. Nanda, *Cultural Anthropology,* 5th ed. (Belmont, CA: Wadsworth, 1994), 142.

123. J. T. Wood, *Gendered Lives: Communication, Gender, and Culture* (Belmont, CA: Wadsworth, 1994), 80. See also J. C. Pearson, R. L. West, & L. H. Turner, *Gender and Communication,* 3d ed. (Dubuque, IA: Brown & Benchmark, 1995), 168–171.

124. D. K. Ivy & P. Backlund, *Exploring Gender Speak: Personal Effectiveness in Gender Communication* (New York: McGraw-Hill, 1994), 48.

125. Ivy & Backlund, 1994, 48.

Notes for Chapter 4

1. "Racist Sect, Activists Square Off at Rally," *San Diego Union-Tribune,* 5 July 1999, A-8.

2. Y. Ling-Ling, "Ethnic Strife Is Not a Geographically Distant Phenomenon," *San Diego Union-Tribune,* 10 June 1999, B-11.

3. J. Leo, "War Against Warriors," *U.S. News & World Report,* 8 March 1999, 16.

4. P. Marshall & L. Gilbert, *Their Blood Cries Out: The Untold Story of Persecution Against Christians in the Modern World* (Word Publishing, 1997).

5. S. P. Huntington, "The Clash of Civilizations," *Foreign Affairs,* 72 (1993), 22.

6. Huntington, 1993, 25.

7. F. P. Delgado, "The Nature of Power Across Communicative and Cultural Borders" (paper delivered at the Annual Convention of the Speech Communication Association, Miami Beach, FL, November 1993), 11.

8. F. Ajami, "The Ancient Roots of Grievance," *U.S. News & World Report,* 12 April 1999, 20.

9. E. L. Lynch & M. J. Hanson, *Developing Cross-Cultural Competence: A Guide for Working with Young Children and Their Families* (Baltimore: Paul Brookes Publishing Co., 1992), 358.

10. E. A. Hoebel & E. L. Frost, *Cultural and Social Anthropology* (New York: McGraw-Hill, 1976), 324.

11. R. H. Dana, *Multicultural Assesment Perspectives for Professional Psychology* (Boston, MA: Allyn & Bacon, 1993), 9.

12. E. A. Hoebel, *Man in the Primitive World* (New York: McGraw-Hill, 1958), 159.

13. R. O. Olayiwola, "The Impact of Islam on the Conduct of Nigerian Foreign Relations," *Islamic Quarterly,* 33 (1989), 19–26.

14. D. L. Pennington, "Intercultural Communication," in *Intercultural Communication: A Reader,* 4th ed., L. A. Samovar & R. E. Porter, Eds. (Belmont, CA: Wadsworth, 1985), 32.

15. T. Bianquis, *A History of the Family*, Vol. 4, A. Burguiere, gen. ed. (Cambridge, MA: Harvard University Press, 1996), 618.

16. R. Bartels, "National Culture-Business Relations: United States and Japan Contrasted," *Management International Review*, 2 (1982), 5.

17. W. S. Howell, *The Empathic Communicator* (Belmont, CA: Wadsworth, 1982), 223.

18. P. Gold, *Navajo and Tibetan Sacred Wisdom: The Circle of the Spirit* (Rochester, VT: Inner Traditions, 1994), 60.

19. S. Nanda & R. L. Warms, *Cultural Anthropology*, 6th ed. (Belmont, CA: Wadsworth, 1998), 275.

20. W. A. Haviland, *Cultural Anthropology* (Fort Worth, TX: Harcourt Brace Jovanovich College Publishers, 1993), 346.

21. S. Nanda, *Cultural Anthropology*, 5th ed. (Belmont, CA: Wadsworth, 1994), 349

22. H. Smith, *The World's Religions* (New York: Harper-Collins, 1991), 9.

23. Haviland, 1993.

24. C. Lamb, "The Claim to Be Unique," in *Eerdmans' Handbook to the World's Religions*, R. PierceBeaver et al., Eds. (Grand Rapids, MI: Eerdmans, 1982), 358.

25. A. W. P. Guruge, "Survival of Religion: The Role of Pragmatism and Flexibility," (paper presented at the Religious Studies Department, George Washington University, Washington, DC, 1 November 1995), 30.

26. R. L. Monroe & R. H. Monroe, "Perspectives Suggested by Anthropological Data," in *Handbook of Cross-Cultural Psychology: Vol. 1 Perspectives*, H. C. Triandis & W. W. Lambert, Eds. (Boston, MA: Allyn & Bacon, 1980), 259.

27. W. E. Paden, *Religious Worlds: The Comparative Study of Religion* (Boston, MA: Beacon, 1994), 170.

28. "One Nation Under Gods," *Time*, Fall 1993, 62.

29. D. L. Carmody & J. T. Carmody, *In the Path of the Masters: Understanding the Spirituality of Buddha, Confucius, Jesus, and Muhammad* (New York: Paragon House, 1994), Preface.

30. Smith, 1991, 3.

31. K. Crim, *The Perennial Dictionary of World Religions* (New York: HarperCollins Publishers, 1989), 665.

32. D. Crystal, *The Cambridge Encyclopedia of Language* (New York: Cambridge University Press, 1987), 384.

33. Crystal, 1987.

34. Crim, 1989, 624.

35. Crim, 1989.

36. Paden, 1994, 96.

37. H. Smith, *The Illustrated World's Religions: A Guide to Our Wisdom Traditions* (New York: HarperCollins, 1994), 210.

38. Smith, 1991, 387.

39. Smith, 1991.

40. Smith, 1991.

41. J. J. Macionis, *Society: The Basics*, 4th ed. (Upper Saddle River, NJ: Prentice Hall, 1998), 319.

42. J. Hendry, *Understanding Japanese Society* (NewYork: Routledge, 1987), 103.

43. D. Crystal, Ed., *The Cambridge Factfinder* (New York: Cambridge University Press, 1994), 343.

44. K. L. Woodward, "2000 Year of Jesus," *Newsweek*, 29 March 1999, 55.

45. D. S. Noss & J. B. Noss, *Man's Religions*, 7th ed. (New York: Macmillan, 1984), 412.

46. Woodward, 1999, 55.

47. T. A. Baima, "Christianity: Origins and Beliefs," in *A Source Book for Earth's Community of Religions*, J. Beversluis, Ed. (New York: Global Education Associates, 1995), 20.

48. *Prime Time School Television: The Long Search* (Chicago, 1978).

49. Carmody & Carmody, 1994, 116.

50. Carmody & Carmody, 1994.

51. M. P. Fisher & R. Luyster, *Living Religions* (Englewood Cliffs, NJ: Prentice-Hall, 1991), 228.

52. Smith, 1994, 212.

53. Woodward, 1999, 56.

54. Woodward, 1999.

55. Woodward, 1999.

56. B. Storm, *More Than Talk: Communication Studies and the Christian Faith* (Dubuque, IA: Kendall/Hunt Publishing, 1996).

57. Smith, 1994, 210.

58. Woodward, 1999, 55.

59. T. C. Muck, *Those Other Religions in Your Neighborhood: Loving Your Neighbor When You Don't Know How* (Grand Rapids, MI: Zondervan Publishing House, 1992), 165.

60. Storm, 1996, 19.

61. Crim, 1989, 171.

62. C. Murphy, "The Bible According to Eve," *U.S. News & World Report*, 10 August 1998, 49.

63. Woodward, 1999, 58.

64. Woodward, 1999, 57.

65. Murphy, 1998, 50.

66. Murphy, 1998, 49.

67. Carmody & Carmody, 1994, 104.

68. Crystal, 1994, 343.

69. Smith, 1991, 271.

70. Fisher & Luyster, 1991, 175.

71. R. Banks, "The Covenant," *Eerdmans' Handbook to the World's Religions*, 278.

72. D. J. Boorstin, *The Creators* (New York: Random House, 1992), 43.

73. D. Prager & J. Telushkin, *The Nine Questions People Ask About Judaism* (New York: Simon & Schuster, 1981), 112.

74. Smith, 1991, 287.

75. *Prime Time School Television*, 1978.

76. Smith, 1994, 193.

77. Prager & Telushkin, 1981, 29.

78. Boorstin, 1992, 39.

79. F. E. Peters, *Judaism, Christianity and Islam: The Classical Texts and Their Interpretation* (Princeton, NJ: Princeton University Press, 1990).

80. Crim, 1989, 732.

81. L. Rosten, *Religions of America* (New York: Simon & Schuster, 1975), 143.

82. Rosten, 1975.

83. P. Novak, *The World's Wisdom: Sacred Tests of the World's Religions* (New York: HarperCollins, 1994), 179.

84. Prager & Telushkin, 1981, 46.

85. Smith, 1994, 189.

86. Rosten, 1975, 575.

87. Smith, 1991, 267.

88. *U.S. News & World Report*, 8 February 1999, 14.

89. J. Blank, "The Muslim Mainstream," *U.S. News & World Report,* 20 July 1998, 22.

90. Noss & Noss, 496.

91. C. Van Doren, *A History of Knowledge* (New York: Ballantine Books, 1991), 20.

92. Novak, 1994, 282.

93. C. Wilson, "The Quran," in *Eerdmans' Handbook to the World's Religions,* 315.

94. Crim, 1989, 346.

95. M. K. Nydell, *Understanding Arabs: A Guide for Westerners* (Yarmouth, ME: Intercultural Press, 1987), 87–88.

96. Novak, 1994, 282.

97. Smith, 1991, 189.

98. Novak, 1994, 306.

99. A. M. Lutfiyya, "Islam in Village Culture," in *Readings in Arab Middle Eastern Societies and Cultures,* A. M. Lutfiyya & C. W. Churchill, Eds. (Paris: Mouton, 1970), 49.

100. A. Esler, *The Human Venture,* 2d ed. (Englewood Cliffs, NJ: Prentice-Hall, 1992), 257–258.

101. Esler, 1992, 250.

102. Esler, 1992.

103. Crim, 1989, 57.

104. L. Schmalfuss, "Science, Art and Culture in Islam," in *Eerdmans' Handbook to the World's Religions,* 328.

105. Fisher & Luyster, 1991, 289.

106. Nydell, 1987, 91.

107. L. Schneider & A. Silverman, *Global Sociology: Introducing Five Contemporary Societies* (New York: McGraw-Hill, 1997), 165.

108. Nydell, 1987, 91.

109. Fisher & Luyster, 1991, 280.

110. Esler, 1992, 80.

111. Boorstin, 1992, 5.

112. R. Smart, "Religious-Caused Complications in Intercultural Communication," in *Intercultural Communication: A Reader,* 5th ed., L. A. Samovar & R. E. Porter, Eds. (Belmont, CA: Wadsworth, 1988), 70.

113. N. Jain & E. D. Kussman, "Dominant Cultural Patterns of Hindus in India," in *Intercultural Communication: A Reader,* 9th ed., L. A. Samovar & R. E. Porter, Eds. (Belmont, CA: Wadsworth, 2000), 83.

114. Boorstin, 1992, 4–5.

115. R. Hammer, "The Eternal Teaching: Hinduism," in *Eerdmans' Handbook to the World's Religions,* 170.

116. R. S. Hegde, "Passages from Tradition: Communication Competence and Gender in India" (paper presented at the Annual Convention of the Speech Communication Association, Miami Beach, FL, November 1993), 5.

117. T. K. Venkateswaran, "Hinduism: A Portrait," in *A Source Book for Earth's Community of Religions,* J. D. Beversluis, Ed. (Grand Rapids, MI: Co Nexus Press, 1995), 40.

118. G. Kolanad, *Culture Shock: India* (Portland, OR: Graphic Arts Center Publishing Company, 1994), 56.

119. Hammer, 1982.

120. Jain & Kussman, 2000, 84.

121. Jain & Kussmam, 2000, 85.

122. Smith, 1994, 21.

123. Jain & Kussman, 2000, 86.

124. R. Brabant-Smith, "Two Kinds of Language," *The Middle Way: Journal of the Buddhist Society,* 68 (1993), 123.

125. Smith, 1994, 68.

126. Thich-Thien-An, *Zen Philosophy, Zen Practice* (Emeryville, CA: Dharma, 1975), 17.

127. Van Doren, 1991, 21.

128. Crim, 1989, 124.

129. Fisher & Luyster, 1991, 103.

130. Smith, 1991, 99.

131. W. Metz, "The Enlightened One: Buddhism," in *Eerdmans' Handbook of the World's Religions,* 231–232.

132. Smith, 1994, 71.

133. Fisher & Luyster, 1991, 110.

134. Fisher & Luyster, 1991.

135. Thich-Thien-An, 1975, 38.

136. Novak, 1994, 67.

137. Smith, 1994, 68.

138. Crim, 1989, 188–189.

139. W. T. Barry, W. T. Chen, & B. Watson, *Sources of Chinese Tradition* (New York: Columbia University Press, 1960), 17.

140. Z. Lin, "How China Will Modernize," *American Enterprise,* 2 (1991).

141. Schneider & Silverman, 1997, 15.

142. Schneider & Silverman, 1997.

143. J. O. Yum, "Confucianism and Interpersonal Relationships and Communication Patterns in East Asia," in *Intercultural Communication: A Reader,* 9th ed., L. A. Samovar & R. E. Porter, Eds. (Belmont, CA: Wadsworth, 2000), 64.

144. I. P. McGreal, *Great Thinkers of the Eastern World* (New York: HarperCollins, 1995), 3.

145. Crim, 1989, 192.

146. Smith, 1994, 110

147. McGreal, 1995, 4.

148. Smith, 1994, 111.

149. Smith, 1994.

150. Smith, 1994, 110.

151. Yum, 2000, 68.

152. G. Chen & J. Chung, "The Impact of Confucianism on Organizational Communication," *Communication Quarterly,* 42 (1994), 97.

153. Novak, 1994, 120.

154. G. Gao & Ting-Toomey, *Communicating Effectively with the Chinese* (Thousand Oaks: CA, Sage Publications, 1998), 75.

155. Yum, 2000, 70.

156. Hoebel & Frost, 1976, 331.

157. Hoebel & Frost, 1976, 331.

158. Paden, 1994, 26.

159. A. Althen, *American Ways* (Yarmouth, MA: Intercultural Press, Inc., 1988), 31.

160. Althen, 1988, 32.

161. W. W. Cobern, "College Students' Conceptualization of Nature: An Interpretive World View Analysis," *Journal of Research in Science Teaching,* 30 (1993), 937.

162. D. Elgin, *Voluntary Simplicity* (New York: William Morrow, 1981), 225.

163. Fisher & Luyster, 1991, 22.

164. Fisher & Luyster, 1991.

165. Fisher & Luyster, 1991.

166. N. C. Asuncion-Lande, "Mediation in Cross-Cultural Conflict," *Informatologia Yugoslavica*, 1985, 160.

167. A. Huxley, *The Perennial Philosophy* (New York: Harper & Row, 1944), 126–127.

168. Smart, 1988, 65.

169. Elgin, 1981, 225.

170. Paden, 1994, 12.

171. D. E. Brown, *Human Universals* (New York: McGraw-Hill, 1991).

172. K. M. Galvin & B. J. Brommel, *Family Communication: Cohesion and Change*, 3d ed. (New York: HarperCollins, 1991), 1.

173. Schneider & Silverman, 1997, 77.

174. A. Swerdlow, R. Bridenthal, J. Kelly, & P. Vine, *Families in Flux* (New York: Feminist Press, 1989), 64.

175. F. I. Nye & F. M. Berardo, *The Family: Its Structures and Interaction* (New York: Macmillan, 1973), 3.

176. A. Burguiere, *A History of the Family* (Cambridge, MA: Harvard University Press, 1996), 9.

177. K. A. Ocampo, M. Bernal, & G. P. Knight, "Gender, Race, and Ethnicity: The Sequencing of Social Constancies," in *Ethnic Identity: The Formation and Transmission Among Hispanic and Other Minorities*, M. E. Bernal & G. P. Knight, Eds. (New York: State University of New York Press, 1993), 106.

178. R. M. Berko, L. B. Rosenfeld, & L. A. Samovar, *Connecting: A Culture-Sensitive Approach to Interpersonal Communication Competency* (Fort Worth, TX: Harcourt Brace Jovanovich College Publishers, 1997), 331.

179. Berko, Rosenfeld, & Samovar, 1997, 331.

180. G. L. Anderson, "The Family in Transition," in *The Family in Global Transition*, G. L. Anderson, Ed. (St.Paul, MN: Paragon House Publishers, 1997), ix.

181. *Comparisons: Four Families (Part I)*, film, I. MacNeill, writer & producer, National Film Board Production: McGraw-Hill Films, 1965.

182. M. McGoldrick, "Ethnicity, Cultural Diversity, and Normality," in *Normal Family Processes*, F. Walalish, Ed. (New York: Guilford Press, 1973), 331.

183. McGoldrick, 1973, 335.

184. M. McGoldrick, "Ethnicity and the Family Life Cycle," in *The Changing Family Life Cycle: A Framework for Family Therapy*, 2d ed., B. Carter & M. McGoldrick, Eds. (Boston: Allyn & Bacon, 1989), 69.

185. Ocampo, Bernal, & Knight, 1993, 14.

186. M. Kim, "Transformation of Family Ideology in Upper-Middle-Class Families in Urban South Korea," *International Journal of Cultural and Social Anthropology*, 32 (1993), 70.

187. Kim, 1993, 70.

188. L. E. Davis & E. K. Proctor, *Race, Gender and Class: Guidelines with Individuals, Families, and Groups* (Englewood Cliffs, NJ: Prentice-Hall, 1989), 67.

189. Hendry, 1987, 5.

190. M. Ferguson, *Feminism and Postmodernism* (Durham, NC: Duke University Press, 1994).

191. E. S. Kras, *Management in Two Cultures* (Yarmouth, ME: Intercultural Press, 1995), 64.

192. C. H. Mindel & R. W. Habenstein, *Ethnic Families in America: Patterns and Variations*, 2nd ed. (New York: Elsevier Science Publishing, 1981), 275.

193. Schneider & Silverman, 1997, 71.

194. Mindel & Habenstein, 1981, 276–277.

195. Dana, 1993, 70.

196. Nanda, 1994, 137.

197. Anderson, 1997, 47.

198. R. Patai, *The Arab Mind* (New York: Charles Scribner's Sons, 1973), 28.

199. Patai, 1994, 31.

200. Patai, 1994, 32.

201. Nanda & Warms, 1998, 221.

202. Lynch & Hanson, 1992, 161–162.

203. Althen, 1988, 48.

204. F. M. Moghaddam, D. M. Taylor, & S. C. Wright, *Social Psychology in Cross-Cultural Perspective* (New York: W. H. Freeman, 1993), 73, 98.

205. N. Nomura, Y. Noguchi, S. Saito, & I. Tezuka, "Family Characteristics and Dynamics in Japan and the United States: A Preliminary Report from the Family Environment Scale," *International Journal of Intercultural Relations*, 19 (1995), 63.

206. Althen, 1988, 5.

207. Althen, 1988, 50.

208. W. A. Haviland, *Cultural Anthropology*, 7th ed. (Fort Worth, TX: Harcourt Brace Jovanovich College Publishers, 1993), 253.

209. S. Wolpert, *India* (Berkeley, CA: University of California Press, 1991), 134.

210. J. W. Santrock, *Life-Span Development*, 4th ed. (Dubuque, IA: Wm. C. Brown, 1992), 261.

211. Y. Richmond & P. Gestrin, *Into Africa: Intercultural Insights* (Yarmouth, MA: Intercultural Press, Inc., 1998), 3.

212. Schneider & Silverman, 1997, 73.

213. A. Valenzula, "Liberal Gender Role Attitudes and Academic Achievement Among Mexican-Origin Adolescents in Two Houston Inner-City Catholic Schools," *Hispanic Journal of Behavior Sciences*, 15 August 1993, 294.

214. R. Shorto, "Made-In-Japan Parenting," *Health*, 23 (1991), 54.

215. Shorto, 1991.

216. G. C. Chu & Y. Ju, *The Great Wall in Ruins: Communication and Culture Change in China* (Albany, NY: State University of New York Press, 1993), 9–10.

217. Nydell, 1989, 75.

218. Lutfiyya, 1970, 55.

219. H. Wenzhong & C. L. Grove, *Encountering the Chinese: A Guide for Americans* (Yarmouth, ME: Intercultural Press, 1991), 6.

220. Hendry, 1987, 24.

221. T. Gochenour, *Considering Filipinos* (Yarmouth, ME: Intercultural Press, 1990), 19.

222. A. J. Rubel, "The Family," in *Mexican-Americans in the United States: A Reader*, J. H. Burma, Ed. (New York: Canfield Press, 1970), 212.

223. G. Arnold, "Living in Harmony: Makah," in *Stories of the People: Native American Voices*, National Museum of the American Indian, Ed. (New York: Universe Publishing, 1997), 48.

224. E. R. Curtius, *The Civilization of France* (New York: Vintage Books, 1962), 225.

225. Curtius, 1962, 226.

226. Anderson, 1997, 265.

227. J. Yerby, N. Buerkel-Rothfuss, & A. P. Bochner, *Understanding Family Communication,* 2d ed. (Scottsdale, AZ: Gorsuch Scarisbrick, 1995), 63.

228. L. H. Turner & R. West, *Perspectives on Family Communication* (Mountain View, CA: Mayfield, 1998), 10.

229. Moghaddam, Taylor, & Wright, 1993, 125.

230. N. Murillo, "The Mexican Family," *Chicanos: Social and Psychological Perspective,* C. A. Hernandez, M. J. Hang, & N. N. Wagner, Eds. (Saint Louis, MO: C. V. Mosby, 1976), 19.

231. Moghaddam, Taylor, & Wright, 1993, 124.

232. McGoldrick, 1973, 341.

233. McGoldrick, 1973, 336.

234. McGoldrick, 1973, 336.

235. R. Cooper & N. Cooper, *Thailand: A Guide to Customs and Etiquette* (Portland, OR: Graphic Arts Center Publishing Company, 1982), 83.

236. Chu & Ju, 1993, 79.

237. Galvin & Brommel, 1991, 9.

238. Galvin & Brommel, 1991, 9.

239. Y. Yu, "Clio's New Cultural Turn and the Rediscovery of Tradition in Asia" (keynote address presented to the 12th Conference of the International Association of Historians of Asia, June 1991), 26.

240. "How the Seeds of Hate Were Sown," *San Diego Union-Tribune,* 9 May 1993, G5.

241. *Time,* 16 May 1994, 63.

242. "Beautiful Dreamers Killed in California," *U.S. News & World Report,* 25 March 1996, 59.

243. B. Kerblay, *Modern Soviet Society* (New York: Pantheon, 1983), 271.

244. Van Doren, 1991, 224.

245. R. G. Del Castillo, *The Treaty of Guadalupe Hidalgo: A Legacy of Conflict* (Norman, OK: University of Oklahoma Press, 1990), 4.

246. *U.S. News & World Report,* 20 March 1989, 9.

247. *U.S. News & World Report,* 20 March 1989, 9.

248. L. Bem, *The Lenses of Gender* (New Haven: Yale University Press, 1993).

249. S. E. Ambrose, *Undaunted Courage: Meriwether Lewis, Thomas Jefferson and the Opening of the American West* (New York: Simon & Schuster, 1996), 36.

250. R. Segal, *The Black Diaspora: Five Centuries of the Black Experience Outside Africa* (New York: Farrar, Straus, & Giroux, 1995), 56.

251. A. Esler, *The Human Venture,* 3rd. ed. (Upper Saddle River, NJ: Prentice Hall, 1996), 526.

252. E. Cose, "Slavery's Real Roots," *Newsweek,* 26 October 1998, 75.

253. M. Angelou, *Wouldn't Take Nothing for My Journey Now* (New York: Random House, 1993), 102.

254. Angelou, 1993, 102.

255. *Newsweek,* 8 December 1997, 63.

256. *Newsweek,* 8 December 1997, 63

257. Van Doren, 1991, 16.

258. A. Esler, 1996, 635.

259. Van Doren, 1991, 16.

260. Van Doren, 1991, 16.

261. R. V. Daniels, *Russia: The Roots of Confrontation* (Cambridge, MA: Harvard University Press, 1985), 55.

262. Esler, 1996, 668.

263. J. Kohan, "A Mind of Their Own," *Time,* 7 December 1992, 66.

264. J. Kohan, 1992, 66.

265. S. Sangren, *History and Magical Power in a Chinese Community* (Stanford, CA: Stanford University Press, 1987), 3.

266. F. Fernandez-Armesto, *Millennium: A History of the Last Thousand Years* (New York: Scribner, 1995), 44.

267. K. Scott Latourette, *The Chinese: Their History and Culture,* 4th ed. (New York: Macmillan, 1964), 22.

268. Esler, 1992, 86.

269. C. Stafford, "Good Sons and Virtuous Mothers: Kinship and Chinese Nationalism in Taiwan," *Journal of the Royal Anthropological Institute,* 27 June 1992, 368.

270. Stafford, 1992, 368.

271. Van Doren, 1991, 9.

272. F. Kaplan, J. Sobin, & A. Keijer, *The China Handbook,* 6th ed. (New York: Eurasia Press, 1985), 37.

273. Wenzhong & Grove, 1991, 1.

274. Wenzhong & Grove, 1991, 1.

275. E. D. Reischauer, *The Japanese Today: Change and Continuity* (Cambridge, MA: Harvard University Press, 1988), 32.

276. Schneider & Silverman, 1997, 2.

277. Reischauer, 1988, 32.

278. Reischauer, 1988, 32.

279. Scheider & Silverman, 1997, 2.

280. Scheider & Silverman, 1997, 2.

281. P. Tasker, *Inside Japan: Wealth, Work and Power in the New Japanese Empire* (London: Sidgwick & Jackson, 1987).

282. H. R. Hays, *From Ape to Angel: An Informal History of Social Anthropology* (New York: Knopf, 1965), 413–414.

283. Reischauer, 1988, 15.

284. Reischauer, 1988, 15–16.

285. Del Castillo, 1990, xi.

286. C. McKiniss & A. Natella, *Business Mexico* (New York: The Haworth Press, 1994), 70.

287. Schneider & Silverman, 1997, 60.

288. J. C. Condon, *Good Neighbors: Communicating with Mexicans* (Yarmouth, ME: Intercultural Press, Inc., 1985), 1.

289. Schneider & Silverman, 1997, 60.

290. L. V. Foster, *A Brief History of Mexico* (New York: Facts On File, Inc., 1997) 2.

291. J. Norman, *Guide to Mexico* (Garden City: Doubleday & Company, 1972) 53.

292. Foster, 1997, 43.

293. Foster, 1997, 65.

294. Foster, 1997, 66.

295. Foster, 1997, 96.

296. Foster, 1997, 72.

297. H. B. Parkes, *A History of Mexico,* 3rd ed. (Boston, MA: Houghton Mifflin, 1969).

298. Foster, 1997, 111.

299. J. Eisenhower, "The War Nobody Knows," *On Air,* September 1998, 17.

300. Del Castillo, 1990, xii.

301. J. Samora & P. V. Simon, *A History of Mexican American People* (London: University of Notre Dame Press, 1977), 98.

302. Samora & Simon, 1977, 98.

303. Esler, 1996, 613.

304. O. Najera-Ramirez, "Engendering Nationalism: Identity, Discourse, and the Mexican Charro," *Anthropological Quarterly*, 67 (1944), 9.

305. Foster, 1997, 156.

306. D. J. Weber, "Conflicts and Accommodations: Hispanic and Anglo-American Borders in Historical Perspective," *Journal of the Southwest*, 39 (1997), 1.

307. Gergen, D. "One Nation, After All," *U.S. News & World Report*, 16 March 1998, 84.

Notes for Chapter 5

1. M. Cartmill, "The Gift of Gab," *Discover*, November 1998, 56.

2. Cartmill, 1998, 56.

3. D. Crystal, *The Cambridge Encyclopedia of Language*, 2d ed. (Cambridge, Cambridge University Press, 1997), 10.

4. Crystal, 1997, 13.

5. Crystal, 1997, 11.

6. Crystal, 1997, 11.

7. Crystal, 1997, 12.

8. Crystal, 1997, 12.

9. Crystal, 1997, 13.

10. Crystal, 1997, 38.

11. J. Edwards, *Language, Society, and Identity* (Oxford, UK: Blackwell, 1985), 15.

12. Crystal, 1997, 34.

13. *San Diego Union-Tribune*, 13 February 1997, A-20.

14. *Newsweek*, 3 February 1997, 4.

15. B. D. Rubin, *Communication and Human Behavior*, 3d ed. (Englewood Cliffs, NJ: Prentice-Hall, 1992), 92.

16. B. Honig, *Handbook for Teaching Korean-American Students* (California Department of Education, 1992), 66.

17. California Department of Education, *Handbook for Teaching Vietnamese-Speaking Students* (California Department of Education, 1994), 29.

18. B. Honig, *Handbook for Teaching Filipino-Speaking Students* (California Department of Education, 1986), 27.

19. S. Nanda and R. L. Warms, *Cultural Anthropology*, 6th ed. (Belmont, CA: Wadsworth, 1998), 69.

20. E. M. Rogers & T.M. Steinfatt, *Intercultural Communication* (Prospect Heights, IL: Waveland Press, 1998), 135.

21. B. L. Whorf, *Language, Thought, and Reality: Selected Writings of Benjamin Lee Whorf*, J. B. Carroll, Ed. (Cambridge, MA: MIT Press, 1940/1956), 239.

22. D. G. Mandelbaum, Ed., *Selected Writings of Edward Sapir* (Berkeley and Los Angeles: University of California Press, 1949), 162.

23. S. Nanda, *Cultural Anthropology*, 4th ed. (Belmont, CA: Wadsworth, 1991), 120.

24. Rogers and Steinfatt, 1998, 138.

25. Nanda, 1991, 121.

26. Crystal, 1997, 15.

27. J. Reineke, *Language and Dialect in Hawaii* (Honolulu: University of Hawaii Press, 1969), 28–30.

28. W. Sloane, "Lapps' Ski-Doos Put Rudolph in Back Seat," *Christian Science Monitor*, 7 December 1995, 7.

29. Sloane, 1995, 7.

30. W. V. Ruch, *International Handbook of Corporate Communication* (Jefferson, NC: McFarland, 1989), 174.

31. E. Chaika, *Language: The Social Mirror*, 2d ed. (New York: Newbury House, 1989).

32. C. Arensberg & A. Nichoff, *Introducing Social Change: A Manual for Americans Overseas* (Chicago: Aldine, 1964), 30.

33. Y. Richmond & P. Gestrin, *Into Africa: Intercultural Insights* (Yarmouth, ME: Intercultural Press, 1998), 85.

34. E. S. Kashima & Y. Kashima, "Culture and Language," *Journal of Cross-Cultural Psychology*, 29 (1998), 461–487.

35. R. Ma, "Saying 'Yes' for 'No' and 'No' for 'Yes': A Chinese Rule," *Journal of Pragmatics*, 25 (1996a), 257–266.

36. Ma, 1996a, 1.

37. M. B. Marks, "Straddling Cultural Divides with Grace," *Christian Science Monitor*, 15 November 1995, 16.

38. R. Ma, "Language of Offense in the Chinese Culture: The Creation of Corrosive Effects" (paper presented at the 92nd Annual Convention of the Speech Communication Association, November 23–26, 1996b, San Diego, California), 1.

39. M. Park & K. Moon-soo, "Communication Practices in Korea," *Communication Quarterly*, 40 (1992), 299.

40. Park & Moon-soo, 1992, 398.

41. P. Matsumoto & M. Assar, "The Effects of Language on Judgments of Universal Facial Expressions of Emotion," *Journal of Nonverbal Behavior*, 16 (1992), 87.

42. Crystal, 1997, 21.

43. Park & Moon-soo, 1992, 399.

44. Richmond & Gerstin, 1998, 75.

45. Richmond & Gerstin, 1998, 77.

46. Richmond & Gerstin, 1998, 77.

47. J. Knappert, *The A–Z of African Proverbs* (London, UK: Karnak House, 1989), 3.

48. K. Yankah, *The Proverb in the Context of Akan Rhetoric: A Theory of Proverb Praxis* (New York: Peter Lang, 1982), 71.

49. Richmond & Gerstin, 1998, 77.

50. A. Almaney & A. Alwan, *Communicating with Arabs* (Prospect Heights, IL: Waveland Press, 1982), 84.

51. J. C. Condon, *Interact: Guidelines for Mexicans and North Americans* (Chicago: Intercultural Press, 1980), 37.

52. A. Riding, *Distinct Neighbors: A Portrait of Mexico* (New York: Knopf, 1985), 8.

53. E. C. Stewart & M. J. Bennett, *American Cultural Patterns: A Cross-Cultural Perspective* (Yarmouth, ME: Intercultural Press, 1991), 45.

54. J. Hernandez, "Computers and Translation: Translation Software," *Translation Review*, 47 (1995), 55.

55. R. Schulte, "Editorial: The Reviewing of Translations: A Growing Crisis," *Translation Review*, 48–49 (1995), 1.

56. E. A. Nida, *Toward a Science of Translating* (Leiden: E.J. Brill, 1964), 160.

57. J. deWard & E. A. Nida, *From One Language to Another: Functional Equivalence in Bible Translating* (Nashville: Thomas Nelson, 1986).

58. M. Shuttleworth & M. Cowie, *Dictionary of Translation Studies* (Manchester: St. Jerome Publishing, 1997).

59. N. B. R. Reeves, "Translating and Interpreting as Cultural Intermediation: Some Theoretical Issues Reconsidered," in *Translation and Interpreting: Bridging East and West*, R. K. Seymour & C. C. Liu, Eds. (Honolulu: University of Hawaii Press, 1994), 33–50.

60. T. Givron, *Mind, Code and Context: Essays in Pragmatics* (Hillsdale, NJ: Lawrence Erlbaum Associates, 1989), 350–351.

61. Reeves, 1994.

62. J. Seidel & W. McMordie, *English Idioms and How to Use Them* (Oxford: Oxford University Press, 1978), 4.

63. S. Basset-Mcguire, *Translation Studies* (New York: Methuen, 1980), 28.

64. Honig, 1992, 32.

65. T. Ogawa, "Translation as a Cultural-Philosophical Problem: Toward a Phenomenology of Culture," *Monist,* 78 (1995), 18–29.

66. T. Tymoczko, "Translation and meaning," in *Meaning and Translation: Philosophical and Linguistic Approaches,* F. Guenthner & M. Guenthner-Reutter, Eds. (New York: New York University Press, 1978), 20–43.

67. H. C. Triandis, "Approaches Toward Minimizing Translation," in *Translation Applications and Research,* R. Brislin, Ed. (New York: Gardner, 1976), 229–243.

68. Triandis, 1976, 229–243.

69. A. L. Becker, "Communication Across Diversity," in *The Imagination of Reality,* A.L. Becker & A. A. Yenogoyan, Eds. (Norwood, NJ: Ablex, 1979), 2.

70. C. W. Stansfield, M. L. Scott, & D. M. Kenyon, "The Measurement of Translation Ability," *Modern Language Journal,* 26 (1992), 455–467.

71. Reeves, 1994, 41.

72. E. R. Clemmens, "An Analyst Looks at Languages, Cultures, and Translations," *American Journal of Psychoanalysis,* 45 (1985), 310–321.

73. R. Setton, "Training Conference Interpreters with Chinese: Problems and Prospects," in *Translating and Interpreting: Bridging East and West,* R. K. Seymour & C. C. Liu, Eds. (Honolulu: University of Hawaii Press, 1994), xi–xviii.

74. Reeves, 1994.

75. C. Freimanis, "Training Bilinguals to Interpret in the Community," in *Improving Intercultural Interactions,* R. W. Brislin & T. Yoshida, Eds. (London: Sage, 1994), 313–342.

76. Freimanis, 1994, 321.

77. *U.S. News & World Report,* November 1998, 24.

78. *Newsweek,* 23 October 1995, 89.

79. D. M. Brown, *Other Tongue to English: The Young Child in the Multicultural School* (London: Cambridge University Press, 1979), 37.

80. E. Folb, "Vernacular Vocabulary: A View of Interracial Perceptions and Experiences," in *Intercultural Communication: A Reader,* 2d ed., L. A. Samovar & R. E. Porter, Eds. (Belmont, CA: Wadsworth, 1976), 194.

81. "Learning American Lingo," *Christian Science Monitor,* 24 October 1995, 2.

82. D. Altman, "For Chinese Women's Ears Only: A Secret Language of Sisterhood Nears Extinction," *Christian Science Monitor,* 11 October 1995, 14.

83. Altman, 1995, 14.

84. A. Rich, *Interracial Communication* (New York: Harper & Row, 1974), 142.

85. L. A. Samovar & F. Sanders, "Language Patterns of the Prostitute: Some Insights into a Deviant Subculture," *ETC: A Review of General Semantics,* 34 (1978), 34.

86. Nanda & Warms, 1998, 78.

87. B. J. Shade, "Afro-American Cognitive Style: A Variable in School Success," *Review Educational Research,* 52 (1982), 219–244.

88. M. L. Hecht, M. J. Collier, & S. A. Ribeau, *African American Communication: Ethnic Identity and Cultural Interpretation* (Newbury Park: Sage, 1993), 5.

89. M. K. Asante, *Language, Communication, and Rhetoric in Black America* (New York: Harper & Row, 1972), x.

90. Hecht, Collier, & Ribeau, 86.

91. Nanda & Warms, 1998, 78

92. Hecht, Collier, & Ribeau, 1993, 85.

93. J. R. Rickford, "A Suite for Ebony and Phonics," *Discover,* 18 (1997), 3.

94. Crystal, 1997, 35.

95. Rickford, 1997, 3.

96. Rickford, 1997, 3.

97. Crystal, 1997, 35

98. Rickford, 1997, 3.

99. Crystal, 1997, 35.

100. Rickford, 1997, 3.

101. Crystal, 1997, 35.

102. Rickford, 1997, 3.

103. Rickford, 1997, 3.

104. Crystal, 1997, 35.

105. Crystal, 1997, 35.

106. Hecht, Collier, & Ribeau, 1993, 86.

107. S. N. Weber, "The Need to Be: The Socio-Cultural Significance of Black Language," in *Intercultural Communication: A Reader,* 7th ed., L. A. Samovar & R. E. Porter, Eds. (Belmont, CA: Wadsworth, 1994), 222.

108. Weber, 1994, 222.

109. Rogers & Steinfatt, 1998, 148.

110. Hecht, Collier, & Ribeau, 1993, 91; Weber, 1994, 224.

111. T. E. Garner & D. L. Rubin, "Middle Class Blacks' Perceptions of Dialect and Style Shifting: The Case of Southern Attorneys," *Journal of Language and Social Psychology,* 5 (1986), 33–48.

112. D. Tannen, *You Just Don't Understand: Women and Men in Conversation* (New York: William Morrow, 1990).

113. J. Elium & D. Elium, *Raising a Daughter* (Berkeley, CA: Celestial Arts, 1994), 21.

114. Tannen, 1990.

115. J. T. Wood, *Gendered Lives: Communication, Gender, and Culture* (Belmont, CA: Wadsworth, 1994).

116. Wood, 1994, 142.

117. Wood, 1994, 142.

118. Wood, 1994, 142.

119. Wood, 1994, 142.

120. Wood, 1994, 142.

121. J. Holmes, "Hedges and Boosters in Women's and Men's Speech," *Language and Communication,* 10 (1990), 185–202.

122. D. K. Ivy & P. Backlund, *Exploring Gender Speak* (New York: McGraw-Hill, 1994).

123. R. Lakoff, *Language and Woman's Place* (New York: Harper & Row, 1975).

124. B. Bate, *Communication Between the Sexes* (New York: Harper & Row, 1988), Holmes, 1990; J. T. Wood & L. F. Lenze, "Gender and the Development of Self: Inclusive Pedagogy in

Interpersonal Communication," *Women's Studies in Communication*, 14 (1991), 1–23.

125. Wood, 1994, 143.

126. Holmes, 1990.

127. Tannen, 1990; Wood, 1994.

128. Wood, 1994, 144.

129. E. Aries, "Gender and Communication," in *Sex and Gender*, P. Shaver & C. Hendricks, Eds. (Newbury Park, CA: Sage, 1987), 149–176.

130. A. T. Beck, *Love Is Never Enough* (New York: Harper & Row, 1988); L. P. Steward, A. D. Steward, S. A. Friedley, & P. J. Cooper, *Communication Between the Sexes: Sex Differences and Sex Role Stereotypes*, 2d ed. (Scottsdale, AZ: Gorsuch Scarisbrick, 1990).

131. Wood, 1994, 144.

132. Wood, 1994, 145.

Notes for Chapter 6

1. D. C. Barnlund, *Interpersonal Communication: Survey and Studies* (Boston: Houghton Mifflin, 1968), 536–537.

2. M. P. Keeley & A. J. Hart, "Nonverbal Behavior in Dyadic Interaction," in *Understanding Relationship Processes, 4: Dynamics of Relationships*, S. W. Duck, Ed. (Thousand Oaks, CA: Sage, 1994), 135–161.

3. J. K. Burgoon, D. B. Buller, & W. G. Woodall, *Nonverbal Communication: The Unspoken Dialogue* (New York: Harper & Row, 1989), 9–10.

4. J. K. Burgoon, D. B. Buller, & W. G. Woodall, *Nonverbal Communication: The Unspoken Dialogue*, 2d ed. (New York: McGraw-Hill, 1996), 5.

5. D. G. Leathers, *Successful Nonverbal Communication: Principles and Applications*, 2d ed. (New York: Macmillan, 1992), 355–356.

6. E. Goffman, *The Presentation of Self in Everyday Life* (New York: Doubleday, 1957), 2.

7. L. A. Malandro & L. L. Barker, *Nonverbal Communication* (Reading, MA: Addison-Wesley, 1983).

8. J. T. Wood, *Communication Mosaics: A New Introduction to the Field of Communication* (Belmont, CA: Wadsworth, 1998), 105.

9. S. Osborn & M. T. Motley, *Improving Communication* (Boston, MA: Houghton Mifflin, 1999), 50.

10. E. T. Hall, *The Silent Language* (New York: Fawcett, 1959), 10.

11. P. Andersen, "Cues of Culture: The Basis of Intercultural Differences in Nonverbal Communication," in *Intercultural Communication: A Reader*, 9th ed., L. A. Samovar & R. E. Porter, Eds. (Belmont, CA: Wadsworth, 2000), 258.

12. Andersen, 2000.

13. P. Ekman & W. Friesen, *Unmasking the Face: A Guide to Recognizing Emotions from Facial Expressions* (Englewood Cliffs, NJ: Prentice-Hall, 1975). Also see P. Ekman, R. Sorenson, & W. V. Friesen, "Pan-Cultural Elements in Facial Displays of Emotion," *Science*, 64 (1969), 86–88.

14. Burgoon, Buller, & Woodall, 1996, 23.

15. J. J. Macionis, *Society: The Basics*, 4th ed. (Upper Saddle River, NJ: Prentice Hall, 1998), 92.

16. P. A. Andersen, *Nonverbal Communication: Forms and Functions* (Mountain View, CA: Mayfield, 1999), 31.

17. "Obesity: A Heavy Burden Socially," *San Diego Union-Tribune*, 30 September 1993, A14.

18. B. D. Ruben, *Communication and Human Behavior*, 3d ed. (Englewood Cliffs, NJ: Prentice-Hall, 1992), 213.

19. E. Berscheid & E. Walster, "Beauty and the Best," *Psychology Today*, March 1972, 42–46.

20. L. A. Vazquez, E. Garcia-Vazquez, S. A. Bauman, & A. S. Sierra, "Skin Color, Acculturation, and Community Interest Among Mexican American Students: A Research Note," *Hispanic Journal of Behavioral Sciences*, 19 (1997), 337.

21. G. E. Codina & F. F. Montalvo, "Chicano Phenotype and Depression," *Hispanic Journal of Behavioral Sciences*, 16 (1994), 296–306.

22. F. Keesing, *Cultural Anthropology: The Science of Custom* (New York: Holt, Rinehart, & Winston, 1965), 203.

23. Malandro & Barker, 1989, 28–29.

24. Y. Richmond & P. Gestrin, *Into Africa: Intercultural Insights* (Yarmouth, ME: 1998), 45.

25. H. Wenzhong & C. L. Grove, *Encountering the Chinese* (Yarmouth, ME: Intercultural Press, 1991), 135.

26. N. Dresser, *Multicultural Manners* (New York: Wiley & Sons, 1996), 58.

27. T. Gochenour, *Considering Filipinos* (Yarmouth, ME: Intercultural Press, 1990), 59.

28. E. T. Hall & M. R. Hall, *Understanding Cultural Differences: Germans, French and Americans* (Yarmouth, ME: Intercultural Press, 1990), 53.

29. W. V. Ruch, *International Handbook of Corporate Communication* (Jefferson, NC: McFarland, 1989), 166–167.

30. E. McDaniel, "Nonverbal Communication: A Reflection of Cultural Themes," in *Intercultural Communication: A Reader*, 9th ed., L. A. Samovar & R. E. Porter, Eds. (Belmont, CA: Wadsworth, 2000), 274.

31. Ruch, 1989, 242.

32. M. K. Nydell, *Understanding Arabs* (Yarmouth, ME: Intercultural Press, 1987), 55.

33. S. M. Torrawa, "Every Robe He Dons Becomes Him," *Parabola* (Fall, 1994), 21.

34. Torrawa, 1994, 25.

35. M. L. De Fleur, P. Kearney, & T. G. Plax, *Fundamentals of Human Communication* (Mountain View, CA: Mayfield, 1993), 384.

36. H. Roberts, "The Exquisite Slave: The Role of Clothes in the Making of the Victorian Woman," *Signs*, 2 (1977), 554–569.

37. S. Ishii, "Characteristics of Japanese Nonverbal Communication Behavior," *Communication*, 2 (1973), 163–180.

38. R. Cooper & N. Cooper, *Culture Shock: Thailand* (Portland, OR: Graphic Arts Center Publishing Company, 1994), 14.

39. G. Kolanad, *Culture Shock: India* (Portland, OR: Graphic Arts Center Publishing Company, 1997), 114.

40. 1989, 279.

41. Cooper & Cooper, 1994, 22–23.

42. For a more detailed account of posture and other nonverbal differences between males and females, see P. A. Andersen, 1999, 106–129; L. P. Arliss, *Gender and Communication* (Englewood Cliffs, NJ: Prentice Hall, 1991), 87; J. A. Doyle & M. A. Paludi, *Sex and Gender: The Human Experience*, 2d ed. (Dubuque,

IA: Wm. C. Brown, 1991), 235; J. C. Pearson, R. L. West, & L. H. Turner, *Gender and Communication*, 3d ed. (Dubuque, IA: Wm. C. Brown, 1995), 126; L. P. Steward, P. J. Cooper, & S. A. Friedley, *Communication Between the Sexes: Sex Differences and Sex Role Stereotypes* (Scottsdale, AZ: Gorsuch Scarisbrick, 1986), 75.

43. M. L. Hecht, M. J. Collier, & S. A. Ribeau, *African American Communication: Ethnic Identity and Cultural Interpretation* (Newbury Park, CA: Sage, 1993), 102.

44. *San Diego Union-Tribune*, 20 May 1992, D4.

45. Andersen, 1999, 38.

46. "Arabic: The Medium Clouds the Message," *Los Angeles Times*, 12 February 1977.

47. D. Morris, P. Collett, P. Marsh, & M. O'Shaughnessy, *Gestures: Their Origins and Distribution* (New York: Stein & Day, 1979).

48. Dresser, 1996, 19.

49. R. G. Harper, A. N. Wiens, & J. D. Matarazzo, *Nonverbal Communication: The State of the Art* (New York: Wiley, 1978), 164.

50. *Handbook for Teaching Korean-American Students* (Sacramento, CA: California Department of Education, 1992), 95.

51. Nydell, 1987, 46.

52. M. Kim, "A Comparative Analysis of Nonverbal Expression as Portrayed by Korean and American Print-Media Advertising," *Howard Journal of Communications*, 3 (1992), 321.

53. Ruch, 1989, 191.

54. See P. A. Andersen, 1999, 118; Pearson, West, & Turner, 1995, 127.

55. Hecht, Collier, & Ribeau, 1993, 112.

56. F. Davis, *Inside Intuition* (New York: Signet, 1975), 47. See also Ray L. Birdwhistell, *Kinesics and Context* (Philadelphia: University of Pennsylvania Press, 1970).

57. Ekman, "Face Muscles Talk Every Language," *Psychology Today*, September 1975, 35–39. Also see P. Ekman, W. Friesen, & P. Ellsworth, *Emotion in the Human Face: Guidelines for Research and an Integration of the Findings* (New York: Pergamon Press, 1972).

58. Andersen, 1999, 35.

59. R. E. Porter & L.A. Samovar, "Cultural Influences on Emotional Expression: Implications for Intercultural Communication," in *Handbook of Communication and Emotion: Research, Theory, Applications, and Contexts*, P. A. Andersen & L. K. Guerrero, Eds. (San Diego, CA: Academic Press, 1998) 454.

60. D. Matsumoto, *Unmasking Japan: Myths and Realities About the Emotions of the Japanese* (Stanford, CA: Stanford University Press, 1996) 54.

61. Matsumoto, 1996, 18–19.

62. Kim, 1992, 321.

63. Wenzhong & Grove, 1991, 116.

64. E. R. McDaniel, "Japanese Nonverbal Communication: A Review and Critique of Literature" (paper presented at the Annual Convention of the Speech Communication Association, Miami Beach, FL, November 1993).

65. Matsumoto, 1996, 54.

66. Dresser, 1996, 21.

67. Cooper & Cooper, 1994, 18.

68. Pearson, West, & Turner, 1995, 123.

69. "The Evil Eye: A Stare of Envy," *Psychology Today*, December 1977, 154.

70. C. Segrin, "Interpersonal Communication Problems Associated with Depression and Loneliness," in *Handbook of Communication and Emotion: Research, Theory, Applications, and Contexts*, P. A. Andersen & L. K. Guerrero, Eds. (San Diego, CA: Academic Press, 1998), 213.

71. D. Leathers, *Successful Nonverbal Communication: Principles and Applications* (New York: Macmillan, 1986), 42.

72. E. W. Lynch, "From Culture Shock to Cultural Learning," in *Developing Cross-Cultural Competence: A Guide for Working with Young Children and Their Families*, E. W. Lynch & M. J. Hanson, Eds. (Baltimore, MD: Paul H. Brooks Publishing, 1992), 19–33.

73. H. Morsbach, "Aspects of Nonverbal Communication in Japan," in *Intercultural Communication: A Reader*, 3d ed., L. A. Samovar & R. E. Porter, Eds. (Belmont, CA: Wadsworth, 1982), 308.

74. Dresser, 1996, 22.

75. Richmond and Gestrin, 1998, 88.

76. Nydell, 1987, 45.

77. For a discussion of homosexual nonverbal communication see J. P. Goodwin, *More Man Than You'll Ever Be* (Indianapolis, IN: Indiana University Press, 1989).

78. "Understanding Culture: Don't Stare at a Navajo," *Psychology Today*, June 1974, 107.

79. M. L. Knapp & J. A. Hall, *Nonverbal Communication in Human Interaction*, 3d ed. (Fort Worth, TX: Harcourt Brace Jovanovich College Publishers, 1992), 310.

80. M. LaFrance & C. Mayo, *Moving Bodies: Nonverbal Communication in Social Relationships* (Monterey, CA: Brooks/Cole, 1978), 188.

81. For a more detailed account of gender differences in the use of eye contact and gaze see P. A. Andersen, 1998, 106–128; M. L. Hickson & D. W. Stacks, *Nonverbal Communication: Studies and Applications*, 3d ed. (Dubuque, IA: Brown & Benchmark, 1993), 20; D. K. Ivy & P. Backlund, *Exploring Gender Speak: Personal Effectiveness in Gender Communication* (New York: McGraw-Hill, 1994), 226; J. T. Wood, *Gendered Lives: Communication, Gender, and Culture* (Belmont, CA: Wadsworth, 1994), 164.

82. D. C. Herberg, *Frameworks for Cultural and Racial Diversity* (Toronto, Canada: Canadian Scholars' Press, 1993), 48.

83. J. D. Salinger, *The Catcher in the Rye* (New York: Grosset & Dunlap, 1945), 103.

84. "The Biochemistry of Touch," 10 November, 1997, 62.

85. P. A. Andersen, 1999, 78.

86. Dresser, 1996, 16.

87. J. Condon, *Good Neighbors: Communicating with the Mexicans* (Yarmouth, ME: Intercultural Press, 1985), 60.

88. D. Rowland, *Japanese Business Etiquette* (New York: Warner, 1985), 53.

89. G. Kolanad, 1997, 118.

90. B. Bates, *Communication and the Sexes* (New York: Harper & Row, 1988), 60. See also Pearson, West, & Turner, 1995, 129; Wood, 1994, 162–163.

91. Bates, 1988, 62.

92. Hecht, Collier, & Ribeau, 1993, 97. See also Burgoon, Buller, & Woodall, 1996, 230.

93. Leathers, 1986, 138–139.

94. Dresser, 1996, 29.

95. Gochenour, 1990, 61.

96. E. T. Hall, *The Hidden Dimension* (New York: Doubleday, 1966), 149.

97. V. P. Richmond, J. C. McCroskey, & S. K. Payne, *Nonverbal Communication in Interpersonal Relations*, 2d ed. (Englewood Cliffs, NJ: Prentice Hall, 1991), 94–109. Also see M. L. Knapp & J. A. Hall, 1992, 331–352.

98. Burgoon, Buller, & Woodall, 1996, 226.

99. Ruch, 1989, 191.

100. Cooper & Cooper, 1994, 31–32.

101. Richmond, McCroskey, & Payne, 1991, 302.

102. McDaniel, 1993, 18.

103. McDaniel, 2000, 275.

104. D. Crystal, *The Cambridge Encyclopedia of Language* (New York: Cambridge University Press, 1987), 24.

105. Crystal, 1987. See also the literature review on accents and dialects by H. Giles & A. Franklyn-Stokes, "Communication Characteristics," in *Handbook of International and Intercultural Communication*, M. Asante & W. B. Gudykunst, Eds. (Newbury Park, CA: Sage, 1989), 117–144. Also see M. J. Collier, "A Comparison of Conversations Among and Between Domestic Culture Groups: How Intra- and Intercultural Competencies Vary," *Communication Quarterly*, 36 (1988), 122–124.

106. Andersen, 1999, 81.

107. Hecht, Collier, & Ribeau, 1993, 113.

108. M. Houston, "When Black Women Talk With White Women: Why Dialogues Are Difficult," in *Our Voices: Essays in Culture, Ethnicity, and Communication*, 2d ed., A. Gonzalez, M. Houston, & Victoria Chen (Los Angeles, CA: Roxbury Publishing, 1997), 187–194.

109. A. W. Siegman & S. Feldstein, *Nonverbal Communication and Behavior*, 2d ed., (Hillsdale, NJ: Laurence Erlbaum, 1987), 355.

110. Pearson, West, & Turner, 1995, 131. Also see Wood, 1994, 164–165; Ivy & Backlund, 1994, 162–163.

111. W. B. Gudykunst, S. Ting-Toomey, S. Sudweeks, & L. P. Steward, *Building Bridges: Interpersonal Skills for a Changing World* (Boston: Houghton Mifflin, 1995), 325.

112. Condon, 1985, 60.

113. Ruch, 1989, 239.

114. Richmond & Gestrin, 1998, 95.

115. Hall & Hall, 1990, 38.

116. McDaniel, 2000, 274.

117. D. N. Berkow, R. Richmond, & R. C. Page, "A Cross-cultural Comparison of Worldviews: Americans and Fijian Counseling Students," *Counseling and Values*, 38 (1994), 121–135.

118. Chen & Starosta, 1998, 96.

119. Hall & Hall, 1990, 91.

120. McDaniel, 2000.

121. L. A. Samovar, "Prostitution as a Co-Culture: Speaking Well for Safety and Solidarity, Part II" (paper presented at the Western States Communication Association Convention, Vancouver, 1999).

122. Leathers, 1986, 236. Also see Andersen, 1998, 115; Wood, 1994, 160–162; Pearson, West, & Turner, 1995, 121.

123. L. A. Siple, "Cultural Patterns of Deaf People," *International Journal of Intercultural Relations*, 18 (1994), 345–367.

124. K. L. Egland, M. A. Stelzner, P. A. Andersen, & B. H. Spitzberg, "Perceived Understanding, Nonverbal Communication and Relational Satisfaction," in *Intrapersonal Communication Process*, J. Aitken & L. Shedletsky, Eds. (Annandale, VA: Speech Communication Association, 1997), 386–395.

125. M. Argyle, "Inter-cultural Communication," in *Cultures in Contact: Studies in Cross-Cultural Interaction*, Stephen Bochner, Ed. (New York: Pergamon Press, 1982), 68.

126. Richmond & Gestin, 1998, 108.

127. Hall & Hall, 1990, 35.

128. R. Brislin, *Understanding Culture's Influence on Behavior* (Fort Worth, TX: Harcourt Brace Jovanovich College Publishers, 1993), 211.

129. P. R. Harris & R. T. Moran, *Managing Cultural Differences*, 4th ed. (Houston TX: Gulf, 1996), 266.

130. Ruch, 1989, 278.

131. R. Levine, "Social Time: The Heartbeat of Culture," *Psychology Today*, March 1985, 35.

132. N. J. Adler, *International Dimensions of Organizational Behavior*, 2d ed. (Boston: PWS-KENT, 1991), 30.

133. E. T. Hall, *The Dance of Life: Other Dimensions of Time* (New York: Anchor Press/Doubleday, 1983), 42.

134. E. T. Hall, *The Silent Language* (New York: Fawcett, 1959), 19.

135. Dresser, 1996, 26.

136. Richmond & Gestrin, 1998, 109.

137. Richmond & Gestrin, 1998, 110.

138. K. Burgoon & T. Saine, *The Unspoken Dialogue: An Introduction to Nonverbal Communication* (Boston, MA: Houghton Mifflin, 1978), 131.

139. J. Horton, "Time and the Cool People," in *Intercultural Communication: A Reader*, 2d ed., L. A. Samovar & R. E. Porter, Eds. (Belmont, CA: Wadsworth, 1976), 274–284. Also see A. L. Smith, D. Hernandez, & A. Allen, *How to Talk with People of Other Races, Ethnic Groups, and Cultures* (Los Angeles: Trans-Ethnic Education, 1971), 17–19.

140. D. Crystal, *The Cambridge Encyclopedia of Language*, 2d ed. (New York: Cambridge University Press, 1997), 174.

141. J. Wiemann, V. Chen, & H. Giles, "Beliefs About Talk and Silence in a Cultural Context" (paper presented at the Annual Convention of the Speech Communication Association, Chicago, 1986).

142. D. C. Barnlund, *Communicative Styles of Japanese and Americans: Images and Realities* (Belmont, CA: Wadsworth, 1989), 142.

143. N. J. Adler, *International Dimension of Organizational Behavior* (Cincinnati, OH: South-Western College Publishing, 1997), 217.

144. N. Jain & A. Matukumalli, "The Functions of Silence in India: Implications for Intercultural Communication Research" (paper presented at the Second International East Meets West Conference in Cross-Cultural Communication, Comparative Philosophy, and Comparative Religion, Long Beach, CA, 1993, 7).

145. R. L. Johannesen, "The Functions of Silence: A Plea for Communication Research," *Western Speech*, 38 (1974), 27.

146. Pearson, West, & Turner, 1995, 134. Also see Doyle & Paludi, 1991, 226–228.

Notes for Chapter 7

1. U. S. Department of Commerce, U.S. Aggregate Foreign Trade Data, March 16, 1999.

2. *San Diego Union-Tribune*, November 23, 1996, C-1.

3. P. R. Harris & R. T. Moran, *Managing Cultural Differences: Leadership Strategies for a New World of Business*, 4th ed. (Houston: Gulf Publishing Company, 1996), 6.

4. E. M. Rogers & T. M. Steinfatt, *Intercultural Communication* (Prospect Heights, IL: Waveland Press, 1998), 258.

5. *San Diego Union-Tribune*, October 27, 1998, C-2.

6. *San Diego Union-Tribune*, June 19, 1998, A-10.

7. Harris & Moran, 1996, 19.

8. Harris & Moran, 1996, 181.

9. Harris and Moran, 1996, 210.

10. G. Hofstede, "Cultural Constraints in Management Theories," *Executive*, 7 (1993), 81–94.

11. R. D. Lewis, *When Cultures Collide: Managing Successfully Across Cultures* (London: Nicholas Brealey Publishing, 1996), 108.

12. Lewis, 1996, 70.

13. Hofstede, 1993, 83.

14. Lewis, 1996, 71.

15. Lewis, 1996, 73.

16. Lewis, 1996, 111–112.

17. Hofstede, 1993, 84.

18. R. B. Peterson, *Managers and National Character: A Global Perspective* (Westport, CT: Quorum Books, 1993), 418.

19. Lewis, 1996, 75.

20. Lewis, 1996, 75.

21. Lewis, 1996, 109.

22. Hofstede, 1993, 86.

23. G. M. Chen, "An Examination of PRC Business Negotiating Behaviors" (paper presented at the annual meeting of the National Communication Association, Chicago, IL, November 1997, 6.)

24. G. M. Chen & W. J. Starosta, "Chinese Conflict Management and Resolution: Overview and Implications," *Intercultural Communication Studies*, 7, 1–11.

25. Chen, 1996, 6.

26. R. Y. Hirokawa, "Improving Intra-organizational Communication: A Lesson from Japanese Management," *Communication Quarterly*, 30, Winter 1981, 35–40.

27. Peterson, 1993, 410.

28. R. Culpan & O. Kucukemiroglu, "A Comparison of U.S. and Japanese Management Styles and Unit Effectiveness," *Management International Review*, 33 (1993), 27–42.

29. Harris & Moran, 1996, 268.

30. Harris & Moran, 1996, 269.

31. M. J. Marquardt & D. W. Engel, *Global Human Resource Development* (Englewood Cliffs, NJ: Prentice Hall, 1993), 232.

32. Marquardt & Engle, 1993, 232.

33. Lewis, 1996, 80.

34. Lewis, 1996, 80.

35. Lewis, 1996, 81.

36. *San Diego Union-Tribune*, July 4, 1999, B-1.

37. G. K. Stephens & C. R. Greer, "Doing Business in Mexico: Understanding Cultural Differences," *Organizational Dynamics*, 24 (1995), 39–55.

38. Stephens & Greer, 1995.

39. T. Gray & B. Deane, "Launching a Diversity Market Effort," *Diversity Marketing Outlook*, Spring 1996, 3.

40. Stephens & Greer, 1995, 42–43.

41. T. Morrison, W. A. Conaway, & G. A. Borden, *Kiss, Bow, or Shake Hands: How to Do Business in Sixty Countries* (Holbrook, MA: Bob Adams, 1994), 232.

42. M. G. Weinbaum, *Egypt and the Politics of U.S. Economic Aid* (Boulder, CO: Westview, 1986).

43. D. Endicott, "Doing Business in Egypt," *Bridge*, Winter 1981, 34.

44. Y. Richmond & P. Gestrin, *Into Africa: Intercultural Insights* (Yarmouth, ME: Intercultural Press, 1998), 128–129.

45. Morrison et al., 1994, 58.

46. Morrison et al., 1994, 326.

47. K. B. Bucknall, *Kevin Bucknall's Cultural Guide to Doing Business in China* (Oxford, UK: Butterworth-Heinemann, 1994).

48. Harris & Moran, 1996, 256.

49. Bucknall, 1994.

50. Bucknall, 1994.

51. Harris & Moran, 1996, 256.

52. Bucknall, 1994.

53. Morrison et al., 1994.

54. Acuff, 1993, 308.

55. Morrison et al., 1994, 208.

56. N. Dresser, *Multicultural Manners* (New York: Wiley & Sons, 1996), 94.

57. Morrison et al., 1994, 411.

58. Harris & Moran, 1966, 40.

59. Lewis, 1966, 116.

60. Harris & Moran, 1966, 40.

61. D. A. Foster, *Bargaining Across Borders: How to Negotiate Business Successfully Anywhere in the World* (New York: McGraw-Hill, 1992), 35.

62. Morrison et al., 1994, 4.

63. Acuff, 1993, 219.

64. Lewis, 1966, 122.

65. Acuff, 1993, 52.

66. Morrison et al., 1994, 131.

67. Acuff, 1993, 156.

68. Lewis, 1966, 116.

69. Lewis, 1966, 117.

70. Morrison et al., 1994, 370.

71. Morrison et al., 1994, 317.

72. Morrison et al., 1994, 131.

73. Morrison et al., 1994, 191

74. Endicott, 1981.

75. Harris & Moran, 1996, 232.

76. Harris & Moran, 1996, 232.

77. Winsor, 1994, 20.

78. Malat, 1996, 44.

79. Richmond & Gestrin, 1998.

80. Acuff, 1993, 294.

81. Lewis, 1966, 124.

82. M. Whigham-Desir, "Business Etiquette Overseas: The Finer Points of Doing Business Abroad," *Black Enterprise*, 26, 142–143.

83. Harris & Moran, 1966, 256.

84. S. D. Seligman, *Dealing with the Chinese: A Practical Guide to Business Etiquette in the People's Republic Today* (New York: Warner Books, 1989).

85. Morrison et al., 1994, 157.

86. Morrison et al., 1994.

87. Morrison et al., 1994.

88. Morrison et al., 1994.

89. Dresser, 1996, 104–105.

90. Foster, 1992, 210.

91. S. Weiss & W. Stripp, *Negotiation with Foreign Business Persons: An Introduction for Americans with Propositions of Six Cultures* (New York University/Faculty of Business Adminisration, February, 1985).

92. H. Quanyu, R. S. Andrulis, & C. Tong, *A Guide to Successful Business Relations with the Chinese: Opening the Great Wall's Gate* (New York: Haworth Press, 1994).

93. F. Fukuyama, *Trust: The Social Virtues and the Creation of Prosperity* (New York: The Free Press, 1995), 26.

94. Fukuyama, 1995, 31.

95. Fukuyama, 1995, 27.

96. *San Diego Union-Tribune*, July 4, 1999, B-1.

97. *Sacramento Bee*, September 15, 1999, A-4.

98. D. B. Wood, "Monterey Spins Itself as Cultural Kaleidoscope," *Christian Science Monitor*, October 6, 1995, 11.

99. T. Gray & B. Deane, "Launching a Diversity Market Effort," *Diversity Marketing Outlook*, Spring 1996, 3.

100. Gray & Deane, 1996, 3.

101. Gray & Deane, 1996.

102. B. R. Deane, "Nordstrom Sets the Pace," *Diversity Marketing Outlook*, Spring 1996, 8.

103. M. Rossman, "Multicultural Marketing: The State of the Art," *Diversity Marketing Outlook*, Spring 1996, 6.

104. *Bloomberg News*, September 2, 1999, A-73.

105. *Atlanta Journal-Constitution*, September 3, 1999, F-2.

106. D. R. Francis, "Bosses Kill Loyalty: What Happens Now?" *Christian Science Monitor*, November 24, 1995, 8.

107. *Wisconsin State Journal*, September 11, 1999, B-3.

108. *Detroit News*, August 5, 1999, B-3.

109. *Spokesman Review*, August 24, 1999, B-1.

110. R. Sandoval, "When Cultures Collide," *San Diego Union-Tribune*, December 18, 1995, E-1–E-2.

111. *San Diego Union-Tribune*, November 23, 1998, A-8.

112. *Providence Sunday Journal*, January 24, 1999, A-01.

113. *San Diego Union-Tribune*, November 30, 1998, C-2.

114. *Sacramento Bee*, April 28, 1999, F-2.

115. L. A. Wertin & P. A. Andersen, "Cognitive Schemata and Perceptions of Sexual Harassment: A Test of Cognitive Valence Theory" (paper presented at the annual meeting of the Western Speech Communication Association, Pasadena, California, February, 1996.)

116. *Columbian*, August 21, 1999, C-2.

117. *Times-Picayune*, September 8, 1999, C-6.

118. *Times-Picayune*, April 23, 1999, A-1.

119. Sandoval, 1995, E-2.

120. D. D'Souza, *The End of Racism* (New York: Free Press, 1995).

121. M. Land, "Where Diversity Survives Hard Times," *USA Today*, January 8, 1992, B-8.

122. S. Evans, "The Prudential," *Cultural Diversity at Work*, March 1992.

Notes for Chapter 8

1. J. Henry, "A Cross-Cultural Outline of Education," in *Educational Patterns and Cultural Configurations*, J. Roberts & S. Akinsanya, Eds. (New York: David McKay, 1976).

2. M. Saville-Troike, *A Guide to Culture in the Classroom* (Rosslyn, VA: National Clearinghouse for Bilingual Education, 1978).

3. S. Lu, "Culture and Compliance Gaining in the Classroom: A Preliminary Investigation of Chinese College Teachers' Use of Behavior Alteration Techniques," *Communication Education*, 46, January 1997, 13–14.

4. B. Honig, *Handbook for Teaching Japanese Speaking Students* (Sacramento, CA: California State Department of Education, 1987), 10.

5. M. J. White, *The Japanese Educational Challenge: A Commitment to Children* (New York: Free Press, 1987), 150.

6. Honig, 1987, 17.

7. B. Honig, *Handbook for Teaching Korean-American Students* (Sacramento, CA: California Department of Education, 1992), 25.

8. Honig, 1992, 23.

9. H. Grossman, *Educating Hispanic Students: Cultural Implications for Instruction, Classroom Management, Counseling, and Assessment* (Springfield, IL: Charles C. Thomas, 1984).

10. Grossman, 1984, 85.

11. *U.S. News & World Report*, 9 September 1997, 12.

12. L. Stefani, S. M. Zormeier, & L. A. Samovar, *The Role of Culture and Communication in Educating Hispanic Students in the United States* (paper presented at the annual meeting of the Speech Communication Association, San Antonio, Texas, November, 1995).

13. Grossman, 1984.

14. S. Headden, "One Nation, One Language," *U.S. News & World Report*, 25 September 1995, 38–42.

15. U.S. Census Bureau (http://www.census.gov/population/estimation/nation/intfile3-1.txt), August 27, 1999.

16. R. L. Contreras, "The Browning of America: As with Other Immigrants, Our Country Will Benefit," *San Diego Union-Tribune*, 24 March1996, E-2.

17. *San Diego Union-Tribune*, 27 July 1977, A-14.

18. P. Gray, "Teach Your Children Well," *Time*, Fall 1993, 68–71.

19. *Sacramento Bee*, 28 April 1999, E-2.

20. *Newsweek*, 2 December 1996, 55.

21. G. M. Chen & W. J. Starosta, *Foundations of Intercultural Communication* (Needham Heights, MA: Allyn & Bacon, 1998), 226.

22. G. Althen, *American Ways: A Guide for Foreigners in the United States* (Yarmouth, ME: Intercultural Press, 1988), 54.

23. C. Calloway-Thomas, P. J. Cooper, & C. Blake, *Intercultural Communication: Roots and Routes* (Boston: Allyn and Bacon, 1999), 193.

24. Calloway-Thomas et al., 1999, 194

25. D. Ravitch, "Multiculural: E Pluribus Plures," *American Scholar*, 59 (1990), 163–174.

26. Bilingual Education Office, *Individual Learning Programs for Limited-English Proficient Students: A Handbook for School Personnel* (Sacramento, CA: California Department of Education, 1984), 5.

27. L. B. Clegg, E. Miller, & W. Vanderhoff, Jr., *Celebrating Diversity: A Multicultural Resource* (New York: Delmar, 1995).

28. C. Letherman, "The Minefield of Diversity," *Chronicle of Higher Education*, 1 April 1996, 57–60.

29. J. M. Schrof, "What Kids Have to Know," *U.S. News & World Report*, April 1, 1996, 57–60.

30. Calloway-Thomas et al., 1999, 199.

31. Calloway-Thomas et al., 1999, 198.

32. E. R. Hollins, J. E. King, & W. C. Haymen, *Teaching Diverse Populations: Formulating a Knowledge Base* (New York: State University of New York Press, 1994).

33. Calloway-Thomas et al., 1999, 199.

34. Calloway-Thomas et al., 1999, 199.

35. D. M. Gollnick & P. C. Chinn, *Multicultural Education in a Pluralistic Society* (New York: Macmillan, 1994), 306.

36. B. P. Leung, "Culture as a Study of Differential Minority Student Achievement," *Journal of Educational Issues of Language Majority Students*, 13 (1994).

37. J. C. Kush, "Field-Dependence, Cognitive Ability, and Academic Achievement in Anglo American and Mexican American Students," *Journal of Cross-Cultural Psychology*, 27 (5), September 1996, 563.

38. Gollnick & Chinn, 1994, 307.

39. Grossman, 1984.

40. Hollins, King, & Haymen, 1994, 19.

41. L. M. Cleary & T. D. Peacock, *Collected Wisdom: American Indian Education* (Boston: Allyn and Bacon, 1998).

42. L. Stefani, "The Impact of Culture on Classroom Communication," in *Intercultural Communication: A Reader*, 8th ed., L. A. Samovar & R. E Porter, Eds. (Belmont, CA: Wadsworth, 1997).

43. H. Grossman, *Teaching in a Diverse Society* (Boston: Allyn and Bacon, 1995), 270.

44. Cleary & Peacock, 1998.

45. B. J. Shade, C. Kelly, & M. Oberg, *Creating Culturally Responsive Classrooms* (Washington, D.C: American Psychological Association, 1997), 23.

46. Cleary & Peacock, 1998.

47. Althen, 1988, 129.

48. N. Dresser, *Multicultural Manners: New Rules of Etiquette for a Changing Society* (New York: Wiley and Sons, 1996), 42.

49. Althen, 1988, 128.

50. Althen, 1988, 128.

51. S. Nieto, *Affirming Diversity: The Sociopolitical Context of Multicultural Education* (New York: Longman, 1992), 115.

52. Dresser, 1996, 39.

53. K. H. Au, *Literacy Instruction in Multicultural Settings* (New York: Harcourt Brace Jovanovich College Publishers, 1993), 96.

54. Au, 1993, 96.

55. Grossman, 1995, 265.

56. Gollnick & Chinn, 1994, 306.

57. Grossman, 1995.

58. Grossman, 1984.

59. Cleary & Peacock, 1998.

60. Cleary & Peacock, 1998, 160.

61. Grossman, 1995, 269.

62. C. L. Hallman, M. R. Etienne, & S. Fradd, "Haitian Value Orientations," *Monograph Number 2*, August 1992, ERIC ED 269–532.

63. Grossman, 1995.

64. M. E. Franklin, "Culturally Sensitive Instructional Practices for African-American Learners with Disabilities," *Exceptional Children*, 59 (1992), 115–122.

65. E. L. Yao, "Asian-Immigrant Students—Unique Problems That Hamper Learning," *NASSP Bulletin*, 71 (1987), 82–88.

66. Grossman, 1995.

67. Grossman, 1995, 273.

68. White, 1987.

69. B. J. Walker, J. Dodd, & R. Bigelow, "Learning Preferences of Capable American Indians of Two Tribes," *Journal of American Indian Education* (1989 Special Issue), 63–71.

70. S. J. Dicker, *Languages in America: A Pluralist View* (Philadelphia: Multilingual Matters, Ltd., 1996), 2

71. Dicker, 1996, 4.

72. Dicker, 1996, 4.

73. V. D. Menchaca, "Multicultural Education: The Missing Link in Teacher Education Programs," *Journal of Educational Issues of Language Minority Students*, Special Issue, 17, Fall 1996, 1–9.

74. P. Leppert, *Doing Business with Mexico* (Freemont, CA: Jain Publishing Company, 1996), 13.

75. Headden, 1995, 25.

76. Headden, 1995.

77. R. Gersten, "The Changing Face of Bilingual Education," *Educational Leadership*, 56, April 1999, 41–45.

78. C. Tanamachi, "Educators Poll: Set Bilingual Time Limit," *Austin American Statesman*, 18 July 1998, B-1.

79. J. Traub, "The Bilingual Barrier," *New York Times Magazine*, 31 January 1999, 32–35.

80. J. Cummins, "Primary Language Instruction and the Education of Language Minority Students," in *Schools and Language Minority Students: A Theoretical Framework*, 2d ed. (Los Angeles: California State University, National Evaluation, Dissemination, and Assessment Center, 1994).

81. Gersten, 1999.

82. D. McKeon, "When Meeting Common Standards Is Uncommonly Difficult," *Educational Leadership*, 51 (1994), 45–49.

83. McKeon, 1994.

84. McKeon, 1994, 46. Gersten, 1999.

85. J. A. Cardenas, *Multicultural Education: a Generation of Advocacy* (Needham Heights, MD: Simon & Schuster, 1995).

86. Menchaca, 1996, 1.

87. Menchaca, 1996, 2.

88. Hollins, King, & Haymen, 1994.

89. P. J. Palmer, *To Know as We Are Known: Education as a Spiritual Journey* (San Francisco: Harper, 1993), 5.

90. M. P. Orbe, *Building Community in the Diverse Classroom: Strategies for Communication Professors* (paper presented at the annual meeting of the Central States Communication Association, Indianapolis, Indiana, April, 1995).

91. Orbe, 1995, 4.

92. Orbe, 1995, 5.

93. Orbe, 1995, 5.

94. M. Saville-Troike & J. A. Kleifgen, "Culture and Language in Classroom Communication," in *English Across Cultures, Cultures Across English: A Reader in Cross-Cultural Communication*, O. Garcia & R. Otheguy, Eds. (New York: Mouton de Gruyter, 1989), 84–102.

95. Cogan, 1995.

96. I. G. Malcolm, "Invisible Culture in the Classroom: Minority Pupils and the Principle of Adaptation," in *English Across Cultures, Cultures Across English: A Reader in Cross-Cultural Communication*, O. Garcia & R. Otheguy, Eds. (New York: Mouton de Gruyter, 1989), 117–135.

97. Malcolm, 1989, 134.

98. R. D. Rhine, *Pedagogical Choices in the Teaching of Communication and Multicultural Diversity* (paper presented at the annual meeting of the Speech Communication Association, San Antonio, Texas, November 1995).

99. I. Cueller, L. C. Harris, & R. Jasso, "An Acculturation Scale for Mexican American Normal and Clinical Populations," *Hispanic Journal of Behavioral Sciences*, 2 (1980), 199–217.

100. J. N. Franco, "An Acculturation Scale for Mexican-American Children," *Journal of General Psychology*, 108 (1983), 175–181.

101. R. M. Suinn, K. Rickard-Figueroa, S. Lew, & P. Vigil, "Asian Self-Identity Acculturation Scale: An Initial Report, *Educational and Psychological Measurement*, 47 (1987), 401–407.

102. Grossman, 1995.

103. L. Murry & J. Williams, *Diversity and Critical Pedagogy in the Communication Classroom* (paper presented at the annual meeting of the Western States Communication Association, Pasadena, California, February, 1996).

Notes for Chapter 9

1. J. A. Graeff, J. P. Elder, & E. M. Booth, *Communication for Health and Behavioral Change: A Developing Country Perspective* (San Francisco: Jossey-Bass, 1993).

2. L. Haffner, "Translation Is Not Enough: Interpreting in a Medical Setting," *Western Journal of Medicine*, 157 (1992), 225–260.

3. G. L. Kreps & B. C. Thornton, *Health Communication: Theory and Practice* (Prospect Heights, IL: Waveland Press, 1992), 2.

4. R. E. Spector, *Cultural Diversity in Health and Illness*, 4th ed. (Stamford, CT: Appleton & Lange, 1996), 4.

5. Spector, 1996, 4.

6. B. Koenig & J. Gates-Williams, "Understanding Cultural Differences in Dying for Dying Patients," *Western Journal of Medicine*, 163 (1995), 246.

7. M. H. Fitzgerald, "Multicultural Clinical Interactions," *Journal of Rehabilitation*, April/May/June 1992, 39.

8. P. Angelucci, "Notes from the Field: Cultural Diversity: Health Belief Systems," *Nursing Management*, 26 August 1995, 8.

9. J. N. Giger & R. E. Davidhizar, *Transcultural Nursing: Assessment and Intervention*, 2d ed. (St. Louis, MO: Mosby, 1995), 121.

10. Angelucci, 1995, 8.

11. Angelucci, 1995, 8.

12. Angelucci, 1995, 8.

13. Angelucci, 1995, 8.

14. Giger & Davidhizar, 1995, 114.

15. Giger & Davidhizar, 1995, 456.

16. N. Dresser, *Multicultural Manners: New Rules of Etiquette for a Changing Society* (New York: John Wiley & Sons, 1996), 236.

17. Giger & Davidhizar, 1995, 465.

18. Giger & Davidhizar, 1995, 404.

19. Giger & Davidhizar, 1995, 405.

20. Giger & Davidhizar, 1995, 405.

21. I. Murillo-Rhode, "Hispanic American Patient Care" in *Transcultural Health Care*, G. Henderson & M Primeaux, Eds. (Menlo Park, CA: Addison-Wesley, 1981), 59–77.

22. Dresser, 1996, 246.

23. R. E. Spector, "Cultural Concepts of Women's Health and Health-Promoting Behavior," *JOGNN*, March/April 1995, 243.

24. Giger & Davidhizar, 1995, 510–511.

25. Giger & Davidhizar, 1995, 404.

26. Dresser, 1996.

27. Dresser, 1996, 234.

28. Murillo-Rhode, 1981.

29. M. E. Burk, P. C. Wieser, & L. Keegan, "Cultural Beliefs and Health Behaviors of Pregnant Mexican-American Women: Implications for Primary Care," *Advances in Nursing Science*, June 1995, 27–52.

30. Dresser, 1996, 238.

31. G. A. Galanti, *Caring for Patients from Different Cultures: Case Studies from American Hospitals* (Philadelphia: University of Pennsylvania Press, 1991), 101.

32. P. A. Twumasi, "Improvement of Health Care in Ghana: Present Perspectives" in *African Health and Healing Systems: Proceedings of a Symposium*, P. S. Yoder, Ed. (Los Angeles: Crossroads Press, 1982).

33. Dresser, 1996, 249.

34. Giger & Davidhizar, 1995, 216.

35. Dresser, 1996, 230.

36. Galanti, 1996, 106.

37. A. Fadiman, *The Spirit Catches You and You Fall Down* (New York: Farrar, Strauss and Giroux, 1997), 4.

38. Spector, 1995, 244.

39. M. A. Miller, "Culture, Spirituality, and Women's Health," *JOGMN*, March/April 1995, 256–263.

40. B. Bhayana, "Healthshock," *Healthsharing*, 12 (3), 1991, 28–31.

41. Miller, 1995.

42. C. G. Helman, *Culture, Health, and Illness*, 2d ed. (London: Wright, 1990).

43. B. S. Nelson, L. E. Heiskell, S. Cemaj, A. O'Callaghan, & C. E. Koller, "Traumatically Injured Jehovah's Witnesses: A Sixteen-Year Experience of Treatment and Transfusion Dilemmas at a Level I Trauma Center," *Journal of Trauma, Injury, Infection, and Critical Care*, 39 (4), October 1995, 683.

44. Nelson et al., 1995, 681.

45. M. C. Gonzalez, "An Invitation to Leap from a Trinitarian Ontology in Health Communication Research to a Spiritually Inclusive Quatrain," in *Communication Yearbook 17*, S. A. Deetz, Ed. (Thousand Oaks, CA: Sage, 1994), 378–387.

46. R. Marquand, "Healing Role of Spirituality Gains Ground," *Christian Science Monitor*, 6 December 1995, 18.

47. Marquand, 1995, 18.

48. Spector, 1996, 4.

49. L. Payer, *Medicine and Culture: Varieties of Treatment in the United States, England, West Germany, and France* (New York: Henry Holt, 1988), 26.

50. B. Qureshi, *Transcultural Medicine: Dealing with Patients from Different Cultures*, 2d ed. (Lancaster, UK: Kluwer Academic Publishers, 1994), vii.

51. G. Reddy, "Women's Movement: The Indian Scene," *Indian Journal of Social Work*, 46 (4), 1986, 507–514.

52. Giger & Davidhizar, 1995, 487.

53. Giger & Davidhizar, 1995, 487.

54. Galanti, 1991, 63.

55. *San Diego Union-Tribune*, October 23, 1998, B-6.

56. Galanti, 1991, 76.

57. L. C. Callister, "Cultural Meaning in Childbirth," *JOGNN*, May 1995, 327–331.

58. Galanti, 1991.

59. Galanti, 1991.

60. Galanti, 1991.

61. R. L. Elliott, "Cultural Patterns in Rural Russia," *Journal of Multicultural Nursing and Health*, 3 (1), Winter 1997, 22–28.

62. Galanti, 1991, 17.

63. K. Witte & K. Morrison, "Intercultural and Cross-Cultural Health Communication," in *Intercultural Communication Theory*, R. L. Wiseman, Ed. (London: Sage, 1995).

64. Haftner, 1992, 256.

65. R. Alcalay, "Perceptions About Prenatal Care Among Health Providers and Mexican-American Commuity Women," *International Quarterly of Communication Health Education*, 13 (2), 1992, 107–118.

66. Alcalay, 1992.

67. Spector, 1996.

68. E. W. Lynch, "From Culture Shock to Culture Learning," in *Developing Cross-Cultural Competence: A Guide for Working with Young Children and Their Families*, E. W. Lynch & M. J. Hanson, Eds. (Baltimore, MD: Paul H. Brookes Publishing, 1992), 19–33.

69. Giger & Davidhizar, 1995.

70. D. Gleave & A. S. Manes, "The Central Americans," in *Cross-Cultural Caring: A Handbook for Health Professionals in Western Canada*, N. Waxler-Morrison, J. Anderson, & E. Richardson, Eds. (Vancouver, BC: The University of British Columbia Press, 1990), 36–67.

71. S. Chan, "Families with Asian Roots," in *Developing Cross-Cultural Competence: A Guide for Working with Young Children and Their Families*, E. W. Lynch & M. J. Hanson, Eds. (Baltimore, MD: Paul H. Brookes Publishing, 1992), 181–258.

72. M. M. Andrews, "Transcultural Nursing Care," in *Transcultural Concepts in Nursing Care*, M. M. Andrews & J. S. Boyle, Eds. (Philadelphia: J. B. Lippincott, 1995), 49–96.

73. E. Dihn, S. Ganesan, & N. Waxler-Morrison, "The Vietnamese," in *Cross-Cultural Caring: A Handbook for Health Professionals in Western Canada*, N. Waxler-Morrison, J. Anderson, & E. Richardson, Eds. (Vancouver, BC: The University of British Columbia Press, 1990), 181–213.

74. Giger & Davidhizar, 1995.

75. Dihn et al., 1990.

76. G. Althen, *American Ways: A Guide for Foreigners in the United States* (Yarmouth, ME: Intercultural Press, 1988).

77. Dihn et al., 1990.

78. A. T. Brownlee, *Community, Culture, and Care* (St. Louis, MO: C. V. Mosby, 1978).

79. N. Murillo, "The Mexican American Family," in *Chicanos: Social and Psychological Perspectives*, C. A. Hernandez, M. J. Haug, & N. N. Wagner, Eds. (St. Louis, MO: C. V. Mosby, 1978), 15–25.

80. A. Montagu, *Touching: The Significance of the Human Skin* (New York: Columbia University Press, 1971).

81. L. Rocereto, "Selected Health Beliefs of Vietnamese Refugees," *Journal of School Health*, 15 (1981), 63–64.

82. M. Muencke, "Caring for Southeast Asian Refugee Parents in the USA," *American Journal of Public Health*, 74 (1983), 431–438.

83. M. B. Marks, "Straddling Cultural Divides with Grace," *Christian Science Monitor*, November 15, 1995, 16.

84. J. Klessig, "The Effect of Values and Culture of Life Support Decisions," *Western Journal of Medicine*, 157 (1992), 316–322.

85. Burke, Weiser, & Keegan, 1995.

86. Fitzgerald, 1992.

87. Galanti, 1991, 109.

88. Galanti, 1991, 102.

89. Fitzgerald, 1992, 41.

Notes for Chapter 10

1. L. Schneider & A. Silverman, *Global Sociology: Introducing Five Contemporary Societies* (New York: McGraw-Hill, 1997), xxi.

2. E. Griffin, *A First Look at Communication Theory*, 2d ed. (New York: McGraw-Hill, 1994), 173.

3. Griffin, 1994, 173.

4. H. Cleveland, "The Limits of Cultural Diversity," in *Intercultural Communication: A Reader*, 8th ed., L. A. Samovar & R. E. Porter, Eds. (Belmont, CA: Wadsworth, 2000), 427.

5. H. Cleveland, 1997, 431.

6. C. M. Berger & R. J. Calabrese, "Some Explorations in Initial Interaction and Beyond," *Human Communication Research*, 1 (1975), 99–112.

7. Berger & Calabrese, 1975, 100.

8. C. Berger & W. Gudykunst, "Uncertainty and Communication," in *Progress in Communication Sciences*, vol. 10, B. Dervin & M. Voigt, Eds. (Norwood, NJ: Ablex, 1991), 23.

9. W. Gudykunst, *Bridging Differences: Effective Intergroup Communication*, 3rd ed. (Thousand Oaks, CA: Sage Publications, 1998), 19.

10. Gudykunst, 1998, 272.

11. W. Lippman, *Public Opinion* (New York: Macmillan, 1957), 79–103.

12. N. J. Adler, *International Dimensions of Organizational Behavior*, 2d ed. (Boston, MA: PWS-KENT, 1991), 74.

13. E. W. Lynch & M. J. Hanson, *Developing Cross-Cultural Competence: A Guide for Working with Young Children and Their Families* (Baltimore, MD: Paul H. Brookes Publishing Co., 1992) 44.

14. D. R. Atkinson, G. Morten, & D. Wing Sue, "Minority Group Counseling: An Overview," in *Intercultural Communication: A Reader*, 4th ed., L. A. Samovar & R. E. Porter, Eds. (Belmont, CA: Wadsworth, 1982), 172.

15. J. J. Macionis, *Society: The Basics*, 4th ed. (Upper Saddle River: NJ: Prentice Hall, 1998), 217.

16. J. Levin, *The Functions of Prejudice* (New York: Harper & Row, 1975), 13.

17. G. Allport, *The Nature of Prejudice* (Cambridge, MA: Addison-Wesley, 1954).

18. J. Feagin, *Racial and Ethnic Relations*, 3rd ed. (Englewood Cliffs, NJ: Prentice Hall, 1989).

19. R. H. Dana, *Multicultural Assessment Perspectives for Professional Psychology* (Boston, MA: Allyn & Bacon, 1993), 23.

20. Macionis, 1998, 217.

21. S. Nanda & R. L. Warms, *Cultural Anthropology*, 6th ed. (Belmont: CA: Wadsworth, 1998), 9.

22. Nanda & Warms, 1998, 10.

23. R. Brislin, *Understanding Culture's Influence on Behavior* (Fort Worth, TX: Harcourt Brace Jovanovich, 1993), 185.

24. Brislin, 1993, 186.

25. R. W. Brislin, "Prejudice in Intercultural Communication," in *Intercultural Communication: A Reader,* 6th ed., L. A. Samovar & R. E. Porter, Eds. (Belmont, CA: Wadsworth, 1991), 386.

26. Brislin, 1993, 191.

27. R. A. Barraclough & R. A. Stewart, "Power and Control: Social Science Perspectives," in *Power in the Classroom,* V. P. Richmond & J. McCroskey, Eds. (Hillsdale, NJ: Prentice Hall, 1991), 1–4.

28. Nanda & Warms, 1998, 226.

29. Nanda & Warms, 1998, 226.

30. J. N. Martin & T. K. Nakayama, *Intercultural Communication in Context* (Mountain View, CA: Mayfield, 1997), 103.

31. E. Folb, "Who's Got the Room at the Top?" in *Intercultural Communication: A Reader,* 9th ed., L. A. Samovar & R. E. Porter, Eds. (Belmont, CA: Wadsworth, 2000), 122.

32. E. Folb, 2000, 122.

33. M. L. Hecht, M. J. Collier, & S. A. Ribeau, *African American Communication: Ethnic Identity and Cultural Interpretation* (Newbury Park, CA: Sage, 1993), 135–137, 144. Also see A. Smith, *Transracial Communication* (Englewood Cliffs, NJ: Prentice Hall, 1973), 118–119.

34. Smith, 1973, 71.

35. G. A. Borden, *Cultural Orientation: An Approach to Understanding Intercultural Communication* (Englewood Cliffs, NJ: Prentice Hall, 1991), 116.

36. J. A. Blubaugh & D. L. Pennington, *Crossing Differences: Interracial Communication* (Columbus, OH: Charles E. Merrill, 1976), 39.

37. C. Storti, *The Art of Coming Home* (Yarmouth, ME: Intercultural Press, 1997), 2.

38. A. Furnham & L. Bochner, *Culture Shock—Psychological Reactions to an Unfamiliar Environment* (New York: Methuen, 1986).

39. K. Oberg, "Culture Shock: Adjustments to New Cultural Environments," *Practical Anthropology,* 7 (1960), 176. Also see P. K. Bock, *Culture Shock* (New York: Knopf, 1970).

40. R. W. Brislin, *Cross-Cultural Encounters: Face-to-Face Interactions* (New York: Pergamon Press, 1981), 155.

41. Lynch & Hanson, 1992, 23.

42. J. T. Gullahorn & J. E. Gullahorn, "An Extension of the U-Curve Hypothesis," *Journal of Social Science,* 17 (1963), 33–47.

43. P. R. Harris & R. T. Moran, *Managing Cultural Differences: Leadership Strategies for a New World of Business,* 4th ed. (Houston, TX: Gulf, 1996), 142.

44. N. J. Adler, *International Dimensions of Organizational Behavior,* 3rd. ed. (Cincinnati, OH: South-Western College Publishing, 1997), 238.

45. I. Kawano, "Overcoming Culture Shock: Living and Learning in Japan Through the JET Program" (paper presented at the Annual Convention of the Western States Communication Association, Monterey, CA, February, 1997), 25.

46. W. G. Sumner, *Folkways* (Boston: Ginnand, 1940), 13.

47. Nanda & Warms, 1998, 6.

48. Nanda & Warms, 1996, 7. Also see D. G. Bates & F. Plog, *Cultural Anthropology,* 3rd ed. (New York: McGraw-Hill, 1990), 17; W. A. Haviland, *Cultural Anthropology,* 7th ed. (Fort Worth, TX: Harcourt Brace Jovanovich College Publishers, 1993), 48.

49. Macionis, 1998, 48.

50. F. M. Keesing, *Cultural Anthropology: The Science of Custom* (New York: Holt, Rinehart, & Winston, 1965), 45.

51. L. Damen, *Cultural Learning: The Fifth Dimension in the Language Classroom* (Reading, MA: Addison-Wesley, 1987), 45.

52. E. C. Stewart & M. J. Bennett, *American Cultural Patterns: A Cross-Cultural Perspective* (Yarmouth, ME: Intercultural Press, 1991), 161.

53. F. E. Jandt, *Intercultural Communication: An Introduction* (Thousand Oaks, CA: Sage, 1995), 43.

54. B. H. Spitzberg, "A Model of Intercultural Communication Competence," in *Intercultural Communication: A Reader,* 9th ed., L. A. Samovar & R. E. Porter, Eds. (Belmont, CA: Wadsworth, 2000), 375.

55. Y. Y. Kim, "Intercultural Communication Competence: A Systems-Theoretic View," in *Cross-Cultural Interpersonal Communication,* S. Ting-Toomey & R. Korzenny, Eds. (Newbury Park, CA: Sage, 1991), 259.

56. B. Spitzberg & W. Cupach, *Interpersonal Communication Competence* (Beverly Hills, CA: Sage, 1984).

57. A. J. Almaney & A. J. Alwan, *Communicating with Arabs* (Prospect Hills, IL: Waveland Press, 1982), 87.

58. E. R. McDaniel & S. Quasha, "The Communicative Aspects of Doing Business in Japan," in *Intercultural Communication: A Reader,* 9th ed., L. A. Samovar & R. E. Porter, Eds. (Belmont, CA: Wadsworth, 2000), 312–324.

59. Lynch & Hanson, 1992.

60. R. H. Dana, *Multicultural Assessment Perspectives for Professional Psychology* (Boston, MA: Allyn & Bacon, 1993).

61. M. Zhong, "Perceived Intercultural Communication Competence in Cross-Cultural Interactions Between Chinese and Americans," *Critical Studies,* 12 (1998), 161–179.

62. Stewart & Bennett, 1991, 175.

63. R. Norton, *Communication Style: Theory, Application and Measures* (Beverly Hills: Sage, 1982).

64. D. C. Barnlund, *Public and Private Self in Japan and the United States: Communication Styles of Two Cultures* (Tokyo: Simul Press, 1975), 14–15.

65. W. V. Ruch, *International Handbook of Corporate Communication* (Jefferson, NC: McFarland, 1989), 76.

66. Adler, 1991, 190.

67. D. Clutterbuck, "Spanning the Communication Gap," *International Management,* October 1975, 18–22.

68. L. M. Skow & L. Stephan, "Intercultural Communication in the University Classroom," in *Intercultural Communication: A Reader,* 9th ed., L. A. Samovar & R. E. Porter, Eds. (Belmont, CA: Wadsworth, 2000), 361.

69. Skow & Stephan, 2000, 359.

70. Adler, 1991, 192.

71. Ruch, 264.

72. P. Kenna & L. Sondra, *Business Mexico: A Practical Guide to Understanding Mexican Business Culture* (Lincolnwood, IL: Passport Books, 1996), 25.

73. R. Cooper & N. Cooper, *Culture Shock: Thailand* (Portland, OR: Graphic Arts Center Publishing Company, 1990), 152.

74. M. K. Nydell, *Understanding Arabs: A Guide for Westerners* (Yarmouth, ME: Intercultural Press, 1987), 121.

75. G. Geo & Stella Ting-Toomey, *Communicating Effectively with the Chinese* (Thousand Oaks, CA: Sage, 1998), 36.

76. Geo & Ting-Toomey, 1998, 36.

77. Geo & Ting-Toomey, 1998, 36.

78. H. Walters, Jr., "Race, Culture and Interpersonal Conflict," *International Journal of Intercultural Relations,* 16 (1992), 447.

79. Walters, 1992, 448.

80. Ruch, 1989, 361.

81. G. Chen & W. J. Starosta, "Intercultural Communication in the University Classroom," in *Intercultural Communication: A Reader,* 9th ed., L. A. Samovar & R. E. Porter, Eds. (Belmont, CA: Wadsworth, 2000), 408.

82. J. Johnson, "The Press Should Show More Sensitivity to Disabled People," *Editor and Publisher,* 22 February 1986, 64.

83. S. Ting-Toomey, *Communicating Across Cultures* (New York: Guilford Press, 1999), 160.

84. B. J. Broome, "Building Shared Meaning: Implications of a Relational Approach to Empathy for Teaching Intercultural Communication," *Communication Education,* 40 (1991), 235.

85. C. Calloway-Thomas, P. J. Cooper, & C. Blake, *Intercultural Communication: Roots and Routes* (Boston, MA: Allyn & Bacon, 1999), 106.

86. G. R. Miller & M. Steinberg, *Between People: A New Analysis of Interpersonal Communication* (Chicago: Science Research Associates, 1975), 167.

87. R. Bell, "Social Involvement," in *Personality and Interpersonal Communication,* J. McCroskey & J. Daly, Eds. (Newbury Park, CA: Sage, 1987), 205.

88. S. Trenholm & A. Jensen, *Interpersonal Communication,* 2d ed. (Belmont, CA: Wadsworth, 1992), 254.

89. D. C. Barnlund, *Communication Styles of Japanese and Americans* (Belmont, CA: Wadsworth, 1989), 162.

90. Trenholm & Jensen, 1992, 255.

91. A. L. Rich, *Interracial Communication* (New York: Harper & Row, 1974), 35–36.

92. Wenzhong & Grove, 1991, 114.

93. J. T. Wood, *Communication Mosaics: A New Introduction to the Field of Communication* (Belmont, CA: Wadsworth, 1998), 25.

94. D. Rowland, *Japanese Business Etiquette* (New York: Warner, 1985), 47.

95. R. Hart, R. E. Carlson, & W. F. Eadie, "Attitudes Toward Communication and the Assessment of Rhetorical Sensitivity," *Communication Monograph* 47 (1980), 1–22.

96. S. Trenholm, *Human Communication Theory* (Englewood Cliffs, NJ: Prentice Hall, 1986), 112.

97. R. W. Brislin, 1993, 215.

98. D. A. Foster, *Bargaining Across Borders: How to Negotiate Successfully Anywhere in the World* (New York: McGraw-Hill, 1992), 253.

99. B. D. Ruben & D. J. Kealey, "Behavioral Assessment of Communication Competency and the Prediction of Cross-Cultural Adaptation," *International Journal of Intercultural Relations,* 3 (1979), 19.

100. Y. Y. Kim, "Cross-Cultural Adaptation: An Integrative Theory," in *Theories in Intercultural Communication,* R. L. Wiseman, Ed. (Thousand Oaks, CA: Sage, 1995), 171.

101. E. Anderson, "A New Look at an Old Construct: Cross-Cultural Adaptation," *International Journal of Intercultural Relations,* 18 (1994), 293–328.

102. A. M. Harper, "Cultural Adaptation and Intercultural Communication: Some Barriers and Bridges" (paper presented at the Annual Convention of the Western Speech Communication Association, Monterey, CA, February 1997), 13.

103. F. T. Leong & E. L. Chou, "The Role of Ethnic Identity and Acculturation in the Vocational Behavior of Asian Americans: An Integrative Review," *Journal of Vocational Behavior,* 44 (1994), 165.

104. G. M. Chen & W. J. Starosta, "Intercultural Communication Competence: A Synthesis," in *Communication Yearbook,* vol. 19, B. R. Burleson & A. W. Kunkel, Eds. (Thousand Oaks, CA: Sage, 1996), 365.

105. P. A. Begley, "Sojourner Adaptation," in *Intercultural Communication: A Reader,* 9th ed., L. A. Samovar & R. E. Porter, Eds. (Belmont, CA: Wadsworth, 2000), 404.

106. Harris & Moran, 1996, 143.

107. Kim, 1995, 172.

108. G. Althen, *American Ways* (Yarmouth, ME: Intercultural Press, 1988), 165.

109. Althen, 1988, 165.

110. R. K. Johannesen, *Ethics in Human Communication,* 4th ed. (Prospect Heights, IL: Waveland Press, 1996), 1.

111. Griffin, 1994, 458.

112. Ting-Toomey, 1999, 273.

113. J. Q. Wilson, *San Diego Union-Tribune,* 29 November 1993, B5.

114. W. S. Howell, *The Empathic Communicator* (Belmont, CA: Wadsworth, 1982), 179.

115. Johannesen, 1996, 244.

116. S. Boorestein, *It's Easier Than You Think: The Buddhist Way to Happiness* (New York: HarperCollins, 1995), 60.

117. O. Tead, *Administration: Its Purpose and Performance* (New York: Harper & Row, 1959), 52.

118. Johannesen, 1996, 257.

119. Y. Chu, "Six Suggestions for Learning About People and Cultures," in *Learning About Peoples and Cultures,* S. Fersh, Ed. (Evanston, IL: McDougal & Littell, 1974), 52.

120. "Bert and Ernie Go to Moscow," *U.S. News & World Report,* 12 February 1996, 4.

121. D. W. Kale, "Peace as an Ethic for Intercultural Communication," in *Intercultural Communication: A Reader,* 9th ed., L. A. Samovar & R. E. Porter, Eds. (Belmont, CA: Wadsworth, 2000), 452.

122. Kale, 2000, 453.

123. J. Beversluis, *A Source Book for Earth's Community of Religions* (New York: Global Education Associates, 1995), 138.

124. Barnlund, 1989, 92–93.

125. J. Wood, "Gender, Communication, and Culture," in *Intercultural Communication: A Reader,* 8th ed., L. A. Samovar & R. E. Porter, Eds. (Belmont, CA: Wadsworth, 1997), 171–172.

126. D. Gomez-Ibanes, "Moving Toward a Global Ethic," in *A Source Book for Earth's Community of Religions,* J. Beversluis, Ed. (New York: Global Education Associates, 1995), 128.

127. W. Booth, "Diversity and Division," *Washington Post,* 2 March 1998, 6.

128. Booth, 1998, 6.

129. J. Krishnamurti, *Krishnamurti to Himself* (San Francisco: CA, HarperCollins, 1987), 60.

130. H. Cleveland, "The Limits to Cultural Diversity," *Futurist,* March–April 1995, 23.

131. Y. Ling-Ling, "Ethnic Strife Is Not a Geographically Distant Phenomenon," *San Diego Union-Tribune,* 10 June 1999, 11.

132. V. Lynch Lee, Ed., *Faces of Culture* (Huntington Beach, CA: KOCE-TV Foundation, 1983), 69.

Index

Chesterfield, Lord Philip, 30
China, history of, 128–29
Chirac, Jacques, 11
Christianity, 99–101
Chung Tzu, 21, 36
Cicero, 211
Clausewitz, Karl von, 9
Clinton, William Jefferson, 2, 262
Clothing, nonverbal communication through, 171–72, 173–74
Co-cultures
    assertiveness views of, 86
    communication between, 47–49
    as cultures, 47–48
    defined, 14, 47
    genders as, 48
    language use by, 154–61, 285, 286
    major U.S., 14–16
    nonverbal communication by, 174, 184, 187
    subcultures vs., 47
    time and, 190
Cognitive styles, 227–28
Collectivism
    as cultural value dimension, 65–66, 67–68
    cultural value orientation toward, 79
    families and, 119–20
Commonalties. *See* Similarities
Communication, 22–30
    as complex, 28–29
    context as specifying rules for, 25–26, 197–98, 283
    defined, 22
    as dynamic process, 23–24
    as having consequences, 27–28, 265, 296–97
    health care and, 241–42, 254–58
    importance of, 22
    making inferences as aspect of, 26–27
    as self-reflective, 27
    similarities/differences between people and, 29–30
    as symbolic, 24
    as systemic, 25–26
    See also Intercultural communication; Nonverbal communication
Communication styles
    in education, 228–30
    knowing your own, 280–82
Competition
    as cognitive learning style dimension, 227–28
    as dominant American cultural pattern, 64–65
Computers, international contact accelerated by, 7, 8
Confucian dynamism, as cultural dimension, 73
Confucianism, 111–12, 117, 202
Confucius, 36, 111, 112
    sayings of, 2, 188, 192, 294, 297

Context
    communication rules specified by, 25–26, 197–98, 283
    elements of, 25–26
    See also Business; Education; Health care
Context orientation, 79–82
Cooperation
    as cognitive learning style dimension, 227–28
    as view toward nature, 75–76
Credibility, cultural perception of, 54
Cultural adaptation, 45–46, 292–94
Cultural patterns, 58–86
    assertiveness-interpersonal harmony dimension, 84–86
    characteristics of, 58–60
    Confucian dynamism dimension, 73
    defined, 58
    dominant American, 60–65
    Hall's context orientations, 79–82
    Hofstede's value dimensions, 65–73
    informality-formality dimension, 84
    Kluckhohns and Strodtbeck's value orientations, 73–79
Cultural values, 57
Culture, 31–46
    as adaptive, 45
    co-cultures as, 47–48
    deep structure of, 90–92
    defined, 33–34
    dominant, 12–13
    as dynamic, 43–45
    education and, 218–24
    family and, 116–22
    functions of, 32–33
    health care and, 249–56
    individual uniqueness within, 17, 30, 58–59, 169
    knowing your own, 280
    language and, 42–43, 139–48
    as learned, 34–41
    nonverbal communication and, 164, 166, 170–71, 285–86
    omnipresence of, 31, 45–46
    perception and, 52, 53–54
    symbolic basis of, 42–43
    as systemic, 45
    transmitted from generation to generation, 41–42
    See also Management culture
Culture shock, 273–75
Curriculum, cultural differences in, 220–22
Customs
    in business, 204–7, 283
    importance of, 283–84

Darwin, Charles, 190
De Forest, Mariah, 203

Deep structure of culture, 90–92
    See also Families; History; World view
Del Castillo, Griswold, 130
Descartes, René, 201
Dialects, 183–84
Diaz, Porfirio, 132
Dickinson, Emily, 266
Differences. *See* Diversity
Diffusion, as changing culture, 44
Directness
    in classroom communication, 228
    of language use, 143–45
Discrimination, 214–15, 270
Disraeli, Benjamin, 22
Diversity
    in advertising, 213
    among cultures, 53
    among individuals, 17, 30, 58–59, 169
    recognizing, 300
    See also Multicultural education
Doing orientation, 78, 100
Domestic contacts, 3, 12–16
    with co-cultures, 14–16
    immigration's effect on, 13–14
Dominant culture, 11–12
Dualistic world view, 114
Durant, Ariel, 89
Durant, Will, 89, 219

Economic sanctions, 11
Economics, in new world order, 11–12, 199–200
Education
    cultural functions of, 218–19
    curriculum, 220–22
    teaching methods, 222–24
    See also Multicultural education
Elderly, the. *See* Age
Eliot, T. S., 23
Emerson, Ralph Waldo, 27, 191
Emotions
    nonverbal expression of, 166, 171, 177
    verbal expression of, 138, 146
Empathy, 286–90
    hindrances to, 287–89
    improving, 289–90
    in multicultural teaching, 238
Enculturation, 34–35
Environmental problems, 9
Equality, as dominant American cultural pattern, 62
Ethics
    of Christianity, 99–100
    defined, 295
    intercultural, guidelines for, 296–301

    relativistic approach to, 295–96
    as religion component, 97
    universalistic approach to, 296
Ethnic discrimination, in workplace, 214
Ethnic groups, communication between, 47
Ethnocentrism
    avoiding, 290
    consequences of, 276–77
    coping with, 293
    defined, 275–76
    nonverbal communication and, 166
    as problem in studying intercultural communication, 17–18
    of this book, 22
Eye contact, nonverbal communication through, 54, 177–79, 254

Facial expressions, nonverbal communication through, 176–77, 254–55
Families, 115–22
    age and, 120–21
    collectivism and, 119–20
    customs regarding, 283–84
    gender roles and, 117–19
    importance of, 116
    individualism and, 119
    Judaism's emphasis on, 103
    roles in, and health care, 250–52
    social skills development in, 121–22
    types of, 116
Feedback, 290–91
Fellini, Federico, 136
Females. *See* Women
Femininity
    as cultural value dimension, 72
    See also Women
Fernandez-Armesto, Felipe, 128
Flexibility, communication, 291–92
Food, future shortage of, 8–9
Foreign languages, 148–54
    learning, 284
    translation of, 149–52, 285
    working with interpreters of, 152–54
Formality
    in classroom communication, 228–29
    as cultural dimension, 83–84
    in health care communication, 255–56
Frank, Anne, 74
Frankfurter, Felix, 62
Franklin, Benjamin, 61, 174, 188
Free choice, 264–65
Freud, Sigmund, 169
Fuller, Thomas, 172

Furniture arrangement, nonverbal communication
through, 186–87
Future orientation, 77–78, 100, 189

Gender
Christianity on, 101
as co-culture, 48–49
discrimination based on, 214
family roles, 117–19, 250–52
nonverbal communication and, 179, 181
See also Men; Women
Gestures, nonverbal communication through, 175–76
Gift giving, in business, 206–7
Gissing, George, 30
Globalization, 11–12, 199–200
Golden Rule, cultural variations in, 299
Greetings, in business, 205–6

Hall, E. T., context orientations, 79–82
Harmony, interpersonal, as cultural dimension, 85–86
Hazlitt, William, 218
Health belief systems, 242–47
on causes of illness, 244
on prevention of illness, 247
on treatment of illness, 245–47
types of, 243–44
Health care, 241–58
family roles and, 250–52
health belief systems and, 242–47
importance of communication in, 241–42
improving multicultural communication in, 256–58
language barriers to, 253–54
nonverbal communication in, 254–56
religion and spirituality and, 248–49
self-disclosure and, 252–53
Heraclitus, 23, 43, 165, 263
Hesse, Hermann, 53
Heyerdahl, Thor, 184
Hidalgo y Costilla, Miguel, 131–32
Hinduism, 106–8
History, 122–32
African American, 126–27
Chinese, 128–29
influence of, 122–24
Japanese, 129–30
Jewish, 127
language's role in, 138
Mexican, 130–32
Russian, 127–28
United States, 124–25
Hofstede, Geert, 59
on management cultures, 201, 202
value dimensions, 65–73
Hoover, Herbert, 61

Hsieh, Tehyi, 218
Hugo, Victor, 182
Hui Neng, 114
Human communication. *See* Communication
Human nature, cultural value orientation
regarding, 74–75
Huygens, Christiaan, 187

Identity
expression of, 138
from deep structure institutions, 92
Idioms, 150, 285
Illness
beliefs about, 242–44
causes of, 244
prevention of, 247–48
treatment of, 245–47
Immigration
as cause of problems, 3
effect of, on U.S. population, 13–14, 224
as worldwide phenomenon, 7–8
Indian Americans, as immigrant population, 13
Individualism
Christianity's emphasis on, 100
as cultural value dimension, 65–66
cultural value orientation toward, 79
as dominant American cultural pattern, 27, 61–62
families and, 119
personal space demanded by, 186
Individuals
identity of, 92, 138
respect for, 297
responsibility of, 300–301
similarities between, 29–30, 298–99
uniqueness of, 17, 30, 58–59, 169
Informality
in classroom communication, 228–29
as cultural dimension, 82–83
in health care communication, 255–56
Initial contacts, in business, 204–5
Innovation, as changing culture, 43–44
Intercultural communication, 46–49
competence in, 277–79
defined, 2, 46
domestic, 3, 12–16
forms of, 46–49
future of, 301–2
guidelines for improving, 279–94
importance of, 3–5
increase in, in business, 198–200
international, 3, 5–12
potential problems in, 265–77
problems in studying, 16–18
Interethnic communication, 47